MEMORY AGAINST FORGETTING

MEMORY AGAINST FORGETTING

Memoirs from a Life in South African Politics

1938 – 1964

Rusty Bernstein

VIKING

VIKING

Published by the Penguin Group
27 Wrights Lane, London W8 5TZ, England
Viking Penguin, a division of Penguin USA Inc, 375 Hudson Street, New York,
New York 10014, USA
Penguin Books Australia Ltd, Ringwood, Victoria, Australia
Penguin Books Canada Ltd, 10 Alcorn Avenue, Toronto, Ontario, Canada
M4V 3B2
Penguin Books (NZ) Ltd, Cnr Rosedale and Airborne Roads, Albany,
Auckland, New Zealand
Penguin Books India (P) Ltd, 11 Community Centre, Panchsheel Park,
New Delhi – 110 017, India
Penguin Books (South Africa) (Pty) Ltd, 5 Watkins Street, Denver Ext 4,
Johannesburg 2094, South Africa

Penguin Books (South Africa) (Pty) Ltd, Registered Offices:
Second Floor, 90 Rivonia Road, Sandton 2196, South Africa

First published by Penguin Books (South Africa) (Pty) Ltd 1999

ISBN 0670 88792 7

Typeset by PJT Design in 10.5/13 point Sabon
Cover design: Bureau Connexion
Cover photographs: Times Media Limited
Printed and bound by Interpak, Natal

For Hilda, without whose courage, persistence and love
neither my children nor I would have come through

And for all those who resisted apartheid and finally laid it low,
but whose courage and sacrifices are now in danger
of being forgotten

*The struggle of man against power
is the struggle of memory against forgetting.*

Milan Kundera

CONTENTS

Foreword ix

Prologue 1

1 Starting Blocks 7
2 Time at the Crossroads 25
3 A Foot in Each Camp 39
4 Across the Divide 53
5 Spoils of War 72
6 Warning Winds 87
7 A Line in the Sand 101
8 Goodbye to All That 114
9 Overground – Underground 129
10 To Speak of Freedom 145
11 Power, Treason & Plot 163
12 Cracking the Fortress Wall 182
13 Exercise Behind Bars 199
14 To Put Up or Shut Up 217
15 Things Fall Apart 237
16 To Sit in Solemn Silence 261
17 In a Deep Dark Dock 283
18 Telling It As It Was 305
19 In A Closing Net 329
20 Over, and Out 344

Epilogue 366
Index 371

FOREWORD

By ANTHONY SAMPSON

The libraries and archives about the South African resistance to apartheid include many remarkable personal records, but there remain large gaps of understanding. There are too many self-serving accounts by people on the sidelines, too few candid records by people at the centre. That is hardly surprising. The demands of the commitment, whether to oppose tyranny in South Africa or to maintain ideological positions during the cold war, inhibited many participants from writing frankly or humorously about their difficulties or doubts. The struggle, like any war, inevitably produced its own clichés and propaganda on both sides – as the Truth Commission's report has helped to reveal – in which truth was sometimes a casualty.

Rusty Bernstein's long-awaited memoirs are all the more welcome, to provide a readable, entertaining and honest account by a man who was close to the centre of events from the forties to the sixties. They turn out to be what many students of South Africa have longed to find – a well-told, unpretentious story of what it was like to live through those extraordinary times.

Rusty and his equally remarkable wife Hilda were always people of unusual modesty and talents, who in other circumstances could have been outstandingly successful in conventional careers. This book convincingly describes how their humanity and sense of outrage drew them into a movement which would soon require extraordinary courage and self-sacrifice, with no prospect of material rewards. But the sacrifices of the Bernsteins and their white colleagues on the left would yield a crucial political reward and significance for South

Africa's future: for it showed the young black nationalist leaders of the forties, including the young Mandela, that there were white people who were prepared to abandon their privileges and identify themselves completely with the Africans' predicament – and thus prepare the way for a genuinely multi-racial society in which nationalism was outmoded and superseded. In a world in which the resurgence of ethnic nationalism is causing such misery and devastation, the multi-racialism of South Africa looks all the more unusual.

It is a story which will fascinate anyone interested in the forty-year epic of the campaign against apartheid; but it has a special interest for observers like myself who watched it from outside the Marxist camp, and who worried about the motivations and objectives of South African communists. As an English liberal journalist, editing *Drum* magazine in Johannesburg in the early fifties, I watched the Bernsteins and their comrades with a mixture of admiration and apprehension: I knew I would never have the courage to commit myself as they did to a programme which was very likely to lead to jail; but I worried about the extent of the commitment to international communism, and could not understand how such intelligent and sensitive people could accept such a rigid and demanding dogma.

But Rusty's story in this book makes that development seem so natural and inescapable that it will make many non-communists understand it more sympathetically – particularly as the machinations of the cold war on both sides become clearer in retrospect. Rusty persuasively shows how the international evils of Fascism and Nazism in the thirties, combined with the callous oppression of the black majority in South Africa, made the Communist Party virtually the only rallying point for those whites who identified themselves with the black majority; and how the Party gave him and others the entrance-key to the black political world from which nearly all whites had excluded themselves.

He explains his own progress in unsentimental terms which make it much more interesting. He vividly describes his cheerless ordeal of trying to sell the left-wing weekly *Guardian* to black readers in the beer halls and to white railway workers in Braamfontein: 'Did we achieve anything at all?' – and answers with characteristic modesty: 'Perhaps when the time came for white South Africa to choose between civil war and majority government, our *Guardian* Sundays might have influenced some of their decisions for the better. Perhaps.'

He describes with equal candour the scepticism of white communists about the ANC with all its incompetence in the early forties, before its renaissance at the end of the decade: 'It is easy to understand why so many Party members regarded it either as irrelevant or a potential handicap in the struggle.'

He retains his candour and modesty as he becomes much more closely involved in the Party and the ANC. He plays down his role in drafting the Freedom Charter in 1956 which would become the key document of the ANC over the next thirty years, and explains casually how he wrote the opening and closing sentences, which he now thinks were overblown. He is critical of the risks involved in Mandela's underground activity in 1961; he admits that the first acts of sabotage in December 1961 'caused only a ripple of concern in the government or the country at large'; and he worries about the carelessness of the Rivonia plotters in 1963. But he remains totally loyal and courageous; and it was not until the end of the Rivonia Trial that he went into exile, from which he and Hilda remained invaluable supporters of the movement.

It is the honesty and credibility of his narrative, without any posturing or self-advertisement, which makes it both a gripping story and a crucial historical document. He poignantly takes his title from Milan Kundera: 'The struggle of man against power is the struggle of memory against forgetting'. But his own memory is unusually reliable and important, in its insistence on truthfulness and uncomfortable facts. His story is not just the record of a heroic movement, told from the inside, important though that is: it is the account of a warm individual and his family, caught up in a challenge they could not ignore, who still retained an individual scepticism and humour as they looked back on the events which turned their lives upside down.

PROLOGUE

1987. I am in Moscow on behalf of the African National Congress and Umkhonto we Sizwe to conduct a series of seminars on the history of South Africa's liberation struggles. My students are young men and women of all races, mostly of the 'Soweto generation'. They are fresh from street battles with the police and are training to be guerrilla fighters. They are self-confident, self-assured, very sharp and questioning, anxious to learn.

We have only two weeks together. I have planned to have two teaching sessions per day. They insist on three. They take nothing for granted, challenge everything, and let no casual phrase or imprecision pass.

I enjoy the challenge. I try to convince myself that it is doing them good, although it is exhausting me.

My Russian interpreter has a request. Would I agree to a filmed interview for a TV documentary? I would, reluctantly. The interview takes place in a meeting room in the hotel. The director and crew speak no English; I speak no Russian. My interpreter is competent to deal with menus, travelling and shopping, but struggles with political concepts. The director knows little about me or about South Africa but thinks the interview will be useful for a film he is only thinking of making.

He wants to explore why people take political action which runs counter to their own class interests.

'Take the Decembrists, for instance,' he says.

All I know about the Decembrists is that they were aristocrats and officers of the Tsar who staged a revolt against him in the late 19th century, challenging the feudal order which provided their own privileged position. I suspected that most of them were executed.

I don't think he is giving me warning of my fate. He is just drawing a tentative analogy between Decembrists and white South African anti-apartheid radicals, though talk of 'aristocrats' and 'martyrs' seems somewhat inappropriate.

Question: 'Why do you, a privileged white South African, risk your life to end white rule, and so bring your own comfort and privilege to an end?'

I have been expecting questions about political history, and have no ready answers. I say that I can give no explanation for the origins of my politics. My childhood was fairly ordinary and my family unexceptional.

He is clearly disappointed. I suggest that he consider instead the life of Bram Fischer, who had exchanged prestige and privilege for a life in the communist underground. And had died in a Pretoria prison, serving a term of life imprisonment. He had been as near to an aristocrat as a South African can get – grandson of a President of a Boer Republic, son of a Judge President, and in his own right a Rhodes Scholar and barrister destined to become a judge. If there is an answer to the question 'Why?' it could well be found here.

The director is dissatisfied. He says something in Russian which my interpreter doesn't bother to translate. I assume it means: 'Don't call us. We'll call you.'

On my last night in Moscow I am having dinner with the doyen of Soviet scholars on contemporary South Africa, Professor Apollon Davidson of Moscow University, who has a formidable knowledge of people and politics.

Hotel table service is Soviet-leisurely; we are drinking mineral water in accordance with Gorbachev's recent reform of the liquor laws, and talking. He tells me many things about the history of our liberation movement which I should know but don't, and I tell him a few things I know which he doesn't.

He wants to know whether I have written my memoirs? I have not. He is short, white-haired and thickset. His face wrinkles up as if he is about to cry.

'But you must!' he says. 'You must! It's a tragedy, an absolute tragedy, all you chaps dying off – Moses, JB, Yusuf[1] – without writing anything. You must! You really must!'

I make vague noises of agreement. I have lived through a time when people have been tortured and killed for their memories of names, places, times.

Survival has required that memory be deliberately suppressed, and every written record burnt, shredded, flushed away or even swallowed. I have no records, no diaries, no appointment books, no letters, no minutes of meetings, no copies of anything I have written.

Lives depended on silence and forgetting.

In South Africa there are indications that things might be about to change. The time may be coming when forgetting is no longer essential, and remembering may start contributing to the overthrow of apartheid.

Davidson has started me remembering some of the things I have been disciplining myself to forget.

I have been shocked at how completely the apartheid years have robbed my Moscow students of their own history. They have little understanding of what has really happened in their own country. In school they have learnt only what was permissible under 'Bantu Education' and its mission to support white supremacy. Their elders have told them little, preferring silence and forgetting as protection for themselves and their families.

They know little more than the anecdotal accounts of their own generation's street battles in the black townships over schooling. They have justifiable pride in their own resistance, but their knowledge of the wider resistance movement ends with the liberation songs and political slogans.

I am thinking of ways to help them fill that void when the ANC calls for help. There is a need for the political education of

---

[1]Moses Kotane, National Executive Committee member of the African National Congress, General Secretary of the Communist Party 1933 to 1968; died in exile in 1972. J B Marks, President of the African Mine Workers' Union, Chairman of the Communist Party until his death in exile in 1972. Yusuf Dadoo, President of the Transvaal Indian Congress, Chairman of the Communist Party 1972 until his death in exile in 1983.

young South African refugees who have made their way to the 'front line states'. In 1989, Hilda and I agree to spend a year at Somafco[2] in Tanzania, doing what we can. Facilities are limited; there is little we can do. I have a lot of spare time on my hands, and start making notes about things I have been forgetting.

The notes are fragmentary, filling some of the gaps in my remembering, but not all. Those notes are the basis of my memoirs. They have not been derived from research or cross-referencing but are purely personal rememberings of some political events in which I participated.

Memory is no substitute for history. But where there are no other records, memory may provide an insight which research cannot or may miss altogether. My memory is, admittedly, subjective. It promotes my own version of things at the expense perhaps of aspects which are more important. Memory is selective and eclectic. My memoirs are neither an autobiography nor a history of the times. They are only a small personal recalling of a small part played in some big political dramas. Many events of equal or greater historical importance find no place in it.

It is more than ten years since Davidson made his plea for my memoirs. In that time many more of the men and women who made the history of those times have passed away leaving no personal written records – not just Marks, Kotane and Dadoo whom Davidson cited, but also Albert Luthuli, Z K Matthews, Oliver Tambo, Tom Nkobi, Michael Harmel, Abram Fischer, Helen Joseph, Duma Nokwe, Ruth First, Joe Slovo, Harold Wolpe, J N Singh, Jack Hodgson, Cecil Williams – the list goes on and on. If the memory of them is not recorded now, when will it be?

I know only part of all their histories. I feel an obligation to record that part on behalf of those who did not survive to tell it for themselves. I am one of the lucky ones. I survived what an old Chinese curse would call 'a life in interesting times'. I have the

---

[2]SOMAFCO – properly the Solomon Mahlangu Freedom College – established by the ANC in 1979 as a refuge and school for South African juvenile refugees at Mazimbu near Morogoro, Tanzania. At its peak, SOMAFCO housed some 800 children of all ages and several hundred adult refugees and invalided MK guerrillas. In 1994 all buildings and installations were returned to the Tanzanians who had donated the site.

privilege of looking back to those times of tension, terror and forgetting, and remembering times which might be beyond the understanding of generations who did not live through them.

Amongst those are my own children, who were shielded from our secret lives but had to pay the personal and emotional cost of living with them. If these memoirs help them to make sense of what was happening to them and around them, they can scarcely compensate them for their childhood in 'interesting times'.

1

STARTING BLOCKS

to 1939

The white rabbit put on his spectacles.
'Where shall I begin, please your majesty?' he asked.
'Begin at the beginning,' the king said very gravely, 'and go on till
you come to the end: then stop.'
From Alice's Adventures in Wonderland

Begin at the beginning! Excellent advice – provided you know where it is. I do not. Could it have been the 1928 elections – a big event in the life of Durban's small white community?

I was eight years old. For a short while, before- and after-school games took on election colouring. We gave up games of cops and robbers or cowboys and Indians, in favour of the gang warfare of SAPs[1] versus Labour. English-speaking Durban was overwhelmingly SAP. Labour Party support was small, and Afrikaner Nationalist support even smaller. For reasons unknown, I declared myself for Labour. I knew nothing about Labour or anything else at issue in the elections. My parents, so far as I recall, had no Labour leanings. I must have been seeking attention for myself. If so, it certainly worked. I was duly chased about the playground by a rowdy nine-

---

[1]South African Party – headed by General J C Smuts.

year-old SAP mob, and was duly scragged in the grass. No one got hurt; when the bell sounded we dusted ourselves off and went in to class together, without any animosity.

Near the school there lived a family with four or five sons in different classes. I grew friendly enough with the one in my class to go to his home one day after school. His mother gave us tea and jam sandwiches. Why should I remember this out of all my childhood? Perhaps I remember – or was I told? – that there was something special about the Hennessys. They were fully accepted at school, but seemed to hold themselves aloof like a clan of their own. The boys were all dark skinned, their mother even darker. I remember suggestions – I do not know from whom – that I should not get too friendly with the Hennessys and should avoid visiting their home. Much later it began to dawn on me that perhaps they were not 'white'.

There were rumours in the air that the mother was Mauritian. Or perhaps even Coloured? 'Coloured' was a new concept for me – interesting but meaningless. The times were not as racially obsessed as they would become later. No one did anything to bar the Hennessys from the school, but as we grew older my friends and I became less and less comfortable in their presence, until they were almost totally isolated. Now I realise that they were clinging precariously to the fringe of white society, always in danger of being swept off by the rising tide of racism. But I did not realise it then. I left the school at the age of eleven and never saw or heard of them again.

Was this, even so, the beginning? I cannot remember when I first realised that 'black' and 'white' were not simply colours but separate categories of people. I knew black people – two of them worked in our family home, a cook named Dick and a gardener John. I don't think I ever knew their surnames. John was my companion. He played games with me, and made me bows and arrows. He could run and jump like a champion, and throw a ball further and higher than anyone. He was a hero figure. I do not think I ever thought of him or Dick as 'black'.

That childhood colour-blindness could not last. Something new and disturbing happened to our comfortable white world. Rumours of it spread through gossip at home and at school. Trouble, it was said, was 'brewing among the natives'. Its nature was unknown to me, but it seemed to be confined to the downtown commercial and industrial areas which were remote from our home on the Berea.

There was talk of a character called Champion who was believed to be the source of the trouble. My favourite weekly comic book was called *The Champion*. It was strong on war heroics and the adventures of 'Fighting Mac at Arras', as well as triumphs in the boxing ring, the motor cycle dirt track and the FA Cup. And it had a fair share of horror stories and drawings of ogres dripping blood and venom. In my childish imagination, Champion the trouble-maker appeared as one of those.

The brewing trouble came to a head in a mass meeting of blacks near the racecourse. A mob was said to have marched on the town; police had barred their way; shots had been fired and men had been killed and wounded, Champion not among them.[2] I either heard or imagined I heard the distant rattle of rifle fire. A momentary frisson of fear and uncertainty upset my parents and our white neighbours – but it soon passed. The 'trouble among the natives' subsided and life returned to normal.

Politics proper began much later. In 1936 I was in my matriculation year at boarding school near Pietermaritzburg. Our debating society was to contest with our 'sister school' a few miles away the proposition: 'The future of mankind depends on a civilisation based on science'. I was asked to second the motion. I searched the school library for inspiration, and in that collection of miscellaneous discards from family bookshelves I turned up a slim red volume called *The Results of the Soviet 5-Year Plan*. How it came to be there I cannot imagine. It was little more than a catalogue of statistics about Soviet industry, agriculture, transportation and so on. It was crashingly boring, but it gave me just what I needed. It presented a picture of all round Soviet triumphs which it attributed neither to luck nor nature but to 'scientific socialism'.

I based my speech on the little red book – the term had not yet acquired its Maoist connotations. I made the bold claim – based on my profound ignorance – that the Soviet 5-Year Plan vindicated scientific planning. The opposition had come prepared for a more

---

[2] As part of a campaign against the Pass Laws a mass rally had been called by the Communist Party on 16 December 1930, then known as Dingaan's Day in celebration of armed white victory over the Zulus at Blood River in 1838. Marching protesters clashed with police, who opened fire. Four were killed, including a Durban communist, Johannes Nkosi, who became a celebrated resistance martyr. George Champion was one of the Natal ANC's leading figures.

genteel case based on morality and learning. I unsettled them, and we won the debate hands down. Overnight, I acquired a totally unmerited reputation as the school Bolshevik. In truth, I knew no more about communism, politics or the USSR than anyone else in the school. But I had read the little red book and they had not.

I was struggling with Latin and the Gallic Wars. My teacher, known as 'Caesar Jenks' was in his mid-twenties. He was a cadaverous, skin-and-bones immigrant from Britain, one of an Oxbridge generation who had awoken early to the Nazi threat and the dangers of the policy of appeasement. Jenks interpolated caustic comments on current affairs into his explanations of the Gallic Wars. His diction, filled with crashing consonants, excoriated Hitler and Mussolini as caricatures of the Roman greats. His aphorisms about the mad dictators and even madder appeasers appealed to me. I recorded many of the best in the back of my Latin book, and left it behind by mistake when I left the school at the end of 1936. Some of his hatred of fascism must have come away with me.

In Johannesburg I found a job as the most junior junior in an architect's office and enrolled for a part-time course in architecture at the University of the Witwatersrand. I had come from a white school into two exclusively white establishments where the only exception was an elderly black employed as the office delivery 'boy'. His status was even lower than mine. There were no black students in the architectural faculty, and almost none in the whole university. I lived amongst whites in a wholly white suburb, and at weekends played hockey in an exclusively white team. Racial separateness was so ubiquitous, so deeply bound by both custom and law, that it never seemed in the least peculiar. What little social consciousness I had was concerned with the 'mad dictators'.

Their rise and rise filled the press and radio. In Germany, Hitler was rearming massively in preparation for war, and his opponents – communist, socialist, trade union or religious – were dying in concentration camps. Japanese armies had overrun Manchuria and were battering China. In Spain, German and Italian forces were in action with General Franco, the democratic Republic was drowning in blood and Madrid was under siege. Austria, undermined by subversion, had been annexed to the German Reich with scarcely a hand raised in the outside world to prevent it. Czechoslovakia was in imminent danger of the same fate. And in Africa Italian armies had overthrown Ethiopia's ancient independence and converted it into an Italian colony.

Fascism was everywhere – in Britain there was Mosley's Union of Fascists, in France the Croix de Feu, in the USA the Ku Klux Klan and German-American Bund. In South Africa, Afrikaner Nationalism had sprouted an undergrowth of Blackshirts and Greyshirts with quasi-military uniforms, swastikas, and Nazi ideology of race mixed up with lingering bitterness carried over from the Anglo-Boer War. They were close to the centre of state power, and tolerated or encouraged by pro-Nazi cabinet ministers like Oswald Pirow at Defence and Eric Louw at Trade. Police and army would stand by while fascist thugs disrupted political meetings. Blackshirts and Greyshirts seemed to be immune from prosecution under the new Riotous Assemblies Act.

I knew of all this; so did my contemporaries. But it was as though it was happening somewhere else, somewhere outside that narrow ring of suburb, office and university in which I lived. It was like a bad smell in the background – something to worry and complain about, but not bad enough to compel me to do anything about it.

One Sunday morning some young people came to my door collecting money for Medical Aid for Spain. I can no longer recall how they persuaded me, but the following Sunday I was with them, carrying a collecting tin, and arguing on doorsteps in Berea. Suburban Johannesburg did not feel itself to be involved in the fate of Spain, nor was it convinced that the war in Spain could be the curtain-raiser for a new world war. A few householders gave us money for the cause, others just to get rid of us. We found a few supporters, and several opponents still holding the Spanish people responsible for the Inquisition and the terrible things done to the Jews. In the arguments, I was out of my depth. I needed to find out much more of what was actually happening in Spain, and what it might mean for the rest of the world.

That was the end of my Sundays at leisure at the swimming baths and the hockey fields. The more I found out, the clearer it all became. Spain was the front line against fascism and war. All our fates were being fought out there. If the Republic fell, there would be no restraining the mad dictators. Peace and democracy everywhere would be in peril, and my generation would become the cannon-fodder of a new war. Campaigning to uphold the Spanish Republic began to take over my life. I even toyed fleetingly with the idea of joining the International Brigade fighting on the Republican side.

Amongst the young people in the campaign for Medical Aid for Spain were members of the Labour League of Youth – the youth section of the South African Labour Party. When I joined them some time in 1937 or '38, they numbered about twenty in all, all around my own age and all white. They were a lively and dedicated group – almost the only lively and growing part of the Labour Party. Hilda Watts, as she then was, was probably the liveliest of them all, and the most politically experienced. She had been a member of the Young Communist League in Britain before emigrating to South Africa. She was an outstanding public speaker, a dynamo who put her formidable energy into the LLY and Medical Aid, carrying the rest of us along in her trail.

The LLY kept us all busy, but as with so many small sects, much of our time went into defining precisely what we stood for, and why *our* politics were uniquely right.

Hilda was sharing a flat with three young men, which was very daring, almost Bohemian for those times. Rowley Arenstein, also a member of the LLY, was a serious, rather humourless legal clerk, a didact who tended to monopolise every theoretical political discussion. Archie Lewitton was already a member of the Communist Party, a natural iconoclast who enjoyed sarcastic sallies against political pomposity, usually at Rowley's expense. Hilda claims they both had designs on her.

But she and I worked well together, and developed a friendship beyond our shared politics. She introduced me to Italian opera in the Johannesburg City Hall, where a very large lady named Betsy Delaporte played the starving and consumptive Mimi in La Bohème. I don't doubt she sang beautifully, but all my attention was on the leading man bracing himself like a rugby forward to take the shock as a dying Mimi fell into his arms; and on the tops of the City Hall organ pipes which stuck up above a ten foot high painted backdrop. Our friendship survived that, and a lot more. We worked together in political causes, and married in 1941.

Spain and the LLY set me on a search for political understanding which led me to the Left Book Club, founded in Britain by the left-wing publisher Victor Gollancz. The Club provided its members with uniformly bound, cheap, red-covered books with an anti-fascist, radical or socialist content. It encouraged members to discuss the books as well as read them, and had sponsored the formation of a Left Book Discussion Group in Johannesburg. Members of various left and radical sects and of none met monthly to discuss the Club's current book choice, or a related topic.

The mainstream bookshops ignored, or perhaps boycotted, Left Club publications whose distribution was confined to a few specialist left-wing and generally obscure outlets. I was introduced to one of the smallest and most obscure of them.

Salmon's bookshop occupied one room on an upper floor in Eloff Street, above Cuthbert's shoe store and the Corner Lounge Café. Mr Salmon was a middle-aged, rather corpulent, Dickensian bookshop proprietor. He had thick spectacles perched on the end of his nose, and muttered to himself in a strong Eastern European accent as he searched the shelves for what he wanted. The shelves were cluttered with dun, blue or grey-bound volumes, many of them in foreign languages or from Soviet publishing houses. Left Club 'choices' with fading red covers gathered dust among the back numbers of *Moscow News*, *Pravda*, and the Comintern's press digest known as *Inprecorr* (*International Press Correspondence*).

There was no space for browsing, but there was a cluttered lobby where one would rub shoulders with customers from other left-wing circles, waiting while Mr Salmon puttered and muttered around the shelves. Books and papers in some disorder piled up on an old roll-top desk where regular customers would wait, chatting and sifting through the latest titles.

Salmon's and the Discussion Group opened up a small world of books which I could have found nowhere else. I had always been a voracious reader. I worked my way through years of Left Club publications, most of them now outdated and forgotten.[3] Together, the good, the not so good and the pretty bad opened my mind to the political theory, history and philosophy which shaped my political development. Through meetings of the Left Book Discussion Group I was gradually introduced to an intersecting – almost incestuous – network of organisations and committees which

---

[3] Such as John Strachey's *Why You Should Be A Socialist*; Hewlett Johnson's *The Socialist Sixth of the World*; Frank Jellinek's *Paris Commune*; Edgar Snow's *Red Star Over China*; and Michael Foot's *Tory M.P.*

constituted the Johannesburg left. Or rather, Johannesburg's white left. If there was a black left – as I think there must have been – there was no more sign of it in the Left Club than in the LLY or Wits University.

In the Faculty of Architecture at Wits there was a lively group of left-wing students a year or two ahead of me. They were developing ideas of socially responsible architecture, especially in relation to housing and town planning, encouraged by one of the senior tutors, Rex Martienssen. Their political inspiration, however, came from an extraordinary third-year student, Kurt Jonas. Jonas was small, soft-spoken and self-effacing. He bore an uncanny resemblance to that popular Hollywood actor of oppressed little-man roles, Peter Lorre. He was a few years older than his colleagues and had been born in South Africa but educated in Germany where he had qualified as a barrister. The rise of Hitlerism led his family to return to South Africa, where he exchanged the study of law for the study of architecture. He was an avowed Marxist.

In short time, Jonas was elected President of the Architectural Students' Society, and re-elected year after year. From that power base, he was transforming the Faculty from a training centre for businessmen-architects into a place of advanced architectural, political and social thinking. He was intellectually brilliant in both his architecture and his politics. In public debate, he dominated by intellect alone despite his apologetic, almost diffident manner. I came to regard him as closer to genius than anyone I ever knew.

At university, our paths seldom crossed, until we met by chance at Salmon's roll-top desk when I was still rather in awe of him. Some months later he asked if I would join a political study group he was starting. I jumped at the opportunity. Anything headed by Jonas had to be stimulating and exciting. There were about ten students in the group. Jonas proposed to start – start! – with Karl Marx's *Capital*, an enormous advance on anything I had read before. My political reading was not far beyond beginner's level. I had no idea what I was letting myself into, but I bought a copy of *Capital: Volume 1* from Mr Salmon, and dipped into Chapter 1, as instructed. I found it dense and incomprehensible.

In weekly sessions, Jonas expounded brilliantly on the mysteries of use value, exchange value, surplus value, commodity production, accumulation and exploitation. But it was small help. I was unready for the intricacies of mind of either Marx or Jonas. I persevered, as we all did, until the class collapsed by mutual consent with only a part of *Volume 1* poorly digested.

I did not dare open *Capital* again until years later, when I had enough of a foundation to be able to read it for myself and to appreciate the monumental scale of Marx's ideas which were still able to shake the world almost a century after he had written them. *Capital* blew my mind. It transformed my interpretation of the world, and transformed my way of living in it. Jonas had tried to explain it to me when I was not yet literate enough. He failed. But he pointed me in the right direction, for which I have been in his debt ever since.

At that time, Johannesburg's first Continental-style coffee house had been opened by some German Jewish refugees. Florian's Café served *real* coffee on a corner balcony in Hillbrow – none of the then standard South African chicory-based brew which had been stewing on the stove for hours. For the price of a cup of coffee, we could move from Jonas's class to the balcony and sit talking politics for hours. It was at Florian's via Kurt Jonas that I first learnt of the invisible world of black workers and their trade unions which existed on my own doorstep.

There, too, I was introduced to the great debate about the interaction of socialism and nationalism. Jonas was an active member of the Zionist Socialist Party whose Zionism came under regular attack over coffee from Jock Isacowitz, as Jewish as Jonas but different from him in almost every other respect. Jock was a prototypical English-speaking South African. He was articulate, argumentative and radical, uninhibited in his hostility to Zionism which he described as Jewish fundamentalism. Even in its Zionist-Socialist colours, for him it was a doctrine of racial apartheid and a contradiction of socialist internationalism.

Jonas made no doctrinal defence of Zionism. His position was purely pragmatic. As a Jew, he had experienced anti-Semitism at first hand in Germany. It had made him feel more at ease in a Jewish milieu than outside it. He claimed that, in the Zionist Socialist Party, he was best able to serve the socialist cause without conceding any of his Marxist principles. I took no part in the fierce disputes between him and Isacowitz on the truth of that claim – I am a better listener than a talker. But I learnt a great deal from it at just the time when I was learning about practical organisation and agitation from my membership of the LLY. Between those schools I was learning to understand something of the central issues of all South African politics – the issues of class and race.

In Spain, Germany tested its latest weapons and blitzkrieg tactics; the Western powers looked the other way, pursuing what they called 'non-intervention'. The Spanish Republic was being battered to death. As its fall became a matter of weeks, then days, a sense of doom seemed to set in amongst the anti-fascists who had held high hope of Spain as the last bastion against the mad dictators. Volunteers from around the world had fought and died in the International Brigade under the slogans 'No pasaran! They shall not pass!' and 'Better die on one's feet than live on one's knees'.

Despite their sacrifices, the war was being lost. The Spanish Republic had been left to fall by 'non-intervention', leaving a sense of mourning and of defeat and hopelessness such as I never felt at any other time – not even during Chamberlain's betrayal at Munich. In our bones we could feel the clock ticking down for the Second World War.

The first battles of that war had already swept across China, Ethiopia, Austria. Now they were coming close in Czechoslovakia as once again the Western powers looked away. While the left campaigned for the world to stand by the Czechs, Europe's old order prepared once again to open the pass to fascism, and encourage it to move eastwards against communism. Hitler's armies were loose and poised for action. Neville Chamberlain flew to Berchtesgaden to trade away Czechoslovakian independence and democracy.

In Johannesburg, an Emergency Committee was cobbled together to call for the West to 'Stand by the Czechs!' At the University, a parallel Students' Emergency Committee was formed, sponsored by Jonas, Isacowitz, and Guy Routh – at that time a sociology student and campus bard of folk and protest song. They convened a students' mass protest meeting at the University on the night of Chamberlain's flight to Munich – twenty-four hours ahead of a citizens' mass rally outside the City Hall. We turned the Architectural Faculty's studios into a painters' workshop and spent the night preparing banners and placards for the city rally. We still had paint on our hands when we made our way to the chemistry lecture theatre for the students' protest.

16

In those days, student meetings were rare and usually concerned with things like inter-varsity fixtures or the annual Rag Days. Most of them went almost unnoticed by the main student body. This time things were different. The hall was packed to capacity, with all the aisles filled. A phalanx of students from the University hostel had taken up position on one side. That was not a good omen. Hostel-dwellers came mainly from the Rand mining towns and tended to be very right wing, rowdy and macho – the scourge of the left and of radicalism.

The chairman attempted to start the meeting. He got a rough ride and could scarcely be heard above the booing and catcalling. After several false starts he gave way to the first speaker – the University Registrar Ivor Glyn Thomas. It must have been expected that his official status would earn him some respect and a decent hearing. From his occasional appearances at the Left Club, I knew he was a committed socialist and – either then or later – a member of the Communist Party. He was slightly built, pale and bespectacled, an intellectual and reasoner with precise language but not much oratory. He did his best. But the heckling grew steadily more raucous as the rowdies realised he could not strike back. After a miserable attempt to make himself heard he retired in defeat.

The chairman called the next speaker. The small, shy figure of Kurt Jonas pushed its way through to the platform. Pale, and with a lick of black hair hanging apologetically over his forehead, he seemed comically misplaced amongst the oversized and sun-tanned rugby-playing audience. He was almost unknown outside the architectural faculty and was greeted with catcalls and mocking laughter. He stood silent at the lectern for a few moments letting the noise wash over him, almost as though he could not hear it.

Then he started to speak in a conversational tone, making no attempt to raise his voice. The noise died away as people strained to hear what this comic might be saying. He talked fluently about Germany and fascism, without any histrionics. The audience began to strain to catch his words spoken softly into the developing quiet.

'Germany,' he was saying reasonably, 'has made an offer to the world.' Murmurs of surprise and dissent. 'It offers peace to its neighbours and peace to the world.' Consternation and murmuring. He raised his voice marginally: 'The peace of the graveyard.' He had taken charge.

He was heard out to the end in mesmerised silence. He delivered a withering and brilliant critique of fascism, and of Chamberlain and the policy of appeasement. It was a *tour de force* not of oratory but of intellect and of psychology. He ended as quietly as he had begun. The applause almost brought the house down. The chairman called for student attendance at the next day's citizens' protest meeting, and we left in triumph at what felt like a great success.

But it was already scarcely relevant. Chamberlain was already in Munich signing the piece of paper on which Hitler guaranteed 'Peace In Our Time', as he told a cheering parliament in London on his return. That same night a vast crowd gathered on the steps of the Johannesburg City Hall. Czechoslovakia had been sold out, though we did not yet know it, and the protest went ahead as planned.

It was my first experience of a street demonstration. We marched off through the city centre, filling the street from kerb to kerb under a sea of banners and placards, most of them from our university workshop. I was carrying a pole at one end of a red banner which stretched across the road. Then the rain came down. We kept marching, but our inexperience as banner-painters was exposed. Red rainwater trickled down on us from our banners – no one had warned us against water-soluble paint – and turned mysteriously indelible as it washed over faces and clothes. My shirt and jacket, stained indelibly pink, became my first real sacrifice for the cause at a time when I was earning £2.10 a month.

In pouring rain we marched down Von Brandis Street chanting slogans, past a high-rise building which housed the local German Club. The upper floors of flats were occupied by Germans, possibly supporters or even functionaries of the Nazi regime. Out of the darkness cups, saucers and plates started to rain down, smashing to pieces around us on the street. Our ranks broke for the cover of overhanging verandas. Alone in the centre of the street, Johanna Cornelius of the Garment Workers, young, athletic, over six feet tall, strode back and forth with her head protected only by a scarf, shouting 'Come on, boys! Don't be afraid!', waving us on while crockery crashed down out of the dark and shattered all around her. She was statuesque, magnificent.

The ranks re-formed behind her – out of range of the bombardment – and marched on to the Union Grounds where there were to be speeches. The grounds were surrounded by iron railings with only a single gateway. It was barred by a line of dripping and fidgety soldiers with rifles at the ready, trying to look fierce. They were one-night-a-week civilian trainees from the Active Citizen Force (ACF) whose headquarters was in the drill hall across the road.

We stood about in the rain while their officers parleyed with the leaders of the march. In the end we all turned around and marched back disconsolately to the City Hall. On the way we discarded washed-out banners and soggy placards in the gutters. It was a dispiriting and damp end to the night, and to all hope of a last-minute stand against barbarism. The lights, as someone said, were going out all over Europe. And we were being dragged protesting into the darkness.

I no longer remember how I came to the Anti-Fascist League. Its original purpose seemed to have been to organise physically fit young men to act as bodyguards and protectors at anti-fascist meetings. Its secretary and only visible public presence was a recent immigrant from Britain, Ephraim Burford – always known as EJ. Short and bespectacled, he looked like a subaltern from the British army in India – thinning sandy hair, sandy military moustache, ruddy complexion, clipped British accent, and a military stomach-in-shoulders-back bearing. He was then, I suppose, in his mid-thirties.

Burford's fierce anti-fascism was born in Spain. He had been there on holiday with his wife. Madrid was peaceful enough until the morning they woke to the sound of rifle fire in the street outside. The hotel staff advised them to keep the shutters closed against snipers. Burford thought they were being rather windy and un-British. When the firing stopped, he stepped out into the street to see for himself and a sniper shot him through the thumb. The Civil War had started. He had been an early minor casualty in it, but now with a major sense of outrage against the fascists.

Republican soldiers came to his hotel to commandeer cars with which to transport their men to the battlefront. Burford stood on his rights. He would not hand over his car but would agree – under duress – to drive it himself. The holiday was over, turned into a short stint of ferrying Government troops to the front. He returned to Britain a staunch supporter of the Spanish Republic and a lifelong enemy of fascism.

In South Africa he became a member of the Labour Party, and the secretary – possibly the founder – of the Anti-Fascist League. He was an efficient manager with great bustling energy. Early in 1939, he involved me in the Anti-Fascist League's most ambitious propaganda venture. He had obtained from somewhere a mock 'Wanted for Kidnapping' notice for the arrest of Adolf Hitler, much like the notices posted up outside police stations. He had found a printer willing to reproduce it without the identifying imprint required by law. It would have to be printed and distributed secretly – defamation of a foreign head of state was a serious criminal offence, and was bound to be dealt with severely by a government that included pro-Nazi ministers like Oswald Pirow and Eric Louw. It would have to be distributed on a grand scale to have a worthwhile impact.

Burford raised the money and masterminded the work. I worked secretly with him and others to compile a massive mailing list of names collected from organisations far and wide, augmented with names taken at random from post and telephone directories for every town and district in the country. We farmed out the work of addressing thousands of envelopes in assorted shapes and sizes, addressed in many different hands and typefaces. When all had been stuffed, stamped and sealed, the entire posting was carried out on a single night. Volunteers posted small batches in every postbox we could find on the Rand, to give no indication of an extraordinary bulk posting which could be intercepted before delivery.

The operation went like clockwork. The handbill itself failed to shake either the German Reich or the South African government. It aroused some comment inside the country, but did little to change public attitudes. The police had neither the numbers, the ruthlessness nor the special powers they would get in later years. They enquired about it in a desultory way, found out nothing and gave up. I had served my first apprenticeship in clandestine political work.

Burford and I got on well together. We were both members of the Labour Party and belonged to the same branch. The Labour Party, which was loosely associated with the British Labour Party, had once had a considerable number of members and working-class supporters – all exclusively white. It maintained a colour bar in its ranks without specifically stating so, simply on the basis that that was how things had always been. The much more recent Labour League of Youth, also all white, had no such tradition and a youthful radicalism. It made regular demands that the Party 'open

20

its ranks' to blacks. That suggestion created constant friction between the Party and its youth section, and contributed to divisions inside the Party itself.

There was a yawning contradiction at the very centre of Labour ideology, between its acceptance of the colour bar and its long-term aspiration of a socialist future. Socialism and democracy can only be understandable if they apply to everyone. But in the Labour Party they were seen as the aspirations of whites only – an incomprehensible anomaly in a country where the majority of the people and the working class is black. Law and custom could be cited to explain away the exclusion of blacks from Party membership, but not their exclusion from the socialist future which was the explicit aim set out in the Party constitution. The aim – I quote from memory – was:

> To secure for the producers by hand or by brain the full fruit of their labours, *due regard being had to the presence of an overwhelming native population* (my italics).

At the end of the First World War the Labour Party had been a serious contender for parliamentary power. By my time, it had lost everything except a last precarious toe-hold on the ladder to power consisting of four MPs, one senator, and a handful of provincial councillors. From a position which gave it no real state responsibility it could almost disregard what it called 'the Native Problem'. All aspects of the colour bar could be relegated to the same league as such particular problems as soil erosion, tariff barriers, cattle culling and deforestation – not fundamental to the social order but simply matters of administration and order which had no bearing on the socialist goal. Socialism would be a change of social order for us, the citizens; not for them, the black outsiders. What it would provide for them could be settled by our administration when the time came. Implicitly it would not be much different from what they already had, though its administration would be more efficient and humane. Labour Party socialism was, in essence, a special variant of white domination and black inferiority.

In the Party conferences of the late nineteen thirties, the Party left was a loose grouping united by a desire for democratic change, and 'fairness and justice for all' – which could extend from a simple relaxation of the Pass Laws to full democratic rights and an end to the colour bar. 'Native Policy' formed the backdrop to most of the policy confrontations between left and right. The left was a constant irritant to the Party establishment, but not strong enough to carry the conference vote against it. Demands for the Party to rethink its 'Native Policy' were fiercely resisted by the hierarchy. As the left grew, debates became steadily more heated and also more personal. They gave rise to the belief that agendas were being manipulated against us, and that defunct branches and dead members were being resurrected to vote in emergencies.

We could never prove any of that. In fact, the Party establishment was probably more representative of the Party's real and ageing membership than we were, even though the whole machine was running down. Former Labour supporters amongst the skilled white workers were retiring, and the new generations coming in from the countryside were turning instead to Afrikaner nationalism. The Party leaders clung doggedly to a labourist class-consciousness untempered by political theory. Opportunism was the order of the day, but their aspirations and ideology were out of tune with the times. Except for a shrinking role in Parliament and local councils, the Party seemed to come alive only at election times; and even then to depend on a corps of temporary paid 'agents' to deliver its message.

As Labour's political arteries hardened, only the left minority still had the purpose and vigour to recruit a new generation of members. Together with Burford and others, I helped resuscitate the Labour Party branch in Hillbrow-Berea where we were both living. It was an area inhabited mainly by white-collar workers and middle-class householders, often with an Eastern European background. It was a good area for us. We attracted members more readily by raising such issues as fascism, the danger of war and race relations than by reliance on Labour's past political record. We broke away from the tired Branch tradition of meetings concerned almost entirely with electioneering and fund-raising, and held regular 'open' meetings on current political topics. We published a monthly bulletin for members titled 'Advance' which was the only official Labour Party publication in the country.[4] We were putting

---

[4] The weekly 'Forward' edited by Labour Councillor Ben Weinbren in Johannesburg was often taken to be the official Labour Party organ. In reality, it

22

Labour back on the Johannesburg map and also revitalising its inner politics. By the end of 1939 we had built what was almost certainly the Party's biggest branch, and its most active.

By 1939 I had been persuaded to act as Secretary of the LLY. It was not very onerous – the whole LLY was little more than a sect with perhaps fifty members organised in only two or three Witwatersrand branches. Amongst other things, I kept in touch with the British LLY and its secretary Ted Willis over mundane matters of printed propaganda material and supplies of their handsome enamelled badges.[5] Labour Party rules entitled the LLY to one representative at all meetings of Party's National Executive Committee. I was delegated to the task, and was able to observe all the Party great and good in action – including all its MPs who attended *ex officio* when in Johannesburg. I do not recall that I ever spoke at these meetings – perhaps I was not entitled to – but I learnt a lot about career politicians, and how opportunism and careerism subvert political principles.

Left-wing Johannesburg was a very small pool in which almost everyone knew everyone else, or knew of them. I had heard of Dr Max Joffe as a reputed communist and the *éminence grise* of its almost invisible Youth League. I received a message that he was anxious to talk to me. It had to be about politics – we had nothing else to talk about. His (CP) Youth League was, I believe, even smaller than the LLY, and had even less of a public presence, but it was said to be more radical, and avowedly Marxist. For reasons of his own, Joffe made our appointment for 10 p.m. in his city consulting rooms – suitably conspiratorial.

At that time of night central Johannesburg was almost dead. The last trams were still running. Occasional cars came by, but there were virtually no pedestrians as a night curfew kept all blacks off the streets except the municipal labourers who were hosing down

carried the Party's views only where they coincided with those of the proprietor and printer George Weinstock. The symmetry of titles 'Forward' and 'Advance' was fortuitous.

[5] Years later Ted Willis was to become an MP, and also the well-publicised writer of a British TV serial 'Z Cars'. When I heard of him again after the war he had become Lord Willis – and I was in prison on trial for treason. One of us appears to have taken a wrong career turn.

the streets and clearing the day's litter. Outside the City Hall my footsteps echoed off the walls in a way suitable for a Raymond Chandler novel.

Joffe's rooms overlooked the City Hall steps from the first floor of a tall building with a pompous Corinthian pilastered facade. He was perhaps ten years older than I, wearing then and always a tight wasp-waisted dark suit and waistcoat. A lock of straight black hair hung down over one eye giving him the romantic air of a wilting poet. He tried to persuade me of the merits of the Communist Party and Marxism, and to get me to join his Youth League. I was only mildly interested, and not totally convinced that the Youth League actually existed. But he did manage to persuade me – perhaps unintentionally – that lurking somewhere in the wings of most local left-wing activity, there was a Communist Party. To which he had the key.

I came to know Joffe and his waiting-room better in subsequent daytime visits when the place was like a railway station, alive with arrivals, interchanges and departures. Everyone hurried. People dashed in from the street looking haunted, exchanged hurried whispers with the receptionist, and were whisked into an inner sanctum with no suggestion that first come was first served. Moments later they would reappear, often through another door, and hurry out without another word. From time to time a harassed-looking Joffe would pop out of one of the doors, stethoscope dangling from his neck, touching his temple with an elegant sigh of exhaustion and suffering, and then scuttle back out of sight.

I always thought of the place as the White Rabbit's Warren. Its atmosphere was furtive and conspiratorial. People spoke in whispers; doors never opened wide enough for others to see in. The waiting-room had no bowls of flowers or back copies of *Punch* or *Tatler*, but – as in every good conspiracy story – there was a glamorous blonde receptionist (whom Max later married), and from time to time her equally glamorous blonde sister whose function was not apparent. Whatever else was going on, it was none the less the waiting-room to a surgery. The comings and goings, I guessed, were about one-third medical and two-thirds political.

2

TIME AT THE CROSSROADS
1938 – 39

Some time later I made a move to track down the Communist Party. It proved more difficult than I had expected. There were no addresses in telephone or street directories. I asked around amongst people who might know. Most of them were rather cagey.

Someone suggested that I try the People's Bookshop. A single small shopfront window gave into a shop not much wider than a passage immediately next door to the Kerk Street entrance of the Labour Party Club in central Johannesburg, which in turn adjoined the Trades Hall, HQ of the Trades and Labour Council. The shop window held a collection of sun-yellowed pamphlets with curling and faded copies of some of the 'Little Lenin Library' series. Inside, the shelves held Left Book Club publications, copies of *Labour Monthly*, *China Today*, *Moscow News*, and works by Marx and Lenin in English, German and Russian – and not much else.

Its staff of young women regarded me with caution, as if I were there for dubious purposes. I made some small purchases and then broached the subject of the Communist Party. The woman I asked looked somewhat startled, but said she would try to get word to the District Secretary. I left my phone number, and a man calling himself Jack Watts duly phoned and suggested we meet at the bookshop at closing time. He turned out to be perhaps a few years older than I, a recent arrival from Britain. We fenced. I wanted to know all about the Party and he wanted to know all about me and why I wanted to know. I must have established my bona fides, because he identified himself as the District Secretary and agreed to pass on my application for membership.

I had expected the Party Secretary would be someone fairly well known in left circles, but none of my colleagues had ever heard of him before. It was a long time before I discovered that Watts was a pseudonym – or 'party name' as I learnt to call it. His real name was Gathercole and, like most of the white Party members at the time, he considered himself to be semi-underground – or, as the jargon had it, 'concealed'.[1]

The Party was not illegal, but it was in a state of deep decline after years of internal strife. It had withdrawn from the light into the shadows, split into factions and sub-factions of factions. Accusations and counter-accusations of 'revisionism', 'Bukharinism' and 'Trotskyism' had been bandied about in a search for ideological purity. Majorities had expelled minorities only to be expelled themselves in due course. Internecine doctrinal strife had displaced public political activity, until ultimately the Central Committee had been moved from Johannesburg to Cape Town lest it too dissolve in the cross-fire.

The Johannesburg Party had withered, with debts unpaid and its offices repossessed by the landlords. Its printing press had been sequestrated and its former journal *Umsebenzi* was defunct. All that remained was a semi-secret sect.

My application for membership was accepted and I was placed 'on probation' for several months during which I would be required to pay regular subscriptions, attend regular members' meetings, and 'carry out all tasks assigned to me'. Every explanation was couched in a jargon which was new to me, filled with references to 'aggregate meetings', 'functionaries', 'democratic centralism' and 'factionalism'. The only meaning of 'aggregate' for me was its building industry meaning: the main component of a concrete mix.

I began to learn the jargon, and discovered that 'aggregate' meant 'general meeting'. I gradually learnt that the jargon was not South

---

[1]Gathercole disappeared from sight soon after. When CP members were facing 'listing' under the Suppression of Communism Act in 1950, some claimed that the Liquidator's evidence could only have come from him.

African but a special variety of international Communist-speak. In its most impenetrable form we called it 'Inprecorr' language after its main user, the journal of the Comintern: *International Press Correspondence*.

In addition to 'aggregates', the Communist Party had 'functionaries' rather than officials or office-bearers, a 'Political Bureau' (or PB) rather than an executive committee, and 'secretariats' in addition to secretaries. The jargon gave the Party a foreign, almost exotic air. But it also gave its members a sense of membership of a select band, much as the rituals and secret handshakes do for Freemasons or Boy Scouts.

My first aggregate meeting was held at the south end of Eloff Street, where the shopping area expired and gave way to urban wasteland. It was in a decrepit office block in an unplanned sprawl of car parks, black municipal workers' compounds, municipal beer halls and cemeteries of dead cars. The Bantu Men's Social Centre – then the hub of the city's black cultural life – was nearby. Further south, there were only huge windswept dumps of white mine sand. The Party office was about as far out of town as one could get while still claiming to be 'in town'.

The building's entrance hall and staircase were unlit. Mice, rats or cockroaches rustled in the passageway. A creaking wooden staircase led to a dimly lit upper landing. The Party 'premises' turned out to be a single room in which were some thirty kitchen chairs and a table, and about fifteen people, black and white. They looked me over briefly and went on gossiping amongst themselves. I recognised only one or two, members of the Labour League of Youth I had not expected to find there. No one introduced me to anyone. I sat hunched down in my chair until the meeting began. Late.

I had never attended a meeting with black people before, or been in a place where there was no apparent distinction between 'us' and 'them'. It was a dislocating experience but not threatening. It all seemed so casual, so natural that settling in to it was quite easy. I had expected to find myself in an exalted political club, but not in a totally new society where black and white participated as equals. It turned my world upside down. The colour barriers which had been an inseparable part of my home, school and working life were missing, and all reason for them gone. The very ordinariness of what was taking place was more disturbing to me than their gaping absence.

I had come with romantic expectations of finding a comradely circle, a dedicated fraternity such as I had looked for and not found in the Labour Party. I had expected a gathering of tolerance and mutuality suitable for my vision of the new socialist order. It was nothing like that. Debate was fierce and adversarial. Speakers snapped at one another, attacked each other passionately and personally. The jargon flew – factional, sectarian, opportunist, revisionist. Could this verbal warfare really lead the way to the new world of socialism?

Only later did I come to understand that these wars of the aggregates were the last skirmishes of the years of feuding and faction-fighting which had brought the Party to its lowest ebb. I knew almost nothing of that past. I did not appreciate that this was a Party in transition, picking away at old sores in the course of rediscovering the essence of a Communist Party. That first aggregate meeting ended with a spiritless singing of the Internationale. The factions separated and left without much more than a curt 'good-night'. Outside it was Saturday night, raining and dark in a deserted neighbourhood. The experience nearly turned me off the Party for ever.

For unexplained reasons aggregate meetings were always held on Saturday nights – perhaps as a show of dedication, or as a hair shirt worn for the good of our souls. For everyone else in Johannesburg, Saturday nights were dedicated to 'a good time' – drinking, dining, dancing and movie-going. Only the Communist Party imposed this monkish self-restraint on itself, and even called absentees to account afterwards.

Suffering the hair shirt, in time I came to know the thirty or so men and women who constituted the 'aggregate' of the Johannesburg Communist Party.

It was 1938. The Central Committee had been removed to Cape Town and General Secretary Moses Kotane had gone with it. A new District Committee had been formed to revive what could be revived of the Party, and to bury the past's factional strife. Some veterans of past factional wars remained – some like Willie Kalk of the Leather Workers' Union and Sam Nikin of the Furniture Workers, still fiercely combative and unrepentant; others seemingly reconciled to the new dispensation, like Issy Wolfson of the Tailoring Workers' Union and Edwin Mofutsanyana – the *éminence grise* of the black membership – and his then wife Josie Mpama (or Palmer). The new

28

District Committee was an uneasy mix of survivors from the factional past and newcomers who had joined the Party after the worst of the internal fray. It was made up of a mix of native South Africans with a good number of first or second-generation European immigrants. Together, they constituted a reasonable cross-section of Johannesburg's population, though English-speaking whites were over-represented and Afrikaners and blacks under-represented.[2]

The only aggregate meeting I now remember from that time was concerned with a new initiative of the Minister of Defence, Oswald Pirow. He had proposed the formation of a National Register of white citizens whose skills could be conscripted by the state in times of national need.

Pirow was the most outspoken supporter of Hitler and National Socialism in the cabinet, and responsible for the Riotous Assemblies Act which seriously curtailed rights of free speech and assembly. His National Register would almost certainly have some hidden anti-democratic purpose. The aggregate meeting debated whether or not to urge people to register. Was the Register a genuine preparation to meet the threat of fascism and war, or the start of a Pirowite corps of stormtroops?

Eli Weinberg was in town, from Cape Town, and led the discussion. He was a small, vigorous and ebullient man who had been imprisoned in Lithuania for political offences while still adolescent. He had emigrated to South Africa without a trade and with very little English. He had hiked his way around the country and particularly the mountains of Basutoland (now Lesotho) getting the feel of it, mastering English and acquiring a working knowledge of Sotho and Afrikaans. He was an active trade unionist and, at that time, the elected Secretary of the Commercial Travellers' Union.[3]

I have forgotten the decision we reached on the National Register

---

[2]Other District Committee members included Archie Lewitton, Hilda (Watts) Bernstein, Michael Harmel, Ray Harmel, Gessie Landman and Max Joffe. In later years also Yusuf Dadoo, Bram Fischer, Alpheus Maliba, Armstrong Msitshana, Michael Diphoko, Rowley Arenstein and me.

[3]Banned in 1948 from all trade union work, he became a professional photographer and built up a large archive of photographs of the political movement. After five years' imprisonment under the Suppression Act (1970-75), he left the country in '76, and died in exile in Tanzania in 1981.

– it was, in any case, of no importance since the whole proposal sank from sight soon afterwards. That such a discussion should be held at all, however, is indicative of the character of the Communist Party. To some people there might be something ludicrous in the picture of thirty ordinary citizens agonising over a legislative proposition as though the fate of the nation depended on their decision. It might seem to echo the spirit of that declaration of the six tailors of Gloucester which began 'We, the people of England . . .' But it was a debate conducted in dead earnest, though no one participating in it could have had any illusion that they would materially influence the fate of the National Register. But that was scarcely the point. The point was to find the 'right line' before exercising the Party influence on events, however small that might be.

The Party took its politics very seriously. The fact of a tiny membership and small public following could not excuse it from its civic responsibilities. That seriousness – which some might find absurd – was the Party's great strength. It reflected an inner conviction that 'nevertheless, the world does move!', that how ever small our own thrust we were helping it move, if not now then some time in the future. This conviction that they were helping to move forward the course of history gave the Party the determination and resilience which was enabling them to pull themselves back from the brink of internecine extinction.

When I joined the Communist Party I thought I was ending my membership of the Labour Party. It did not work out like that. I was called to a routine new member's interview with the CP Secretariat, and explained the reasons for my decision to leave the Labour Party. The Secretariat agreed with my criticisms of the Labour Party but thought it was capable of being changed for the better – from the inside. My best contribution to the cause of socialism, they decided, was to continue to fight the good fight inside the Labour Party and, at the same time, maintain 'dual membership' in the Communist Party. I was only half convinced, but agreed to give it a try.

I was assigned to a Party group and required to continue with all Labour Party activities 'not incompatible' with membership of the Communist Party. In today's vernacular this would be termed 'entryism' or 'boring from within'. In fact my objective had been 'exitism'. Though I had been temporarily talked out of it, I had little faith in the prospect of breathing life back into a moribund Labour Party.

My CP group was made up of seven or eight others, all also members of the Labour Party or the League of Youth. Hilda was one of them. It was far removed from the crusading socialism I thought I had joined. It was concerned almost entirely with the same issues as those which had concerned that Labour Party left which I had wanted to get away from. Only the Communist Party's constant concern with international affairs presented a sharp contrast to the near total disinterest which the Labour Party had displayed on such matters.

The threat of imminent war dominated the agenda and the thinking of the Communist Party. Talks on an Anglo-Soviet treaty of mutual defence against Hitlerism were leading nowhere; negotiations had been relegated to a junior Foreign Office official with no power of decision. Germany was rearming apace. The Labour Party, completely wrapped up in its own local political concerns, seemed oblivious to the dangers. The Communist Party, by contrast, seemed focused on the war threat and the need for an Anglo-Soviet treaty above everything else.

Late that year, Stalin issued a warning that – in the absence of such a treaty – the USSR would not be prepared to 'pull the chestnuts out of the fire' for the West. To us in the Communist Party that was a signal. We were keenly aware of the imminence of war, but were taken by surprise by the manner of its coming. A surprise Soviet announcement that it had negotiated a mutual non-aggression pact with Germany caught us totally unawares. Perhaps we had been giving so much attention to the menace of fascism at home that we had not foreseen the possibilities of radical changes of scene abroad. Even so, the Soviet change of direction created little upheaval in our ranks, although the shock waves split the Communist Parties in many other countries and led to mass membership defections. In South Africa, remote from the epicentre of the event, there were only minor rumbles.

The loudest of those rumbles I can recall broke without warning at a Saturday night 'aggregate'. There was nothing on the agenda to prepare us for a dramatic denunciation of 'Soviet betrayal', made by one of the Party's intellectual eminences, Hymie Basner. He was a radical lawyer and formidable orator, a short, stocky, red-faced man with a choleric disposition, and a fine flow of language. In a burst of passion he spoke of his bitter disillusion with the Soviet Union and the Soviet Communist Party. He condemned the immorality and opportunism of the Soviet-German pact – and then dropped his bombshell. He was leaving the Party for ever.

Those who knew him better than I may have been forewarned. To me, his speech came as a shock, almost as a blasphemy. But no one chose to reply. In dead silence he rose and started to stamp out; then turned in the doorway and fired a parting shot: 'Leave me alone, and I'll leave you alone!'

What he meant I do not know, but inside the Party his departure created a minor stir. Outside, in all the turmoil of impending war, it passed almost without notice. Nothing more was heard of it until months later, when Basner broke silence in a letter to the press, repeating his denunciation of the USSR and defending his defection from the Party.

Few Party members followed him. If the Soviet-German pact had caught us unprepared, we were mentally prepared for war when Hitler's armies launched their attack on Poland, and Britain formally declared itself at war with Germany. It was the end of an era of appeasement in Europe.

In South Africa, war brought to the surface all the strains in parliamentary politics which had been hidden for a decade by the Smuts-Hertzog coalition. During the pre-war economic crisis of the 1930s, contradictions between SAP and Nationalist factions had been papered over by the creation of a single party of white supremacy, the 'United Party'. UP government had mitigated the effects of the depression on whites by intensifying the exploitation of blacks. It had ensured the supply of plentiful, cheap black labour for both farms and mines. Only a die-hard Afrikaner nationalist faction had hived off, to form a 'purified' National Party without the Hertzogite compromisers. This was the 'official opposition', led by doctor of divinity D F Malan.

. The strains of war opened up once again the contradictions between SAP and Nat in the Smuts-Hertzog coalition. The cabinet, faced with the need to define South Africa's position in relation to the war, split apart. Five ministers voted with Hertzog for South African neutrality; six with Smuts for a South African declaration of war on Germany. No one knew how Parliament would vote. The reckoning between war and peace hung in the balance. Malan's National Party would certainly throw its weight behind Hertzog. But the final outcome might depend on the votes of two minority parties – a small Dominion Party of Empire loyalists who would undoubtedly stand with Smuts; and the four Labour Party MPs.

At the height of its popularity in 1924, Labour had been party to a pact with Hertzog against Smuts and his resort to martial law in the 1922 General Strike. That alliance had ousted the Smuts government and installed a 'pact' government under Hertzog's premiership, in which Labour ministers had served. Some years later the Pact had been superseded by the United Party government of Smuts and Hertzog, with Labour left on the sidelines of power, and its present loyalties uncertain. Labour's vote on the issue of war or peace could be the most significant decision in its history.

The Labour Party National Executive Committee met in emergency session in Johannesburg. Its three MPs and its Minister – Walter Madeley – had flown up from Cape Town, along with its lone Senator – Party chairman Jimmy Briggs. I was present as 'fraternal' representative of the League of Youth.

The meeting was dominated by the parliamentarians who all supported Smuts and the declaration of war. Compared with the CP debates, their speeches were strangely shallow, and made little reference to the politics of the war, to the nature of fascism, to the fascist threat to trade unions and democratic movements or to the independence of nation states. They were couched in terms of indignation, and of unquestioning patriotism – or more correctly jingoism or Britishism. Instead of serious analysis of the origins or possible consequences of war there was a lot of tub-thumping of the my-country-right-or-wrong type.

That is, until M J van den Berg, who represented a West Rand mining constituency in Parliament, claimed the floor. He was a burly former miner, fluent in English although his first language was Afrikaans, and the undisputed leader of Labour's Afrikaner members. He chose to speak in Afrikaans, though he must have known that some of the NEC members would have difficulty in following. His oratory and bull voice brought an uninspired meeting to life – and to real politics. All the bitterness of Afrikaner nationalism poured out in his attack on the advocates of war; all the pent-up grievances of British concentration camps, of the destruction of the Boer republics, and of the deportations of those who refused to 'hands-up' at the end of the Anglo-Boer War. In a tirade filled with 'blood-and-soil' references, he bellowed that the Boerevolk would never be prepared to fight Britain's wars or accept Smuts's call to arms. The Labour Party should give Smuts a simple, answer: We will not join your war! Not now! Not ever!

His rant was heard in silence. No one seemed willing to respond except city councillor Ben Weinbren, who had learnt his politics as a one-time member of the Communist Party. His was the only substantial political speech of the evening, based on the crucial issues of the nature of fascism, its threat to peace and progress everywhere, and the need for international unity to halt it.

No one was prepared to follow him. The chairman called for a vote. Every hand except Van den Berg's was raised in favour of war. Van den Berg spoke again to make a short and bitter denunciation of a Party which had sold its soul to British imperialism. Then he stormed out of the meeting, leaving a shocked silence behind him. His exit, it was obvious, would mark the end of his Labour Party membership and the reduction by one fourth of its parliamentary caucus. It seemed inevitable that most of the Afrikaners in the Party would follow him out. The meeting broke up, more concerned with the electoral implications for itself than with the fate of the country. Within days, the Party's next most prominent Afrikaner, Dr Venter Odendaal, Party leader in the Transvaal Provincial Council, followed him out, taking many of the Afrikaner members with him.

When Parliament resumed, Hertzog's neutrality motion was voted down and Smuts's pro-war amendment carried with a majority of thirteen, Smuts took over as Prime Minister and the Labour Party leader, Walter Madeley, entered the cabinet as Minister of Labour. Little was heard of Van den Berg for several weeks. Then there was a brief announcement in the press that M J van den Berg MP had been commissioned as Captain in the South African Army, and would be involved in army recruiting on the home front.[4]

---

[4]He never returned to the Labour Party. After the war he won his constituency seat as a Nationalist in the 1948 election, and became a cabinet minister in the Malan government.

At Labour's decision-making I was a silent observer, but in the Communist Party's, a participant. Labour's decision had been pragmatic, settled in a single evening. The Communist Party's required weeks of uncertainty before the debate came to a final conclusion. Ironically, Labour's quick decision might well have tilted the country's balance between neutrality and war. The Communist agonising over 'the right line' could have no real influence whatsoever on the national decision.

Until the Soviet-German treaty the Party line had been clear. It had been for a broad international alliance against fascism, if necessary by means of war. But in our view, the Western powers were more concerned with containing the USSR and socialism than confronting fascism – hence appeasement, the betrayal of Spain and Czechoslovakia and the foot-dragging over the Anglo-Soviet treaty. But the Soviet-German non-aggression treaty clouded the certainty by taking the Soviet Union out from its central position in any anti-fascist alliance. The prospects of an east-west alliance was obsolete. And before our policy could be reconsidered in this new situation, there was war. The Nazi armies crashed into Poland. Britain and France declared war.

Our policy which had seemed so clear for so long was suddenly muddied over. Political parties change direction just as cumbrously as ocean liners. Ours was no exception. Our change of course was complicated by a tradition of deference to the greater political expertise and experience of the Soviet Communist Party. Before words of wisdom on the new 'line' were forthcoming from the Party leadership, our groups struggled on their own to adjust themselves.

George Findlay came to my group from the District Committee to help us through the maze. George[5] was a barrister with a golden tongue, a wonderful precision of word and impeccable logic. 'The line', we were assured, was not changed. We were still for a resolute world stand against fascism. The Soviet action had not invalidated

---

[5]Findlay was from Pretoria, at that time part of the Johannesburg District. He and his wife Joan drifted out of the Party some years later. He became an acting judge, but was threatened with 'listing' under the Suppression Act. His response, published in the press, was a refusal to apologise for his past, and, in effect, 'List and be damned!' He went on to become a distinguished judge.

that, though it had been a surprising eleventh hour tactic to safe-guard the Soviet's own frontiers from a Nazi attack. The appeasers had been drawn against their will into a phoney war, still hoping for the communist and fascist armies to bleed each other to death. We were for an all-out war – not phoney war. That policy remained, even in these new circumstances.

He argued his thesis brilliantly. But the question that bothered us all was this: How can it be that we seek to prosecute a war to the utmost while our Soviet comrades and allies move in precisely the opposite direction? Findlay had – as always – a clear and logical answer. When two armies set out to make a co-ordinated attack on an enemy citadel from opposite starting places, one army must march east while the other marches west. QED. That impeccable logic did not allay all doubts. We might have left the meeting spell-bound but we were not quite convinced. Doubts remained until we received confirmation of sorts from a press report. Harry Pollitt, Secretary of the Communist Party of Great Britain, had also declared the war to be an 'anti-fascist war', to which his Party too would give its full support.

That carried a lot of weight amongst us. Our Party had enjoyed a close fraternal relationship with the CPGB for many years. Our view of world events had been greatly influenced by the analyses published as 'Notes of the Month' in the British Party's journal, *Labour Monthly*, written by its chairman, R Palme Dutt. Divergence of view between us and the CPGB would have been quite as confusing as divergence from the Soviet Party. We were settling down to the idea that our policy was, after all, right and clear when there came a contrary declaration from the Soviet Communist Party. It declared the war to be reactionary and 'imperialist', and urged communists everywhere to follow Lenin's advice of 1914 and 'turn imperialist war into civil war'.

This was startling stuff. We had no formal links with the Soviet Party but their views carried enormous authority – they had made their revolution and were building socialism while the rest of us were still only talking of it.

We went back to serious study of Lenin's writings on the First World War. They did not translate easily to a different war in a different age. There were few analogies between Smuts's white supremacist regime and the Tsar's Imperial autocracy. Or between the all-volunteer South African and Tsarist conscript armies. Lenin's war had been drawn from a reasonably clear clash of rival imperialisms over territory. We were dealing with a more complex war whose substance was inextricably tied up with issues of democracy and national independence.

We were still arguing our way through this thicket when confusion was worse confounded by a new statement from the CPGB. This repudiated Pollitt's characterisation of the war and announced that he had been relieved of his position as Secretary. Before the implications of that had been fully taken aboard, a definitive communique from our own Central Committee laid down 'the line'. The war was, in essence, a struggle between rival imperialisms. It was neither 'people's war' nor 'anti-fascist war'. Whether they had arrived at that conclusion independently or out of deference to the combined decisions of the Soviet and British Parties was never clear to me.

At least we now had a formal 'Party line' which conformed to Clausewitz's aphorism that 'war is the continuation of politics by other means'. We would continue the fight against white supremacists, the Smuts government, *and* the war. We would not assist the war effort but concentrate on developing a mass people's movement against white supremacy, for all-out resistance to South African fascism and for the victory of a non-racial democracy in our own country.

To some commentators, this on-again off-again Party vacillation over the war has been interpreted as evidence of a Party following the dictates of Moscow, like puppets. It did not feel like that from inside. Soviet views were always factors in our policy decisions. The indecisions and vacillations were our own, indicative of our own seriousness when we made political decisions rather than subservience to Soviet instructions. Whether the CC's line also wavered before settling down as the District Committee's had, I do not know. But if it did, it had the courage to correct its errors. No political party can honestly claim that it never makes mistakes, though few others ever have the integrity to admit or reverse them when they become apparent.

Once our policy was firm, it committed us to a twin-track attack on both white supremacy and the war effort. That put us on a collision course with both factions of white politics, government and nationalist opposition, who were equally determined that the war would not be allowed to interfere with white supremacy. But they were not omnipotent. The social, economic and political consequences which followed South Africa's entry into war could not be kept – like the vote in Parliament – as just white man's business. In the end, judgement on Parliament's decision and its sole right to take it would be critically affected by that black majority which it had ignored and disregarded.

The Party would be working to bring that majority's aims and aspirations into the reckoning. That was certain to guarantee us a rough ride in a country where politics has always been a rough business.

3

A FOOT IN EACH CAMP

1939 – 40

Though the country was at war, nothing much seemed to change – no black-outs, no air-raid sirens, no conscription. Young white males were signing on for full-time service, and in the countryside young black men too – but only for non-combatant duty as cooks, stretcher-bearers and drivers. There were no calls for full-time service of the Citizen Force part-timers, no gas-masks, no food rationing.

In Johannesburg, a white hooligan mob set out on an alcohol-assisted round of 'patriotic' mayhem, setting German cars alight in the streets, beating up German civilians and trashing the German Club. Outside of the city, a retaliatory spate of random assaults on lone soldiers started. A mob of soldiers from their Potchefstroom camp replied in kind by smashing National Party premises.

For a short while it seemed that Lenin's idea of turning imperialist into civil war was coming into its own. But the frenzy passed. Unthinking mob violence gave way to organised violence by secretive armed pro-Nazi groups, one of them led by an ex prize-fighter, Robey Leibbrandt, who had been trained in Nazi Germany and been returned to South Africa by German submarine.

In parallel with the clandestine groups, a quasi-military organis-ation was organising and drilling militant white republicans. Calling itself the Ossewa Brandwag and playing on nostalgia for the Boer Republican commandos, it was rejecting parliamentary politics and preparing for a quasi-military confrontation. The Smuts government showed little sign of concern. It appeared to accept that the OB, for all its militarist bluster, was nevertheless part of a fundamental consensus that political power was to remain a white preserve.

Only the Communist Party stood outside that consensus. The black majority, still mainly rural, lacked an organised voice strong enough to influence the course of politics. That too was changing. War was bringing rapid industrial expansion, drawing armies of rural men and women to work in the cities, especially to the Vaal triangle. In Johannesburg, the black population was growing inexorably into a majority. Once impotent and barely visible organisations were growing in confidence. Trade unionism was spreading, as was a new sense of national identity. Urban blacks were starting to flex their muscles and to make their demands with a new-found militancy.

Most Communist Party members were involved either in the trade union movement or in the Party's most important activity – the running of night-schools for adult black workers. A growing network of these schools was providing basic tuition in reading, writing and arithmetic from unlikely places like domestic garages and outbuildings in the white suburbs, or unused store-rooms and offices in the central city.

Black adults would arrive after work to be taught by Party members who generally had themselves no teaching qualifications but a good deal of dedication. The schools were neither philanthropic nor charitable ventures. They had a serious political purpose. Through them, the Party was making contact with serious and responsible men and women, and introducing them to social and political ideas through the teaching of the three Rs. It was proving to be a fruitful field. Many of the students were taking on active roles in the community and in trade unions, and providing a steady flow of recruits to the Party.

In its attitude towards the left, the Smuts government was proving little different from its predecessors. We did not share the reverential view which had given Smuts a near-saintly status in pro-war circles at home and abroad. His dismal record included responsibility for the massacre of 190 men and women at Bulhoek in 1921 over non-payment of taxes; and the crushing by martial law of the 1922 Witwatersrand miners' strike with the loss of some two hundred lives. He had collaborated with avowed pro-Nazis like Oswald Pirow and Eric Louw in the coalition government right up to the eve of war. There was little in his choice of cabinet to suggest that he had changed. His government, as we had expected, was proving itself white supremacist and anti-democratic at home even while it portrayed itself as anti-fascist and democratic.

Not long after his government took office, 'detention camps' were set up for the first time since the South African War, ostensibly for enemy agents. Internment without trial of ethnic Germans and Italians began, and before long the distinction between enemy agents and local anti-fascists faded. Internment widened, and extended to some anti-fascists and members of the Party, like Dr Max Joffe and his brother Louis, a veteran of the South African army in the First World War campaign in South West Africa, and Issy Wolfson of the Tailoring Workers' Union. Non-Party trade unionists like Max Gordon, a Trotskyist and organiser of black workers' unions on the Witwatersrand, fell victim, and then Arnold Latti, an elderly Italian communist and veteran of the struggle against Mussolini; and Fritz Fellner, an anti-Nazi refugee from Germany, trade unionist and husband of Johanna Cornelius of the Garment Workers' Union. And also E J Burford, secretary of the Anti-Fascist League and member of my own branch of the Labour Party.

There was no obvious reason why they had been picked out. Their internment passed almost unnoticed by press and public, though Burford's case drew the loudest protest because of his high-profile in anti-fascist campaigns. His only other political activity had been in the Labour Party which was a part of the Smuts government coalition, but it drew scant protest from the Labour Party hierarchy or its cabinet member, Walter Madeley. Other internments of anti-fascists might be attributed to excesses on the part of the security services. But in Burford's case, people inside and outside the Labour Party suspected connivance of the Party leadership in whose side he had been a radical thorn.

I had that suspicion myself, though now I am not so sure it was fully justified. Anger over the Labour leadership's failure to protest certainly was. Whether they were complicit in Burford's internment must remain in doubt. Their man in the cabinet, Walter Madeley, appeared to me to be an honest man as career politicians go, but he was no radical. His politics were limited and parochial. To him the term 'the working class' appeared to mean the class of the skilled white artisans – black workers were not part of it, though he probably understood their disabilities and deplored them. I doubt if he had a hand in Burford's internment, but I felt far less charitable towards those of his colleagues in the Party leadership who constituted what we called the 'Headquarters Clique'.

The Headquarters Clique was a cabal of Party cronies. Almost all of them held public or Party office. They hung out in the seedy, beery, smoke-laden Labour Party Club on the floor below the Party head office. It was exclusively male. It had no amenities except a bar, where they hobnobbed with a similar group of cronies and bureaucrats from the Trades and Labour Council next door. The financing and administration of the Club was a closely guarded secret. The radical left, which never used the place, believed that its profits which should have gone into Party funds were being secretly siphoned off to pay the election expenses of the insiders. We had no proof. At annual National Conferences, the left would ask to be shown the Club's balance sheet, and annually the procedures would be manipulated or filibustered to frustrate the demand.

The Club's finances were not important in themselves, but the refusal to disclose them exacerbated political animosities. The annual National Conferences became more confrontational year by year. A left-right division overshadowed almost every debate on policy – whether on such matters as strikes and civil liberties, or on social and economic policy. By tacit agreement, both left and right avoided debate on the basics of the war effort for fear of an irreversible split. On other, less fatal issues, Burford had been a regular combatant. For a short time, his internment and the role of the Party leadership in it, became one of the divisive issues.[1] But the fundamental and lasting conference confrontations were over so-called 'Native Policy'. That lay hidden at the heart of almost every matter in dispute.

The Labour Party's socialism was explicitly for whites only. It did not extend to voting rights or equal citizenship for the black majority, or necessarily include the abolition of pass laws, segregation laws and the rest of the props to white supremacy. All such matters were lumped together under the rubric of 'Native Policy'. The

---

[1] Burford – and most of the others – were released without explanation after some months in internment.

loose left grouping was agreed on the need for radical revision of the Party's 'Native Policy', but could never muster enough Conference votes to obtain it. Headquarters – that is to say the Party establishment – was better managed, and not averse to reviving dead branches and members to ensure a majority vote for the status quo. We believed that we won all the arguments, but still we lost all the significant votes.

The annual Labour Party Conference after Burford's release from internment was an especially ill-tempered and hostile affair. I was a branch delegate – I do not remember taking any part in the debates. When it ended, left and right joined in the customary chorus of: 'We'll keep the red flag flying here!' and went off to face another year of temporary inner-party peace.

What we got was something like a firing squad. Curt letters arrived to inform our Branch that it had been dissolved by the National Executive Committee – no reasons given; members who wished to do so could apply for admission to other branches. Burford and I both received personal letters informing us that the NEC had expelled us from the Party. There had been no hearing; we were given no explanations.

By that time we had built the Hillbrow-Berea branch of the Party into the liveliest and largest branch in the country, and the only one with a regular organ of its own. The NEC's blow against us could only be motivated by fear of a possible incipient challenge to its reign. It was a leadership whose democratic arteries had hardened. It was clinging to its power even by means which could only weaken and dispirit the Party.

Labour was sinking ever deeper into decline at just the time when the Communist Party was succeeding in hauling itself out of its own. The Communist Party Central Committee had been successfully reconstructed in Cape Town; it had sponsored the revival of vigorous District Committees in all four provinces. Archaic practices like the use of pseudonyms and of 'concealed' membership were being phased out, and dual CP-LP membership was being reconsidered.

At about the time of my excommunication from Labour, all CP 'dual members' were required to end that long-standing Party practice by choosing one party and opting out of the other. With two exceptions, all the members of my group chose to opt out of the Labour Party. The exceptions were Alex Hepple, who was a Labour provincial councillor and prospective parliamentary candidate, and his wife Girlie. Alex was slightly older than the rest of us in the group. He had inherited a small factory which made him a small-time 'employer' and 'industrialist', an anomaly in the Communist Party.

The Hepples' loyalty to the Party was unquestionable, but in the circumstances they were unlikely ever to be considered for any public leadership role. They felt that they could probably do more for the cause of socialism from the front ranks of the Labour Party than from the back benches of the CP. We agreed. The decision was a difficult one for them both, but in the end they decided to end their membership of the Communist Party. We had been in the same CP group for some time. I liked them both and had a high regard for their honesty and commitment. We remained friends.

Alex went on to become the Labour MP for Rosettenville and a principled member of the shrinking Labour group in public office.[2] By that time Labour's decline was near terminal. The white-supremacist cancer had eaten away its core; its supporters had dribbled off towards the National and United Parties. It had been displaced from its niche by narrow nationalist and chauvinist factions. Its final knell sounded in the 1948 General Election, when the Smuts government was turned out of office, taking the Labour remnants with it.

Labour had been born out of a white artisan class which had, by now, lost all socialist orientation. It had outlived its time, and for all practical purposes died in tandem with the Smuts government.[3] Whether it was ever formally wound up I do not know.

To me, expulsion from the Labour Party had come as something of a merciful liberation. I had repeatedly petitioned the CP District Committee for permission to resign from it, and had been repeatedly

---

[2] Years later, together with Canon John Collins of St Paul's Cathedral, London, he formed the International Defence and Aid Fund (IDAF) which assisted South African political prisoners and their families through the long years of apartheid.

[3] The mixed-race Labour Party formed at the time of the Nationalists' 'Tricameral Parliament' had no connection with the South African Labour Party except the name.

turned down. Now the decision had been made by Labour. I could concentrate my political activity in the CP as I wanted to do.

It was a good time for it. The CP was coming out into the public light from its reclusive and semi-clandestine past. It had moved from its hole-in-corner premises to new offices in Progress Buildings, close to the heart of the city where the Carlton Centre now stands. It had replaced the press sequestrated in the times of decline with a new electric duplicator. It was starting publication of a new monthly *Inkululeko* (Freedom) to replace the former, now defunct, *Umsebenzi* (The Worker): the change of title indicated some shift of orientation.

Inkululeko had pages in the main African languages as well as English. It was typed on wax stencils and duplicated in the party offices. Hilda drew me into the production team in which she did skilled things like drawing the illustrations and hand lettering the headlines, while Archie Lewitton typed the stencils with two fingers, and Mofutsanyana edited. I was only a gofer.

We met at the office once a month, early on Sunday morning, and spent the day wrestling with the Gestetner machine, and collating and stapling the pages as they rolled off the press. By the time we came up for air in late afternoon, coated in printers' ink, a stack of some 1 200 copies would be ready for distribution and sale. For me it was the start of an unplanned career as a propagandist.

Inkululeko helped bring the Party out of the shadows and into the streets. Members were expected to hawk it at factory gates, railway stations and municipal compounds. Once such street-vending became a regular practice, it was logical to make it a weekly affair by adding the *Guardian* to our vending stock.

The *Guardian* was not a Party organ but an independent and radical weekly, produced in Cape Town under the editorship of Betty Radford. It was the only regular publication to give space to the news and views of the trade unions, the national liberation movements, and the Party. It was already being sold by paid street vendors and commission agents. We joined them, in part to help boost sales, but chiefly in an attempt to turn the Party outwards away from its concentration on internal doctrinal minutiae, towards public activity in the real world outside.

For months, perhaps for years, I did my stint of vending at

midday on Saturdays at the entrance to the Mai-Mai municipal beer hall at the south end of Von Wielligh Street. At the time, the sale or supply of any form of alcohol to blacks was totally prohibited, the only exception being sorghum beer – so-called 'kaffir beer' – for on-consumption at municipal beer halls. Municipalities with total monopolies saw no reason to make their beer halls anything more than comfortless drinking sheds. Mai-Mai's was a bleak corrugated iron shed baking in the sun in a bleak wasteland of swirling red dust. My sales were quite brisk. The men – the customers were almost all men – would insist on seeing a page in their own tongue before they would spend a penny on a copy of *Inkululeko*. It was always strangely easier to sell a two-penny *Guardian*, all in English.

But whichever I was selling, it was an ordeal which I forced upon myself as a matter of Party duty. Although I hated everything about selling, I came to enjoy the noise and liveliness of the Mai-Mai crowds and the exchange of banter with sober men coming in from work, and with rolling drunks coming out. My pitch was shared with a bustle of women street-traders roasting mealies and chicken legs on pavement braziers. Alongside us there were pavement barbers giving alfresco trims and razor-cuts to customers sitting on soap-boxes.

Everywhere else in Johannesburg, paper selling was done only by blacks, usually teenage blacks, and the buyers were almost all white. Here the standard order was reversed – an adult white man was selling to black buyers. Just being white in such an all black environment made me a curiosity. Men would stop and stare in disbelief. Occasionally some inebriated fellow might jeer, but I was never threatened or even felt threatened.

There at Mai-Mai I first learnt to feel at ease in the midst of black people, and to move amongst them without self-consciousness. The psychological baggage of a life lived in exclusively white surroundings rubbed away as blacks ceased to be 'others' – menials, servants or 'victims of underdevelopment' – and became simply people, individuals.

After some years of Mai-Mai I moved to a different Party branch, handed over the Mai-Mai pitch to others, and transferred my paper selling to the branch area of Braamfontein. In those days before it was 're-developed' with an unlovely mix of shops, high-rise offices and University overspill, it was a working-class area of small semi-detached brick cottages occupied by white railwaymen, some with student lodgers.

Branch members trudged door to door with the *Guardian* every Sunday morning. We learnt to know where there might possibly be a buyer, where we would get a political argument on the doorstep but no sale, and where it was best to pass rapidly in silence before being spotted by hostile residents or even more hostile guard dogs. To me it was a cheerless activity, with none of Mai-Mai's compensations. Only missionary zeal kept me at it, and a belief that sooner or later one of my regular buyers would develop democratic, radical or even left views, and become 'educated' as our jargon had it.

That belief was constantly undermined by experience. My most regular customer was an Afrikaans-speaking railwayman who had an adult son. Every Sunday, one or other of them duly handed over twopence and chatted on the doorstep about the state of the nation. The chat was costing me my Sunday morning leisure, but in the good cause of their 'education'. Eventually the question of crime came up on the doorstep. Every white claims to be an expert on what they portray as a specifically black phenomenon, and to have an instant solution for the crime wave. My favourite Braamfontein customer gave me his: 'Follow Paul Kruger!' he said. 'Tie the kaffir to a wagon wheel and give him a thrashing he will never forget!' The educational payoff for my Sundays with the *Guardian*!

Did we really achieve anything at all by all that expenditure of time and energy? Did we really effect even a subliminal change in our buyers' thinking, or were we mortifying our flesh for the good of our own souls? I am not sure of the answer, or of what our Braamfontein customers were thinking when they handed over their twopence. Were they looking for alternative news? Getting rid of us cheaply? Or were they perhaps being charitable and helping out an apparently poor white boy in need?

I like to think that perhaps we did help to change some of their ideas and counter some of their prejudices. Perhaps when the time came for white South Africa to choose between civil war and majority government, our *Guardian* Sundays might have influenced some of their decisions for the better. Perhaps.

Whatever the reality, those hours of paper-selling were not totally wasted. We had spread information and ideas which might possibly have helped Braamfontein railwaymen and Mai-Mai beer drinkers to look at their country in a new way, perhaps to start adapting their minds to a new South Africa which was still fifty years away.

It was not just a one-way process. While trying to 'educate' others we were educating ourselves. We were learning to work collectively, to listen to what 'the man in the street' was saying and thinking, and to present our political ideas to them in non-dogmatic ways. Through paper vending we were also rebuilding the Party as an open organisation in the public light, just like any other political party.

Opposing the war effort had its price. Early in 1941, Yusuf Dadoo in Johannesburg and Dawood Seedat in Durban, both prominent members of the Party, were arrested and charged with subversion and anti-war incitement. Their arrests triggered the biggest protest campaign of meetings, handbills and posters that the Party had managed for years. My group was assigned to help campaign in the Sophiatown area where our local organisation was under strength. Sophiatown now exists only in memories. It was bulldozed in one of Verwoerd's worst racial excesses to make space for an exclusively white suburb provocatively named Triomf (Triumph).

At that time it was a multi-racial residential area where black people could own their own homes and live unencumbered by the red tape and round-the-clock controls of the municipal townships. It was a tight huddle of small run-down cottages which had once been single-family homes. As the war-time population grew, houses had been divided and re-divided until almost all were in multiple occupation, often with one family per room. Backyards had been built over with unauthorised annexes occupying every remaining inch of open space. It was a lively bustling place where people of all races and colours shared minimal facilities and deprivation. By night, householders locked themselves in, leaving the yards to jazz clubs and illegal shebeens, and the streets to petty gangsters, drunks, and packs of mangy dogs.

Night after night, our group trudged the streets around midnight, with our stacks of protest leaflets. The people were asleep but the dogs were loose. We worked in pairs, up and down the streets, slipping leaflets under every door. Dead of night may have been chosen as the best time to avoid police patrols and roving gangsters; or perhaps out of revolutionary romanticism. It was very scary. The streets were badly lit and pot-holed, and crossed by foul-smelling open ditches and overloaded drains. We crept guardedly to the front doors on dark front porches where lean mean guard dogs lurked in the shadows.

That too was a part of our learning and party-building – by ordeal. We gained a first-hand knowledge of the living conditions of a sector of the black working class. We learnt to rely on one another for support and morale, and developed a Party bond which cannot be created by rules alone. In that activity, the Party developed the exceptional levels of unity and voluntary discipline which became its most distinct characteristic. Whether we affected the fate of Dadoo and Seedat is hard to say. Both were found guilty and sentenced to short terms of imprisonment, making them the first martyrs of the years of the Communist Party revival.

Open-air political meetings had been held intermittently on the steps of the City Hall since the time of World War One, and throughout the white workers' strikes of 1913 and 1922, but the practice had withered. Meetings there had become irregular and infrequent until the Party District Committee decided to revive the tradition.

We started to hold public meetings there every Sunday evening. The steps provided a natural podium with speakers at the top of the steps and the audience spread along the pavement at the foot. We took our pitch in the centre of the podium, facing the clock on the old Rissik Street Post Office across the road, and simply held forth to anyone who happened to be passing – and often initially to no one at all.

We had no better claim to that prime site than anyone else. On Sunday evenings there were precious few passing pedestrians – almost no blacks lived in the city proper, and even they were kept off the streets by a night curfew unless they had a 'special pass'. The meetings were thus an all white affair which all our city members were expected to attend to form the nucleus of a crowd. That gave us an advantage over our lone-wolf competitors. The speakers were white, and the audiences white except for the occasional black straggler who paused momentarily to listen from the outer fringes. But not for long – the white audience would soon make him feel alien and uncomfortable. The Party which was waging a consistent and resolute fight against the colour bar everywhere, never managed to banish it from its own meetings on the steps.

We had only a few experienced public speakers. Novices like me were simply thrown in at the deep end – without tuition and without any public address equipment. Our veteran speaker was Issy Wolfson of the Tailoring Workers' Union, endowed with a voice like a fog-horn which drowned out the noise of hecklers and passing traffic, and echoed back from the Post Office across the road. He seemed never to use notes, but the words flowed effortlessly, conjuring up instant slogans and drawing intermittent applause.

Hilda was our most eloquent speaker. She too could conjure up the applause and rousing perorations, but always from a base of meticulously prepared notes.

Most of our speakers had learnt the art in the trade union movement. Betty du Toit of the Food and Canning Union, equally at home in English and Afrikaans. Willie Kalk of the Leather Workers pacing furiously like a caged lion; Danie du Plessis of the Building Workers' Union. The rest of us learnt as we went along, including the District Secretary Michael Harmel, Archie Lewitton and several others. I was probably the most reluctant of them all.

Attendances fluctuated between fifty and several hundred. Occasionally someone from the crowd would apply to join the Party, but recruiting was not the main aim. The purpose was to build ourselves a regular public forum in the centre of the city as a step towards establishing the Party in the mainstream of political life.

In time, the Steps on Sunday Nights came to be known as the Party's platform. Other speakers, some of whom had been there from time to time before us, would also exercise their rights, and take advantage of what we considered to be *our* audience. These irregulars were a strange mixture. There was an elderly, vituperative, tub-thumping socialist radical named Dunbar, who thundered out minor variations of a sermon he had been delivering since the 1920s and the days of the International Socialist League (ISL). An altogether more tolerant old socialist and veteran of the 1922 General Strike,

Jimmy Brown, preached the social panacea of 'One Big Union'.

Most vituperative and hostile of all our rival orators was a lone Trotskyist named Saperstein, a white-coated pharmacist during the week and a proto-proletarian with greasy leather lumber-jacket, patched jeans, checkered sweat-shirt and day-old stubble on his chin on Sundays. He arrived with no discernible message of his own only to deliver a fiery 'revolutionist's' condemnation of all things communist.

No doubt they all believed in their messages as much as we did in ours, but only sheer cussedness can account for their persistence in the face of cruel heckling and howls of rejection from the audience. Our meetings would start strictly on time, regardless of who else might be speaking a few yards away. We could rely on Wolfson's fog-horn to persuade the others to shut down for the night.

As the Steps became known as the Party's platform, audiences of hundreds would appear from nowhere whenever there was an event of importance to give the gathering immediacy – such as Rommel's capture of South African soldiers at Tobruk, the fall of Paris to the Nazis, or the German invasion of the USSR.

Johannesburg still carried some birthmarks of its mining camp beginnings. Political meetings were rowdy, and often rough. The Steps meetings became both, and a focus for hooligans looking for a punch-up with communists. Gangs of young fascists took to mingling with the crowd, bringing a vicious tone to the jeering and heckling, shouting fascist slogans and trying to provoke a fight. As their confidence grew, they took to assaulting any of our members whom they found in the street alone on the way to or from the Steps. They made random assaults on any passing blacks, and staged violent forays against the speakers on our platform. Sunday evenings on the Steps became a regular battleground.

We had either to abandon the meetings or defend them physically. We chose defence and organised a corps of our fittest and toughest members to protect the speakers, and to guard members coming to or from the meeting. That helped us feel safer, but made our meetings more fraught. While our speakers balanced precariously at the top of the steps, fists flew and bodies clashed while the police who were regularly there in force stood idly by.

We were seeing the beginning of new-style policing, based either on surreptitious encouragement of the right-wing thugs or on positive protection of them. Sunday nights for us became ordeals of stomach-knotting anticipation of minor brawls and running street-fights. They regularly ended either at our casualty clearing station in Max Joffe's surgery overlooking the Steps, or in a march to Marshall Square to bail out comrades arrested for 'assault' or 'public disorder'.

The City Hall Steps meetings tested our nerves to the limit, but gave the Party a real presence in the city's politics. Unlike the Steps meetings, growth was not confined to the white arena. In the black areas of the city, a parallel growth in Party confidence and activity was taking place with the recruiting of new members proceeding faster than amongst whites. Black Party members were advancing into leading positions in the trade unions, in the liberation movements and in township community organisations. The whole Party was growing up, and changing from a predominantly white sect into a predominantly black mass party. For the first time in its history, its membership began to mirror the real racial and class composition of the population as a whole.

4

ACROSS THE DIVIDE
1940 – 43

The Communist Party was functioning in a non-racial enclave of its own. Inside the Party there was a total black-white equality which could be found nowhere else. But we were not utopians seeking to create a perfect place of our own, shut off from the world. We were trying to engage with that world, challenge its fundamental mores and customs, and ultimately change them.

But there was a paradox. The more we involved ourselves in that wider world, the greater became its pressure on us to conform to its practices. Inside the Party and its committees, conferences and members' meetings, there was no colour differentiation. But the more we moved out of our own closed circles into the social and political mainstream, the more we were driven to divide into black and white streams – fraternal, nominally equal, but separate.

There was no way for us to grow outwards and avoid the great racial divide. Society imposed its racial division on our organisational forms and on our political activities. Our residentially based branches were inevitably either predominantly black or predominantly white according to the race pattern of the area. Trade unions we belonged to were either 'white' or 'black' to accord with industrial laws. Election campaigns were restricted by law to white candidates and voters only, or to black. The languages used at meetings had to be either English or Afrikaans in a white area, or Zulu or Sotho in a black. Society locked us into its established racial net. We had either to conform or cease to function at all.

I was seconded to assist the Party branch in Vrededorp – a racially mixed slum area with close-packed cottages where single rooms were rented out by absentee landlords. The branch members were all new recruits, black, mainly middle-aged men, with no prior Party experience. The only member with a place big enough to hold ten or twelve people was a very large and forceful woman who had two back rooms and a kitchen. She was known as a 'shebeen queen': that is to say, she kept an unlicensed drinking place with a stock of hard liquor, and was a vendor of home-brewed beer stored in old petrol drums buried in the yard. Illegal things, including brewing of beer and the sale of alcohol to blacks, went on in her kitchen.

Our branch met in her parlour each week, always in fear of a police liquor raid. Occasional drunks would lose their bearings and blunder in and out. It was all very new to me, both socially and politically. I was only to guide, advise and facilitate. In theory at least, I was an ordinary member, equal with all others. In practice, there was no disguising my separate status. I was the only one who knew and understood the Party ropes. I was the only white, and the only one who did not live in the area. I felt like an outsider, an intruder into the community and not really part of it. But the others showed no signs of resentment or distrust. They accepted me fully – a rare experience for a white in such a black circle, and for the few hours I spent each week in Vrededorp, it was as though there was no racial divide.

But that was an illusion. Outside there was white supremacy everywhere. And inside the group, a deeply ingrained habit of black subservience which holding a Party card did not cure. When any difference of opinion arose, the members would invariably defer to my opinion, not because of my Party rank but because of my racial status. I knew it, and tried to combat it. But there was a fatal contradiction. Our black members were being encouraged to act as full equal citizens inside the Party, at the same time as they were being compelled to live in racial subservience and inequality outside it. I began to understand that though I was trying to help them develop self-reliance and a sense of equality, my very presence among them inhibited both.

It was a paradox. My mission in Vrededorp was to assist, but to do that I needed to diminish my own role and allow them to discover how to stand on their own feet.

I am not sure that I was successful, but the Vrededorp branch was eventually up and running and I was transferred to another struggling branch in Alexandra Township. It was my Vrededorp experience revisited, but in rather different circumstances. In Alexandra our meetings were held in a quiet detached cottage occupied by a comrade named Tommy Peters. There were no blundering drunks or threats of police liquor raids, but outside there was tension and real danger.

Alexandra was a sprawling slum, much smaller than it is today, with dusty, rutted roads and little sign of drainage or garbage removal services. Dilapidated cottages and shacks stood amidst vacant plots of weeds and litter. There was no street lighting. By night the streets were dangerous and intimidating, with roving bands of gangsters with lethal weapons made from sharpened bicycle-spokes. After dark it was perilous and foolhardy to walk alone, and not quite safe in a car.

Meetings were never held on Friday nights – the bicycle-spoke gangs would be out waiting for men coming home with a week's pay in their pockets. Members would never leave meetings singly; always in groups. On Sundays when the sun dispelled some of the menace in the air, we held open-air public meetings on a dusty, litter-strewn bus terminal known as Number 1 Square. It had none of the vibrant liveliness of Mai-Mai or even of the streets of Vrededorp.

From time to time I would be one of the speakers. I was always ill at ease, even in the sunshine; the place always felt hostile. Those passers-by who stopped to listen for a few minutes would walk off often shouting something derisory or dismissive. Whether the hostility was caused by my white presence or by the meeting's message was not clear. It was always a relief when the meeting was over and I could get away – by car to my side of the racial divide, leaving my comrades uneasily on theirs.

Just as in Vrededorp, so in Alexandra. Inside the branch meeting I was amongst equals; outside an intruder. Inside there was comradeship and trust without regard to colour; outside, distrust and hostility. Inside we were working together to change the old order; outside we were trapped in its racial coils on separate sides of the divide.

Yet the Party was expanding on both sides of the divide. At the Johannesburg centre it was outgrowing its resources, and I was asked to take up full-time work as a 'Party functionary' engaged mainly in publicity and propaganda activities. I agreed. I could carry on with my part-time course at university, with lectures before and after work.

I soon learnt that there was little difference between full-time Party work and any other office work, except that the hours were unlimited and the pay about that of an unskilled labourer.

Party work produced a special variant of Parkinson's law: meetings proliferate to fill the time available for them – including meal hours and all hours of day and night. And an addendum which gives meetings precedence over everything else. My home life became erratic. I kept irregular hours and ate irregular meals, but I learnt something about the art of propaganda, and became a competent committee clerk, copy-writer, reporter, and occasional sub-editor.

Inkululeko had outgrown the wax stencil and Gestetner machine and was about to change to a regularly printed fortnightly. It was edited in the Party office by Edwin Mofutsanyana who could read most of the African languages, with Michael Harmel writing most of the English language articles and the editorials. Edwin was a veteran of the leadership of both Party and ANC, best described as an egghead. He was quiet, shy to the point of diffidence, an intellectual and a thinker – his critics might say a slow thinker. As newspaper editor he was neither an inspirer nor an administrator.

Edwin was cautious and slow of speech. He edited *Inkululeko* systematically and with careful attention to political correctness, but without much verve or originality. For flair *Inkululeko* depended on Harmel who wrote easily and well but was even less of an administrator than Mofutsanyana. Between them they planned and edited, but gradually left almost everything else to me.

I knew just enough about newspaper production to be the office boy – if the editor knew more than I did he did not show it. He gave me no instructions, merely explained the procedures, suggested what I might do, and left me to it. I found myself gradually saddled with layout, headlining, and seeing the paper through the press. And when Edwin was away on Party or ANC business as he often was, I was left to do the proof-reading of articles in languages of which I was wholly ignorant.

I learnt to do it by making a tedious letter-by-letter comparison with the manuscript. In time I could manage a syllable-by-syllable check, and finally a word-by-word. It is not the way to learn a language, but in the end I could recognise most commonly used words by phonetics without reference to the script, and without understanding them. Over the years I picked up a smattering, but no more, of several languages. By the time I completed my university course and received my diploma, I had little practical experience of actual building, but considerable experience of newspaper production and printing, and of dashing off a piece of journalese at short order. I had become a Party propaganda specialist.

Harmel, Mofutsanyana and I worked out of two small offices. The corridor access was locked by a steel grille at night. The Party's confrontation with fascists at the City Hall steps and elsewhere was intensifying. One night, petrol or something similar was poured through the grille and set alight. Before the building's night watchman realised it, flames had burnt through the door and into the offices, where what was not incinerated was reduced to pulp by his fire-hose.

We salvaged what we could and moved into the only other space available in the building. It was a much larger suite of four offices and a boardroom large enough for meetings or small conferences, and much more expensive. The Party treasurer bit the bullet, and the Party operated from there until its demise in 1950.

The Party and *Inkululeko* were both growing and needed more hands. A young comrade, John Nkadimeng, joined us and took charge of *Inkululeko*'s distribution and sales, and John Kepobetsoe came in as filing clerk, messenger and general factotum. By 1941 *Inkululeko* had grown sufficiently to move up from fortnightly to weekly publication, putting severe strain both on the Party finances and on the capacity of part-time volunteer writers and reporters.

It also strained the capacity of our printers who had only one linotype machine operator. He was a morose but co-operative Afrikaner who had learnt to set type in the African languages by the same letter-by-letter process without understanding that I had used. He was a high-speed, high-quality operator, but our weekly issue proved to be the straw that broke the camel's back. After a few months he issued a *démarche*: no more weekly *Inkululeko*! Either our weekly went or he did. Our printers gave way to *force majeure. Inkululeko* was more dispensable than their linotype operator. We reverted to fortnightly production, and all heaved secret sighs of relief.

Party propaganda services were expanding in several directions. On the trade union front discontent was growing amongst the black workers. Prices were rising fast but wages were not, and the unions were struggling to cope with a rash of industrial disputes and spontaneous strikes. The Party, in concert with the unions, launched a campaign for a national minimum wage of ten shillings a day – equivalent to one rand. By today's standards it is a risible amount. At that time it was way beyond what any part of the establishment would even contemplate. It was said to be unrealistic and revolutionary, more than the country could afford and a recipe for bankruptcy. But the ten shilling claim brought an instant response from the black workers. It was adopted by all the black trade unions and by the national liberation organisations.

As part of the campaign for that minimum wage, I wrote my first pamphlet for the Party titled – slightly misleadingly – *How To Get More Money*. It sold in thousands for a penny a copy and was translated into several languages. Its message – more precise than its title – was: If you want better wages, join and build your trade union! The slogan of 'Ten Shillings a Day' caught on fast, the trade union message rather more slowly.

But the campaign and the pamphlet gave a tremendous spurt to trade union growth, and a focus for rising militancy amongst black workers at a time when white trade unions were slowly declining with defectors gravitating to right-wing Afrikaner nationalism. Even so, the white trade unions' Trades and Labour Council (TLC) barred all affiliation by black unions.

On the Rand the black unions had come together to form their own independent Council of Non-European Trade Unions (CNETU), under whose aegis new and fast-growing black unions were being built. An unprecedented influx of black workers was coming into the Party, recruited from the factories and townships, and also at public meetings. There the rush to join could get out of hand.

We held periodic mass meetings on what was then the Newtown Market Square – now a weekday car park and Saturday flea market opposite the Museum Africa. Meetings would end with a call for recruits and the handing out of membership application forms.

After one such meeting at the height of the 'ten shilling' campaign, we received a mass of completed application forms which appeared to represent almost the whole black labour force at the Castle Breweries compound not far from our office. The applicants were all called to the customary interview before acceptance. That was almost a mass meeting in its own right. The applicants were almost all Shangaan speakers. Our best Shangaan interpreter was appropriately named – English Tschauke.

It was soon apparent that the brewery workers made no distinction between joining the Party and joining the claim for ten shillings a day. Perhaps our public speakers were themselves allowing the edges to blur. Tschauke spelt out the difference to them, and persuaded them that what they really needed was a way to deal with grievances at work. That meant a trade union – not the Party. There was no union in the brewing industry, but if they would support one Tschauke and the Party would organise one. They agreed and went off happy; Tschauke underwent a short course of intensive training, and became a founder and full-time organiser of the new Brewery Workers' Union. It was typical of the times.

Trade union growth was being paralleled, perhaps exceeded, by simultaneous growth of the national liberation movements. In theory, the Party had always supported a liberation movement, but in the locust years of inner Party doctrinal strife, the relationship of nationalism to socialism had become a matter of fierce dispute. Now, when the Party was deliberately seeking to integrate itself into mainstream politics, the debate had to be resolved. Practical political work had to be carried on wherever there were politically aware people.

Accordingly, almost all eligible Party members were active members of the Indian or the African National Congresses, though there remained a small minority core who would not join. Some argued a dogmatic, allegedly 'Marxist' view that nationalism was simply 'bourgeois', and the national movements a 'reformist' distraction from class struggle and revolution.

The main source of opposition to joining the ANC, however, was its sorry organisational state. The ANC had proved itself to be the most durable and representative African national body. But despite wide popular support, organisationally it was a broken reed.

Its active membership had declined to the level of a sect, and feeble public appearances had reduced it to not much more than a current of opinion, rather than a serious contender for political power.

The ANC's Transvaal Secretary at that time, C S Ramohanoe, would call at the Party office from time to time to borrow ink, paper and duplicator with which to produce notices of his committee meetings. We both knew that none of the loans were ever likely to be returned. If he had an office of his own, it must have been about the ANC's only asset.

It is easy to understand why so many Party members regarded it either as irrelevant or as a potential handicap in the struggle. It required real political insight to see in this enfeebled organisation the once and future representative of the nation. The Party, to its credit, had that insight. It had to fight a consistent campaign inside its own ranks to convince the sceptics. In the end, aided by the spectacular renaissance of the ANC membership in the late '40s, the objections were laid to rest once and for all.

Although the Party and the mass movements were moving boldly out into the public arena – or perhaps because of that – harassment by police and fascist irregulars carried on. The right to speak and organise was always under threat, and the prospect of a state clamp-down seemed real enough to move the District Committee to defensive preparations. It decided to establish a clandestine printing press, just in case.

Someone in the upper echelons made a discreet purchase of a machine known as a 'Multilith', and a small group which included Hilda and me was given responsibility for it. The apparatus looked simple enough. It turned out to be fiendishly difficult. Hand-set type had to be composed letter by letter and locked into a drum. Sheets of paper had to be fed in individually by hand, strictly synchronised with the hand-rotated drum – a trick calling for the same knack as is called for in rubbing one's stomach in a circular pattern with one hand while patting the top of one's head with the other. Its action was heavy. We never managed to get the thing moving at much more than a crawl, and even at that speed it made enough noise to waken the dead.

We found a secluded house to let in an acre of overgrown garden in Orchards, far enough away from neighbours to muffle the noise. Hilda and I hired the place, and moved in with the Multilith. Our group practised on the machine each evening, and mastered it well enough to produce some small Party handbills.

Success with what it called 'the Party press' went to the District Committee's head. We were ordered to print multiple copies of a speech by Soviet foreign minister Molotov which explained the USSR's armed incursion into Finland. It was, I suppose, an important speech. It had passed almost unreported in the press. It would run to twelve of our pages, though we had only enough type to set two pages. So two pages had to be printed and the type recovered first before any more could begin to be set.

We were into a long job, and stuck at it determinedly while the war rolled on faster than our Multilith. At last we had the whole thing printed except the cover page and its title in bold: THE SOVIET UNION MAINTAINS NEUTRALITY! We spent nights churning away at the handle and watching the words flash past interminably: 'The Soviet Union maintains neutrality . . . maintains neutrality . . . maintains neutrality.'

Only it did not. Just as we reached the end of our print run, Hitler's armies blasted their way across the Soviet border, and the Soviet Union was fighting for its life. June 22nd, 1941, and neutrality was dead. So was the first and only pamphlet from our secret press, which was mothballed and disappeared from sight. Hilda and I abandoned the cottage retreat and returned to ordinary living.

By this time, Party membership in Johannesburg had grown to around three hundred, rooted in the trade unions and the national liberation movements. The Pretoria branch had grown into a separate District, and new branches had been established in several Rand mining towns. Fraternal relations had been established with Lekgotla la Bafo, a radical peasant movement in Basutoland (now Lesotho) led by the remarkable brothers Maphutseng and Josiel Lefela; and with small communist sects in Moçambique and in Southern Rhodesia.

The internecine schisms of the 1930s and the strife which had dictated the removal of Party headquarters to Cape Town were things of the past. Johannesburg was the industrial and commercial heart of the country. The resurgence of national liberation movements and trade unions made it also the political heart. The siting of Party headquarters in Cape Town had always been an anomaly, dictated solely by the need to restore Party stability and unity. The geographical and political distance between the Cape Peninsula and the rest of the country remained. The Peninsula was uniquely different. It was the only part of the country where Africans were a minority, and thus where the CC would be insulated from the gale of political growth and change which was blowing up amongst the black majority everywhere else.

When the move to Cape Town had taken place, it had not been intended to be permanent. By 1941 there was general agreement that the time had come to prepare to move our headquarters back to the political centre of the country. Two members of the Johannesburg District Committee – Harmel and Lewitton – were seconded to Cape Town to learn the CC ropes and provide for continuity when the move back to Johannesburg came about. That left Johannesburg without a District Secretary. I was elected to the post at the next District conference. It made little difference to my work except to load me down with *ex officio* attendances at innumerable additional sub-committee meetings, and with extra secretarial duties.

From time to time, Moses Kotane would arrive in Johannesburg on a political mission. During one of his visits my work at the office was interrupted by a middle-aged white man I did not know. He was small, wrinkled, and wore an ice-cream coloured suit and pince-nez. He wanted to see his 'old friend Moses Kotane'. Kotane was not in. I told the visitor he would be back shortly, and suggested he wait.

After a time, I took pity on the poor fellow and phoned Kotane to tell him a friend was waiting for him. Kotane was just leaving Dadoo's home less than half a mile away. A few minutes later he stepped into the office, and stopped as though pole-axed. His little 'friend' stood up and said: 'Hello, Mr Kotane. I have a warrant for your arrest!' He was from the Special Branch, Cape Town, and marched Kotane off in a state of shock.

I was as shocked as he was – by my own naïvety. We started an immediate campaign of protest, but Kotane remained locked up for some weeks on allegations of incitement before being released without charge. Afterwards he made black jokes about it, but never held any grudge against me. I had earned myself a niche of sorts in history as the only Party official who ever shopped his own General Secretary – and got away with it.

Kotane and I got on quite well together. He was a man who spoke his mind bluntly, and many people found his manner abrasive, intimidating, or sometimes just downright rude. For that reason he was not always popular, but he was our best known public figure and much respected in the Party and beyond. He was also a member of the ANC National Executive and one of the founders of the Council of Non-European Trade Unions. His status in the movement was built on a solid base of incorruptibility and personal integrity, combined with an independent mind, plain speaking and remarkable political acumen.

There was no sensible reason for his sudden arrest. It was a clumsy blunder at a time of growing pro-Japanese sentiment in the black community, based on Japan's sweeping victories in the far east. Their military triumphs were being widely interpreted in black political circles as the ascendancy of the non-white people over white imperial power, and thus a harbinger of South Africa's coming liberation.

The Party was the only organisation challenging this simplistic thesis head on. Kotane had been in the forefront of that challenge. He had attacked the myth from many public platforms, and had written a Party critique of Japanese fascism, published under the title 'Japan: Friend or Foe?' His arrest created widespread protest – not just from the Party, but from other pro-war and establishment circles. The charge was dropped within weeks by order of the Minister of Justice, Dr Colin Steyn, and he was released. That was a sign of how the political climate had changed since the campaign only two years before for the release of Dadoo and Seedat.

As we saw it, the character of the war was also changing, which accounts in some measure for our open campaigning against the pro-Japanese camp around us. To some, that stance coupled with our persistent critique of the anti-democratic and racist actions of the Smuts government appeared to have us facing both ways at once. It was a tricky balancing act. But it was indicative of a policy in transition. A changing world was calling into question our overall characterisation of the war. It might once have been correct, but was it ever adequate? I think now that it had always been too simplistic. It dealt only with the predominant and overall character of the war, and skated over the contradictory and complex aspects of it.

From the beginning there had been genuinely anti-fascist struggles and localised struggles for democracy or national independence mixed up in the imperial struggle. As the war went on, these struggles were gathering importance in the overall equation. Genuinely popular struggles were taking over centre stage in almost every Nazi-occupied country, moving the centre of gravity from imperialist war towards people's war.

We were responding to that shift, instinctively and almost certainly too slowly because we were so far from the scene. But refugees, partisans and resistance fighters from some of the people's struggles were beginning to arrive among us, along with soldiers bringing new ideas and attitudes from the war fronts in East and North Africa. We were being made to appreciate that the character of the war – like everything else – was subject to change. And that our policies needed to change to keep in touch.

Servicemen were returning to South Africa for leave or re-grouping after the battles in the Western Desert. Men in army uniform would drop in to the Party office for an argument or a discussion, amongst them Jack Hodgson in blue army hospital fatigues. He was about my age, but gaunt and hollow cheeked as though all flesh had melted off his bones. He had a slight stutter as his thoughts raced ahead of his tongue. He had served in the Western Desert with an irregular armoured car unit known as the Desert Rats, roving behind the enemy lines, hitting and running wherever opportunity offered. It had left him with seemingly incurable stomach ulcers. Army medics had tried every cure they could think of – surgery, psychiatry, drip-feeds, drugs. Nothing had worked. He was waiting on an army Medical Board to decide about his future.

Jack lacked the temperament for waiting. Convalescence in hospital was driving him mad. He was looking for some useful activity in the Party. He had learnt something about communism when he had worked on the Northern Rhodesian copper mines during the great depression of the 1930s. An expatriate British miner, Frank Maybank, had introduced him to socialist ideas and Marxism. They were both militant members of the Mine Workers' Union.

Soon after the outbreak of war, and together with another South African, Chris Meyer, they had been prominent in a strike of the white miners. Northern Rhodesia's Prime Minister, a Labour man and former railway worker, Sir Roy Welensky, who Jack referred to as 'that fucking Labour baron', had imposed martial law. Maybank, Hodgson and Meyer were all declared to be *personae non gratae* and deported back to their home countries. Jack had joined the army.

I took an instant liking to him. His family were sharing a small Bellevue house with the Meyers and an army of children. We struck up a close friendship which lasted, in South Africa and in exile in Britain, until the end of his life. He was an unassuming man with no personal ambitions, utterly unshakeable in his political convictions, and incurably optimistic about the future despite the ill health which dogged him to the end of his life.

At that time not much was known in South Africa about an organisation which had started amongst the soldiers 'up North' calling itself the Springbok Legion. Jack provided the facts. It had started as a type of soldiers' trade union concerned with conditions of army service, the welfare of their dependants, and the provisions for ex-servicemen after the war; and had been at pains to avoid possible accusations of 'conduct prejudicial to good military order and discipline'.

The South African army was not a likely breeding ground for such a body. Most of the ordinary soldiers had joined the army too young to have been trade unionists before. They were all volunteers. Their service conditions were neither as harsh nor as repressive as those of many conscript forces, and their family backgrounds were generally conservative or thoroughly reactionary. Army service abroad had changed their ideas and radicalised them.

In Egypt, they had had some contact with the radicalism which was spreading in the ranks of the British and other armies, and with a regular political forum functioning amongst them in Cairo known as the Soldiers' Parliament. Amongst the 'Parliament's' founders were British serviceman Leo Abse, later to become a distinguished Labour MP; James Klugman, one of the British CP's leading Marxist theoreticians; and Basil Davidson, the British 'Special Operations Executive' liaison man with Tito's partisans, and later populariser of Africa's lost history. The Soldiers' Parliament's debates on the shape of a possible brave new post-war world, had helped broaden the South African minds, and revive faded folk memories of a classless (white) South African frontier democratism.

The Springbok Legion was an idea whose time had come. Among its founders was Jock Isacowitz who had received an introduction to Marxism with me from Kurt Jonas at Wits University. He had returned from 'up North' with the rank of Sergeant Major, and the Springbok Legion as his inspiration. He was a powerful public speaker who travelled in uniform from one public meeting to another, introducing the Springbok Legion to South Africa. A packed meeting with a white audience in the Johannesburg City Hall started funds and pledges of support rolling in; the Legion began recruiting black servicemen from segregated black camps and units inside the country, and started building a 'Home Front League' for soldiers' dependants and ex-servicemen of earlier wars. It also started a lively newspaper called *Fighting Talk* which circulated quite widely in the army camps at home and abroad.

Jack Hodgson was discharged from the army on medical grounds and pensioned. He became the national secretary of the Legion with an office in Johannesburg.[1] The Legion was fast becoming a force to be reckoned with. Most of its members in uniform were cutting their political teeth in the Legion, and developing their first flush of political consciousness which brought a number of them also into the ranks of the Communist Party.

The war was also casting up on South African shores many refugees fresh from political struggles in Europe, particularly Holland, Yugoslavia and Greece. Between them, these diverse groups were loosing a fresh wind in the ranks of the Party. Those who came our way were generally very left wing, very militant, and fired with the partisan spirit. Amongst them were twenty or more veterans of the anti-Nazi resistance in Greece, members of the Greek Seaman's Union, and partisan fighters who had escaped when their country fell to the Germans. At least one of them had been sentenced to death in Greece *in absentia*. Most of them spoke poor English, so when they joined the Party en bloc it was decided to form them

---

[1] The Legion's foremost fund-raiser was a former army nurse, Rica Gampel, whom he later married. Jack went on to become the first technical expert and instructor to Umkhonto we Sizwe. In 1963 they escaped from twenty-four hour house arrest and left the country. In London, Jack remained an active participant in MK until his death. Rica became one of the key members of the International Defence and Aid Fund (IDAF), and returned to South Africa to become Walter Sisulu's private secretary at ANC headquarters.

into a special branch of their own.

Shepherding them became one of my tasks as Secretary. They were lovely people, wonderfully untamed spirits with an irrepressible partisan enthusiasm, but temperamentally different from most of our Party members. Right from the start, I sensed that they found us disappointingly mild and legalistic – not at all what they thought communists ought to be.

Our Greek comrades all found jobs at the Van der Bijl steelworks in Vereeniging – just how I never discovered. Not long afterwards, a dispute erupted between the white workers and the company, in which they were all deeply involved – possibly even the makers of it. The company fired them all. They claimed they had been victimised simply for exercising their union rights – which was probably true. Through a leak of information from the company office, they learned that they had been blacklisted and their names sent out in a 'do-not-employ' warning to other employers in the area. They brought their troubles to the Party office.

I could not see that the Party could do much about it, so suggested that they take it up with the steelworkers' trade union. They agreed, but without visible enthusiasm, and decided instead to lay hands on the blacklisting letter and make it public. One of them arranged to get himself locked into the plant office for the night. He searched the files until he found the letter and removed it. When they reported in triumph on their coup, I tried to explain that, proud as we were of their initiative, it was not quite our style. We were still battling to prove that we were a legitimate political organisation and not a criminal conspiracy. The last thing we needed was to be accused of the theft of company documents. Once again I urged them to try and involve the union and the Trades and Labour Council. Again they went away unenthusiastic.

I do not remember how things went after that, except that they never got their jobs back at Van der Bijl, and found work elsewhere. We suggested that they give some thought to ways of drawing the sizeable local Greek community into progressive politics. For this they showed some enthusiasm, and went at it Greek style. Within weeks they had either founded or resurrected a body called the Pan-Hellenic Progressive Union. It gave them a forum from which to vent their contempt for their Queen Frederica who was in South Africa as the special refugee guest of General Smuts. To them, she was the deeply hated, unacceptable face of the Greek ruling class which had betrayed their people to the Nazis.

The next time they came to my office, they brought the first issue of a new Pan-Hellenic Progressive Union newspaper. They were triumphant, and we shook congratulatory hands. It was printed in Greek. I had no idea of the contents – I could only read the subheading below the mast-head which used the Latin alphabet: 'Organ of the Communist Fraction of the Pan-Hellenic Progressive Union'. Once again I had to explain that this was not quite our style. We had abandoned the Bolshevik practice of forming 'fractions' in other organisations, and were working to win support through open debate and persuasion – not secret caucuses or 'fractions'. Total disbelief and incomprehension. That had never been the way of the Party in Greece.

I admired their spirit. While we were fighting for a legitimate foothold in the political arena, they were – in spirit – fighting a partisan war for patria and freedom. Our ideals were in tune but our tactics were out of sync. Nevertheless, they stayed loyally with us, despite their disappointments. They were revolutionary revolutionaries in a way we were not. I do not think they learnt anything much from us; we certainly had a lot to learn from them. When they did go home when the tide of war had turned and Greek partisans were once again armed and fighting for the liberation of their homeland, our Greek comrades left as suddenly and as secretly as they had arrived to rejoin their revolution, no doubt in their own exuberant style.

They were the liveliest of our immigrant groups. There were also Hollanders, equally bitter about their Royals who had abandoned the people when the Nazis came. And Yugoslavs, fiercely critical of the aid reaching General Mihailovich and his fascists from the West. Together, their presence helped us reappraise our characterisation of the war, and to give proper weight to the spreading popular anti-fascist struggles encompassed in it.

The German attack on the USSR in June 1941 finally tilted the balance, and changed our political landscape. The 'Soviet menace' turned instantly to our Soviet ally, creating a new climate in which communism could come in from the cold, even in South Africa. It was as though the bars of a cage had fallen away. For the first time we could throw off the mantle of outcasts and operate in every political field with the same freedom as any other party.

We were forced to confront questions which had seemed scarcely relevant before. Should we be entering into racially based and discriminatory election contests? Why stay away from white elections and yet take part in black elections for the Natives' Representative Council and township Advisory Boards? What purpose if any was served by such token institutions which had no meaningful power but still gave an illusion of self-rule?

Many new possibilities were opening up for us. We could enter elections we had never ventured to enter before, even those we knew we were unlikely to win. In 'white' elections our non-racial policies would still tell against us, and in black elections our opposition to tribalism and outworn custom. We decided to campaign – and usually duly lost, but we were making a new mark. In Johannesburg, with an all white electorate in Hillbrow-Berea, Hilda won election to the City Council. In the Cape Peninsula where there were still some coloured voters on the electoral rolls, Party candidates won Council seats, and a lone seat as 'native representative' on the Provincial Council.

Everywhere, we were breaking new ground. For the first time we were breaking through the nationalist monopoly of Afrikaner support, and starting to recruit white artisans from the building and mining industries. At meetings in white areas we were drawing large audiences – on one memorable occasion two thousand people, filling the Johannesburg City Hall and donating some two thousand pounds to the Party coffers in response to Hilda's appeal.

All other sectors of the radical movement were also racing ahead. An organising drive amongst black miners, initiated by the ANC and headed by J B Marks, brought into being a new African Mineworkers' Union which cracked the country's hardest anti-union barrier and penetrated the compounds housing 340 000 black workers. Black miners' wages set the base-line for all other industrial wages. The new union was positioning itself for a direct challenge to that base, and to the whole structure of indentured labour and below-subsistence wages.

The ANC was also forging ahead under the modernising presidency of Dr A B Xuma and a new constitution. Branches were growing everywhere, many in previously untapped rural areas. A formal pact between Drs Xuma and Dadoo had raised co-operation between African and Indian Congresses into a standing alliance. Moves at the annual ANC National Conferences to debar communists from membership died away, and communists like Kotane and Mofutsanyana on the NEC were joined by many others at provincial levels, including J B Marks, David Bopape, Dan Tloome and Duma Nokwe on the Transvaal Provincial Committee.

These were times of exciting all-round growth for the whole movement, but I was growing ever more restless in the role of a Party official. The longer I held that office the more frustrating I found the great black-white divide which we could not bridge. As District Secretary I was supposedly as much the representative of the black members as the whites. But the ingrained separation forced upon us by the apartheid of life and of language outside belied that position. When I visited branches in the black townships, I still came as an outside visitor or an official – an outsider. Only within the apparatus of Party administration, in its committees and sub-committees did I truly feel that I was accepted as equal amongst equals. Elsewhere, at the general membership and branch levels, apartheid society imposed its divides and inequalities.

As our attitudes to the war shifted, I became ever more convinced that I should be in the army rather than the Party office. The Party's slow response to the changing international situation strengthened that conviction. The Springbok Legion experience had proved that military service did not exclude overt radical political activity, and left me feeling that I was losing touch with and becoming alienated from my connections with the white middle class. Even though, in exchange, I was enjoying an acceptance and rapport in the black community which I could not have earned anywhere else.

I knew that, in many ways, I was an unsuitable choice for the post of District Secretary. My personality was not right for it. I was capable enough for the purely administrative tasks, the paper work and the committees. I could 'make the trains run on time'. But those were not the essentials. The post called above all else for someone to inspire, galvanise and organise people. That is not in my nature; I lack the easy rapport with people, the outgoing personality and the oratory.

For some time I saw myself as eminently replaceable as District Secretary, and applied several times to be released in order to join the army. All my applications had been turned down by the District

Committee. The Party, it had been said, was desperately short of safe and experienced hands, while the army could obviously manage without me.

All of which was true. But even here the balance was shifting. Our membership had grown much larger, more stable and united. More hands were becoming available. Harmel, who had been Secretary before me, had returned from secondment to the CC in Cape Town and could easily take up the post again. The committee could no longer claim that I was an irreplaceable cog in the machine. I applied once again to be released, and some time in 1942 the Committee finally agreed.

I resigned as District Secretary of the Party and became a gunner in the South African Artillery.

5

SPOILS OF WAR
1944 – 47

I went through the same army experience as thousands of others –
base camp, training in the desert outside Cairo, and on to a regiment
on the Italian front. There were good moments and bad, none of
them memorable or relevant enough to be recounted here.

A few years on: Spring 1945. We were south of Bologna, at the
foot of the Appenines in what Churchill had once described as 'the
soft underbelly of Europe'. The 6th South African Armoured
Division ground to a halt for the winter. Our 25-pounder guns
stood in deep snow, black as sentinels in a leafless apple orchard.
On the farm where we spent the whole winter we lived together
like troglodytes, hibernating in dug-outs under a deep cover of
earth and snow. Each morning, one of my gun crew would crawl
out to collect breakfast for the rest of us who clung to our sleeping
bags until it was time for lunch. Then we would emerge into the
weak sun, and eat an alfresco meal on a bank overlooking a deep
valley below.

We were like the front-row audience to a war. A German 88mm
gun was tucked away in the mouth of a disused railway tunnel on
the mountain side high above. As regular as the lunch bell, its black
muzzle would poke out from its lair like an animal nosing the air,
and wait for a vehicle to appear on the valley road below. There
was a low-level bridge across a frozen stream. For fifty yards it
would have to run the gauntlet in sight of the German gunners

before it disappeared from our sight and from the German gunners. We knew, and so did our divisional drivers, that at midday every day that stretch of road would be under fire. It had become a ritual. German ammunition must have been as strictly rationed as ours because of supply difficulties across snow-bound mountain roads. We were limited to irregular firing of eight to ten rounds per day. The orderly Germans used theirs only at midday.

We would watch the trucks emerge on to that stretch of road and make a dash for safety across the bridge. From where we sat we could see the muzzle flash from the 88, and hear a shell tearing by above our heads. The Germans had been there long enough to have the bridge precisely zeroed in; there was nothing problematic about where the shot would land, only about its timing. It would hit the bridge, but would it hit precisely when the truck was on it?

Afterwards, the drivers who played this perilous game of Russian roulette would shrug the whole thing off. For them and us, the familiarity of it all made it feel more like theatre than war – lots of suspense but little blood. When the day's ammunition had been expended, the gun would pull back into the tunnel, and the performance was over for the day. We were left with the only other thing there was to do – games of poker.

If war is ever totally pointless and pursued purely out of habit, this must have been it. The German gun was a nuisance with little strategic purpose. It was invulnerable to attack from ground or air, and was there presumably only to remind us it was there. In the mindless nature of the game, we were obliged to show that we were there too. We would fire off our own ration of shells at odd hours of day or night at targets we could not see, working only from map references. We never knew what we were aiming at and were scarcely ever told whether we hit or missed.

Between these random bursts of activity, it was back to the poker table to kill time. There was little alternative. Reading matter was scarce, radio reception abysmal, and alcohol almost unobtainable. Some men tried skiing the hillside on improvised planks until the incidence of broken bones prompted a Divisional order banning recreational skiing at the front.

In the poker games, Allied Military Government (AMGOT) banknotes with the 'Four Freedoms' printed on the back changed hands in thousands and hundreds of thousands of lire, but with nothing to spend them on. Poker was our opiate against war. I had never been a keen card player, and have not been able to face a game since that overdose.

Spring came. The icy roads turned into glutinous churned-up skid-pads. Munition trucks bogged down in deep mud and had to be extricated by hand, but stockpiling went steadily ahead. Orders came through for an almighty barrage. For three days and nights, every gun in the Division blasted away at the German positions in the Appenines. Massed flights of bomber planes passed over us without any German challenge. We could see great bombs slowly turning over in the air as they dropped, and feel the percussion as they hit the ground. Great sheets of flame flashed across the mountain side. We decided they were petrol bombs, but they were probably napalm which we had not yet heard about.

After all that sound and fury, the front moved forward. We seemed to meet little resistance, as if the German army and its feared 'Gothic Line' had melted with the winter snow. We rolled on across the Appenines, past Bologna, into the plains of Lombardy. The Germans pulled back before us, across the Po into North Italy and then across the borders and into Germany. By mid-summer, the war in Italy was virtually over.

We were camped near Venice when Army Intelligence reported German divisions preparing to counter-attack from the north. The entire Division set off in convoy of nose-to-tail guns, tanks and trucks across Lombardy to confront it. Our motorised force rolled through newly liberated territory like a triumphal procession. In every town and village, in the choking dust churned up by tyres and caterpillar tracks, cheering crowds threw flowers and passed up flasks of home-made wine. Word passed back along the convoy that the Commander in Chief and Prime Minister, Field Marshal Smuts, would take the salute as we passed through the next town – Mantua? Padua? Verona? I no longer recall.

In accordance with army codes of seniority, the Artillery headed the convoy. My battery was almost at the head, with a truck carrying our field kitchen and regimental cooks close behind us. The cooks belonged to the unarmed Cape Coloured Corps. They were a raucous and bawdy crew with the rich vernacular wit of Cape Town's District Six. On the back of their truck they carried our battery's pride and joy – a three-hole wooden toilet seat which had been lovingly carved by one of our craftsmen and had travelled with us through the Italian campaign.

We drove through the main street of Padua – or was it Verona – sitting rigidly to attention, eyes right, as we rolled through a vast cheering crowd outside a magnificent Renaissance pile, perhaps the Town Hall. Smuts stood at the top of the steps taking the salute, goatee-bearded and stiff as a ramrod, in full uniform. As our kitchen truck passed in front of him, our three-hole toilet seat slid slowly off the back, bounced on the road, and came to rest. As far as we could see, no one in his entourage had the wit or courage to move. The entire 6th Division swept past in full military style, in apparent salute to a toilet seat. The cooks swore it had been an accident, but it was wonderfully in tune with their zany anti-establishment sense of humour.

They were not alone in their irreverence. In the liberating atmosphere of an imminent end to the war, a wave of anti-establishment feeling was sweeping through the ranks. The Division, so the soldiers put it, was 'going Bolshie'. It was an atmosphere in which the Springbok Legion could start to articulate their inchoate desire for social change.

The 'intelligence' which had started the convoy on the road towards Milan turned out to be false. There were no die-hard German divisions about to strike out. We had become an army without a war, and with nothing to occupy our time. We were outside Turin in what felt like holiday time. The sun shone; it was a good time for unauthorised walk-about or sightseeing expeditions, which the army tolerated but did not encourage.

A few of us hitched a ride to the shores of Lake Como which was also in holiday mood at the prospect of peace. Crowds eating water-ice were strolling in the sun, mingling with servicemen from all the Allied armies who were, like us, holidaying unarmed. In the crowd, a scattering of partisans with red neck scarves – some genuine partisans and some just pretending – all demonstratively armed and showing off their Sten guns, Tommy guns and revolvers.

We hired a rowing-boat and pottered out on to the lake – the war might still be going on somewhere beyond the Alps, but not at Como. We were well away from the shore when a rifle shot rang out across the water and echoed back from the surrounding hills. Then another and another, followed by a regular crackle of small-arm fire from the shore. A grenade exploded near the water's edge; spent bullets fell like hail in the water around us. We thought the rumoured German counter-attack must have begun, with us in a rowing-boat in the centre of it, unarmed. We were panicking and uncertain what to do.

Then the church bells started ringing, first in Como and then followed from a dozen little churches in the hills. The firing tapered off as we rowed back towards the shore. The crowds had grown thicker – the whole town must have been there, cheering, shouting and singing. The end of the war in Europe had been announced by radio and Como was in the full madness of an Italian-style celebration. Partisans were still firing celebratory shots in the air as we made our way through the crowds, being bear-hugged and kissed by strangers as though we had won the war from our little rowing-boat. Famous for fifteen minutes.

Back at our camp they were celebrating. Alcohol was flowing freely, and drunken soldiers were reeling and falling about. Everyone sober enough to walk seemed to be making for somewhere else like Milan or a pub, or just away from there and the army.

I wanted to make a record of the day and my feelings about it before they were lost. I sat writing late into the night for some forgotten purpose – perhaps as a letter to Hilda or just for my own record. By morning it was done and posted off to Hilda. It appeared later in pamphlet form, published by the Party in Johannesburg without my knowledge, titled 'Letter from Italy'. It sank without trace.

The Comitato di Liberazione Nazionale – the broad alliance of all Italy's anti-fascist groups – was organising a fiesta in Milan in celebration of Italy's liberation. In the morning I called in at the office of the communist daily paper, *L'Unita*, for a chat. I had become friendly with one of the editorial team which had restarted the paper illegally some time before the fall of Mussolini. He insisted I accompany him and his friends to the evening's celebrations.

I do not like crowds. But that night in Milan there was a vast crowd in a mood of such companionship and joy as I had never experienced before. It seemed that the great city's entire population had crammed into the cathedral area which had been closed to traffic. The Piazza del Duomo and all the galleries leading off it were crammed.

People were threading their way through the crush with difficulty, for no other purpose than to be there and join the rejoicing at that moment. They were singing, laughing, joining hands and shouting greetings in sheer pleasure at the sense of liberation and togetherness. Wherever they could find a space there were brass bands and string orchestras, pop groups and singers with guitars, just making music which no one except themselves could possibly hear above the noise.

At the intersections of the great Gallerias there was music of some sort, and heaving crowds of dancers. Wine was everywhere. Bottles passed from hand to hand, from friends or strangers, but with no drunkenness, and none of the rough rowdyism I would have expected in a South African crowd.

It was a wonderful night of warmth and joy, a triumphal celebration in gentleness and togetherness, as though an entire people was telling itself: Liberation is just marvellous! The dawn sun was coming up before I could tear myself away. It was an unforgettable experience to have been part of. I have never felt that way again – except perhaps on a memorable day fifty years later when the people of South Africa came out into the sun together to vote in South Africa's first free and non-racial election.

The army had nothing more to do in Italy but wait to be repatriated and demobilised. Armies are no good at idling. They feel compelled to keep the 'other ranks' busy in useless, time-consuming routine. Almost the only escape from boredom was offered by educational courses at the Army Education College in Florence. For a few weeks, I went on an organised study tour of Northern Italy's architecture, while other men from my unit went off to the College for residential courses. Naval Lieutenant Cecil Williams was the college principal. We had been friends since the time when I had been a pupil at King Edward VII School in Johannesburg and Cecil was a trainee teacher there for practical experience towards his teaching certificate.

I did not see much of him in the following years, during which he became one of the town's professional actors and a well-known theatre producer. When we did meet our status had been turned around. I was the Party District Secretary vetting new applicants for membership; he was there for the test, which he passed. Thereafter we worked together in a variety of political activities, and developed a close friendship. When he joined the navy early in the war we lost contact – until we met up again through the Springbok Legion in Italy.

While the war had been going on there had been little scope for doing anything more than talking about the Legion. Now that the army was both stationary and idle, we could hold meetings and start recruiting and building. Cecil fired enthusiasm for the Legion amongst the men on short courses at the Florence College. They returned to our unit raring to go. We started holding regular open Legion discussions in the regimental canteen, and we produced a wall newspaper which was open to anyone with anything to say. The same thing was happening elsewhere in the army. The official army newspaper started carrying news about Legion doings, suggesting we were becoming recognised and accepted.

Acceptability was a new experience. We were wary that it might lead to assimilation by the army establishment, and before long came the troubling news from South Africa that talks on the amalgamation of the Legion and the British Empire Service League were under way. The BESL was a carry-over from the First World War. It was supposedly non-political and provided useful charitable services for ex-servicemen and their families. It had a decidedly Blimpish and blinkered British Empire patriot image. To us in Italy, talks about amalgamation with the Legion seemed absurdly ill-conceived.

Out of the blue, a telegraphed order arrived at my unit instructing me to report to Army Command in Rome immediately. It gave no hint whether for transfer, court martial or promotion. My regiment provided a jeep and driver, and we travelled through the night to Rome. I discovered that I had been summoned to attend a Legion consultation on the BESL merger – which only strengthened the feeling that we were already being assimilated into the establishment.

There were about twenty Legion activists at the consultation. Some I was meeting for the first time. Others were old comrades like Cecil Williams, Brian Bunting and Fred Carnesson. Almost all of us had grave reservations about any merger with the BESL, although our opinions were not likely to influence the negotiations in South Africa which seemed to be already far advanced. We recorded our opposition, and broke up to return to our separate units, only to hear that the merger talks had been broken off for undisclosed reasons. There were no regrets amongst my Legion colleagues in Italy. Merger between a conservative welfare-oriented BESL and a radical trade-union type Legion had always seemed improbable. How it had even come to be considered remained a mystery.

Regiments in Italy were beginning to unravel. Men with the longest overseas service were being peeled off and transferred to Egypt for flights home, and demobilisation. Everyone assumed that the rest of us would soon follow. We were wrong. Several planes carrying men home from Egypt crashed at Entebbe, and further flights were suspended. A new period of waiting began, and went on with no end in sight. South Africa had no shipping of its own, and was a long way down on the Allied priority allocations. Many of the men who had left Italty on the 'first in, first out' principle had managed to get no further than the transit camp at Helwan outside Cairo.

Amongst them were men who had previously staffed my unit's Orderly Room. I assume someone went through our records of pre-war employment to find replacements for them. Orderly Room duty calls for nothing much more than simple office work. My army record gave my pre-war occupation as 'secretary'. The search apparently failed to note that that had been in the Communist Party. I was ordered to take on Orderly Room duty where all communications, secret or open, operational or political, would pass through my hands.

Having some regular occupation was welcome, but petty, mindless and irritating bureaucratic army procedures were not. I spent the days strained and impatient in an office, operating a primitive telephone exchange and reading and passing messages. It was deadly boring.

A message arrived one day from headquarters: 'Gunner Bernstein to report on OC's Orders, 10 a.m. tomorrow.' Ominous. OC's Orders generally involved breaches of discipline or offences too trivial for a full court martial. I could not recall doing anything more criminal than falling asleep on duty, but duly polished my boots and buttons better than usual and reported as ordered.

The Regimental Sergeant Major marched me in in proper style: 'Quick march! Left turn! Right turn! Halt! Salute!' I stood at attention while the OC stared through me as if I wasn't there – until he grew tired. Then he picked up a paper from his desk and read from it without looking up and without any expression. There were to be no further Springbok Legion meetings whatsoever anywhere on or around army premises. Understood? I understood. But what about prior permission? He repeated, as if talking to a retarded child: No meetings whatsoever. With or without permission. May I ask the reason? No reason. Orders from Army Command in Rome. Dismissed! The RSM barked another 'Salute! About turn! Quick march!' And that was it.

I had no idea what it was all about. Later I learnt that there had been a riot in the South African army camp at Helwan in Egypt, and the army had reacted to trouble in typical South African fashion by banning all meetings. If there had been a riot, then agitators must have been responsible; and if there were agitators, who other than the Legion?

Months later I learnt from my close friend and next-door neighbour, Ivan Schermbrucker, what had really happened. He had been one of those waiting at Helwan for the transport home which never came. They were given no information. Anger boiled up over endless waiting in the heat, the wind-blown sand and the flies. In the evening, several hundred men were sitting on the sand in the camp's open-air cinema. The film broke mid-reel – as usual. The men reacted with whistles, jeers and lewd insults about the Arab operator's ancestry. This was the moment chosen by an officer to take the stage and announce that a ship was available at last. Many of them would be leaving in the next few days.

Pandemonium. Ivan, who was young and very volatile, made the first public performance of his life. He jumped on to the stage in his excitement, flung his arms in the air, and shouted, 'We're going home!' It was, he said, like magic, as if he had conjured fire from the air. Flames leapt up everywhere; in minutes the whole place was alight, with the flames leaping to the tinder-dry tents, huts and offices. The breeze took charge and the camp burned to the ground. For an instant, he said, he felt what it was like to have the power to change the world.

Without even Legion meetings, army life was more boring than ever. We were billeted in a small fishing village on the Ligurian coast, where the only amenity was a pub, and the only entertainment watching the fishermen haul their nets across a wintry beach. The regiment had changed since men with long service had left for home. New recruits fresh from school had arrived to replace them. They were too young to have learnt to fend for themselves or to make their own lives. They were simply dumped amongst us without any experience of work or work disciplines, and left to their own devices. After morning roll call they would spend the day on their beds, bored out of their minds, gossiping while their morale collapsed.

Out of inertia and boredom they were turning their faces to the wall rather than face another day. One of my duties was to circulate notices of any entertainments, outings or sports in the neighbourhood, all free and with transport laid on. There was not much on offer – a few cinema shows and concert parties, but there was little response. The indolence of post-war army life was defeating them. A generation was wasting away without any noticeable concern from the army, perhaps because of disruption created by piecemeal repatriation, but mainly, it seemed to me, because of a military culture which places little value on individuals other than their utility in war.

I was lucky. My strict hours on duty protected me from soul-destroying idleness. I was also making contact with the civilian world outside the army enclave.

Everything about Italian civil society was in a fascinating ferment of change. Partisans and freedom fighters all around us were unmaking fascism and struggling to create a new democracy – in their centre the communists and left radicals with whom I shared an ideology. I was striking up friendships with some of them outside the army, while inside the army such relationships and commonality were withering away. The army was no longer united in war. Bonds of solidarity were dissolving as men left separately for home and their units were being rolled together into *ad hoc* formations. In these new and temporary formations men scarcely knew one another or their officers, and the officers did not stay long enough to get to know the men. *Esprit de corps* and all sense of unity was going.

In its place came black marketing. What had once been a united and disciplined force was gradually turning into a body of free-booting traders. The locusts were taking over. Anything the army had which wasn't actually bolted down was being carried off and sold. The struggle against fascism was past, and the present was becoming a time for black-market transactions with Italy's spivs, petty gangsters, and the last survivors of the fascist order. Years before, when I had been a new recruit, the whole Potchefstroom camp had been paraded to hear court martial sentence passed on a sorry-looking private for selling army-issue cigarettes on the black market. His regimental badges had been struck from his shoulders with full military pomp, and he had been marched off for a term of solitary imprisonment to be followed by a 'dishonourable discharge'.

That was then. But now the black market infection was spreading like a disease, though it could have been nipped out if anyone in authority had cared enough.[1] Official indifference made black marketing appear acceptable. What had started with cigarettes spread to food, soap, petrol, boots, clothing and medical supplies. In the end the epidemic extended to army vehicles, and to weapons which were seized on by the new Italian mafia. The army was becoming a pipeline which siphoned anything in short supply on to the black market for the highest price that could be obtained. It was helping to fuel Italy's runaway inflation, and to further impoverish the already starving civilian poor. And it was giving petty gangsters the economic leverage with which they would inherit the power of the fallen fascist bosses.

Indifference in the army hierarchy fostered corruption lower down. What appeared to be accepted at the top quickly became acceptable everywhere. Selling off army goods – public property – ceased to be a crime or even a misdemeanour; it was no longer theft or looting but a joke, 'nicking' or, more cynically 'liberating'. The epidemic was at its height when the orders came to pack up everything the Division had and deliver it to base. Regiments started to collect in all stores and equipment, and to transfer their heavy-duty equipment and vehicles to a vehicle park in Genoa in preparation for trans-shipment to South Africa.

The store adjoining my Orderly Room slowly filled up with miscellaneous bits and pieces – coils of electrical wire, field

---

[1] An army HQ circular which crossed my desk informed unit commanders that the monthly value of South African postal orders sold by army post offices was exceeding the sum total of the entire Division's pay.

telephones, first-aid kits, medicines, drugs, radios, uniforms, tools. I kept them under lock and key. No procedures had been laid down for recording what came in or from where. Soon everyone realised that items could 'fall off the back of a truck', as they said, without any check.

A dispatch rider I had not seen before arrived at the office. He claimed to be under orders from a major I had never heard of to collect all our field telephones. I was feeling bloody-minded and made up my own regulations. Nothing could go out without a signed requisition. He left in a rage.

Later the major arrived and made an 'official' request for the telephones. I repeated my own regulations. He could have used his rank – there is nothing in the artillery more lowly than a gunner – but he wrote out a requisition and a receipt, signed them both with his name, rank and unit, and went off with his loot. I doubted that the details were genuine. I had no quick way to check, and we both knew that he would be back in civilian life and untraceable long before a check could be made through the army's bureaucracy.

Stores continued to come in. Some went out and my file of on-the-spot requisitions and receipts filled up. No one ever came to check, or to find out what still remained in the store. What I was doing made no sense. It was just a private protest. If field telephones were going to the black market, their copper and magnetic innards might be recycled into something useful. But what useful purpose would be served returning them to moulder in a South African army warehouse instead? The dilemma was still unresolved when an alleged captain phoned to ask what medical supplies were in store – especially penicillin and sulpha.

I stalled, and offered to call him back. He wouldn't have that. He would come by the following day to collect what we had. All round us Italians were dying painfully for lack of such vital medicines. On the black market scarce supplies were being adulterated and diluted down until they were useless. I checked what we had, and went off to the local hospital on the hill behind the village. It was run by an order of nuns; the medical director was a man. I offered him the drugs, no questions asked. He nodded sagely and waited for me to name the price. I had difficulty persuading him that the price was that he keep his mouth tightly shut about the source – no word to nuns, medics or anyone else.

That night I delivered the whole stock to him. He embraced me and seemed close to tears. I felt smugly righteous. The doubts came later. What would he actually do? Pass the drugs to the hospital for nothing, or to the black market for his own benefit? And then, why was I any more entitled to dispose of the army's penicillin as I chose than the claimant captain?

There were no satisfactory answers, but I repeated the transaction several times with anything I felt should be kept from the black market. Soap, foodstuffs, chemicals and tools I handed on to the local Communist Party secretary for distribution to the civilian population. He was the most concerned and apparently honest citizen I had found in the area, and I took him on trust.

Meanwhile, all the Division's guns, tanks, armoured cars and trucks were being collected at a vehicle park at the Genoa docks. It was a great empty tract of land enclosed by a high brick wall to keep out thieves and the sea. The vehicles were neatly parked, row on row, more closely than in the meanest car park. There was a constant armed guard at the gates day and night, but thieving went on inexorably. Anything which could be removed – batteries, lamps, mirrors, tyres and wheels – vanished.

There is an old story about a soldier who arrives at a guarded gate each evening pushing a barrowload of waste. Each evening the guard searches the barrow and finds no contraband. Long afterwards the soldier and the guard meet again. 'I knew you were pinching something,' said the guard, 'but I could never discover what.' 'Wheelbarrows,' said the soldier. The origin of the story is said to have been the Genoa vehicle park.

The spring tides came and waves crashed over the wall of the vehicle park. Through indifference or incompetence, the escape drainage outlets had been blocked. The water rose to the top of the wall. The neat rows of guns, tanks and trucks were submerged in seawater. Only the muzzles of the anti-aircraft guns projected above the water to mark where they had drowned. Corrosion and slime seemed like an epitaph on the army's last rites in Italy.

My army service was turning sour. I had joined with the belief that military service would be a continuation of the struggle for democratic change which had been the purpose of my life. Perhaps it had been – but only while the war lasted. Now, in the post-war, I could no longer believe that it did – or could be. Italy did not need even my do-gooding which would change nothing. Italy needed profound political and social changes which the war had made possible. But the peace time army had lost its way and was no longer assisting that process. It had ceased to be a crusade and had become a vehicle of tragedy – or farce.

Black market money sloshed around everywhere. Some of it ended in our unit canteen whose profits belonged to the men, not to the army. The final winding up in Italy was under way; the accumulated canteen profits had to be disposed of along with all else. We convened the only 'authorised' meeting we had held since the ban on the Legion, and voted almost unanimously to divide the money fifty-fifty between the Red Cross and the Springbok Legion. Our Legion work had paid off via the black market. My last Orderly Room duty was to make sure that the cash was dispatched to the proper places and not simply recycled to the black market.

Christmas 1945. My number had come up for repatriation. I spent a miserable Christmas in a miserable transit camp in Foggia, drinking bad wine with Monty Berman who had turned up there from places unknown. We bought the wine from a local peasant, across the fence. It dyed our enamel mugs deep purple but did nothing to raise our spirits. From there by air to Egypt and Helwan camp, another wait, and then finally by ship from Alexandria to Durban, and an overnight train back to Johannesburg where the Mayor would welcome us at the station. From there we would be marched off to the old Wanderers Sports Ground nearby, where our families would be waiting.

That year the Mayor was Jessie MacPherson, one of the last honest, down-to-earth Labour Party socialists. She was on the platform wearing her mayoral chain and her usual black 'garden party' hat. Hilda, now a city councillor, was on the platform with her. Nepotism has its uses. We embraced to the good-natured chorus of catcalls and cheers from the men who were forming up to march to the Wanderers. My daughter Toni hid her face in Hilda's skirts, wishing this unknown stranger in khaki would go away and leave her alone with her mother – as she had been ever since she had learnt to walk.

I tried to get friendly with her in the weeks before I was formally demobilised. We spent a holiday week at Uvongo Beach in Natal where I became a handy porter to carry her over the rocks and dunes. Most of the time it rained. We were confined to the glazed hotel veranda. Children played between the rattan chairs and tables, tripped over adult feet, knocked their heads and shins, and cried. We took the train home. On Durban station friends came to greet us carrying a gift of greenish bananas. While we chatted we left the bag on the seat next to Toni. She ate her way quietly through several of them while our backs were turned. Stomach pains hit her just as we reached Pietermaritzburg. She started screaming, and screamed her way across Natal and into the Transvaal. Distressed passengers kept coming up to ask why we were torturing the poor child.

It was not a memorable holiday. But within days of our return I was out of the army for good. VE Day was almost a year behind us as I began to pick up the threads of life as a civilian.

6

WARNING WINDS
1946 – 47

Adjusting to Johannesburg was not easy. Italy had been moving to the left, but here there had been a drift to the right which seemed to concern no one except the Springbok Legion.

In the days after the war's end, the National Party had staged a march through the city streets to a public meeting in the City Hall. It had been intended as a show of strength in a traditionally anti-Nationalist city. There had been great protests about it so soon after the war, and the Legion had called for the lease of the City Hall to be cancelled. The Council had refused. The Legion had tried to bar the streets to the Nationalist marchers by organising a counter-demonstration in which hundreds of white citizens including many soldiers and ex-servicemen took part. There had been pitched battles in attempts to bar the Nationalist parade through the streets leading to the City Hall, but the Nationalists had fought their way through, abetted by the police, and held a triumphant 'victory rally'.

The Legion viewed the event as a major set-back for the anti-fascist cause, though they seemed to me to be exaggerating its importance. The Nationalists were far short of a parliamentary majority, but they had given clear warning that they had come through the war years with enhanced strength and confidence. White attitudes towards them were altering as uniforms were exchanged for civilian garb, and war-time anti-fascism for peacetime conservatism and political apathy. As soldiers became civilians, the Legion was struggling to adapt. Its quasi trade union activities were declining, and political campaigning was moving to the forefront of its agenda.

In a fortuitous symmetry with the Nationalist march to the City Hall there had been a far bigger, predominantly black march through the city's streets to celebrate VE Day. That had passed off peacefully. It, too, had been a show of strength, but by a coalition of liberation movements, trade unions and Communist Party which had brought thousands of people out to claim the freedom of the streets. And, more significantly, to demand for themselves the freedoms so eloquently promised in the Allied nations' Atlantic Charter but so completely denied them by the state at home.

I knew about these events only at second hand. There was little sign that they had made much impact on white public opinion. White society wore the same old blinkers. Except in the Legion, there was no recognition of the rise of the National Party, or of the black majority pushing its way out of the wings on to the centre of the political stage. Elsewhere politics was still regarded as a white affair.

The growth of radicalism in the African National Congress, and especially its Youth League, seemed to be passing unnoticed. There was no attention to its new Charter of African Rights, intended as a programme for a new South Africa in the spirit of the Atlantic Charter. And no recognition of the calibre of a new black generation with leaders like Nelson Mandela, Oliver Tambo and Walter Sisulu. Only the stock-market speculators seemed aware of the rash of wild-cat strikes spreading along the Rand amongst the black mine-workers.

At the end of 1944, before I returned from Italy, there had been a flexing of black muscle which no one in Johannesburg could have missed. The people of Alexandra Township had taken to the streets in a daily protest over a one penny rise in bus fares, walking nine miles to work and nine miles home again day after day. It had been the greatest and longest bus boycott the country had ever seen.

Clearly there had been more than money at issue. There had been pride, dignity, and a refusal to be pushed about any longer by faceless authority. The daily procession of thousands had clogged one of the city's chief traffic arteries for weeks on end, with the unspoken message: Thus far and no further! Some few white citizens noticed the suffering; some offered the marchers lifts in private cars, but few seemed to have got the political message.

I needed to acclimatise to this society so changed in spirit from the one I had left and yet so unchanged in its life-styles. I also needed to break the last of the ice with my own daughter, and to accustom myself to being referred to as 'Councillor Watts' husband'. And to earn a living.

The Communist Party suggested that I return to full-time political work. I declined. I was out of touch with current political developments and a stranger to the new generation of activists. My professional competence as an architect had been mothballed for some seven years. If I did not start working at it again soon, everything I had learnt about architecture would be lost. So I turned down full-time Party work, and returned to the firm where I had worked seven years before.

I also returned quite quickly to the Party District Committee – whether by election or co-option I do not recall. It too had changed. Danie du Plessis had become District Secretary, Yusuf Dadoo Chairman and Bram Fischer Treasurer. Amongst the committee members was J B Marks, a former school teacher who had been caught up in the inner Party turmoils of the early thirties, expelled on dubious grounds, and later reinstated to the general satisfaction of the membership. JB was a big man physically and an excellent public speaker with great presence and the common touch. He was more approachable than Mofutsanyana, less abrasive than Kotane, and was liked and admired by the younger generation who called him Uncle JB. He was also the elected President of the Transvaal ANC, and President and spokesperson for the African Mine Workers' Union.

The District Committee agenda was dominated by matters new to me. The Alexandra bus boycott was over and won, but other crises of several kinds were developing. Mofutsanyana and others in the black townships were confronting a housing crisis. The population had outgrown the available housing space. It had swollen close to bursting point, with no action by government or City Council to relieve it. Relations between the homeless and the authorities were becoming explosive.

Marks was trying to cope with an even more explosive crisis maturing on the mines. Wages and conditions had remained largely unaltered during the war years, despite the soaring cost of living and the men's rising expectations.

When the African Mine Workers' Union had been formed and started organising, there were few if any working miners in either the ANC or Party. The union idea had to be brought to workers in the compounds by activists from outside, who had to overcome the conservatism and ethnic diversity of a mainly illiterate contracted labour force. They met with organised obstructionism from both employers and the state, and with scepticism from many of the migrant workers to whom trade unionism was a foreign concept, far removed from their own experience and traditions.

Yet conditions for it were ripe. Cost of living for miners, and more especially for their families back in the rural 'reserves', had risen inexorably while wages had remained fixed. Mining companies had sought to offset their own rising costs by economising on the food and amenities which were a substantial part of a miner's remuneration. By 1943, friction was threatening the stability of the country's golden economic lifeline, demanding government intervention.

Governments which have no intention of doing anything camouflage their inaction by appointing Commissions of Inquiry. A Commission headed by Justice Lansdowne was appointed to inquire into the wages and conditions of black miners. All interested bodies and individuals could submit evidence. The exercise was intended to shunt the whole matter away from the employer-worker arena on the mines and on to accountants, economists, sociologists and other experts, until it had been buried under an overlay of economics and statistics.

The intention had misfired. Marks and his Union had spread the word through the mine compounds that the workers' own grievances and demands were going to be put by the Union directly and publicly to the Commission and the government. The miners were called on to speak for themselves. That idea struck a chord.

Blanketed men in mining boots, ill at ease in the city, found their way to the Union offices for their grievances to be taken down in their own words. From them, the Union compiled a unique, first-hand account of life and work in the mines, a living history of disputes about clothing, food, recreation, safety, medical treatment and wages. That oral testimony became the substance of the Union's testimony to the Commission. It was the first major public exposure of a regime of stark and inhuman exploitation which had previously been hidden in the closed mine compounds.

Almost my last Party task before I went off to the army was to present the Communist Party's views to the Commission, together with Mofutsanyana. As I remember it, we dealt largely with the depressive effect of low mine wages on all other wage rates in the country; and on the ability of the industry to pay a living wage from its above-average profits.

We claimed that real wages had been manipulated steadily downwards and profits and dividends upwards through increasing exploitation and manipulation of the gold price. We endorsed the Union's demands for radical improvements, and put forward the principle that an industry which could not or would not pay a living wage had lost all justification. We were subject to some aggressive cross-examination by counsel for the Chamber of Mines, but the Commissioners sat silent and stony-faced. I doubt that we influenced their opinions at all. And I went off to the army.

I was abroad in 1943 when the Commission presented its findings to the government, dismissing out of hand the Union claim for a ten shilling daily minimum wage. It recommended some petty changes such as a boot allowance, overtime pay, and a wage rise of fourpence a day for surface workers and fivepence for underground workers. Even so, the Smuts government hesitated for months before rejecting even these niggardly proposals late in 1944, and ordered an even more miserly increase in the daily rate in lieu of all other improvements.

The miners felt, justifiably, that they had been tricked and betrayed. The government increase had already been more than wiped out by rising prices since the Commission was first appointed. The rash of strikes and riots which had been temporarily quelled by the appointment of the Commission, began again with added fury.

Disputes flared up all across the Rand, some in the form of short local strikes, others as violent riots with the wrecking of mine buildings and offices. The compounds which had once been the bedrock of the national economy had become the site of seething confrontation.

The Chamber of Mines blamed everything on the Union. In fact, far from causing the strife, the union came to the scene after the event, like an ambulance from outside. The Party's involvement in the Union was considerable, and had been so ever since it had been founded on the initiative of the ANC. In addition to J B Marks as its President, Party members like Eli Weinberg became the Union adviser, Hosea Tsehla a full-time organiser, and T W Thibedi – said to be the first black ever to have joined the Party – a member of the committee. The Union secretary was James J Majoro, a non-communist, blue suited, collar-and-tie lawyer's clerk. Together they headed an unlikely team to take on the state-within-a-state which was the Chamber of Mines. But they had managed to carry their message into the compounds, warning against unorganised anger and teaching that in Union there is strength.

By 1946, the Union was being bombarded with demands from the men for strike action. Marks reported to the District Committee that the Union was unprepared for a major strike, but unlikely to be able to avoid one. His Union had called a mass meeting of miners to consider what should be done, and strike action was bound to be proposed. The District Committee had no direct role to play. It decided to support whatever action the miners might take, and to mobilise its members to assist the Union action in any way it could. Du Plessis was to inform the Central Committee accordingly.

There were hundreds of miners at the Union meeting on the Market Square. When the Union officials explained the government's response to Lansdowne's proposals, there were shouts of anger and protest. A miner pushed his way through the crowd, climbed on to the speaker's platform and demanded that the Union call a strike. His proposal was carried by acclamation and a near unanimous show of hands. That was a gauntlet thrown down at the feet of all the power centres – government, mining and finance – and notice to them that the black working class had come of age. The only response when the strike started on the following Monday, 12 August 1946, was a declaration of war.

The strike started slowly, on only a few of the mines. During the week it leapt like a veld fire from mine to mine, flaring up in new places just as it was beaten out in others. It involved more black workers than any strike in South African history. The Smuts government met it with the resort to force which had been his style in confrontations in the past. Company and government police combined to crush the strike brutally with unrestrained force, as if it challenged the very foundations of white power.

Except for the miners, Day One of the strike was a normal working day for all others. In downtown Johannesburg there was no indication of the battles that were being fought out in the sprawling mining areas along the Reef. At midday there was little news on radio, and not much more in the afternoon newspapers. But the sheer scale of the strike gave black workers everywhere some evidence of the power that lay in their own hands. And the ferocity with which it was being met reinforced their smouldering anger and sense of grievance.

After work I made my way to the Party office. Everyone who wanted to be useful was being redirected to the Union office. There, only a few junior officials were on hand in a hubbub of noise and confusion. The senior Union officers were out on the mines and no one knew when or whether they would be back. The word was that the compounds had been sealed off from outsiders, and from each other. No one in any of them could know what was going on elsewhere, and police were preventing anyone from leaving to find out. Union organisers had been refused entry to talk to the strikers; some had been taken away and were believed to have been arrested.

No one in the office had any plan – everything was being improvised. One of the officials with a fistful of papers said it was vital that the Union make contact with the men in the separate compounds and let them know that they were not alone.

'Take these,' he said to me, 'and make us a Bulletin to go out to them before midnight.' The papers were scribbled bits of news and rumour which had reached the office during the day. I found an unused desk and set out, in the midst of the confusion, to write a report on the progress of the strike so far as we knew it, and to add an exhortation from the Union for the strikers to remain firm.

There were typewriters, an electric duplicator and a stack of paper in the office. Some volunteer two-finger typists got to work, typing the material out as fast as it was ready, and passing it on to others to run off. Before midnight, Strike Bulletin No. 1 was ready in thousands of copies. During the evening and night, volunteers – almost all ANC or Party members – drifted in unsummoned, many of them wrapped in blankets and prepared to pass themselves off as miners or camp-followers. Someone organised them into teams with cars and drivers, and they took off with the Bulletins into the night, to try and penetrate the defences of the mine properties.

For most of them it was a venture into an unknown alien territory. Their plan was to intercept working miners as they walked across the veld between compound and shaft. It was going to be dangerous, and they were experienced enough to know that the police would not stand on ceremony with them if they were caught.

They were magnificent men and women – nervous but calm, ready for what they had decided for themselves they had to do. Years of apprenticeship in the movement lay behind their confidence in themselves and one another. No one protested that the task was too risky. No one opted out. Everyone knew that if they did not reach the miners at midnight when the day and night shifts changed over, the Bulletin would go to waste.

Only a handful of us remained in the office, exhausted in an atmosphere thick with stale cigarette smoke, waiting for the teams to report back. It was almost dawn before we could make a tally of Bulletins successfully distributed, of seizures and confiscations by police, and of volunteers arrested and taken no one knew where. They would be on their own until lawyers could locate them.

Before it was light, we moved duplicators, paper and typewriters out of the office to a safe place, hours ahead of the police who raided the union office in the morning, seized all its records, arrested what was left of its staff and locked the place up. By then I had snatched an hour's sleep on a settee at home and staggered back into town to work. On the way, an old comrade – Harry Bucholz of the Hairdressers' and Barbers' Union – restored me to life with a hot towel and a shave and passed me fit to face another day.

The Bulletin became my nightly responsibility for the rest of the strike. With the union office locked and its officials under arrest or gone to ground, the District Party office became the focus of events for the rest of the week. On the mines, strikers were being driven out of the compounds to the shafts by force. Some who were forced underground staged sit-down strikes until driven out again by force.

Neither the Chamber of Mines nor the government made any attempt to talk to the strikers or the union, or seek a settlement. They treated the mine properties like enemy territory, with the miners as the enemy. There were no holds barred as the workers were steadily bludgeoned back to work. No one knows how many were shot, wounded and killed in the process. But each night the Strike Bulletin went out, and more of our volunteers were arrested.

In the end, *force majeure* told. By Thursday, isolated groups of strikers began to surrender and return to work. We produced and distributed the last Strike Bulletin as the return to work gathered pace and the strike petered out.

The other trade unions had been unprepared for the strike or its scale and determination. The brutal treatment meted out to the miners shocked them into action. At a hastily convened meeting, the Council of Non-European Trade Unions (CNETU) took a hasty and poorly considered decision to call for a general strike of protest and solidarity throughout the Witwatersrand.

They were moved more by anger than by realism. There had been no real preparations for such an action; only hope that the masses would respond spontaneously out of anger. It proved to be a false hope. Most workers probably never even knew about the call. Only a tiny number who did responded. For one day there was a fizzle of small local strikes, and then nothing more. By the end of the week the great mine strike was over.

The Union had suffered a shattering blow which might perhaps prove fatal. Prices of mining shares which had suffered a panic fall at the start of the strike, recovered. Just as it seemed that the storm had blown over, police raided the Party office, seized all the records, and arrested the secretary, Danie du Plessis.

A few days later, all members of the Party District Committee were summoned to police headquarters and threatened with arrest although no charge was laid. By later police standards, it all sounds unbelievably polite. These were the last days of the old police security regime before the bully boys and thugs took over and turned it into the National Party's ideological stormtroop force.

Bram Fischer and I went to Marshall Square together. Detective Sergeants Boy and Day, whom we knew well – they had been present at our public meetings for years – were two of the last straight Special Branch men left over from former times.[1] They interviewed

---

[1] After Hilda was elected to the City Council, we were plagued with late night phone calls which continued for several hours with voices and noises in the background but no one speaking. We left our phone off the hook until warned of permanent disconnection by the operator. We asked for and were refused an ex-directory number. Hilda mentioned the matter to Sergeant Boy, whose response was: 'What's it got to do with me?' The calls stopped the same day and were never resumed. They must have originated from someone in the police – someone who was warned off by Boy.

us separately about a copy of a letter seized in the raid on the Party office a few days before. It purported to inform the CC in Cape Town of the District Committee's attitude to the forthcoming mine strike. For reasons impossible to understand, Du Plessis had resorted to a simple and obvious code with words like 'the operation' for the strike, and 'the doctors' for the Union or possibly the Party. It spoke of fears for the health of 'the patient' and the need for 'surgeons' to take a hand. It read like adolescent fiction – and for no reason at all. The miners' strike had probably been illegal – a War Measure banning all strikes by black workers had never been repealed – but taking part in one could be, at worst, a trivial misdemeanour. The 'doctor's letter' managed to make it seem like a major criminal conspiracy.

All members of the District Committee[2] declined to comment on it, except to say that they had never seen it before. Days later, we were all arrested, formally charged with 'Conspiracy to Commit Sedition', and released on bail.

Du Plessis had been a bricklayer, a union organiser and a prominent critic of the conservative leadership of the Building Workers' Industrial Union. He helped found a militant rank-and-file union grouping called the Job Stewards' Movement, joined the Party early in the war, and was elected in my place when I was in Italy. He was a powerful orator in Afrikaans, a popular figure in the Party, and in many ways better suited to the post than I had been. I lacked his outgoing personality and his natural rabble-rousing talents. He had no prior experience of office administration or formal secretarial work, which probably accounts for what came to be known as 'The Doctor's Letter'.

Though the whole District Committee had repudiated the letter at first sight, Du Plessis would never accept that it put a false slant on our decisions. He believed he was being unjustly turned into the 'fall guy' for the Committee's decisions. A sense of grievance soured his relations first with the Committee, then with the whole Party, and finally with communism. By 1950, when the Suppression of

---

[2]Marks, Mofutsanyana, Harmel, J N Singh, W Roberts, Hilda and possibly others. Fischer had been away on holiday, and Dadoo in prison during the strike for 'passive resistance'; CC members Kotane and Bunting had been in Johannesburg and were also treated as members of the District Committee.

Communism Act was enacted, he had severed all contact and returned to the building industry as a contractor and employer, and – so his employees said – was something of a slave driver and a pillar of the Dutch Reformed Church.

Fifty-two of us stood trial. Apart from the District Committee, the Miners' Union officials and those arrested while distributing the Strike Bulletin, there were a number of others picked up randomly in the streets for possession of a copy of the Bulletin. We were charged together with 'Conspiracy to Commit Sedition' for which the penalty was unlimited and could include sentence of death.

It was the first mass political trial of the post-war. The dock was too small to hold us all, so the public were evicted and the public gallery turned into a dock. Days passed while policemen and compound managers gave evidence of the strike happenings in their neighbourhoods. After the first one or two had been heard, the others were repetitive and extremely tedious. The press lost interest and so, to a considerable extent, did the accused.

We had been given large printed numbers cut from a wall calendar, to be pinned to our lapels for identification, and were seated in the dock in strict numerical order. In the second week, a black youth appeared in the seat next to mine – a total stranger but wearing the proper lapel number. He explained that he was just 'sitting in' for his friend who had something important he had to do elsewhere. No one noticed the substitution, and by that time I doubt if anyone cared.

The most telling evidence came from the Secretary of the Chamber of Mines, who read a letter he had received from the Union years before. It requested a meeting to discuss workers' grievances. The Chamber, he said, had taken a decision not to make any acknowledgement or reply to it, or to any subsequent communication from the Union. It had stuck to that policy to the end, even though it knew there was widespread discontent amongst the miners, and growing malnutrition and poverty in their families in rural areas.

Sergeant Boy confirmed that, at the Union meeting on the Market Square, the call for strike action came not from the platform but from an unidentified miner who had come out of the crowd and been given almost unanimous support. The charge of conspiracy thus came to depend on documents seized from Union and Party offices. Reams of such documents were 'read into the record' by a succession of policemen who spoke with all the animation of speak-your-weight machines. The more they read, the less substance there seemed to be for a charge of either conspiracy or sedition. As the case began to fall apart, the prosecution proposed a deal: they would withdraw the charge of conspiracy and sedition if we would plead guilty to 'Assisting an Illegal Strike'.

The court was cleared to allow our lawyer, Vernon Berrange,[3] to consult us. He advised acceptance. The reduced charge would cut proceedings short; it would allow for summary trial in the magistrate's court instead of a preliminary hearing followed by committal for trial in the High Court. That would enable us all to go back to work and earn a living.

But the decision had to be unanimous. Few of us had any qualms about acquiring a criminal record. Pass laws and political repression had done that for most of us already. We were about to vote when one young man objected.

'Mr Berrange, why should I plead guilty when I was just arrested in the street. I did nothing in the strike.'

Vernon fixed him with his cold blue eyes. 'And why didn't you?' he snapped in the steely tones he normally reserved for hostile witnesses.

The young man shrivelled back into his seat. We voted. His hand went up with all the rest and the deal was agreed. We returned to court to plead guilty to assisting an illegal strike in breach of a War Measure.

We did not quite appreciate what we had let ourselves in for. The rules required that all evidence already given be read from the stenographer's records into a record of the new case. The dreary reading began and went on interminably. Policemen, prosecutors and defence lawyers all took turns until their voices ran out, while

---

[3]Berrange was a slim, short man with military bearing, a specialist in criminal law renowned for his cross-examination. He liked living dangerously. He had been an RAF fighter pilot in the First World War, later a racing driver on the old Earl Howe circuit near Johannesburg, and had joined the Springbok Legion's Home Front League and the Communist Party during the Second World War. His Party membership was never made public.

everyone else struggled to stay awake. It came to Berrange's turn. He started reading at tremendous pace, turning the pages without perceptible break. No one seemed to be capable any longer of paying attention – except perhaps the magistrate.

'I think you turned over five pages there, Mr Berrange.'

'Oh, did I, your worship?' Berrange said in a voice of pained surprise, and went back reluctantly to the missed pages.

The reading lasted for three whole days, but it felt like a lot longer.

In view of our admission of guilt, the lawyers advised against any evidence for the defence. Almost everyone agreed. I did not. Police evidence had grossly distorted the meanings of some important documents. I had a gut feeling – no more than that – that we ought to put the record right while we still had the chance. That was probably just my natural stubbornness, not any special insight. I had a feeling that somehow, somewhere, the distortions and misinterpretations might come back to haunt us.

There was another consultation, where I tried to persuade the others, but was heavily voted down. Harry Snitcher, a Cape Town barrister and member of the Party CC who was in Johannesburg at the time, was there with our lawyers. He was a fine debater with a great flow of words, something of a prima donna; but not a good listener. I always found him rather glib. His advice was that we make no rebuttal of the state evidence at all. That seemed to be based on the convenience of the lawyers and the accused rather than on any principle.[4] He was not directly involved but he was persuasive enough for the documents to be left unchallenged.

The case closed, and we were all duly convicted – including Dadoo and Fischer who had declined to excuse themselves. The Union officials and District Committee members were fined £50 each or four months' imprisonment, half suspended; and all others £15 each or three months, two-thirds suspended. All our fines were paid by a Defence Fund formed for the purpose. The case which had started with the bang of conspiracy, sedition and possible death sentences ended with a whimper.

---

[4]His legal advice also contributed to the decision of the CC in 1950 to dissolve the Party. Later, in the Nationalist government's time, he was appointed a judge.

I tried to resist saying: 'I told you so!' But some weeks later I did, *sotto voce* when all the members of the Party Central Committee in Cape Town were suddenly arrested and also charged with sedition, the prosecution resting largely on the unexplained and undefended documents from our case – including the 'Doctor's Letter'. I felt like a prophet in my own time. How Snitcher felt amongst the CC accused I never discovered.

The case went on in fits and starts in Cape Town for several months, with two separate indictments. The defence, master-minded by the Party's foremost thinker and political theoretician, Jack Simons, saw the first and the second indictments dismissed by the court on technical grounds. And then the case was simply abandoned.

But those crucial documents survived in the state archives, their meanings still undisputed, only to be resurrected to justify the state's final and fatal assault on the Party – the Suppression of Communism Act. The experience should have persuaded us that however badly we may need lawyers for their expertise, we should be wary of their political guidance. Laws and courts are not the best guides to political action. If we had troubled then to look back, we might not have made the same mistake again. But the Party was never good at looking back. It was always too busy looking forward.

7

A LINE IN THE SAND
1947 – 50

Johannesburg was in the throes of the worst housing shortage it had
ever known. Public as well as private house-building had ground to
a halt, strangled by material shortages and War Measures. Newcomers
to the city sought desperately for any sort of accommodation. The
lucky and the early arrivals had found rooms for hire in township
family homes, on a supposedly 'temporary' basis – only for both
tenant and landlord to discover that 'temporary' would, in time,
become permanent, and single rooms become homes for entire
families.

Municipal regulations prohibiting subletting fell into disuse and
were by-passed with impunity. Two- and three-roomed houses were
split and split again to accommodate two or three families or dozens
of lodgers. Single rooms were in turn divided by makeshift curtains
and hessian partitions. But nothing could relieve the growing
pressure for accommodation.

Conditions of life in the townships declined. In freehold areas
like Sophiatown and Alexandra, where all pretence of local authority
restraint had collapsed, homes were being 'converted' down. Front
porches were being enclosed in hardboard or corrugated iron to create
additional rooms; rear annexes of small rooms were being added
unplanned, until all backyard space had been eaten up.

Overcrowding became chronic. Without any growth in essential
services, public health and sanitation standards plummeted, crime

and vandalism soared. Local authorities went through the motions of planning but built no new houses. Township Advisory Boards protested and proposed action but had no power to act. Everyone who knew the townships sensed that tensions were reaching breaking point.

The District Committee received regular inside information about the crisis from Mofutsanyana who was a member of the Orlando Advisory Board (now a major part of Soweto). Since Hilda had been elected to the City Council in 1944, an unholy alliance of Labour and Ratepayer members (the UP in municipal disguise) had kept her off the Council's important Housing and Native Affairs Committees. But she was entitled as of right to attend their sessions where Council policy was really being made. She amplified Mofutsanyana's reports with inside information on the wheelings and dealings between Government and the City Council, and about what the township politicians were thinking and doing. They provided the background information for the District Committee's policy as the housing crisis developed.

Things might have been different had our views been shaped by people who were themselves under the accommodation hammer. They might have known less about the Council end of the matter but more about the explosive head of steam building up at the grass roots in the townships.

Very few of our members were themselves amongst the townships' desperate and homeless. Most of them were settled urbanites, with reasonably steady jobs and reasonably acceptable if meagre housing which they had acquired before the great war-time influx. Few of them lived with the full trauma of homelessness or overcrowding. Though they lived amongst the homeless and the desperate, they were not of them.

We were slow to recognise this fact, and to discover that we did not have our fingers firmly on the pulse of the explosion which was coming.

In Orlando, a charismatic and idiosyncratic character, James Mpanza, responded to the times with a call for direct action to house the homeless. From the back of his white horse, he canvassed the township promising to lead the people to a new life. At his signal, the homeless and the desperate should pick up their belongings, leave the places where they lived, and follow him out to a better place.

There they would have land on which to build homes for themselves. His call had a messianic ring to it – a promised land for those bold enough and with sufficient faith to die for the cause. His slogan – '*Sofazonke!*' (Let us all die!) sounded suitably militant, defiant and apocalyptic.

Mpanza had long been a lone campaigner in Orlando. Our members in the area had little confidence in him. Some thought him to be a clown, others a charlatan. But doubts about his character played only a small part in the Party's negative response to his plan of action. On the face of it, it seemed to be reckless and adventurist. It might even be no more than a racket to raise subscriptions from the gullible. In principle we were in favour of direct political action, but doubted that the action he was proposing could have any real prospect of answering the people's desperate housing needs. Even if the action was taken, what would be the consequences for the families who had burnt their boats behind them?

Mofutsanyana was a cautious man. His view necessarily carried a lot of weight on the District Committee. He was our most senior member; he lived in Orlando and was a recognised elder statesman there. He should know better than any of us whether the people were likely to respond to Mpanza. The rest of us could only enter the municipal townships with difficulty or surreptitiously, and had little first-hand contact with people inside the fence. And Mofutsanyana was totally opposed to Mpanza's scheme, and had powerful arguments against it.

Unauthorised occupation of municipal or private land would be forcibly resisted by police and the local authority; the people would inevitably be beaten back, having already lost whatever house-space they had previously occupied. Winter was coming on; people in Mpanza's makeshift shelters on the open veld would fall ill and die in the bitter highveld cold. Encouraging such action would be irresponsible on our part. And anyway only a few reckless and easily influenced people would be daft enough to follow Mpanza's call into the wilderness when it came.

Mofutsanyana's case convinced the District Committee. Mpanza's instant army was not being properly organised or prepared; his action would almost certainly go off half-cocked. And yet, Mpanza was suggesting something new. Our own campaigns for official action on the housing front had achieved nothing over the previous years.

All our political instincts told us that Mpanza's action was unlikely to succeed, and might do no more than provoke the Council to crack down with force against all housing protesters. And yet we were not happy with Mofutsanyana's advice that we should campaign actively against it. We were still uneasy and undecided when Mpanza announced his Day of Destiny had come.

Its appeal was most compelling for those who had come last to the housing queue. Our members were generally not amongst them. They and we were taken by surprise at the scale of the response. Hundreds, perhaps thousands, of families answered Mpanza's call, took their belongings on their backs and followed the man on the white horse in exodus from Orlando.

The promised land turned out to be an unused municipal tract not far away which was earmarked for Council housing in the indeterminate future. On that site, they started constructing shacks and shelters out of whatever they had – cardboard, hessian, corrugated iron, blankets and gum-poles. There were no services, no layout plans. Shacks were thrown up almost randomly, higgledy-piggledy, separated only by narrow meandering passages. Mpanza's immediate entourage was busy from the first, heavy-handed in collecting 'permit fees' from every site.

Our judgement had been wrong. The Party, which always aimed to lead in mass action, had been out-flanked and by-passed. Our members who had always been the organisers of popular action had been reduced to spectators. In one thing only were we right; the Council fought back with no holds barred. Council squads were employed to clear the squatters away, tearing down their shelters and hauling their 'building materials' away. Some of the haulage trucks mysteriously caught fire and were reduced to ashes.

But the City Council had underestimated the people, just as we had. Once the first shelters had gone up, the doubters and the cautious were emboldened to emerge from the wings and join the squatters. While the Council squads demolished one clump of shelters, others were being erected by a steady stream of new squatters flowing out of the overcrowded townships. Do-it-yourself housing had been started, and squatting had been seen to work. The idea caught on.

It would be simplistic to assess the squatters' movement as a mere exchange of the municipal 'law-and-order' of Orlando for the new order of Mpanza's strong-arm squads. For all its inadequacies, something new and hopeful had happened on the housing front, and been seen to work. Ripples of interest and excitement generated by the Sofazonke squatters spread out from Orlando to places as far away as Alexandra. New squatters' movements sprang up in different places, with leaders who were prepared to seize the moment. New camps mushroomed on empty urban sites as the desperate and the homeless of the Witwatersrand began to shoulder their belongings and claim living space for themselves.

Members of the Springbok Legion, including several Party members, started a new squatters' camp of their own on a site near Mpanza's. They called it Tobruk and tried to run it on military lines. The Legion leadership, which may have been behind their action, restricted its own role to matters of policy and left the camp to the autonomous administration of Legion members on the spot.

Amongst those who joined in was the Reverend Michael Scott, the first and only white to become a 'squatter'. He was tall, handsome and ascetic. His parish seemed to be all of suffering humanity, and his motivation a deep sense of outrage over the cruelty and injustice of life under apartheid. He was close to the Party in political spirit and on friendly footing with many of us, but a loner by temperament, ill suited to the rules and disciplines which Party membership would have demanded of him.

At much the same time, a squatters' camp sprouted on a tract of baked red earth in the middle of Alexandra. Its promoter and leader, Schreiner Bhaduza, was a Party member acting on his own initiative independently of the local Party Branch. He was middle-aged, with a military bearing and a military moustache which made him look like Field Marshal Kitchener in that First World War poster: 'Your country needs you!' He carried much of the Party style of work into his camp, basing discipline on consensus and explanation rather than on charisma or strong-arm persuasion. His camp expanded rapidly until every inch of the site was filled and the shacks were starting to encroach on the yards and gardens of surrounding houses. Something had to give.

Bhaduza took a bold strategic decision to move his entire settlement with all its people to a better place. The preparations were kept secret. On a weekend, his community struck their shelters, shouldered homes and possessions, and made a surprise long march to a new site in Moroka township (now part of Soweto) miles away – a strategy perhaps suggested to him by the Chinese 'long march' to Hunan. It took the authorities by surprise. Before they could be stopped, Bhaduza's people occupied yet another tract of municipal land near Orlando, and a new squatters' settlement had come to stay.

Experience showed us that our response to Mpanza's initiative had been wrong. We began belatedly to correct our position and to involve ourselves in the squatters' movement through our links with Bhaduza and the Springbok Legion. But we were late. A vast people's movement had developed without us, and we were coming to it from behind. We threw our weight into campaigning on two fronts at once, stepping up the campaign for building of permanent houses while pressing for urgent interim provision of proper services to the squatters' camps. We used what influence we had to combat the gangsterism and 'protection' rackets in the camps and to establish democratic control of camp administrations. It was something – but not enough to compensate the Party for having missed the tide.

The District Committee was in session when news reached us that Bhaduza was planning another mass march – this time to enter and occupy an estate of almost completed houses in a new municipal estate near Moroka. His plan had been leaked to the City Council, and security around the site was being strengthened. The Committee decided to make an eleventh-hour attempt to warn Bhaduza that he was leading his people into a trap; and that occupying houses scheduled for allocation to people on the Council's housing waiting list would set his squatters on a collision course with other township people. I had the only car close by, and I went off with Joe and Ruth Slovo to deliver the message.

Our informant guided us to Bhaduza's camp. We parked in the bushes in the pitch darkness a few hundred yards from the camp. It was already after ten o'clock. Groups of armed police were moving about. The camp was buzzing like a beehive. People were scurrying about in the dark between shacks, calling softly to each other while we searched for Bhaduza. Something was wrong, but we didn't know what. Unseen people hissed warnings to us – '*Polisi!*' – as we stumbled blindly along winding passages. The electric torches of police posses flickered amongst the shacks; every corner held the danger that we would blunder into one, but unseen hands reached out to pull us into dark recesses when the police came close. Our guide was using a single magic password: '*Khomanisi!*' (Communists!) It was enough. Unseen people rallied to the magic talisman and took us in. All the years of our political work, which often seemed to bear so little fruit, now paid off handsomely. We were *Khomanisi*! We belonged – in a way few white people could ever have known.

Bhaduza could not be found. We searched and dodged for perhaps half an hour till there was no more point. He must already have taken off with his followers from one part of the camp at about the time we entered from another. As we discovered later, hundreds of men and women had crossed the veld in the dark with him. They had been intercepted and driven back by a waiting cordon of police. Pursued and beaten with batons, they had broken up and fled back to the camp from which they had come. As with all our interventions in the squatters' movement, we had arrived too late.

We walked back to the car through veld strewn with evidence of the rout: discarded possessions, building materials, clothes and shoes. Near the car were a few policemen who stared in disbelief as we emerged from the bushes. They leered at Ruth as if they thought we had been having a roll in the hay.

'You must *pasop* here!' they told us. 'There's bloody kaffirs everywhere!'

We nodded our agreement and left. A useless exercise at the tail-end of a botched political campaign.

1948 brought the first post-war elections. They would test the white electorate's support for the Smuts government – or for the National Party. The vote would, as usual, be weighted in favour of rural constituencies where the numbers of voters was small and support for the National Party strong – which meant that the Nationalists might just possibly win. That would be the worst possible outcome – on that the Party and Springbok Legion were fully agreed. But we differed on how best to exert our own small influence on the election.

The Legion's black membership had declined as men had been discharged from the army and returned to civilian life. Its remaining membership was almost totally white and their concerns also overwhelmingly white. Ensuring the defeat of the Nationalists at the polls was their primary concern. Which meant that all the Legion's energy would be thrown into campaigning for Smuts and his United Party, which they looked on as the front-line of the struggle against fascism.

The Party, conversely, operated largely in the black arena, where people were excluded from the vote. There, the outcome of the election would also be important, but not *all* important. A defeat for the National Party would not mean a victory over either white supremacy or racism. As we saw it, the real anti-democratic threat did not depend on which party controlled a parliamentary majority. It depended on a ruling class which aimed to suppress all radical political change and if possible destroy the trade unions and black liberation movements – an aim shared by the United and National parties, and supported by the whole financial-industrial complex headed by the Chamber of Mines.

Whichever party won the election, that threat would remain. It could only be countered by a struggle for the extension of equal democratic rights to all. For us, that was the key – though a Nationalist victory would undoubtedly make its realisation more difficult.

We followed our convictions; the Legion followed theirs. They swallowed their doubts about Smuts and threw themselves fully into the UP election campaign. We set out to make the voice of the disfranchised majority heard in the election, and in the post-election political dispensation. Something innovative and imaginative would be called for if the black majority was to be heard from and considered at all in the frenzy of the exclusively white election. The Party and its allies in Johannesburg entered the election contest not in order to sway the voting but to strike out against the white monopoly of the vote and to claim an equal right for all. They decided to organise a mass non-racial conference to challenge the very concept of 'whites only' elections and the white monopoly of Parliament. It would have a single focus: Votes for All!

The trade unions, ANC, Indian Congress and the Party in Johannesburg formed a joint committee to sponsor the event, and to organise the selection of delegates from all sorts of groups and organisations in the Transvaal and Orange Free State.[1] To give it its maximum political impact the conference would be held as close

---

[1] Nothing similar happened in Natal or the Cape Province. Perhaps the Party CC was fully occupied with the sedition case against it, or influenced by the fact of a small number of black voters on the Cape voters' roll.

to election day as possible. I was part of a small team of young people which was made responsible for the advance publicity and propaganda of the conference. The team went to work with extraordinary energy. Amongst its members were two Natal students reading law at Wits University, Ismail Meer and J N Singh; also Vella Pillay, then a student of economics; two young Chinese brothers known as Alec and Dougie Lai; a young factory worker Paul Joseph; and most tireless and enthusiastic of us all, a lad still at high school and probably truanting from classes for the duration, Ahmed 'Kathy' Kathrada.

We were all novices, learning as we went along in our first experience of a major non-racial event. And – as they boast in the construction industry – we brought the project in on time and within budget. It proved the capacity of a loose collective of the Congresses, Communist Party and trade unions to mount a broad popular campaign, and served as a model for many other such political campaigns in later years.

Three to four hundred delegates of all races came together in the Gandhi Hall in Fordsburg on the weekend before the mid-week general election. That sounds pathetically small by comparison with some of the mass gatherings that the same coalition would gather on many occasions in later years. But the significance of that Transvaal-OFS 'Votes for All' conference went far beyond its numbers. Though we scarcely realised it at the time, we were changing the course of liberation history. The 'Right to Vote' had been claimed by black organisations often enough before, but always as a long-term aim, an aspiration for the future. Here for the first time 'Votes for All' was turned from a distant aspiration into a demand for immediate change.

Now, with hindsight, the Votes for All Assembly can be seen as the end of that chapter of black liberation politics which sought only reform and betterment; and the opening of a new one in which the claim for a full share of political power was writ large. It was there that the modern struggle for the vote and for majority rule really began, though its historic significance has often been missed and commentators have treated it as just another of the movement's conferences in a long line of them.

It was my first experience of a conference where the over-whelming majority was black. For the first time I saw the depth and richness of black political consciousness which I had known existed but had never come up against. The speeches formed a rich tapestry of black political and social opinion.

Amongst the speakers were some almost mythical figures who I had heard about but had never seen before – amongst them Clements Kadalie, the ageing figure-head of the mighty ICU of the thirties and still a formidable orator; and also in neat blue suit, collar and tie, that menacing ogre from my Durban childhood, George Champion.

There was little controversy. The gathering was more a demonstration than an opportunity for debate. There was near universal agreement that the time had come for the vote to be extended to everyone without exception. No one, so far as I recall, even suggested that a 'liberal' franchise with educational or property qualifications would be acceptable. The right to vote was, quite simply, a citizen's right which was owed to every adult. It was a matter of simple justice, not an abstract right; a remedy for concrete grievances of their everyday lives – pass raids, cattle culling, migratory labour, starvation wages, housing and much else. They were not 'speaking bitterness', but throwing out a direct challenge to the status quo, and to the immorality of the imminent white election.

There was minor discord only on the pavement outside, where a Trotskyite group took the opportunity offered by 'our' conference to peddle the journal of their 'Fourth International'. It disparaged 'Votes for All' as bourgeois reformism when nothing less than social revolution was needed. Some of our young militants took exception, and burnt copies of the paper in the gutter outside, while inside the hall the delegates adopted a near unanimous resolution and a call for a vigorous follow-up campaign, and then staged a short triumphal march through the Sunday streets of Fordsburg before dispersing.

The whole event passed almost unnoticed by press and radio. It was scarcely mentioned by anyone in the course of the white electioneering, and could not have had any measurable effect on the white vote. Yet it had taken the core issue of South African democracy out of the closet of future-dreaming, and set it down firmly in the centre of the national political ring. Neither I nor anyone else could have known that we had blazed a trail which would lead the country, many years later, to its first truly universal non-racial voting, and to the election of an ANC majority government.

I had worked myself to a standstill in the campaign. Two days after the conference and a day before the general election, my family and I set out on holiday. We would, in any case, not be casting our votes: the UP candidate in our area had been returned unopposed as usual since there was little local support for the National Party. The possibility of an overall Nationalist victory seemed remote. Even our Springbok Legion colleagues who had been in the thick of the electioneering were fairly confident that Smuts and the UP would scrape home.

We were in the Hluhluwe game reserve on the day after the election, trying to catch the news on a crackling portable radio. There seemed to be some talk of a National Party victory, which sounded unlikely, but the reception was poor. We went in search of a better radio, and sat sipping drinks on the veranda of a nearby hotel when a news broadcast came through loud and clear. The National Party *had* won; Smuts had lost both his own seat and his Party's majority; the leader of the National Party, Dr D F Malan, was selecting his cabinet.

We knew our lives would never be the same again. Just how uncomfortable it would be for us and our comrades we could only guess at.

The Nationalists had committed themselves to taking action against 'communism' as soon as they were elected. Malan made clear that he was in earnest by appointing the most openly fascist ideologues amongst his followers – Oswald Pirow and Eric Louw – to key ministerial positions. By the time our holiday was over, the prospects looked decidedly menacing. For several months there was no dramatic change in our lives – nothing more than an increase in police harassment and surveillance. There were also no dramatic initiatives from the movement either, as though it had drawn in its horns while waiting to see what would happen. Political activity continued but on a very low key; the uplifting influence of the Votes for All Assembly wore off, and the general mood turned to one of resignation without confidence in the future.

I was at the crossroads in my professional career. My firm had become involved almost exclusively in large commercial developments on behalf of two entrepreneur brothers who were speculating in the development of city-centre properties, backed by – or possibly on behalf of – the Nationalist-oriented Volkskas Bank. I found them and their architectural ventures singularly unattractive.

I was looking for some way out when my eye fell on a newspaper advertisement. The Kenyan government – at that time in reality the British colonial office – required architects for the Nairobi Public Works Department. On offer were two-year contracts, together with fares and free family accommodation. I applied without great enthusiasm. It might give me a way out, an opportunity to get to know another part of Africa, and, at the end of the contract, two months' holiday anywhere in the world on full pay.

I was called to an interview with Kenya's chief architect in the old Carlton Hotel. There were six or seven others 'short-listed'. The chief architect gave us a short talk about the work involved, and about the conditions of Kenyan life and service. Someone asked a question about the cost of living. He regretted that he couldn't do a proper comparison since he had never lived in South Africa, 'But a bottle of Scotch, for instance, costs x shillings in Kenya.' That seemed to cover the important matters. It was time for us to be interviewed separately so that our c.v.'s and draughtsmanship could be examined.

My turn came. I seemed to pass muster. The chief architect, who had been quite jovial, suddenly turned serious. 'Now I have to ask you some rather personal questions.'

I said to go ahead. I was expecting questions about my politics or my religion, or possibly even about whether I beat my wife.

'Do you play any games?' he asked.

Games! What on earth was the man on about? I muttered something non-committal about tennis and hockey.

'Ah, good! Good! Very important out there, you know.'

End of interview. Some time later a letter arrived to say I had got the job. Ship's passage for my whole family had been booked. All I had to do was arrange for a medical certificate, inoculation, and passports.

I did not have a passport. I had applied for one on the eve of the war and had received no reply – travel abroad was, in any case, impossible in war time so I never pursued it. I now made a new application, and in quick time my application fee was returned with a curt note stating that the South African government was not prepared to grant me the facilities asked for. No reasons given. I was probably the Malan government's first refusenik.

I wrote to the Kenyan government explaining why I would not be taking up the appointment, and received a formal acknowledgement without any expressions of regret. Perhaps they recognised that they had been saved from an embarrassing mistake.

I had too, though I only realised it later when civil war flared up in Kenya and all able-bodied white civil servants were pressed into military service against the Mau Mau. How I would have dealt with that I do not know. I cannot even imagine myself on the side of Empire against the Mau Mau, Kenyan independence and self rule – with or without the inducements of games and Scotch whisky.

In May 1950, the Nationalist government had begun to implement its election pledge to root out communism. A 'Suppression of Communism Act' was given its first reading in Parliament, and received almost unanimous support in the house. The 'communist' net was cast wide enough to cover almost any extra-parliamentary action designed to change the status quo. The Communist Party and all its offshoots or successors would be declared illegal, and their members made liable to 'listing' and multiple restrictions on their liberties without prior hearing or trial. The government would have powers to outlaw other organisations, ban newspapers and periodicals, and banish or restrict listed 'communists' by decree.

Sam Kahn, the lone communist in the house, was the only opponent of the proposed law. The 'opposition' United Party climbed on the anti-communist bandwagon, and proposed to include the death sentence amongst the other penalties for 'communism'.[2]

The amendment was not accepted, and the passage of the Bill went steadily ahead on its parliamentary route to becoming law. The time had come, as we had known it would, when we would have to put up a fight for the life of the Party, and possibly for our own.

---

[2]Someone once explained the difference between United Party and Nationalist policy to the radical British MP, D N Pritt QC. He grasped the essentials at once. 'If the NP proposes to legalise the killing of blacks, the UP would move an amendment to limit the length of the blade to three inches.' Just so.

8

GOODBYE TO ALL THAT

1950 – 51

May Day had been celebrated in Johannesburg for as long as I could remember. It was the 'workers' day of unity', celebrated in a uniquely South African way with rigid black-white separation.

On May Day mornings, white trade unionists would parade through the city with union banners and slogan-decorated trucks. In the afternoon, they would adjourn with their families to a sports meeting with beer and speeches before going home. Then, after working hours, black workers would gather in thousands for their May Day at the Bantu Sports Ground. Each year – until 1950.

The white event was regularly organised by a so-called 'United May Day Committee' composed of representatives of all the supporting bodies – mainly white trade unions. For some years I represented the Labour League of Youth on it, and then later the Communist Party.

Between summers, the committee would hibernate until summoned back to life by its perennial honorary secretary, Cissy Grootewal. If she had a life beyond the Committee, I heard and saw no sign of it. She would vanish like the cuckoo on a Swiss clock as soon as the day was past, and reappear only when the next one was coming close. She was a gaunt, school-mistressy lady who nurtured and managed the Committee and annual celebrations almost single handedly. She was tireless, and meticulous over detail. Without her, white May Day would probably have vanished into dust.

My own part on the committee was slightly schizophrenic. For weeks beforehand, I would take active part in the design and construction of the decorated motorised 'floats' for the parade. There my involvement with the 'United' May Day ended, and the excitement of the black rally at the Bantu Sports Ground at the bottom of Eloff Street took over.

The starting time was flexible and waited on enough men and women to arrive after a full working day. Singing started in the great open-air stadium while the tiers filled slowly with thousands of people. By the time the master of ceremonies opened the formalities the sun would be down and the audience in total darkness under an amazing canopy of stars. A flat-bed truck parked in the centre of the arena served as the speakers' rostrum, with speakers and master of ceremonies Gana Makabeni 'spot-lit' by the headlights of two cars.

Before and between the speeches there was massed unaccompanied singing such as I had never heard anywhere else – bass, baritone and soprano in perfect, unrehearsed harmony. I do not remember the speeches – they were probably not very memorable – but the singing was magical and unforgettable. May Day at the Bantu Sports Ground was an experience that has stayed with me for life.

1950 changed all that. The white working class had drifted steadily to the Nationalist right, losing its class heritage and spirit. The United May Day Committee, if it met at all that year, was near to its end. It staged neither street parade nor picnic and sports. In the evening, when the black workers ended their day's work, the gates of the Bantu Sports Ground remained shut and the streets outside deserted. May Day celebrations there had been indefinitely suspended. Instead, the workers had been called on to stay at home. The day which for years had been a working day followed by an evening rally, had been turned into a general strike in protest at government policy.

A stay-at-home had been a new idea, still untried. No one was sure whether it would succeed. There were those who argued that strikes *had* to be organised at the place of work; that few workers would sacrifice a day's pay just by way of protest, or remain steadfastly at home when others might be going to work. A stay-at-home could turn out to be a show of weakness rather than a show of strength, a leap in the dark, a gamble.

But people were demanding forceful protest, and the Council of

Non-European Trade Unions and the Communist Party together had decided to make the call. If the ANC was asked to join with them, nothing came of the request, or of any approach to the ANC Youth League which was still small and fairly new. It had yet to prove itself to be a serious player in the wider political scene and was either deliberately or accidentally by-passed. It had cause for complaint. The call to strike had been made without them and over their heads, although it was aimed at the black urban population which they claimed as *their* constituency. When the sponsors set out to organise for the stay-at-home, the Youth League set out to organise against it.

Their stance was a signal to the movement that a new tide of self-assertiveness and national pride was welling up amongst the black youth. Youth Leaguers heckled pro-strike speakers and disrupted public meetings. They were not influential enough to affect the campaign seriously, but feelings between them and us ran high.

At one such open-air meeting in Newclare I first came across Nelson Mandela who appeared to be heckler and disrupter-in-chief. I had heard reference to him in Congress circles as an up-and-coming leader and potential political heavyweight. It was easy to understand why. He stood out from the gaggle of jeering, heckling Youth Leaguers, partly by sheer physical presence but mainly by the calm authority he seemed to exercise over them. The Youth Leaguers made considerable noise, showed a good deal of anger, but made little other impression on the township residents. They had no counter proposal to the idea of a stay-at-home, and gained little support by simply opposing it.

May 1st, stay-at-home day. On the Witwatersrand, most factories and shops were working, but often with only skeleton staffs within. The trains and buses bringing working people from the townships to the city ran strangely empty. I had agreed to take a well-known British journalist whose name I have forgotten to see what was going on in the townships.

We set out for Alexandra before it was properly light. The streets were silent. At that hour they would normally have been busy with people making their way to the bus stations. In the deserted grey dawn there were only a few loners walking with heads down, talking to no one. At the bus station the buses stood empty under police guard. Few house chimneys were giving off the smoke that normally hung like fog over the township in the early mornings.

On to Sophiatown – much the same. At Orlando it was already light. Thin files of people were making their way to the railway station, nothing like the usual morning rush-hour crowds. Groups of young men hung around on street corners, watching, occasionally calling out, but not interfering.

As we drove around looking we were stopped by a police patrol and escorted to the Orlando police station. We were in the township without a permit, a breach of a municipal by-law – not much more serious than a parking offence. I had been involved in this sort of hassle before, and it had invariably been settled over the counter by a signed admission of guilt and a small fine. My companion had not. He was not accustomed to life under apartheid and insisted on standing on what he considered his rights. He was on legitimate business, a bona fide journalist, a visitor, and a British subject. None of that impressed the Orlando police. He insisted on his right to call a lawyer.

That extended our stay for several hours. When his lawyer finally arrived, we reverted to the rules of the game, admitted our guilt and paid small fines. By that time there was nothing more to see around Orlando – only small children playing in the street, stray dogs, a few elderly women sunning themselves and some men hanging about, smoking, gossiping. Nothing for him to report, so we drove back to town and missed the events of the evening when those who had gone to work came home again.

At the bus and rail stations they were confronted by angry strikers in hostile mood. Confrontations were ill-tempered. Police intervened and succeeded only in raising the temperature. The peaceful day closed with an evening of clashes and minor riots, arrests and casualties. But, by any measure, the stay-at-home had been a substantial success. It had pioneered a new form of non-violent political struggle which had been seen to work. It set a precedent which would be repeated through the next decades. May Day 1950 put down a marker for the future by burying the traditional May Day celebrations for ever.

The Suppression of Communism Bill was going through Parliament with no likelihood of any substantial alteration. The title deceived neither the liberation movements nor black trade unions who saw that it put their future on the line just as certainly as ours. 'Liquidation' of the Party would merely prepare the way for the elimination of the government's next irritant.

The ANC convened a meeting of leaders of all the threatened Johannesburg organisations so that a united stand could be arranged. At the meeting, hatchets were buried, including that between the Youth League and those who had convened the stay-at-home. A unified council of war was set up to run a joint campaign – something the movement had previously been unable to do. The government had created the first formal all-inclusive alliance against its own policies.

There is little reference to that meeting in the histories, yet there – unnoticed – the foundation stone was laid for the ANC-led coalition that would come to dominate the next decades of South African liberation politics.

Despite a vigorous campaign of protest and opposition, the unamended Suppression Act moved steadily towards completion of its parliamentary path. An emergency session of the Party's full Central Committee[1] was convened in Cape Town to decide how the Party would respond. When its members returned to Johannesburg they were tight-lipped. We had expected them to return with a definitive plan for the Party after the Act, but all they brought back was the simple message: Continue the campaign against the Act to the bitter end! Which we were already doing. But what we wanted to know was: What next? What will happen when the Party has been outlawed? They provided no answers.

We were a disciplined body. We toed the line, even though we knew there had to be something to tell which was being withheld from us for security reasons. The CC *must* have decided on its future course. Steps *must* be under way and would be disclosed to us in good time – probably at an emergency general meeting to be held to coincide with the passing of the Act.

The campaign went on. General Secretary Kotane arrived from Cape Town. I was called to a meeting with him and Bram Fischer

---

[1]The full CC had nineteen members, at least seven of them resident in Cape Town and constituting the Political Bureau (PB). This served as the CC's executive body between plenary meetings. To simplify this text, I have referred to the PB as 'the CC' – as, in effect, it was between plenary or 'full' sessions.

who had been at the CC meeting. The three of us had been appointed by the CC to dispose of all Party assets in the District before the Liquidator could lay hands on them in terms of the Suppression Act. I was used to the limitations of 'need-to-know', and did not ask about the future.

The immediate task was fairly simple. We separated the Party's Johannesburg assets into things we could get rid of at once and those we needed for working purposes until the legal end. We disposed of all the office furniture, equipment, vehicles and so on by donating them to needy organisations, delivery deferred until D-day. We gathered in all the Party cash and paid off all outstanding accounts, including advance payments to all the employees. That emptied the coffers. It was all quite legal, though kept very quiet so as not to undermine the members' zest for the political campaign. So far as I know, no one ever asked where the assets had gone – not even the 'Liquidator'.

Our only problem was with the People's Bookshop which had grown out of the hole-in-a-corner place where my search for the Party had started. Under the guiding hand of Julius Baker, lawyer, bibliophile and Party activist, it had been transformed into one of the biggest and best bookshops in the centre of the city. Some time after the war, I had been co-opted to the Board of Management. Its stock had been vastly expanded to include fiction as well as serious works on art, science and politics. It still stocked a wide selection of the best Marxist and Left Book Club publications.[2] Its total share capital was registered in the name of the CC, so the Bookshop would have to be disposed of to keep it out of the Liquidator's hands.

The Party's ownership was a matter of public record, but there were several ways to avoid seizure. We could try to sell it hurriedly as a going concern. We could simply give it away for nothing. Whether the decision was ours, whether it was imposed on us by the CC, I

---

[2]Its only real rival and the city's premier bookshop was Vanguard Booksellers, also founded by Party members, including Julius and Tilly First, and Fanny Klenerman. Klenerman later broke from the Party and took over control of the shop. Thus the city's two quality booksellers in the war and post-war years testify to the Party's contribution to the cultural and literary life of this business and sports-oriented city.

cannot recall, but for reasons I cannot now fathom, we did neither. We agreed that on the day the Suppression Act was passed, the People's Bookshop would close for ever. But before that, we had responsibility for its stock of Marxist literature which included all the classic texts. After the Act, possession of that stock would be illegal, and its replacement impossible. But it would be invaluable for any Marxist group which survived or developed – legally or illegally. It was destined for the rubbish removal men unless we secreted it away first.

Over the last few days of the parliamentary debate, Julius Baker, our accountant Natie Marcus and I got to work in the shop after trading hours. We sorted out the essential and irreplaceable books and packed them into cartons. Early on the last possible Sunday we hauled the dozens of cartons up the stairs and packed them into a small borrowed panel-van. We had underestimated the total weight. The van's springs sagged until the floor of the van almost scraped the axle. We started out with difficulty, the van wobbling like a pregnant duck until we came to the hill at the Houghton Wilds. There the van coughed, and expired in the middle of the traffic with its load of highly suspect communist literature, and at the height of public anti-communist hysteria. It was not good for our blood pressure.

Cursing and sweating, we manhandled the van around and ran it back through the traffic until we could coax the engine back to life and find a less hilly route to our destination. When we finally got there, the cartons seemed to be more numerous and greatly heavier. We transferred them all unopened into a windowless store-room. And there the last unburied remains of the People's Bookshop stayed, gathering dust while the Suppression Act passed into law.[3]

The evening that happened, the last general meeting of Johannesburg Party members took place in a hall in End Street occupied by our Johannesburg East branch directly opposite Dr

---

[3]For the next three years only small batches were removed as and when needed by the movement. Due to a misunderstanding between the three of us, the rent then went unpaid for some months; the building changed hands leaving the new owners with no record of who owned the stock. Eventually they broke in, recovered the room and sent its contents – presumably unread – to the municipal incinerator.

Dadoo's surgery and home. Almost every one of our three to four hundred members crowded in to discover what was to happen now after forty years of legal Party life and struggle. There was great seriousness and great expectancy. Now unquestionably, the CC's plan for our own and the Party's future would be revealed. There had to be life after death.

Dadoo took the chair; Kotane, the only speaker, was as always blunt and direct, without visible emotion or resort to oratory. His address is best described as a communique from headquarters. The meeting of the CC, he told us, had received a considered opinion from its barristers on the meaning and implications of the Act. That had set the framework in which they had considered the action they should take when the Act reached the statute book.

There were options. Option one: to do nothing and wait for the curtain to fall. In that event, the legal advice was that the Party would be deemed to have continued after it had been outlawed; and every member who could not prove to have resigned would become liable to criminal prosecution for remaining in it. The CC had not been prepared to take on the responsibility for that.

Option two: to claim to have dissolved and to reconstitute the Party secretly for underground operations. The majority had decided against that, partly because almost all our members were known to the police, had no experience of underground ways of work, and would therefore have little chance of underground survival. It would be a defiant gesture but no more, with extremely serious consequences. The CC was not prepared to take responsibility for that either.

In the end it had been agreed, almost unanimously, to dissolve the Party formally on the last day of the parliamentary debate on the Act. An announcement of that decision was being made in Parliament by Comrade Sam Kahn as we were meeting.

Kotane added a few low-key words of regret, and sat down. The meeting sat silent, stunned. We had been speculating about what we might hear, but no one had anticipated it would be no more than hail and farewell. The business of the meeting was over – a *fait accompli*. Superfluously, the chairman asked for any questions. No one moved. Discussion? None. We had come expecting a message of courage, hope, perhaps defiance or confrontation; but not cold surrender without a whimper.

Had we, even now, been told the truth? Was Kotane not covering the existence of an illegal successor to the Party which was already being developed? We all had questions, but not ones that could be answered in public. What we wanted to hear, what we hoped to hear could not be spoken. We knew that. There was nothing left to say. Finis. We sang the Internationale without enthusiasm for the last time, and went out into the night as though from a funeral. All our years of work and dedication had disappeared in dust – without warning. Only uncertainty and doubt about the future remained.

We never had the chance to meet together like that again. We met almost by chance in small numbers at legal meetings, conferences and social gatherings, but never where the key question of that meeting could be reopened, though it buzzed in our minds: had the CC started building an underground apparatus or not? If it had, who would be told? How could one know? It was almost impossible to believe that our leadership had simply abdicated from its obligation to lead the way. The truth *must* be being kept from us for security reasons. Of that I was sure.

Since that time, I have questioned many of those who had remained silent as I had at that general meeting. I have found none who did not share my belief that Kotane had told us only what it was safe to tell. And that the truth was that an underground was being built up somewhere in secret, until the time came when each of us would be drawn into it individually.

Sleep-walking. Delusion. Yet we were political activists. We kept up our political activities in the trade unions, the liberation movements and the remaining legal organisations, but it was no longer the same. The bonds had been cut, leaving us as separate operators without the cohesion and discipline of Party membership. We had lost the collective strength which had given the Party its special distinguishing quality.

By way of compensation, there was a positive spin-off. Suspicions that communists were plotting secretly or 'boring from within' to some sinister end of their own, withered away. We were seen now to have no separate organisation of our own, no separate caucuses. Mistrust faded. We began to be accepted individually in a new way in the mass movements, and to become integrally rooted in them. We kept up our political work while waiting for signs of the underground. None came. Slowly the realisation dawned that none was going to come. We had deceived ourselves.

Some of my close friends had been at that final CC meeting. There was no reason for them to dissemble further. Neither Dadoo, Harmel nor Fischer could explain the reasoning behind the decision to dissolve except as a response to that 'legal opinion' which had been accepted almost as holy writ. But why? How could one make oneself guilty of membership in a body which had already been extirpated and declared dead by act of Parliament? And even if such a legal contortion was possible, how could a public declaration of dissolution by the CC change anything? If membership before the Act were to be proof of membership after it, how far back did the contagion go? To last week, last year, or right back to the Party's foundation in 1921? I was not a lawyer – just a layman who knew that the law was sometimes an ass. But surely not *that* asinine.

Bram Fischer was one of my closest friends. He was too honest a man to seek to uphold the validity of a piece of legal nonsense – even though he had once voted for it himself. Slowly we began to unravel the real sources of the act of dissolution which lay behind the fig leaf of that legal opinion.

For years, the Party had had to fight for its legal rights. It had done so too well. Its very success had corroded its political sensitivities and given rise to the illusion that its legal rights had been won for ever. Safeguards against possible future illegality could have and should have been in place, but were not. Attention had been focused solely on open and legal activity, so that in the moment of crisis, past sins of omission caught up with the CC. Forty years of legality had coated its revolutionary edge with fat, and principle had been overtaken by pragmatism. By the time the CC met to see to its defences they had already fallen into disuse. It had clutched at the 'legal opinion' like a drowning man at a straw.

I was reminded of that other legal opinion in the Mine Strike case. At that time my resistance to it had been instinctive. This time it had been thought through, but too late. Bram himself was coming to accept that it had been flawed, as had Michael Harmel who had also been at the CC meeting. He had been District Secretary for most of the time when I worked in the Party office. We had worked closely together in various writing, publicity and propaganda activities. I regarded him as the District's most original political thinker.[4] Piece by piece I extracted from him the story of what had happened at the Cape Town meeting. In addition to consideration of the legal opinion, there had been a broader political discussion. Fundamental differences of opinion had surfaced over the principles which should guide the Party. Was a separate and independent Communist Party a necessity in all countries and all circumstances? Did the Chinese experience not indicate that the broad national movement might serve the cause of socialism just as well? But the legal opinion had been the crux, and had been generally accepted at its face value.

Nevertheless, Harmel had opposed the dissolution of the Party which he regarded as a lawyer's decision, not a politician's. He had moved a counter-proposal to preserve the Party and construct a new underground apparatus for it. Characteristically, his proposal was well supported by political theory and precedent but weak on practical suggestions for the means to carry it out. Only the Party Chairman and grand old man, W H (Bill) Andrews, had voted with him against dissolution, but whether he agreed with the rest of Harmel's proposition is not clear to me.[5]

The practical problem of creating an underground political organisation was now obvious and formidable. Even though Suppression had been in the wind for ages, there had been no planning for such eventuality. There were no stockpiles of equipment, no secure meeting places, no communication systems, and virtually no potential members who were not already on police suspect lists. Harmel had argued, optimistically, that even so the feat could be managed – if the will was there. But on the CC, clearly, it was not. The CC had clutched at its legal straw without even asking itself how it happened that the Party had no alternative to this whimpering finale.

---

[4]He was not easy to work with. He kept up an undergraduate life-style, working erratic hours, often sleeping till noon and then working late into the night. He missed appointments and mislaid documents. Method and detail escaped him, but he had high standing in the Party for his original and critical mind and his total dedication.

[5]In later years when his health was declining, Kotane sometimes claimed that he had voted against dissolution. This is disputed by everyone else I have spoken to, though he did turn against that decision later and took part in the resuscitation of the Party.

In later years, I never heard any CC member offer any *political* justification for the decision to dissolve. And, by contrast, I never found a single ordinary member who had not believed that the decision as reported by Kotane was anything more than a 'security' cover for underground preparations.

Our illusions died hard. The Suppression Act went through its final reading. In Parliament Sam Kahn made the surprise announcement that the Party had been formally dissolved. The death was real, but the Party ghost or spirit lingered on amongst the members who pursued their political activities even more single mindedly without the competing demands of purely Party tasks. The Party control at the helm might have gone, but the Party style of collective work and self-discipline lived on.

We lived in anticipation of an immediate heavy crack-down. It did not come. We met in the course of normal political activity, and every discussion between former Party members sooner or later arrived at the same point: how was the Party to be resurrected? Resurrection was not going to be easy. Who could take the initiative? And with what authority now that the CC had abdicated and dissolved the District Committees? We were steeped in the tradition of consultation and majority consent before every action. Without those preliminaries there could be no legitimacy and no mandate for such a perilous venture as an underground Party which would risk the life and liberty of all involved. Everyone looked to others to bell the cat, though no one was positioned to do so. Self-discipline and consensus had always been our strength. Now it had become a recipe for organisational paralysis.

Stalemate. As we agonised over the dilemma, two small groups shook off all inhibitions and started new embryo Communist Parties without general consultation. The most advanced of them was composed of Wits University students headed by Joe Slovo, Ruth First and Harold Wolpe. Both embryos were tiny sects, but their existence raised the prospect of the emergence of several competing Parties – a dilemma resolved fortuitously by the intervention of the government 'Liquidator' appointed under the Suppression Act. More than fifty former Johannesburg Party members received formal notice that the Liquidator intended to include their names on the official list of 'communists' unless they could provide evidence to convince him otherwise.

'Listing' sounds fairly innocuous, but it could be the gateway to multiple forms of repression. Without trial or hearing, the Minister could prohibit 'listed' people from being in any place, communicating with any other 'listed' people, taking part in teaching, writing or publishing anything, or attending any gathering or belonging to any organisation. And so on. The penalties for any breach of such prohibition order could be severe. In effect, we were being offered an opportunity to repudiate our past actions and allegiances in the hope of a possible grant of immunity. It might have been tempting but for the experience of those Americans who had been offered the same bait by Senator McCarthy – and had impaled themselves on the hook with disastrous consequences.

We saw the invitation as a challenge to our own integrity and to the bonds of communist solidarity. Our response could not be a personal matter. Its results would be too far-reaching to be taken privately, without consultation between us all. That was essential – and the only way it might legitimately be arranged was by way of a consultation with lawyers. We arranged it quietly by word of mouth, and forty or fifty of our comrades gathered in barristers' chambers in His Majesty's Buildings, Commissioner Street.

Bram Fischer and Vernon Berrange, who had both received the Liquidator's letter, explained the law. Any former member who denied membership could be charged with perjury if evidence of membership was forthcoming – and could in any case still be 'listed'. We could each demand the Liquidator's evidence before replying; but that would probably be refused, and the courts were unlikely to order such disclosure. In any case, regardless of the weight of evidence, the Liquidator would be the sole judge and his decision whether or not to list could only be challenged if malice could be shown.

Our only alternative was to ignore the whole thing and wait and see what happened. A few of us might never have given any public indication of membership of the Party. They would be stupid not to demand the Liquidator's evidence and, if false, challenge it. But for most of us there had never been any secret about our Party membership. A demand to be shown the evidence might satisfy our curiosity but do little else. We did not take long to reach a consensus. We would not dignify the Liquidator's witch-hunt by entering into legal arguments. But nor would we either admit or deny Party membership. We would carry on in the spirit of our campaign against the Act – to resist to the end and refuse to collaborate.

We were the first group to face this challenge; we would certainly not be the last. Whatever we did would be a precedent of sorts for others. We decided to make a joint reply, repudiating the Act which denied due process of law, and telling the Liquidator in effect to list and be damned.

A small committee was elected to draft the reply, to give everyone who wished to a chance to sign, and to ensure that it be given wide publicity. Kotane, Dadoo, Harmel, Fischer, Berrange and I were voted in. Apart from Berrange, all of us were former members of the District or Central Committees, sometimes both. Berrange came in on the strength of his legal record in our cause.

We fired off a blunt reply to the Liquidator signed by some forty people, and with copies to the Press, hoping it would create a political stir. It turned out to be only a small squib which did not shake the Liquidator or the country. But the log-jam which had blocked the path to the resurrection of the Party had been broken. For the first time since dissolution we had – fortuitously – an elected committee with some sort of a mandate from a substantial number of former Party members, including members of the Central and the District Committees, who could give substance to a claim to be the legatees of Party's past traditions and prestige. The reply to the Liquidator had discharged our remit. We decided to usurp an empty throne and appoint ourselves as midwife to the birth of a new Communist Party.

At least half of the committee had been parties to the decision to dissolve the old Party. We put that behind us. What had been done could not be undone – our concern was with the future. Our credentials might well be challenged, so we decided to clear our position by consultation with all those formerly in leading Party committees regardless of whether they had previously voted for dissolution. They would all be invited to rethink their positions, and to join us in the new Party organisation.

The process of consulting individually with the members of the former CC and District Committees proceeded slowly in secret. The majority of them agreed to come aboard, though some prominent people including Snitcher, Jack Simons and Horvitch from Cape Town and Wolfson, Du Plessis and Mofutsanyana from

Johannesburg did not. Some argued, like Mofutsanyana, that our circle had been so riddled with what he called 'pimps and spies', that we would certainly be arrested before reaching first base. Others, like Simons, considered that all our political purposes could be fully achieved through the legal national and trade union movements, without the need for an independent Party. And Du Plessis retired to nurse his grievances.

When the consultations were complete we were confident we had an adequate mandate to proceed, with the backing in principle of the majority of former leading comrades in all Districts. We decided to end the delays and the agonising and start building a new, secret and illegal Party.

9

OVERGROUND – UNDERGROUND
1951 – 55

It was slow work, but not as difficult as we had imagined. We had a legacy of ready-made policies and styles of work, as well as a pool of past members to draw on.

Secrecy was the key. If word leaked out we would all be prime suspects for our past records alone. We adopted two rigid rules: to keep totally silent about the existence of the Party; and to require a unanimous committee vote before anyone was approached to join. We developed new ways of meeting surreptitiously in unlikely places such as borrowed homes and offices, moving cars, country picnic sites and even night clubs by day.

We persuaded the two embryo Party groups to integrate their unattached members into the more representative body we were forming, and started systematic recruiting of activists in all provinces from those known to us from their political past. Before long, there was a thin network across the country of groups with not more than four members each, unknown to each other without any contact between them.[1]

The committee still had no formal authority, and no real political programme. The members had accepted the rules of secrecy, but

---

[1] Many commentators refer to these units as 'cells'. It is a jargon word used by the Bolsheviks and the Comintern. It was never used in South Africa while I was in the Party.

had to take the Party's political policy and a faceless, self-appointed leadership core on trust. By 1952, the organisation seemed stable enough for the holding of a formal founding conference where these things could be rectified in a democratic way. Bringing together delegates from every group would be unwieldy and bad security. Somehow groups which did not know each other would have to be combined to select one delegate.

Ex Africa semper aliquid novi. We devised a procedure. Every group would propose one of its own members as a putative delegate, and then add the names of others it *guessed* might be members. The committee would trim the list of nominations to eliminate wrong guesses, and provide a final list, balanced to reflect the racial, gender and geographic character of the membership. Not quite Westminster style democracy, but as close as we dared go.

An Indian merchant in a rural part of the Eastern Transvaal offered us the use of the house at the rear of his family shop. It was an isolated place on a dusty road, some distance from the nearest village. He moved his family out for a long weekend leaving us with the run of the house, while it was business as usual in the store in front.

Arrangements for the delegates to arrive and depart without creating curiosity outside was my responsibility. The logistics were complicated. The delegates, who had no idea where they were going, were collected by car at pre-arranged times and places and taken to the venue at irregular intervals. It was hoped they would pass unnoticed amongst the store's customers – a few white farmers who came in cars to collect their week's essentials, and black peasant farmers who drifted in out of the bush on foot, and sat chattering under the trees outside.

There were about twenty-five delegates in all, prohibited from venturing outside again once they were in. Total silence had to be maintained whenever a knock on the store wall warned that a customer was on the other side. It went off without a hitch. There was a great deal for us to settle, but it was done with less argument and dispute than at former 'legal' Party conferences. There was a sense that the odds were stacked against our small band of well-known communists succeeding in building an underground Party which would last. If we failed, it could well be the last attempt for a long, long time to come – perhaps for ever. That created the atmosphere of seriousness which enabled the essential business to be completed in good time.

Basic principles of organisation and programme were settled; the code of absolute silence about our existence would continue. Rules of membership and security were adopted, together with a short statement of aims to serve as an interim programme. The organisation was formally named 'The South African Communist Party' (SACP), which would distinguish it from its dissolved predecessor, the Communist Party of South Africa (CPSA), without abandoning all connection with it.

Last on the agenda was the leadership election. Once again, security and democratic process were at odds. Every Party member, whether present or absent, should be eligible for election – but for security reasons the membership list could not be revealed. We decided on a new model election. A chairman and secretary would be elected from amongst those present. Delegates would each submit nominations of known or 'presumed' members, which the two elected officers would use as guide to the selection of a suitably balanced committee of the right size. Their names would not be revealed. Dadoo and Kotane were were unanimously elected chairman and secretary respectively. Their headquarters would be in Johannesburg.

That type of election could only be acceptable because of the fundamental unanimity of purpose between us. It was used again at all the subsequent underground Party conferences, without anyone objecting in principle. With it, the new Party was formally constituted to take over from where the self-appointed *ad hoc* founder group left off.

It survived, underground, for some forty years, holding larger and more representative conferences at roughly two-year intervals. The venues varied: a factory closed for the weekend, a suburban cottage specially hired, a garden marquee designed for a wedding party. The members of the Central Committee changed over the years as ill health, exile and imprisonment took their toll. In time the chairman's mantle passed from Dadoo to J B Marks and then to Joe Slovo; the secretary's from Kotane to Moses Mabhida and to Joe Slovo. The committee included, at one time or another, Ahmed Kathrada, Chris Hani, Dan Tloome, Josiah Jele, Reg September and others.

The security rules proved their worth. Despite the Suppression Act, no one was successfully prosecuted for membership of the underground Party until almost twelve years later, when the state abandoned traditional policing and turned to systematic use of torture for extracting information.

Those twelve years confirmed that the CC's legal opinion of 1950 had been completely wrong. Throughout the years, members of the underground Party remained as active and visible in the national and trade union movements as they had been before the Act. They continued to distinguish themselves by the high levels of activity, self-discipline and collective style of work that anyone who had known the legal Party would have recognised.

Many non-Party colleagues in the movement did, and deduced that the Party lived again somewhere. But there was no hard evidence. The Party made no public pronouncements and issued no written documents. Its members remained totally silent about its revival, and about their own or others' membership. In reality the Party was active; its members were out in the open and their profile high, but the Party itself remained hidden.

Invisibility was never intended to be permanent. It had been a temporary defence of our unreadiness to survive a full frontal attack from a strong and ruthless state. Everyone recognised that, sooner or later, as numbers and confidence grew, the veil of secrecy would become unnecessary and would have to be lifted. The Party would eventually once again be able to present itself and its policies publicly.

Within a few years, the timing of that event became a matter of sharp dispute in our ranks. Some, including several members of the CC, claimed that we had proved our ability to survive, and that we were sacrificing the chance of giving the Party back its proper role as an independent militant political voice. That view was not accepted by all, but controversy over it simmered on until the National Conference in a factory in Industria, around 1959. There a resolution was proposed that the Party make an immediate public announcement of its existence, and thus 'emerge' to campaign publicly for its own policies in its own name.

Conference divided down the middle. The supporters of the resolution argued that our cloak of secrecy was spreading the illusion that socialism could be achieved without an independent party of the working class. Lenin was much cited in support. Those against were less concerned with ideology than with the practical consequences of 'emergence'. They claimed that our invisibility had dispelled our allies' fears of a separate, and perhaps rival, communist agenda. 'Emergence' would be, at best, a gesture; but it could disrupt the established relations of trust between communists and the rest of the mass movement, and might well induce the legal organisations to repudiate co-operation with us in order to protect themselves.

There was weight on both sides of the argument which was creating a schism we could not afford. Members were taking sides. Those in unions and national movements seemed generally satisfied with the status quo, and opposed 'emergence'. Those who were not, usually for reasons of ineligibility,[2] were for 'emergence'. Unfortunately, that meant that those against were mainly black and those for largely white. It seemed possible that those demanding 'emergence' might break ranks and take unilateral action.

The possibility was creating some personal animus between factions which we needed to resolve before it got out of hand. I was against emergence, and so – when it came to the vote – was a slender majority of the conference. But that could not be the end of the matter. Neither faction had convinced the other, and both were digging themselves into entrenched all-or-nothing positions – total secrecy or total disclosure. The issue needed to be defused.

Even before the conference I had been thinking about the prospect of circulating some communist educational and theoretical literature without any Party imprint. It seemed a good time to put such a proposal forward. The publication of a regular journal of Marxist views on African and international affairs, without any identifying Party label, seemed to take the middle ground. I made the proposal; both sides agreed to it, perhaps as much as a gesture of peace as for its intrinsic merit. 'Emergence' was deferred *sine die* and the go-ahead was given for what was to become *The African Communist*.

The first edition, typed and cyclostyled, appeared in October

---

[2]At the time, membership of trade unions and national liberation organisations were racially exclusive. Blacks could not join 'white' movements nor whites 'black' movements – not even the Congresses.

1959, describing itself as a quarterly '. . . started by a group of Marxist Leninists in Africa . . .'[3] It had been produced and distributed entirely by the Party in Johannesburg in its first independent but anonymous public action. Harmel edited it, various people wrote articles, and Mlangeni and I organised the production and distribution. Copy printing by wax stencil limited us to around one thousand copies. Before the first issue had been disposed of, it was obvious that we could distribute many more if we were to meet the local demand as well as distribution in other parts of Africa.

We had no alternative means of printing, and turned for assistance to a small group of South Africans politically active in London. They had set themselves up to campaign for British solidarity with our liberation struggles, and to raise financial support for the Cape Town *Guardian*. They were mainly students. Several of them had belonged to the legal Party before they had left South Africa.

They put our problem to the Communist Party of Great Britain, who responded with a grand fraternal gesture – arrangements for the printing and dispatch of future issues from Britain under the control of the South African group. All editorial matter remained our responsibility in South Africa, but in another act of solidarity, a member of the CPGB, Ellis Bowles, agreed to act as nominal publisher to comply with British law. *The African Communist* became a printed quarterly, with distribution to many parts of Africa and to subscribers around the world.[4]

In the early part of 1952, The African and Indian Congresses jointly demanded that the government repeal six specific apartheid laws. If they failed to do so, the Congresses would launch a mass campaign of defiance of apartheid laws by way of protest. Their demand fell on stony ground. The government made no reply, and

---

[3]After the 'emergence' of the Party in 1960, this was changed to 'Organ of the South African Communist Party'. At the time of writing, *The African Communist* is in its thirty-seventh year of publication.
[4]The operation soon outgrew the London group's resources. In yet larger generosity and solidarity with South African communism, the Communist Party of the German Democratic Republic took on the printing, with copies sent in bulk to London for distribution. This arrangement lapsed only with the collapse of the GDR itself.

the enrolment of a corps of Congress volunteers began, with Nelson Mandela as Volunteer-in-Chief. Disciplined groups of volunteers would break selected apartheid laws after notifying the authorities of their intention to do so, and invite arrest. They would offer no resistance to arrest nor pay any fines. The campaign was intended to serve notice to the whole country that the days of black patience and waiting were over. From here on, apartheid would no longer be meekly tolerated.

Press and radio paid scant attention to the first volunteers who took up positions at 'whites only' counters in post offices and railway stations on 26 June 1952, and sat on 'whites only' park benches. They were duly arrested, offered no resistance and were tried and jailed. There were few adult black males who had not been shuttled through the prisons by pass and poll-tax laws. For them, short-term imprisonment was nothing new, but inviting arrest as a political act was. The concept quickly caught on. Volunteers began to flock in, the numbers jailed rose into the thousands, and the prisons filled to overflowing. Apartheid was under direct challenge as never before. But only by black men and women.

White radicals could not fail to ask what part if any they could play in the challenge to unjust laws, even if they were not themselves subject to them. Their exclusion from the campaign was also concerning the Congresses. Defiance appeared to be separating them from the white minority just when their integration in black political campaigning could be vital. Apart from its occasional collaboration with the Communist Party, the Congresses had only tenuous contacts with the white population. They now set out deliberately to widen them.

By the time the number of black defiers had reached around six thousand, a small number of white volunteers had been enrolled to join them. Amongst them were several communists, including Betty du Toit, Percy Cohen and Albie Sachs, and also a leading luminary of the recently formed Liberal Party, Patrick Duncan. They broke the law, were arrested and jailed. Their act of defiance remained a fairly low key affair with not much public attention; but it marked a significant shift in the Congress orientation towards white citizens.

Like many others, I temporised over the idea of volunteering but did nothing about it. I was still dithering when the government struck back against the campaign with a new unjust law. This created a new and peculiarly South African crime: 'An offence by way of protest', with penalties including long-term hard labour or the imposition of lashes.

It posed critical decisions for the Defiance Campaign leaders who were already approaching a different crisis of their own. In some few places, volunteers had lost their cool and reacted violently to provocative acts of police violence. Peaceful acts inviting arrest had been turned into minor riots. The new law could only stoke up the fires of violent confrontation. Any use of the state's new and brutal powers would further inflame the volunteers' sense of anger and encourage the decline into violence. Continuing the defiance in these circumstances would be reckless. The Congresses decided, responsibly, to call a halt to the campaign.

Defiance had not brought the repeal of a single unjust law, but it had left behind a new mood of black self-confidence and assertiveness. The state decided nevertheless to take reprisals, and charged and convicted the campaign's leaders retrospectively with incitement – for which they were duly convicted.

At the height of the campaign, the ANC and Indian Congress had invited a select list of liberal and anti-apartheid whites to a meeting in Johannesburg where they would be challenged to take a stand in the confrontation between the black population and the government. More than two hundred men and women came to the Darragh Hall in response. Bram Fischer had been asked to take the chair; Oliver Tambo and Yusuf Cachalia would speak.

The meeting began dramatically. Bram was in the midst of his opening speech when Cecil Williams[5] intervened from the floor. Was this meeting by invitation only? Bram, slightly taken aback, confirmed that it was; anyone present without an invitation should raise a hand. No one did.

Cecil rose and pointed a dramatic accusing finger at someone in the audience. 'You sir! Do you have an invitation?'

[5]Cecil Williams was a leading member of the Springbok Legion and a well-known actor and producer. I met him when he was teacher in training at King Edward VII School. I was in Form III. He provided a welcome change from the dusty orthodoxy of the other members of staff. He was outspokenly iconoclastic and immensely popular with the boys.

Colonel Spengler, head of the Special Branch, in civilian clothes!

Every head in the place swivelled around. Spengler sat his ground for a moment, his ruddy complexion turned purple, and then he made a rush for the exit shouting something like 'Over to you!' as he went. That got the evening off to a bright start.

Tambo's address was delivered with great eloquence and charm. He explained the aims of the Defiance Campaign, and the way the African, Indian and Coloured communities had responded to it. But where did white South Africans stand – especially those liberal and democratic white South Africans who opposed apartheid? If they remained silent and uninvolved while a struggle was under way to end unjust laws, those engaged in the struggle might well interpret their silence as collusion with racism and injustice. Their antagonism to the state could turn into anger against the white community as a whole. The Congresses opposed all racism, including black racism against whites. But it could not fight it alone. The time had come for those who sincerely shared the Congress aim of ending apartheid to take up their share of the burden.

The audience was composed of two broad groups: a mainly Party-Springbok Legion group of people who had already identified themselves with the Congress movement; and a larger group of miscellaneous liberals and progressives who had various reservations about the Congress position on such matters as extra-parliamentary politics, on extending the right to vote without some property or educational qualifications, and on co-operation with communists. Whatever their reservations about Congress policies, they feared that public association with the Congresses would lose them credibility in the white community.

Tambo had called for them to take a firm public stance in support of the Defiance Campaign. They would not go that far. Sympathy, yes. But no concrete suggestions for action other than, perhaps, sponsoring some social projects to 'build inter-racial bridges'.

What was not said – though many of us knew it – was that, behind the scenes, some of them were already making preparations together with 'unaligned' – that is non-Congress – blacks for the launch of a new, non-racial Liberal Party. Public links with the Congresses might prejudice that project. Some of us in the pro-Congress group had come prepared to respond to Tambo's expected call. We had discussed a proposal to form a Congress-aligned white organisation which would campaign with the Congresses for democratic change. I had been delegated to put that proposal to the meeting.

One of the liberal group spoke from the floor about an ongoing 'bridge building' exercise in the comfortable northern suburbs – the development of a park where black nannies and domestic servants could get together on their afternoons off. When my chance came to speak I poured some scorn on it. We had been challenged to make a principled stand against apartheid and the status quo; a park for nannies seemed to me to be a dismal and insulting response.

My words must have been less than diplomatic. Some of the prime movers in the Liberal Party project took deep offence. I made my proposal – there were no others. We were all there as individuals. There could be little point in taking a vote which could not commit anyone to anything. But the chairman called for a show of hands anyway, and fewer than half voted in favour of my proposal. We left the meeting in peace, but antagonisms between the pro-Congress and the offended liberal factions had been reinforced. That would have political consequences in the future.

Soon afterwards, our Congress-oriented group launched a new organisation, unmistakably aligned with the Congress movement, calling itself the 'Congress of Democrats' (COD). Almost simultaneously, others launched a new non-racial Liberal Party of a parliamentary type. The differences of view which had shown themselves at the Darragh Hall meeting crystallised into disparate programmes. COD adopted a policy of votes for all adults without any qualifications; the Liberal Party settled on a non-racial franchise restricted to those with suitable educational or property qualifications.

Both bodies faced tricky issues of membership. The Liberal Party, by recruiting black members, would appear to be putting itself into direct competition with the ANC and the Indian Congress. For COD, the decision was just as sensitive. If it was to recruit black members it would be diluting the fundamental aim of providing a white partner for the black Congresses. But to debar black membership would undermine its basic stance of opposition to race and colour bars. The Liberal Party opened up a lasting breach between itself and the Congresses. COD devised a fudge. Membership would be open to all races on a basis of equality; but in view of the existence of the ANC and SAIC, recruiting and political activity generally would be concentrated in the white community. It fell to me to explain this proposition to the first COD conference, on behalf of the founding committee.[6] It was adopted there, was never subsequently revised, and was accepted in good faith by the other Congresses.

Personalities contributed to the COD-Liberal split, but its essence was political and thus unavoidable. The split divided the already small white opposition to apartheid and diminished its impact on the course of political events, then and also into the post-apartheid era. COD grew very slowly and was never much more than a sect. But it built up close fraternal relations with the other Congresses and came to be commonly accepted as the 'white wing' of the movement and an accepted part of the Congress Alliance.

The Liberal Party, conversely, grew steadily and became the main organised expression of white progressive and liberal anti-apartheid opinion. But without Congress support it made little inroad into the black community except for a handful of the black elite. By locking itself into competition with the Congresses it effectively locked itself out of black – that is, mainstream and majority – South African politics.

In this period I was writing more than ever before, always with the same basic message: South Africa was approaching its last chance to make a peaceful transition to democracy. Dire consequences would follow if it missed its chance. The demand for written material – for handbills, pamphlets, press releases and policy statements from all the radical organisations was insatiable. I contributed regularly to periodicals like *Liberation*, the *Guardian* and its successor *New Age*, and above all to the Springbok Legion's organ, *Fighting Talk*. I wrote pamphlets for the COD and the Legion with titles like 'D-Day for Democrats', 'Action Stations', and 'Where the Devil Drives', all distributed in thousands of copies. They gave the

---

[6]COD elected Committee included Cecil Williams, Helen Joseph, Piet Beyleveld, Rica Hodgson, Ruth First, Eddie Roux, myself and others. The first chairman, Bram Fischer, was almost immediately banned, as were other committee members thereafter, and COD was itself outlawed by decree in September 1962.

organisations a good focus for their campaigning, but whether they brought any perceptible change in public attitudes is hard to say.

Fighting Talk had been born during the war to take up issues of concern to soldiers and their dependants. Inevitably in a time of war against fascism, every such issue had a political undertone. *Fighting Talk* was partisan and anti-fascist. It brought an anti-fascist slant to bear on the character of an alleged democracy which refused the majority of its people the right to vote or bear arms. While the war was on, such political matters took second place in *Fighting Talk* to such matters as the conditions of servicemen and their families. After the war, when the army was being demobilised and soldiers' special concerns were merging into the general concerns of the whole community, the more political matters like civil rights and economic and social justice began to take over *Fighting Talk*'s editorial space.

I had been co-opted on to the *FT* Editorial Board after the war, when the Legion's membership and its resources were declining. *FT* was shrinking; it no longer circulated in army camps; some of its talented contributors, including two of the country's best cartoonists, Abe Berry and Vic Clapham, had departed to civilian fields, and *FT* was in serious danger of sinking altogether.

Around 1948, the Legion Executive decided it would no longer carry it. *Fighting Talk* would have to be abandoned unless its title and financing as a going concern were taken up by others. Cecil Williams, Joe Podbrey and I, who were already on the *FT* Board, took up the challenge. We persuaded some non-Legionnaires to join us – the *Guardian*'s Johannesburg reporter Ruth First; Dennis Brutus, poet and campaigner for non-racial sports; and Paul Joseph, Indian Congress activist. Together we constituted the new *Fighting Talk* Board, took over control and converted it into an independent monthly, edited for most of its subsequent existence by Ruth.

We ran a strictly spare-time operation without staff, financed by donations and constant jumble sales, cake sales and social functions. After the cutting of the umbilical cord to the Legion, people took *Fighting Talk* to be a limb of the COD – which it was not. It was wholly independent, Congress aligned, but answerable only to its own Board.

Ruth was an energetic editor who wrote little herself but persuaded others to do so. Paul Joseph took charge of circulation and sales, and the rest of us planned, decided policy and wrote. Scarcely an issue passed to which I did not contribute an editorial and other pieces under several pseudonyms; and when Ruth was unavailable I stood in as interim editor.

The Congresses had no journal of their own. We attempted to plug that void, but without the resources necessary to achieve a mass circulation. Gradually we established *FT*, not as the Congress voice but as the thinking Congressite's guide to the political scene. Ruth brought in several new and talented radical writers to contribute occasional original pieces – it was here that some later well-known writers first saw their work in print. That made *FT* also the only cultural voice in the movement, even though not a loud one. Prohibitions and bans on our other political activities proliferated, but writing is not easy to prohibit. Banned or unbanned, producing and writing for *FT* became one of my main political activities, and my link to prohibited and unprohibited radical organisations.

The end of the Defiance Campaign left a quietus on the Congress political front, as though everyone was taking time out to recuperate and regroup. The Campaign had proved that there was a solid core of loyal and disciplined supporters in all parts of the country looking to Congress for political leadership. Their energies had not been dispersed or exhausted when the Campaign had been called off while in full flow. They had been left with a sense of waiting, an interregnum, before a new round of struggle could start from where the last had ended.

The waiting came to an end in 1954 when the ANC summoned its allies – SAIC, COD, SACTU (SA Congress of Trade Unions) and the recently formed CPC (Coloured People's Congress) – to a joint meeting in Natal to discuss next moves. Each organisation would have a delegation of eight.

The meeting was held in a rural school for Indian children, near Stanger where Chief Luthuli had been confined by ministerial decree. A meeting at leadership level without Luthuli was unthinkable. Mahomet could not come to the mountain, so the mountain came to Stanger. Luthuli presided over some forty delegates who tucked themselves uncomfortably into children's desks. The classroom, murky enough with its dusty windows by day, was even murkier when lit only by storm lanterns by night. The atmosphere was somewhat conspiratorial since several of those present were there illegally in breach of ministerial bans.

Such a high-level meeting of all the Congresses – these days it would be called a 'summit' – was quite unprecedented but it was not, and could not be, a media event. Its legality was uncertain. It was a unique opportunity for us all to meet and get to know Congress activists from other parts of the country, as individuals and not just as passing faces at a conference. There was no agenda and no prepared proposals; just an opportunity for all to have an equal say on the matter we had all been temporising over: What do we do now?

Delegates were, in effect, asked to think aloud, to throw out ideas 'off the top of their heads'. Most of the ideas were uninspired and had been aired many times before – proposals for an anti-pass campaign with mass burning of passes; a nationwide petition; a mass conference; a day of stay-at-home. All sounded tired and routine, and seemed to be a step backwards from the high confidence and militancy of the Defiance Campaign.

Finally Professor Z K Matthews revived a proposal he had made to the ANC's Cape Provincial Conference months before. There it had been accepted, passed on to and approved by the National Executive, and then appeared to have run out of steam as Conference resolutions often do. He put it forward again. He proposed that we join forces to convene a Congress of the People where a Freedom Charter would be adopted.

Though it was already slightly second hand, in the absence of any other inspiration it came as a breath of fresh air. Z K Matthews – 'Prof' as he was known in the movement – had been principal of Fort Hare University, which had been the *alma mater* of a whole generation of ANC militants and Youth Leaguers including Oliver Tambo, Duma Nokwe, Nelson Mandela and others. He was a highly respected and respectable ANC veteran. He looked professorial – short, heavy, always impeccably dressed in dark suit, with white collar and tie, a man of gravitas, moderate, even conservative, and trusted right across the Congress spectrum from left to right for a lifetime of dedication to the cause of liberation.

The ANC's failure to act on his proposal when it was first made is probably evidence of the poor state of its organisation even at the height of its popularity. Or it could have been that the idea was too new, too sharp a turn away from acts of mass confrontation with the authorities which had been the ANC's hallmark. Or perhaps it had been deemed too moderate, too conservatively constitutional, not confrontational enough.

Here, in his stolid reasoning way, the Prof explained it all again. The Congress of the People would be a great step forward. Its Freedom Charter would fill a gap in our politics. It would provide a detailed programme of fundamental social, political and economic change, which could point the way to an alternative South Africa and a constitution endorsed by the whole country.

He added detail I do not think he had ever proposed before. The campaign could start with a nationwide canvass to enrol all adults on a single non-racial voters' roll; it could then delimit suitable constituencies, and arrange constituency elections for seats at the Congress of the People; the COP would draw up a Freedom Charter as a blueprint of a new constitution for a democratic, non-racial and unified South Africa.

It was an exciting vision, even when set out in unemotional professorial tone. It seemed to have just the sweep of vision which we needed to break out of the quietus, and to inspire the movement with new enthusiasm. It felt like an idea whose time had come. Everyone present supported it.

As he was expounding his ideas, a small internal voice was telling me that it sounded suspiciously like treason, of which I had only a hazy notion. But he was the Professor of Law, not I. If he was prepared to advocate it, so was I.

We adopted his idea in principle, and elected a Resolutions Committee to formulate it in detail. Nelson Mandela would be the convener, with Dr Zami Conco, myself and others as members. The Committee met that night. No one mentioned treason – none of us knew as much about it then as we would have reason to later. Practical implementation of the Prof's plan appeared to us to call for nothing less than the resources of a small state for its execution. The Congresses together could never muster the manpower or other resources needed. We would have to trim the concept down to a manageable size without denuding it of its inspirational quality.

We returned next day to a plenary session with a stripped down proposal. The idea of a national voters' roll was gone, together with the idea of formal constituencies. In their place, a modest but manageable proposal for a nationwide campaign to persuade people everywhere to formulate their own proposals for the content of a Freedom Charter. A Congress of the People would be composed of delegates elected on a free-for-all basis by any and all organisations and groups. It would debate and adopt the Freedom Charter. In that truncated and expurgated form, Prof's proposal was approved *nem con.* I presume he voted for it himself.

A National Working Committee was elected to mastermind the whole campaign. It would invite all other national parties to join the Committee on a basis of equality with the Congresses. It would be charged with responsibility – with or without others – for bringing the plan to fruition. Oliver Tambo was elected chairman of the Working Committee, and its initial members would be Walter Sisulu (ANC), Yusuf Cachalia (SAIC), Adam Daniels (CPC), Piet Beyleveld (SACTU), and myself (COD). We would be joined by one person from each other national body which decided to come in.

The meeting broke up before the full import of what we had embarked on had time to sink in. Most of us were case-hardened to optimistic resolutions taken at conferences. This could just be one more for the list.

I faced an all night drive back to Johannesburg, during which my passengers could sleep it off while I stayed awake. The enormous possibilities opening up out of the COP idea ticked away in the back of my mind, generating a feeling of excitement. I began to realise it was not going to be just another campaign. It would be a step up to another political plane, the opening of a new and inspirational phase in the democratic struggle. That helped me stay awake. Rica Hodgson who was sitting next to me did the rest. She had been part of the COD delegation at the meeting, not speaking very much. Now she came to my aid, and talked and talked and talked to me non-stop through the night – just one of her special talents. We reached Johannesburg in time to go to work as the sun came up.

10

TO SPEAK OF FREEDOM
1954 – 56

Politics is not a controlled happening. The Prof had proposed
something new without intending to cause a revolution.

But that was what happened. Relationships between Congress
and the people had to be turned on their head; the people had to
be encouraged to speak for themselves, and for the first time
Congress activists had to learn to listen. From that process came a
radical Freedom Charter, and the first outlines of a revolutionary
new South Africa.

It is a paradox that this revolution was triggered by the most
conventional, respectable and thoroughly bourgeois activist of us
all, Z K Matthews. And equally paradoxical that it should have
been started in a schoolroom in rural Stanger. From these unlikely
starts, the Congresses set out on the revolutionary years which
would culminate in that radically new South Africa forty-five years
later.

The Prof and four other great men set their stamp on that
revolutionary period. The father figure of them all was ANC
President Chief Albert Luthuli who commanded a unique respect
across all sectors, from the old guard to the new young militants.
The others were Nelson Mandela, Oliver Tambo and Walter Sisulu,
who together formed a remarkable triumvirate. All their familial
and cultural roots were in the Transkei. Their contrasting
personalities complemented each other so fully that their combined

influence on the period was far greater than the sum of their individual parts. They had come together in Johannesburg in the early days of the new nationalism, and cut their political teeth in the ANC Youth League. They were all men of exceptional ability and total dedication to their ideals, without regard to self. South African liberation history thereafter is, in considerable part, *their* history.

Were it not for politics my path would probably never have crossed any of theirs, and my life would have been poorer for it. We met quite casually, in encounters at occasional conferences and meetings, but in the course of the COP campaign I worked with them and came to know them well and to appreciate their extra-ordinary qualities.

By that time, Luthuli, the 'man of respect' with great dignity and high principle, had already been stripped of his tribal chieftain-ship by government, but he remained always 'Chief' to all who knew him. He was more than the ANC's titular head. He was the movement's greatest statesman, its internationally recognised figurehead whose Nobel Peace Prize celebrated his own no less than his organisation's contribution to the cause of peace and national freedom.

When I came to know Luthuli and the Prof, the members of the triumvirate were still up-and-coming leaders, men to watch but as yet without the national and international recognition they would have in later years. Until the COP campaign, I had never worked closely with any of them, or been part of their ANC circle. But for the COP, I probably never would have.

Before the Stanger meeting, I knew Mandela only as a charming and friendly fellow, with whom I exchanged occasional pleasantries, but no more. In the COP Resolutions Committee, where we spent the night reshaping the Prof's proposal, I learnt to know him also as very serious and very self-confident. He was already then a chairman who would wait until all the views had been heard before he decided his own position, and would then seek to reconcile differing views and competing egos without giving way on principles. He seemed, even then, slightly larger than life, physically and in his quiet authority.

After Stanger, I saw little of him, but a great deal of the other members of the triumvirate – Tambo and Sisulu. They were such different people that I found it hard to understand the obvious closeness between them except their shared belief in the cause of liberation.

Tambo was the complete diplomat, a gentle man, quiet, undemonstrative, with impeccable diction and manners. His greeting was always accompanied by a great smile of pleasure, as though he had been hoping for just such a meeting. It was not turned on specially for me; it was his way with all his colleagues, and it was not an act. He carried himself with great reserve which concealed a natural warmth. And he had a clear, logical mind with no room for generalities or political clichés.

At the first meetings of the Working Committee, I began to sense that he had reservations about me. We were miles apart ideologically. He was a devout and practising Christian who was finding himself, probably for the first time in his life, working in close harness with a white, non-ANC communist. I had the impression that he assumed that, as a communist, I had to have an agenda of my own. But he had great integrity and honesty. There was no occasion when he ever allowed his reservations about me or about communism to get in the way. He gave me and all my suggestions the same open and honest consideration as all others.

Ideology never came between us. As we grew used to working together, his wariness towards me dissolved. We found ourselves in total agreement about almost everything all the time. I believe he came to accept that my commitment was different from but no less than his own, though we started from different political premises. I developed a respect and admiration for him such as I have had for very few others, and which lasted till the end of his life.

Walter Sisulu was much closer to my own ideology. He was a small stocky man, light complexioned, and extremely quiet, almost self-effacing. He had neither Mandela's physique, Tambo's striking good looks, or their educated social ease. He was a man of compassion and of love for people which showed through his every decision – not on the surface but in the depths of the matter. Mandela once spoke of him as 'the father of us all'. Correctly. Amongst all the Congress activists, he was always the quiet counsel and adviser, the strategist to whom everyone – including Mandela and Tambo – turned as to an elder statesman. Work on the mines had endowed him with a wide experience of working and of life in the big city. It had widened his thinking beyond simple nationalism, and brought him close to my own radical socialism. Through working with him I, too, came to recognise him as the greatest strategic and tactical thinker of that ANC generation. The Congresses knew his great wisdom and gentleness. But without either Mandela's or Tambo's public persona and charisma, he was always hugely under-recognised by the world outside.

The separate talents of this triumvirate complemented and enlarged each other. Mandela's endurance and charisma made him the symbol of our liberation struggle for all the world. Tambo's single mindedness and diplomatic skills sponsored the worldwide campaign against apartheid, and held the diverse Congress exiles solidly united through all the years when their colleagues languished on Robben Island. And Sisulu, 'the father of them all', set the strategic directions and the standards of humanity and comradeship which characterised the South African liberation movement, even on Robben Island and thereafter.

If great men ever mould a nation's history, the interconnection of these three great men shaped ours through the decades of struggle which led to the new South Africa.

The chance happening of the COP linked my politics closely with theirs – and much of my life thereafter. That entanglement literally changed my life, accounting for its moments of political triumph and – in part – also for its moments of personal and political disaster. All in all, it was the greatest privilege of my life to have been involved with and to have worked with extraordinary men like these; to have been friends with and to have been befriended by them. There are few rewards in extra-parliamentary politics. For all my years in politics, this has been mine.

Programmes and resolutions like those from the Stanger meeting are routine in Congress politics, and seldom arouse much excitement amongst activists. At first the COP resolutions were taken calmly. Their departure from Congress norms was not instantly apparent. Congress members were accustomed to making calls for government to change the laws and the social system. Now, for the first time, they were being asked to get the ordinary people themselves to state *their own* demands and to take *their own* initiative to realise them.

That was a fundamental departure from the established style of Congress politics, and was not easily understood. It took time for the Congress membership to acclimatise to the radical change. It meant campaigning in a radically new way – no longer telling people: 'This is what *we* stand for! Support us!' but instead asking them: 'What do *you* want? What should we be fighting for?' It required that they listen to and learn from the people rather than exhort or instruct them.

Enthusiasm for the new style developed slowly. Until the members themselves could be fired with enthusiasm for it, the COP campaign marked time. The idea of the COP and the Charter had to be sold to the Congress rank and file before it could be sold to the people. While that was going on, the Working Committee published a nationwide 'Call', explaining the concept of the COP and asking people everywhere to collaborate in setting the terms of the Freedom Charter.

As the only regular writer on the Committee, the drafting of the Call was delegated to me. It was a somewhat daunting task which could make or break the whole operation. It not only had to explain, but it also had to inspire a vision of a new South Africa in which all our lives could be changed for the better. I wrestled with it until a slogan which seemed to crystallise the essence of the COP came to mind: *'Let Us Speak of Freedom!'*

That was the breakthrough. After that, through constant repetition of the slogan, the Call almost wrote itself. I came to understand just how far we were departing from our past political style, and branching out on to a new one. This time we would not be campaigning for our own ready-made programme but searching for a national consensus. In today's jargon, we would be setting out to 'empower people'.

I drafted until I felt satisfied, gave the draft Call to the Working Committee and they passed it on to the Congresses, recommending its acceptance. The joint Congress Executives were recalled to Stanger. Chief Luthuli, with the tone and rhythm of a lay preacher, read the draft to the meeting during a night session. It was like theatre, the audience sitting in the dark and the reader on a platform illuminated by a single storm lantern. Voice and setting made the Call sound better than it really was – it never sounded quite as good again. There was silence when he ended as though we were waiting for the curtain to come down,[1] and the draft was accepted unanimously without a vote.

The slogan *Let Us Speak of Freedom!* became the keynote of the campaign. It provided the agenda for thousands of meetings up and down the country where 'demands' for inclusion in the Freedom Charter were collected over the following months.

The first demands arrived disappointingly slowly as the Congress activists gradually warmed to the task. 'Let Us Speak of Freedom' invited almost any kind of response. Most of the 'demands' were not as we had imagined them – at least not in the written form in which they reached us. Most were one liners dealing with a single issue of daily life – homes, jobs, living standards, civil liberties. Some verged on political generalisations – We want land! No more passes! The police must leave us alone! – which had been summarised from large and small, often open-air, meetings, often by not too well educated activists.

Most of the scribes lacked the sophisticated skill of summarising the sense of the meeting in a single sentence. They wrote their summaries on scraps of paper, backs of envelopes, pages torn from school exercise books, and often the backs of our own handbills. There were only a few carefully formulated opinions about such general issues as the economy, civil rights, democracy and racism.

We stuffed them away together in an old cabin trunk, just as we received them, to be pondered over later – not for lack of seriousness but because, at that stage, the Charter seemed far off. We were concentrating on the COP itself, on the election of delegates and on the logistics of such a gathering. In our daily tasks, the Charter seemed to become an incidental spin-off from the new political culture of listening to and learning from the people. Tacitly, we deferred collating the demands into a draft Charter in order to focus on what seemed like the core issue.

The Stanger meeting had envisaged a COP campaign directed by a far wider group than the Congresses alone. It had hoped to include as many other national bodies as possible in a broad non-

---

[1] I also wrote much other COP material, some of it reprinted in the book *Thirty Years of the Freedom Charter* by Jeremy Cronin and Raymond Suttner (Ravan Press). Even guidance circulars for the campaign workers seem to have caught my sense of urgency and pioneering at that time.

partisan directorate together with the Congress founders. The Working Committee did its best. It sent letters of invitation to the United, National, Dominion and Liberal Parties, asking them to join the Working Committee on an equal basis. That fell on stony ground. None of them bothered to reply. Perhaps the whole COP idea of working together with representatives of the black majority was too advanced for them.

We tried a different tack: if they were unready to join in on the Working Committee, would they care to make their own proposals for the shape of the Charter? Silence. And yet another: would they like to present their views on the Charter from the platform at the COP itself? Still silence.

Clearly, white South African politicians were too fearful of the future to venture outside their own laager. It was rumoured that opinions in the Liberal Party had been divided over the invitations, but they produced no response or communication. We went ahead without them.

During preparations for the COP, it was suggested that there was a need for a special Congress award to recognise outstanding individual service to the cause of South African freedom. The Congresses agreed, and some of their historians suggested we revive a defunct Xhosa award for heroism – the *Isitwalandwe*. We had already adopted a four-spoked wheel as the logo of the COP campaign, symbolising the unity of the four Congresses and the country's four racial groups. That logo served as the design for the *Isitwalandwe* medal. The Congresses nominated Chief A J Luthuli, Father Trevor Huddleston and Dr Y M Dadoo as the first recipients, to receive the award at the COP itself.[2]

The still uncollated 'demands' for inclusion in the Freedom Charter accumulated while the date for the COP was settled, and the search for a suitable venue began. It was one thing to resolve to hold a mass, non-racial assembly. In South Africa it was quite another to find a place for it. We soon discovered that there were scarcely any places of public assembly, indoors or out, which had not been designated for a single racial group in terms of the Group Areas Act. The few pockets of land not so designated were either so

---

[2]The *Isitwalandwe* has become a standing ANC award, conferred on a distinguished few ever since.

inaccessible or so polluted as to be ruled out for our purpose. All arenas, sports stadiums and public parks were controlled either by white local authorities who would not give us use of them, or by Sports Associations who would not let anything less than the Second Coming interfere with their fixture list – and probably not even that.

Our options diminished until there was only one place on offer – a vacant privately owned site in the mixed-race area of Kliptown, not far from Soweto. A friendly Indian owner offered us the use of a piece of wasteland, a few acres of red dust, scattered tufts of scrub grass, khaki-weed and 'blackjacks'. On it, boys had set out empty oil drums as goal-posts for makeshift football games; pedestrians took short cuts across it, and stray mongrels foraged through the litter and used it as a latrine. It was bounded by the main rail line to Soweto on one side, and a dirt road on the other. It was rather discouraging, barely acceptable, but it had to do.

There was much to do to make it acceptable as the COP site. It had to be fenced; water, and electricity to power minimal lighting and public address equipment had to be brought in; sanitary accommodation and rubbish removal had to be arranged, the site cleared, a platform erected, and some sort of seating arranged for an unknown audience which could run into thousands. And after all that, there were the logistics of the day itself – the feeding of the delegates and the provision of overnight accommodation for those who would come from afar. It was a project which would strain the resources of a minor town council, but it would have to be done with very little money and a volunteer corps of unpaid Congress workers.

Somehow, it was all done – not always to the highest professional standards and often at the eleventh hour. That it was possible at all is a tribute to the enthusiasm and voluntary effort which Congress activists could muster when required.

There was a division of labour. The Women's Federation and the ANC Women's League met the delegates from outside areas and found them overnight accommodation in the townships; the Indian Congress collected donations of foodstuffs, and organised the catering services on site; the ANC provided overnight guards and the corps of stewards for the gathering; and the COD took on the construction work on site. I helped to plan the COD's share of the work, but when the time came for the work to start on site I had been served with a Suppression Act order banning me from taking part in the activities of the Congresses and some twenty other organisations; from attending any gathering whatsoever, entering any factory or school, leaving the magisterial district of Johannesburg, publishing or writing anything for publication, and so on and so on.

By that time I was one of a growing body of 'banned persons'. All of us faced the dilemma of whether to ignore the ban and face a punitive fine or imprisonment; or to comply with it and retire from virtually all political and social activity. Most of us found compliance unthinkable. It would achieve the government's aim of weakening, perhaps even breaking the opposition to the apartheid state.

On the other hand, defiance *per se* could be no more than a sacrificial gesture unless it was done deliberately and only when it served a sensible political purpose. Citizens of more democratic countries are predisposed to obey the law; South Africa's political activists were predisposed not to. The law had been subverted from a code of public order into an instrument of minority power. It had forfeited all respect. Conscience dictated that we break our bans as necessary, and continue whatever political work could be done without endangering others.

So I remained a somewhat furtive member of the Working Committee, but took no further visible part in its public functions.[3] Time was running out. It was urgent that we turn our thousands of bits of paper into a draft Freedom Charter. We had delayed that to the last moment largely because no one had any idea about how it was to be done. We had neither precedent nor plan. The Working Committee decided that it was 'just a writing job', and handed it on to me. I had no more idea of where to start than anyone else, but I dusted off the cabin trunk and made a start.

With a team of volunteers, we sorted thousands of the individual

---

[3]As a result, these memoirs deal chiefly with things I could still do. There were many I could not, which may leave an impression that my writing was the Committee's main work. In reality, unbanned others bore the brunt of the Campaign and its public meetings, collection of 'demands', and financing. They carried the Campaign. In its later stages, I merely wrote about it.

written demands into topics, until an entire living-room floor had been covered with mounds of paper, each labelled Labour, Land, Civil Rights, Votes, Education, Living Standards, and so on.

One step forward. What next? We tried breaking down the mounds into molehills, with more specific labels like: Land Owner-ship, Land Rights, Land Workers, etc.

That worked for some topics, not for others. Some 'demands' were too general, and others too limited. Some were no more than expressions of desire: 'Freedom and Equality'; 'Justice for All'; or 'No More Racialism'. Others were opaque, like 'Every Vote must be Counted'; or obscure like 'We're not Moving'; or simply unclassifiable like 'Life too Heavy'.

The volunteers took it as far as they could, admitted defeat and went home. I stayed on and went through them all again to get the general flavour, and then stuffed them all back into the trunk to be kept for reference. No one now remembers what happened to the trunk thereafter. It was lost for ever together with all the 'demands'.

I started to outline a skeleton Charter. It was impossible to accommodate all the topics and sub-topics. The range was too wide. Instead of a skeleton I was juggling with a museum's warehouse of unsorted bones. My knowledge of anatomy extends only to the thought that '. . . the thigh bone is connected to the leg bone . . .'. So I put the skeleton idea aside and tried to arrange a limited number of individual limbs, using those demands which seemed to fit the concept, and discarding those which did not.

I almost abandoned the whole exercise before I realised that it was quite irrelevant how many pieces could be fitted in. This was not a straw poll where each demand counted equally with every other. I began to select out of the maze some general categories of demands rather than all the categories. That made the construction easier, but it still left it misshapen and lopsided, with a host of parts labelled, say, 'Labour' and only one or two marked 'Land'.

There was nothing for it but to trim, shorten or stretch the limbs to fit together into a rough approximation of a workable skeleton. Along that blundering unmapped route, an outline of the Charter began to emerge.

The most difficult part of the exercise was to keep my own opinions from determining the final draft. On many of the topics covered by the 'demands', I had strong views of my own. I am strongly biased towards a socialist economy, in which the main productive resources are held in common for the common good. There was little in the demands which would justify that proposition's inclusion in the Charter. But also little to justify inclusion of either an alternative free market or private model economy.

There was no point in making a count; the Charter required that a compromise or a consensus be read from – or read into – what was on the paper; not what was in my mind. I would like to think that I was always perfectly balanced and objective in my reading, but that must remain a matter of doubt. Although I tried.

In the end, the skeleton had ten limbs, each of which could be summarised in a single phrase such as: 'The People Shall Govern'; or 'All Shall be Equal Before the Law'. Good enough as far as it went. But for public presentation purposes it lacked both a head and a tail. It seemed to cry out for an oratorical flourish at the start – something like 'We hold these truths to be self-evident . . .'– and a call to action at the end. I added what seemed like suitable paragraphs without any of the agonising and hesistancy which had gone into phrasing the demands. They were, after all, only the decorative trimmings of the Charter, not its essence. Perhaps I took them too casually.

Now, in retrospect, both introduction and finale strike me as considerably overblown. But the thing was done. I was satisfied enough with it to show it to a few colleagues whose judgement I valued. I made a few amendments they suggested, and passed it on to the Working Committee. They in turn approved it without alteration. It was ready for the COP only days before the great event itself.

There are different memories about what happened next. Some assert that the Joint Executives met on the eve of the COP, and made amendments to the Draft before it was unveiled at the COP. If there was any such meeting, my bans would have kept me from it. It seems inherently unlikely. By the eve of the COP the Draft Charter was already printed and ready for distribution; we had no facilities for an overnight reprint. It had to be issued as it was, with or without formal approval from the Congresses.

Perhaps it only matters to historians who are bothered by the question: Whose Charter was it? If it was the draft of the Congresses, as is often said, how was that imprimatur obtained? The only possible forum where it could have been given was the Joint Executives – which was a purely consultative body, without power of decision except after unanimous agreement of each of its constituent bodies. It is clear that they were never asked to do so before the COP.

Which leaves the question: Whose document was it? The answer to that question only became a matter of importance after the COP event. I believe that the Charter had drifted out of the Congresses' control – and for lack of foresight had taken on a free-floating life of its own. For all practical purposes it was – temporarily – the creature of the Working Committee and no one else – not even the ANC.

That was something that had not been foreseen. It left the Draft without formal Congress approval, and left open the question whether any of the Congresses would be bound by the Charter once it had been approved at the COP. As I remember it, we became aware of this constitutional loose end only at the last minute, but it seemed unimportant and also too late for anything to be done about it. The Draft was ready, and so was the site. Seating on bare boards laid on concrete blocks was in place, and so were essential services. Anything unfinished would have to stay that way – until afterwards.

Saturday, 25 June 1955. COP Day. Hilda and I were both banned from gatherings. Breaking the ban could mean up to five years' imprisonment, but we could not persuade ourselves to stay away. There was too much of that year's life and hopes invested in it. We had to see it for ourselves. We went as close as we dared. Friends in the area took us to a yard adjoining the site, where coal had been piled high against a corrugated iron fence. By clambering up the coal, we could peer over the fence and into the site to see the delegates queuing up at the gate to present their credentials and receive their copies of the Draft Charter.

It was nearly time for proceedings to start, but time was only notional on such occasions in South Africa. Train and bus schedules for black travellers were erratic. Delegates could be expected to straggle in throughout the day.

For days we had been receiving reports of delegates meeting

serious obstacles on road and rail. Passes were being demanded everywhere en route. Buses and taxis hired at considerable expense were being systematically intercepted by police, and turned back on specious grounds that they were not 'roadworthy', or lacked a licence to carry fare-paying passengers.

Inside the site it was all very relaxed and peaceful. Delegates were taking the sun and socialising. Outside it was different. Police were deployed in strength at railway stations and road junctions around Kliptown; people without valid passes or tax receipts were being arrested and taken away. No one knew how many delegates had been snatched or been left stranded at the roadside in unfamiliar places.

But the show had to go on. Political activists who have lived their lives in a police state have learnt to cope. They might be delayed, but most of them would find a way through, early or late.

Some Special Branch men began to take an interest in our heads showing above the fence. We decided to leave while we could. Our legal position was uncertain. Were we 'attending' the gathering? Could a 'gathering' extend beyond its fence – and if so, how far? To the limits of Kliptown, or beyond? Did we share a 'common purpose' with the delegates? And could looking on from across the fence constitute 'taking part in the activities'?

Such questions were not fanciful; the legal meaning of the banning orders was uncertain enough to confound lawyers. Walter Sisulu had been charged with 'attending a gathering' for sitting down to tea with a friend. Others had been convicted of 'participating in the activities' for owning an aluminium mug with the letters ANC scratched on its side; or an ANC badge pinned out of sight behind a jacket lapel in a wardrobe. Such fine legal subtleties formed the border between liberty and prison. We were breaking our bans regularly, almost daily, but only for good political reasons. Staying around just to satisfy our curiosity did not qualify. So we left.

The little I had seen of the COP had been deeply disappointing. In my enthusiasm for the project, I had imagined thousands of delegates filling the site and overflowing into the streets outside. It had not been anything like that. The numbers we had seen were still growing, but they were far below my expectations. Yet disappointing as it was, it was still the biggest delegate gathering the country had ever known and should make a tremendous impact throughout the country.

We were at home throughout the weekend, waiting for news. It was the time before television; there was almost nothing in the press, and until Sunday evening nothing on radio – a propaganda arm of the state. And then only a short report of a large police raid on a gathering at Kliptown, where many people were being held for questioning.

We learnt later that the police had descended on the site in strength, and allowed no one to leave before they had been searched and identified. Every scrap of paper they could find had been seized and taken away. The noise and confusion they had created had held up proceedings for some time, after which the meeting and the speeches went on despite them and around them.

The timetable had been wrecked. It had provided for each Chapter of the Charter to be debated, if necessary amended, and voted on before discussion started on the next. In a hurried consultation, the leaders on the platform decided to telescope the procedure to fit the time remaining. Instead of taking one chapter at a time, the Charter was opened for discussion as a whole.

Even so, proceedings lasted until well after dark. The whole, unamended Charter was put to the vote and approved by acclaim, with triumphant ululating from the women delegates. Counting was impossible, and superfluous. So far as anyone could judge, the vote had been virtually unanimous. The delegates sang for hours afterwards, while the police doggedly collected every document in sight and recorded every name and address.

We ought to have prepared a great campaign to publicise the COP and the sweeping democratic prospects it had opened up in the Charter. Attention had been focused too closely on the event itself so there was no plan for a follow-up. The glow of enthusiasm inspired at the COP gradually wore off, and the movement slipped back into an uninspired routine of meetings and more meetings.

The Charter was reprinted in thousands of copies, and distributed nationwide; organisations of every kind were called upon to endorse it and adopt it as their own, but the momentum had gone, and enthusiasm had dribbled away even from the Congresses themselves. A few minor organisations endorsed the Charter, but not enough, and even the ANC, which had started it all, delayed endorsing it. The truncated procedure at the COP seemed to have cast a shadow over events.

At the COP, debate on the Charter had been cut short. None of the controversial issues in the Charter had been argued out in depth, and controversy had been left to fester. I had foreseen some of the contentious issues when I was working on the Draft, and had tried to arrive at formulations which could enable a consensus to emerge.

I had struggled, for example, with irreconcilable 'demands' for nationalisation of all land, and others demanding the return of the land to its historic owners. Perhaps mistakenly, I had settled for the vague proposition: *'The land shall be shared by those who work it.'* Though it was unlikely to satisfy everyone, there would be time at the COP for it to be debated and refined – or so I thought. But that had not happened. Inevitably, after the COP, my formula ran into heavy criticism for being either too radical or too imprecise, or even for being meaningless.

The same happened with the chapter on the economy. There had been 'demands' for nationalisation of mines and banks, and 'demands' for the ending of barriers to black private ownership and share-holding. There was no ready compromise, so I cobbled together a formula which did not expressly support either demand but might synthesise their shared implications. My formulation *'All shall share in the nation's wealth'* left supporters on both sides dissatisfied. Yet the Working Committee had approved it without demur, perhaps thinking as I did that it was, after all, only a Draft to be argued over at the COP.

Since there had been no real scope for argument and resolution at the COP, the controversial elements of the Charter inspired argument and disagreement after it, both inside and outside the ranks of the Congresses. Critics claimed that the clauses dealing with the land and the economy represented a concession to a socialist agenda – particularly the single sub-clause which proposed nationalisation of banks and monopoly industry.

The criticisms were ill founded, and sometimes malicious. Nationalisation is not necessarily a gateway to socialism – the country had already nationalised railways, electricity supply and other major sectors of the economy. Despite that, white supremacy had ensured gross economic injustice and inequality. Nationalisation of the commanding heights of the economy might help correct that legacy which could not be corrected by simply ending race discrimination or liberalising markets. More radical steps would be needed, including state intervention, though nationalisation was not necessarily the best or only way to achieve it.

Amongst Congress activists, debates over economic policy and the relative merits of capitalism and socialism were everyday stuff. The Communist Party had popularised the idea of a socialist society; Marxists had initiated a debate about whether apartheid and racism accounted for the specially repressive character of South African capitalism, or whether it was capitalism which accounted for the special racism of apartheid. The debate over the economic clauses of the Charter was not much more than an additional element in an ongoing debate.

More surprising and unexpected was the fierce debate which arose from what I had regarded as the least controversial paragraph in the Charter – the preamble which declared that *'South Africa belongs to all who live in it, black and white'*. I had intended it to be a straightforward summary of the whole ethos of the Charter, and of its vision of a non-racial, democratic and egalitarian state. I had not expected any turmoil over it; it had not been questioned or criticised by any of those who read and approved the Draft.

The storm broke immediately after the COP. The slogan of independence movements elsewhere in Africa – *'Africa for the Africans!'* – had found an echo in the most nationally minded elements in the ANC and its Youth League. They fiercely denounced the Charter and the colour-blind direction taken by the ANC. South Africa, they insisted, did not belong 'to all who live in it'. It belonged to the Africans! And the reason for the ANC's fall from grace could only be the influence of communists upon it.

Many of the most vociferous new 'Africanists' were students, entering politics for the first time. They had not taken part in the steady ANC progress from an exclusive nationalism to an uncompromising non-racialism – a journey of learning from experience, not from political theory. It had been a journey on a long road which stretched continuously from the first Xuma-Dadoo pact of 1947 to the Freedom Charter.

But most of the Africanists had not travelled it. They espoused an often poorly defined 'Africanism' against what they called

'Charterism', thus creating their own theoretical entanglements. Who were these 'Africans' to whom South Africa belonged exclusively? Did they include such non-white minorities as Indians and Coloureds who suffered lesser discrimination than blacks? Or such whites as had put themselves unequivocally on the side of black liberation? The arguments became esoteric, Talmudic wrangles over such concepts as 'black consciousness' and negritude.

The ANC in turn was forced to make a clearer definition of its own ideology. It finally committed itself to the Freedom Charter and incorporated it formally into the ANC programme. The other Congresses followed, and the breach over the 'Charter' widened to a point of no return.

The 'Africanists' crystallised out into a number of organisations of their own, and broke away from the ANC altogether. They were a small but vocal and articulate group and won a substantial following amongst black students. Their separate, often hostile, organisations – the Pan Africanist Congress (PAC), and a string of youth and student organisations (AZAPO and others) – sought to wrest the support of the black community away from the ANC; many of them rejected the very idea of a Union of South Africa and renamed their country 'Azania'. The Charter had changed black politics in a way no one had foreseen or intended.

More Joint Congress meetings were held from time to time. They were low-key affairs. The COP Working Committee, with nothing more to do, disappeared, so after the frenzied months of the COP campaign I had nothing special to do in the movement except write. It was not enough.

I was unhappy, separated from the heart of the political action, and discontented with my architectural career which had always been something of a sideline to my politics. I had been with the same firm for over ten years, climbing the career ladder by seniority, and had finally been made a partner in the firm in 1952. For me, that proved to be a mistake. My interest in architecture was always for the construction side of the profession. I had no interest in the commercial and financial aspects of it, yet as a partner in the firm, I was being drawn ever further from actual building into office administration, cost studies and consultations with clients.

By the end of 1955 I had had enough. I gave my partners six months' notice, as required by our partnership agreement, and in

July 1956 parted from them on amicable terms. The agreement had prohibited my seeking any professional work of my own during those six months. I was free, but with no clients, no professional commissions, and no income.

I hired a single office – part of a young insurance broker's suite.[4] His receptionist would answer my phone when I was out. I put my name on the door, brought in the absolute minimum of furniture and equipment, and sat down to wait for something to happen. Nothing much did. I produced a few speculative house plans to be offered for sale by the Institute of Architects but no buyers showed up. I spent most of the year waiting for the phone to ring.

---

[4]He turned out to be as political as I was, but from the other end of the political spectrum. During the war he had supported General Hertzog, and joined the quasi-military terrorist body, the Ossewa Brandwag. Despite our political differences we got along famously, recognising each other as fellow citizens but not 'fellow travellers'. It was a bizarre friendship. He took care of my interests and my office while I was in prison for treason against 'his' government.

11

POWER, TREASON & PLOT

1956 – 57

Government ministers are talking of communist plots to poison the water supplies and overthrow the government. We are expecting new arrests, but they have cried 'Wolf' too often and there is no panic in the movement. The Congress movement is quietly adopting the Freedom Charter as the definitive statement of aims of the whole liberation struggle. It could be the best of times except for the regular police raids on homes and offices with the seizure of books, documents and typewriters. Everything seems tranquil, though the seizures go on without any explanation or discernible purpose.

At the end of 1955, the police arrive at our house again in the early morning. We have been raided and searched several times before, but nothing like this. Plain-clothes police study every book on our shelves. They seem unsure about what they are doing and ask each other questions like: 'Do we want books by Karl Marx?' They study every piece of paper they can find in files and drawers, and pile up suspect items for confiscation.

Amidst the political matter on the pile there is a children's tale of a horse, *Black Beauty*, and *A Post-War Plan for The City of London*. They are slow readers and slow to decide. As the morning passes I no longer find it funny and grow angry and hostile. At midday they are still working doggedly through the desk and shelves in our living-room with the rest of the house to come.

There are books in every room. It is going to be a long siege. If we do not starve them out they will never finish. The family take their meals and afternoon tea in the kitchen. I take mine on my lap, ostentatiously, watching them at work in the living-room and offering them nothing. By late afternoon they begin to wilt, with two bedrooms, a garage-junk room and outbuildings still unsearched. They get ready to pack up and go, but I am not ready. I insist on an itemised receipt for everything in the removal pile. It is dark before they have painstakingly written an itemised receipt for over three hundred books, papers, letters, documents, and two typewriters, and carried it all away.

The gaping voids in our bookshelves are slowly filled by new additions. My architectural practice is proving very slow to start. Between that, the effect of my bans and the end of the COP campaign, I have more time to spend at home than I have had for years. I am not naturally gregarious; the feeling of isolation does not bother me much, but our financial straits do. I have had no earnings since the end of June 1956, and have no prospect of any until I have completed work on my first commission – to design a drive-in cinema for Nairobi. Hilda is heavily pregnant with our fourth child and will soon have to give up her editorial work for a family magazine.

Early December. Dozens – perhaps hundreds – of overnight arrests of 'political suspects' are reported from across the country, with further arrests expected. We have little hard information about those who have been taken, and our bans on 'communicating' make it difficult to move about and find out. We are still unsure what is going on when Hilda goes into labour in the middle of the night. We leave our teenage daughter Toni in charge of house and children, and rush off to the maternity home where our fourth child, a son, is born during the morning. I am allowed to look in on him but only through a viewing window.

The maternity home has strict visiting hours. Hilda is in good shape but our time to talk is limited. We speculate about the meaning of the arrests and what their implications may be for us. We know we are both on the 'possibles' list if there are any more, but we fill the permitted hour arguing about the name we will give the boy. Our ideas differ. I favour a one-syllable name which cannot be shortened to a babyish diminutive. Hilda thinks this reduces the choice to Al or Bud, and puts forward other choices which I don't like. We leave it for another day, and I go home to see the children into bed and then pass the news to relatives and friends. I am dead tired after a night without sleep, but only get to bed late.

3 a.m. There is someone hammering on the front door again, and the door-bell ringing in the kitchen. Two Special Branch detectives are at the door with a warrant for my arrest on a charge of treason. They keep their eyes on me while I dress and collect a change of clothes and some toilet articles.

Toni is awake and so is Bessie Kubheka, our maid, family friend and occasional surrogate mother for all our children. I can tell them no more than that I will be away for a while; I do not know any more myself. They will have to let Hilda know and take care of house and children. The younger children are still asleep when I am driven away through the sleeping suburbs to the Johannesburg Fort. It *had* once been a fort at the time of the Kruger Republic; its staff still boast that the young war correspondent Winston Churchill had been held here during the South African war. The squat stone fortress walls enclose an untidy scatter of miscellaneous offices, cell blocks, and yards enclosed in steel mesh to mark its transformation from republican fort to apartheid prison.

Inside the walls, apartheid rules. The only apparent master plan is to segregate blacks from whites, but in the apartheid manner. In the white zones there are black menials – convict menials – to do much of the labouring, fetching and carrying as blacks do everywhere outside. The cell block to which I am taken already holds some twenty-two white male political prisoners. Most of us know each other from politics 'outside'. We know that in all there are some 150 politicals under arrest – including black men, black women and white women. Those from outside the Transvaal have been flown to Johannesburg and are housed somewhere in this rabbit warren of a place. That suggests that we will all be tried together on the charge of Treason. Why Walter Sisulu and I and some thirteen others have been seized a few days later than the rest is a mystery.

I have been under lock and key in police and prison cells before. It is part of the standard apprenticeship in radical politics. But this is different. This arrest is not a temporary inconvenience like the previous ones but a total disruption of all normal life for an indefinite period. I am amongst friends, but the physical conditions are primitive and fairly sordid. We are quarantined from the criminal prisoners, perhaps more for their protection than for ours. The prison staff handle us with a mixture of hostility and awe; they are not used to prisoners who are articulate, argumentative and litigious, or are not properly humble at the prospect of retribution for their misdeeds. For us, prison is proof that we have managed to rattle the confidence of the regime. That gives us a sense of moral superiority over the establishment and sustains our morale despite the demeaning physical conditions.

There is nothing in my memory which distinguishes one day in the Fort from any other of the weeks spent there. The single exception is the day when Jack Hodgson, Joe Slovo, and I – perhaps others – are summoned without warning and taken under guard to the Visitors' Room. This is a bare concrete box, furnished only with a solid counter with a plate glass screen above which divides it into two. We are locked in on one side; some twenty of our friends and relations packed two and three deep on the other. I can see my elder brother Harold among them, half a head taller than the rest. He is a liberal-minded but conventional accountant, without any political involvements except some minor part in four-yearly parliamentary elections. His presence in this low-life place is totally unexpected. It must be utterly repugnant to him, but with him is Hilda carrying a blanketed baby in her arms. She pushes her way to the counter and holds the bundle up for my inspection.

People on both sides of the counter push forward to see, all talking at once, greeting and asking questions. It is bedlam. Someone shouts out: 'Talk softly and we'll all be able to hear!' The noise level drops momentarily, but there are several separate conversations going on together, all reverberating off the bare walls. First one and then another raises the volume; within moments everyone is shouting to be heard once again – including some shouting at others to pipe down.

The noise drowns out all sense. Hilda has come directly from the maternity home with a still nameless baby. We shout to each other about what we are going to name him while friends on both sides press in to look at him, make baby-talk through the glass, and join in our deliberations. Somehow, I am not quite sure how in all the din, we agree to call him Keith – it is probably the only name we can both hear. But Keith he is, the Treason Trial baby, firmly linked by fate and an umbilical cord to the Trial where he will become a mascot of sorts.

Days later, we are all packed into the high-sided, closed police pick-up vans known locally as kwela-kwelas. We join a convoy of similar vans coming from the parts of the Fort where the white women politicals and the black men and women have been held. We cross the city surrounded by outriders with sirens blazing, bringing all other traffic to a halt. Some of us push arms through the closely barred windows, to wave and call greetings to people on the footway as we pass. There are only blank stares in response. No one on the streets seems to know who we are, or care. There is nothing that links us in our sealed steel box to them out there in the real world.

The convoy reaches the Union Grounds[1] and the vans nose their way slowly through a vast crowd of slogan-chanting people who are being held back by a massive police cordon. The demonstrators fill the street from side to side, holding aloft a forest of placards with the slogan: 'We Stand By Our Leaders!' Our arms reaching out through the kwela-kwela's barred windows are being answered with shouted greetings, cheers, clenched fist salutes. Some of the crowd start singing liberation songs and push against the police cordon to reach up and touch hands. We are back amongst our own people. The police shepherd us from the vans, through the crowds and the clamour, and into the Drill Hall where the public are not being allowed entry.

Inside the hall, prisoners, lawyers, police, court orderlies and press reporters are milling about. It is a gloomy, utilitarian barn of a place. Echoes bounce off the red brick interior walls with their barred windows crusted in green Public Works Department paint. Sound reverberates from the corrugated iron roof and steel roof trusses above, and from feet clattering on the wooden floor below. There is a platform at one end, and immediately in front of it a row of tables and behind that 156 hard wooden chairs set out in

---

[1] A dreary patch of baked red earth enclosed by utilitarian iron railings, used as the parade ground for the part-time Active Citizens Force (ACF) whose headquarters was the Drill Hall directly across Twist Street. At the time of writing, planners and traffic engineers have encroached on it to create a tangle of roads and a taxi underpass, as unlovely and litter-strewn as ever.

militarily precise rows which are rapidly being pushed aside as people push their way through to greet others. No one is paying any heed to the court orderlies who are calling vainly for silence and order.

The greetings and introductions make the scene look and sound more like a club reunion than a court of law. The air is one of excitement and anticipation rather than dread. It is scarcely possible to believe that, despite the bizarre setting, we are in a court of law to be charged with almost the most serious crime in the book, treason. When things finally settle down and order is restored, we are formally charged, enter a formal response of 'not guilty' and are shepherded out again, through the crowds to the kwela-kwelas, and back to the Fort.

Day 2: Back to the Drill Hall. The crowds are larger, and so is the police presence. The magistrate takes his seat at a table on the platform, with prosecutors, defence lawyers and press reporters arrayed at tables between him and the accused. The crowd noise from outside makes it impossible for us to hear the exchanges between the magistrate and lawyers. There is no public address system. We pass the lawyers a note of protest, they confer with the magistrate and the court adjourns for the day again. Back to the Fort.

Day 3: Inside the hall there is now a special South African design of dock to hold the accused and keep everyone else away from them. It is a ten foot high cage of stout diamond mesh on a framework of steel scaffolding. There is only a single entrance gate, guarded, and inside it 156 chairs. We each have a designated seat – arranged alphabetically and by province.

It must look good on paper. In practice it is not so good. The orderlies persuade a young Indian Congress activist to take up Seat No.1, front row left. He acquires instant historic fame through the case known formally as 'The State vs Faried Adams and others'. One hundred and fifty-five of us have still to be seated in our ordained places. All are self-willed adults, unused to kowtowing to petty authority, distinctly unamused and uncooperative. While some are being persuaded to take their proper seats, others already seated lose patience, get up and wander about to chat. Those tired of standing take a rest in the vacated chairs and reduce the exercise to a shambles. The most bloody-minded of our number install themselves where they should not be, like schoolboys bent on sabotaging a class photograph.

The orderlies struggle to restore the system and to move people along from seat to seat to get the order right. It becomes an ill-tempered and, on our side, a malicious game of musical chairs as some kind of protest.

A public address system has been installed overnight, so that we can hear what is going on. Before anything else can begin, the defence lawyers who have been assembled for us by others, issue a *démarche*: they will not proceed with the case while their clients are caged 'like wild beasts'. If the cage does not go, they will. The court adjourns again. We spend the morning chatting and smoking in the small yard adjoining the Hall while the magistrate and lawyers confer. It is agreed that the cage will be removed; in the mean time, the locked gate is left open and the sides of the cage are reduced to waist height. We return to our seats and the case can finally begin.

The prosecutor's outline of his case runs to eighteen thousand words, which he reads in an interminable drone. The heat is rising in the hall, and the accused doze off. Outside, the crowd noise rises. A police officer hurries into the hall and calls his men out. They are followed by Bishop Ambrose Reeves who has occupied one of the few public seats behind the cage. We lose track of whatever it is that the prosecutor is saying. There is the crack of a rifle shot from the street outside, followed by a fusillade of others. Accused, lawyers and spectators are all on their feet. Outside there is pandemonium, the sound of screaming and running, and a police officer shouting 'Stop that firing!' The magistrate adjourns the court again, leaving us locked in the hall.

When the noise outside dies away the hearing starts once more. The tiny figure of Bishop Reeves returns, walking slowly past the front row of the 'dock'. He looks pale and shocked but is casually tossing some bright brass cartridge cases from hand to hand to make sure we can see them. Later we learn that twenty-two men and women have been taken to hospital with gunshot wounds.

The prosecutor resumes his recital and now, for the first time, we learn the basis for the charge of treason. It is alleged that we are all either office bearers or active members of organisations which make up the Liberation Movement; that we organised the Congress of the People and the Freedom Charter in order to set up a communist state which was to be achieved by force and violence, the incitement of hostility between white and black, and the revolutionary overthrow of the government with the aid of foreign powers. The reading ends; the court adjourns again for a Christmas recess and will only resume in the second week of January. Back to the Fort once more.

Arrangements for our defence are taking shape. A Defence Fund has been established on the initiative of Canon John Collins of St Paul's Cathedral, London. It is raising funds to foot the legal bill, and to help sustain our dependants. Mary Benson and Freda Levson have taken on the administrative tasks and have gathered an impressive list of bishops, retired judges, university chancellors, MPs and others as patrons. A legal team has been assembled, comprising old friends and colleagues like Bram Fischer, Vernon Berrange and George Bizos who have been regulars in previous political trials, together with others who are ready to assist and will appear on special aspects if and when needed.

Two days before Christmas, the lawyers apply to the Supreme Court for bail for us all. We know very little about it and are not present, but the application succeeds. At short notice, we are hustled out of the Fort and transferred to large cells in the basement of the Magistrate's Court while the documentation and cash guarantees for bail are being organised. Bail in a case of treason, which might well end with death sentences, is rare, probably unprecedented. That it has been granted at all implies that, even in the inner apparatus of the administration, there is some recognition that this is not an ordinary case to be dealt with in the ordinary way.

Despite the severity of the penalties for treason, bail more suitable for a traffic offence is set – and in a peculiarly South African way: £250 each for whites, £100 each for Indians, £50 each for Africans and Coloureds. Miraculously, the Defence Fund has found guarantors for all our bail bonds, from people who know little more about us than that we are 'Congress people'. Equally miraculously, a team of magistrates who would scarcely be thought to be sympathetic to our politics have volunteered to work on late into the night to see the paper work completed. By the time we are released, one by one, the city around the Magistrate's Court is dark and deserted. We will all be home for Christmas.

In mid-January, back to the Drill Hall, this time unescorted and without the panoply of police cordons and kwela-kwelas. There are no demonstrators outside, and only a small audience of friends and relations inside. The atmosphere is like that of a return to boarding school after a vacation – a sinking feeling of depression mixed with pleasure at seeing the same old gang again.

There are so many old comrades here – Jack Hodgson, Moses Kotane, Joe and Ruth Slovo, Lilian Ngoyi, Nelson Mandela, Oliver Tambo, Walter Sisulu, Kathy Kathrada and others – that it is like a class reunion, but with many familiar faces missing: Yusuf Dadoo, Monty Naicker, J B Marks, Ray Simons (Alexander), the Cachalia brothers, Hilda, Michael Harmel, Bram Fischer and others. They have all had a hand in the COP campaign, often clandestinely, but had been banned before the start of the 'conspiracy' as fixed by the indictment. They are not all happy to be excluded; some seem to feel that it reflects unfairly on their right to be included on what is being regarded as the 'honours' list of enemies of the state.

The euphoria of our first appearance at the Drill Hall has gone. The dusty echoing hall is as cheerless as a prison cell. We have been detached from the world of home, family and work, and look set to moulder here for no one knows how long. Yet all 156 of us have turned up, justifying the trust placed in us by our bail guarantors.

The atmosphere of crisis has evaporated; magistrate and court orderlies are more relaxed, and the rows of men and women in the dock seem as relaxed as an audience at a lecture. Berrange makes a short opening statement for the defence, castigating the case as a political attack by government on us, on our ideas and on everyone who supports our policies. The defence, he says, will take issue with the state on the political motives and the real content of our political actions.

Strictly speaking, this is not the real trial. It is only a preliminary hearing to enable a magistrate to decide whether to commit us for trial in the High Court. We are under no obligation to answer any part of the evidence. We may, if we choose, simply listen to the state case and reserve our defence for the High Court trial. We have agreed that we will not dispute any of the facts about the COP, the Freedom Charter or the official policies and statements of any of our organisations. We will let the prosecution explain its case, and only challenge lies or distortions in the evidence.

The prosecution has a mountain of evidence, a quite extraordinary mountain for what is, in all respects except size, a run-of-the-mill preliminary hearing. In size, it is an extra-ordinary affair, a block-buster of a case with 156 accused, 10 000 documents and hundreds of witnesses. The official record of the state case alone will run to 8 000 pages. Yet in all the testimony and all the documents, there is not anything which has been done in secret. If, as alleged, there was a 'conspiracy', it was conducted in full sight and presence of the police at public meetings, conferences and demonstrations. Everything said or proposed has been recorded and been seen to have been recorded. Every handbill, booklet and periodical has been legally printed and distributed; all documents, minutes and resolutions have been kept accessible for all who want them.

This is certainly the most open 'conspiracy' in political history – and yet, even so, this 'preliminary' hearing is set to be the longest in South African legal history.

The majority of the state witnesses are policemen who testify to what they have seen or heard at meetings, or who 'hand in' documents they have acquired over the years. It is a deadly slow, dry-as-dust process which grinds on relentlessly, day after day, for weeks.

As in a timeless cricket Test, there are arcane regulations which prolong the agony but appear to bring a result no closer – especially rules that every word in every document and note must be read out in full 'for the record', even where there is no dispute about their authenticity. Readings from the witness stand drone on endlessly, in expressionless monotones.

It is scarcely possible to concentrate on it all. Meaning is lost; attention wanders; days and weeks of sonic murmur blend in the background fog; in the airless Drill Hall heat, minds glaze over and eyes close. What is being read does not matter – we know almost all the documents from before; I have written more than a few of them myself. We know the words, but their relevance to the charge of treason is not explained or fathomable.

Days pass into weeks and weeks to months, and the parade of witnesses becomes a sort of a charade, apparently important to the prosecution but without any meaning to us. Only occasionally is it amusing or even interesting. We give up trying to extract any significance from the words, and turn our minds to better things like reading books and newspapers, writing letters, solving crossword puzzles while the sounds flow over us.

The magistrate knows we have switched off, but says nothing. He himself appears to stay awake like a silent supervisor of the evidence production line. From time to time, someone reminds us that this production line could end at the gallows. The warning cannot be taken seriously when we are really only being bored to death and waiting for the clock to signal a break for lunch or tea.

Even our legal team shows signs of wilting. Senior counsel appear only for special sessions, leaving a junior to hold up the defence end somewhat like a cricketing night-watchman. John Coaker is a portly young barrister with a rather Dickensian turn of phrase. Those of us who are seized by a call of nature during a court session pass him an SOS, and he rises to his feet with due gravitas and informs the magistrate: 'Sir. Accused number x is in distress.' X is granted leave to exit temporarily while the case proceeds. Coaker gradually tempers the phrase to 'acute distress', and ultimately, during a minor epidemic of stomach troubles, to 'dire distress'.

The magistrate bends the rules; those in dire distress may leave the hall quietly, without personal permission. Random comings and goings between dock and toilets in the yard add a small semblance of life to an otherwise moribund process. 'Dire distress' becomes standard Treason Trial speak for every emergency or crisis.

Eventually, the flow of documents dries up, and gives way to a parade of police witnesses reading 'into the record' notes made in their handbooks at meetings. They are wonderfully compressed précis. Hours of speech are reduced to a few paragraphs, often freely translated from the original language spoken. Most of them are simply unbelievable, others no more than gibberish.

They are grist to the lawyers' mill. Vernon Berrange especially enjoys tormenting policemen, much like a small boy pulling wings off insects. He takes on the cross-examination when the evidence is patently false or nonsensical. The police are intimidated by his reputation, though he never bullies them or raises his voice. He is very cool, the complete master of the cross-examiner's art. He enjoys deploying his talent to serious ends – and occasionally also for his own and our amusement.

His performances provide rare breaks in the weeks of tedium, but the relevance of the police notes to the charge of treason remains as obscure as that of the documents before them.

Slotted in at random between police witnesses are a few lay witnesses to events they claim to have seen or heard – many of whom are bogus. Amongst some sober citizens there are clowns, fraudsters, liars and charlatans. They are all gravely presented by the prosecution, and give Berrange the opportunity for virtuoso performances.

One is a sanctimonious savant in whose mouth butter wouldn't melt who turns out to be a convicted criminal; another an alleged cleric complete with black jacket and dog-collar who turns out also to be a jailbird and convicted con man. There is the chief of an Evaton criminal gang known as 'The Russians', who nonchalantly tells Berrange that he became chief by killing his predecessor; and a professional informer who produces an unlicensed revolver from his pocket when challenged on the witness stand by Berrange. There is a detective who demonstrates how he came to write his notes with three different pens while sitting on his motor cycle – two pens in his mouth as stand-by for when the third ran dry; and a detective who will soon rise to the top ranks of the Security Police, who made short-hand notes for half a day while crouched inside a cupboard during a meeting in the Trades Hall.

And there is Professor Murray from Grahamstown University – an 'expert on communism' – who identifies phrases in the court exhibits as 'straight from the shoulder communism' or 'one hundred per cent communism'. And when put to the test by Berrange, interprets sentences taken from the writings of Gandhi, Churchill and himself in the same way.

These are the rare moments of light relief as the evidence deals with the happenings of several years, and the exhibits accumulate like material for a jumble sale. Documents range from the utterly mundane to the weird and irrelevant, and ultimately to the bizarre 'Soup with meat' and 'Soup without meat' – placards seized from the COP catering stall. Into the mix there is thrown a mountain of private letters, books by Karl Marx and Mao Tse-tung, and pamphlets about cattle culling, pass laws, taxes and socialism. The public has deserted this theatre of the absurd; the gallery is empty; the press has abandoned the search for a story line and carries almost no reports. As a public spectacle, the case is dead.

There has to be some purpose to this idiotic process which the prosecution is orchestrating with such solemnity. It cannot be simply to establish a clear prima-facie case for our committal to a higher court. For that, the prosecution team are intelligent enough to select the most telling bits of testimony and documentation, and to confine their case to those. But they have chosen to bury whatever solid evidence they may have in this crazy overlay of dross, as if its sheer quantity will obscure its shoddy quality. The only explanation I can find is that this is not an exercise designed to establish guilt or innocence. It is a demonstration of police muscle in a political battle.

We are in the atomic age, when 'overkill' has become part of basic strategy. Perhaps this is why so many 'conspirators' have been charged together; why so many organisations and committees are cited as 'co-conspirators'; why the state is being so profligate with its regiments of witnesses gathered without regard to cost or time. War is not a time for concern over such trivialities; the only concern is to bring the enemy to its knees, and if possible destroy it.

But in translation from battlefield to court, the strategy loses all rationale. Intended to shock or kill, it only causes yawning indifference; intended to destroy morale, it creates only boredom. Yet no one in the chain of command has either the authority or the wit to order a halt. Long after the prosecution itself appears to have lost enthusiasm for its own strategy, it continues to repeat its actions over and over again like a clock-work toy.

Even the best of clock-work mechanisms eventually runs down. It is over a year since the prosecutor confidently explained his case. Now neither he nor we can penetrate the fog to see whether treason or anything else has been proved. He no longer has any confidence, only resignation as he declares his case complete. It is the turn of the defence.

We have decided to leave the matter in the confused uncertainty the state has created, and reserve our defence for what we hope will be a greater sanity in the High Court. The magistrate closes the book in which he has been making notes throughout the year, and adjourns the court for four months while he considers his finding.

The trial by ordeal which opened a year before with an almighty bang ends with a murmur. Bail is continued and we are free to go. It is not the end, but only an intermission after Act 1. A million words have passed. Neither guilt nor innocence has been established, yet we have all lost a year of our lives.

The law has laboured mightily and produced nothing; not a single new point of law, not a single important ruling or important precedent. It has been an exercise in futility, suitable for the Guinness Book of Records by virtue only of its size and duration.

Law had never been the point of the exercise. It had been intended as a public stage for the destruction of the liberation movement after all other attempts by way of Suppression Acts, police raids, bans, banishments and individual trials had failed. Concepts of justice and truth had been subordinated to political ends in the belief that the ends would justify the means. But even that had gone wrong. A simplistic idea fashioned out of simplistic thinking by a security-intelligence establishment had failed to take into account the possible fallout.

Political fallout had started from Day 1, as evidenced by the scale of protest demonstrations outside the Hall. It continued less visibly thereafter, its effects so silent and subtle that even we who were within it scarcely registered. On Day 1 we were a loose assemblage of people from different places and different organisations. We knew each other – if at all – only from casual and intermittent contact, and had been thrown together like students on their first day at a new school. We shared pro-Congress leanings but were separated by differences of race, culture, class and ideology.

The Drill Hall fosters a collegiate spirit as we sit together, shoulder to shoulder, day after day. We take tea breaks together and lunch together on the food provided for us by a group of supporters outside. We fill the breaks and adjournments together, talking, consulting, arguing and singing our own songs which are being composed by some musicians amongst us. We learn to know and appreciate each other's special qualities, and to know one another's families, friends and lovers. We become involved in each other's concerns over jobs, money and health as well as family illnesses, births, deaths, marriages and school reports.

We are sharing more waking hours together than we do with our families; and the same economic hardships. The few professionals amongst us are more fortunate but also more harassed.

Mandela and Tambo rush back to their offices the moment court ends in the afternoon, to work late into the night attending to clients who have spent the day waiting patiently, filling their waiting-room and overflowing down the staircase into the street. I manage by catching the first dawn tram to town, working in my office until it is time to race off to court; and then returning after court to work on alone until I can no longer keep awake.

Yet we are the fortunate ones. Others have no routine life outside the court. I scarcely see my children – they are usually asleep when I leave and asleep when I return. Hilda and I meet up only late at night. She is writing rhyming couplets for an advertising agency by day, and coping with Keith's feeding troubles by night. Real life is no longer lived at home but in the Drill Hall.

Those of us whose homes are in Johannesburg are lucky; and those who can still work doubly so. Most of us depend entirely on the Defence Fund for survival. It provides the needy with enough for the rent of a Soweto room and some minimal subsistence. We are all living on the edge. Before long, the last of my architectural work is done. There is no end of the case in sight, and I can no longer meet my office rent. There is nothing for it but to close down my stillborn practice. I am so broke that after court each day I by-pass the tram stop opposite the Hall and trudge a long way up the hill in the afternoon heat. That way, I save twopence a day on the fare home.

Hilda is also moonlighting, making knitwear to order on her home knitting machine. She goes out to deliver a finished garment, pushing Keith's pram. On the way home her cheque for £3 goes astray in the folds of the blankets. She is not easily distressed when things go wrong, but this loss is so catastrophic she bursts into tears in the street. And yet we are in better straits than most of the others.

Day by day, fallout is changing the Drill Hall regulars imperceptibly from a company of strangers into something more like an extended family, or perhaps life-members of our own exclusive club. It is shaping us into a close-knit Drill Hall fraternity, and transforming our movement, especially the ANC's National Executive Committee which is its recognised head and directorate.

The ANC has a history which goes back to the first years of the Union of South Africa, but its organisational and administrative structure has never matched its real status as the leadership of the black majority. Its presidents have functioned from their home towns – now Stanger and before that ThabaNchu, Basutoland, while its secretaries and headquarters have operated from

Johannnesburg.[2] The structure had obstructed effective leadership, ensured long gaps between NEC meetings, and difficulties in convening short-notice or emergency sessions. Communications with regions and districts had been cumbersome; NEC directives trickled down slowly, by post or even more slowly by word of mouth, to local officials who were often without access to a telephone.

Lack of a day to day hands-on leadership had hobbled the ANC. Its actions seldom measured up to its potential. At critical moments, the members had often been left leaderless. Despite widespread popular support, the ANC was, in truth, much more of a mass frame of mind than a centralised modern political body. The Treason Trial arrests could have made matters worse by immobilising key personnel from all levels of the organisation, and decimating the ranks of local leaderships. Instead they make things better by bringing many leaders together in one place – National President Luthuli, Secretary General Sisulu, and senior National leaders like Professor Matthews and the Reverend Calata and Kotane, as well as their putative successors and provincial leaders Mandela, Tambo, Dr Zami Conco, Lilian Ngoyi, Duma Nokwe, Henry Makgothi, Robert Resha, Vuyisile Mini, Caleb Mayekiso and others. The ANC leadership, if it is to function at all, must do so from inside the Drill Hall.

In this new setting it is able to overcome many of its structural and organisational weaknesses. For the first time, the leaders are concentrated in one place, always available for meetings and accessible to ordinary members. They can gather together at the next court break by way of a message passed along the rows of the accused.

The quality of the leadership is transformed, and brought closer to their members and supporters than ever before. Soon everyone inside and outside the movement knows how and where to make contact with them without any protocol. Delegations and individuals make the journey to the Drill Hall in search of advice or assistance. Bus boycotters from Alexandra and Evaton come to consult on whether to keep on walking or accept a compromise offer on fares. Delegates from the incipient guerrilla movement in the Ciskei known as 'The Mountain' arrive to ask for assistance in acquiring firearms. The

---

[2]Even this is a Westminster-style improvement brought about by ANC president Dr A B Xuma to replace an archaic, unworkable 'Cabinet' system with departmental ministers scattered around the country.

place is becoming the political centre which the liberation movement has always lacked.

The new conditions are changing relationships inside the movement too, between its separate, ethnically based African, Indian, Coloured and white components. Co-operation and a sense of unity between them which had germinated in shared campaigns like the COP, had been mainly at committee level. Even the closest and oldest relationship, between ANC and Indian Congress, has scarcely percolated down to the membership below committee level. Separate ethnic organisation has kept alive mutual distrust, and doubts about the commitments and motives of others – doubts which are strongest against the latest entry to the partnership, the COD.

Though communism is an established minority opinion in all the Congresses, its influence is visibly greater in the ranks of the COD. Many COD members are new in this milieu and have cut their first political teeth only recently in the COP campaign. With their background in white society with its advanced technology, they often lack appreciation of black sensitivities and are impatient with the slower, low-tech ANC pace. Their pressure for greater urgency and efficiency often fuels new fears that, even here in Congress, whites think they can direct everything and take over everything.

Inter-racial trust and co-operation is a difficult plant to cultivate in the racially poisoned soil outside. It is somewhat easier here where racial discrimination and privileges have been set aside, and leaders of all the ethnic fractions of the movement are together[3] and equal; and where they have the time and opportunity to discover and explore each other's doubts and reservations, and to speak about them without constraint. Coexistence in the Drill Hall deepens and re-creates their relationships.

The protocol and formality which have surrounded their earlier contacts slip into a natural informality; prearranged appointments

---

[3] *Inter alia*: Monty Naicker and 'Kathy' Kathrada of the Indian Congress; Billy Nair, Leon Levy and Leslie Massina of SACTU; Bertha Mashaba and Helen Joseph of the Women's Federation; Alex Laguma and Reg September of the Coloured People's Organisation; Moses Kotane and M P Naicker of the Communist Party; Jack Hodgson and Piet Beyleveld of the Springbok Legion and Congress of Democrats.

and pre-set agendas make way for instant meetings and for decision by consensus rather than majority; joint meetings of the separate Congresses become a regular part of normal politics, and debates become more brisk and businesslike to suit the short time available in court breaks. Secrecy between leaders and rank and file disappears when everyone, whether in the leadership or not, knows what is being discussed and decided, and so comes to feel fully part of the process.

The Congress machine is undergoing root-and-branch change, and as the mechanism changes so the politics moves on from joint declarations of policy to a truly integrated and united, all-inclusive alliance.

The fallout is having unforeseen results which are precisely opposite to those the Treason Trial was meant to achieve. The leaders it was intended to cripple are more united and effective. The activists it was intended to demoralise and disperse have found new strength in unity. The inter-racial Congress front which it was intended to shatter has emerged stronger and closer. And frictions between communists and the rest which it was intended to enlarge have been resolved and laid to rest.

The political fallout from the Treason Trial has turned it from a clumsy legal blunder into the most complete political reversal the state has suffered in its war against the liberation movement.

For those of us who have had to endure it, it has not been a triumph but an ordeal. Despite the impression given in works of fiction, there are few things more tedious than a long trial; the Treason Trial was longer and more tedious than most, and an account of the detailed evidence is now of little interest to anyone except historians. The most interesting and important passages have been described by several other writers,[4] and do not merit repetition. What *was* important about the Treason Trial was not its misconceived legal process but its political fallout, which provided the conditions for a new-style Congress movement and so set the agenda for the next three decades of South African political struggle.

The Drill Hall had taken a year of our 156 lives, and at the end

---

[4] *The Treason Trial* by Lionel Forman and E S Sachs (John Calder); *The Treason Cage* by Anthony Sampson (Heinemann); and *If This Be Treason* by Helen Joseph (Andre Deutsch).

of it the legal case was no closer to finality than when it started. The issues between the movement and the state remained precisely as before, but the politics had matured, and would never be the same again.

The Drill Hall had given rise to an extraordinary fraternity which became the bedrock from which the modern Congress was sprung. That close fraternal spirit was the core which held together the enduring unity of the liberation movement for the next forty years, and kept it free of the factionalism and strife which destroyed so many movements in so many other countries. It was the matrix of the singleness of purpose which distinguished Congress, inside and outside the country, in prison and in exile, until the end of the apartheid era.

If the movement had come through the First Act in better shape than before, the 156 were not quite so fortunate at the end. It was as though the club we had been living in had closed, and flung us out, impoverished and slightly punch-drunk, to wait like unemployed boxers for the next bout. There was little incentive to try and pick up the threads of work and life; the bell might sound for another round as soon as the indeterminate adjournment ended. Few had jobs to go to or even prospects of a job. I had nowhere to go except back to my undusted office, to sit and wait and debate the state of the nation with my Ossewa Brandwag friend and landlord.

12

CRACKING THE FORTRESS WALL
1957 – 60

A few small architectural commissions come my way – none of them enough to keep me fully occupied. My clients, mostly small businessmen or industrialists, are in no way political. They know my politics and that I am out on bail awaiting trial for treason, but never speak of it. They seem to have no qualms about employing me on small projects like extensions, alterations and renovations to their properties – which are something that any architect in town could do competently without much effort.

I do not think of it as an act of charity. There is a radical streak amongst Johannesburg's white middle class. It thrives in this ugly, commercial town surrounded by white mine dumps whose sands whip across the city in the wind. Somehow within its brash materialism there is not only a wonderful climate but also a heart. The middle classes are no different from other South Africans in their acceptance of black oppression and white supremacy. But beneath it there is a libertarian sense, and a bias against the establishment. It does not manifest itself in partisan politics but in occasional acts of compassion or humanism.

It reveals itself in small ways – in offering work or jobs to the Treason Trial accused; in overtime work by the magistrates who process our bail applications. In part it is the last hangover of the frontier democracy and cosmopolitanism of the mining camp which spawned the city on this bleak and treeless hillside. In part, a folk memory of past experience of racial persecution and resistance in the ghettos of Eastern Europe from which many of them came.

We who adhere to the cause of black liberation or of communism are, nevertheless, a freak minority. We are tolerated, generally accepted and sometimes even welcomed. Even at the height of anti-communist hysteria, we are not the untouchable pariahs which our counterparts became in the USA during the McCarthy era.

When the Treason Trial Defence Fund is badly in need of funds, it applies to the City Council for a permit to hold a street collection, and gets it. Street collections are very tightly controlled and have to be competed for. Only two per week are allowed, only sealed municipal collecting tins may be used, and takings must be counted and certified by a Council officer. Ours coincides with one of the many court adjournments. We are out on the streets all day in the central city area, shaking collecting tins. Many people pass by head down, refusing to look at us. Some mutter refusals or protests, but not a single instance of aggression towards us is reported. By the end of the day, there is close to £2 000 in the tins. Johannesburg is that kind of place.

We are still marking time in the four-month court adjournment when, close to Christmas, all charges are withdrawn against sixty-five of the accused, including two of the most prominent partici-pants in the Congress of the People – Chief Luthuli and Oliver Tambo. There is no explanation. There may be inadequate evidence against some of the sixty-five, but not against these two. Dropping all charges against these two practising Christians can only be a political decision to deflect growing international criticism of the trial. Now there are ninety-one of us who return to the Drill Hall for its continuation.

There is no euphoria, no celebration, only the tired feeling of returning to school for another boring term. Surprisingly, the prosecution team has been refurbished with a new leader – Oswald Pirow QC – who is better known as the former Minister of Defence in Hertzog's pre-war government than as a lawyer. He has always been an admirer of Hitler and still sponsors an openly pro-Nazi periodical called *The New Order*. The only reason to recall him from legal obscurity must be to try to restore some credibility to the state case. It is also a tacit admission that this case is more about politics than about law.

If it is intended that Pirow's reputation will add weight and respectability to a case which is losing its way, it misfires. If he had once been a legal luminary, it is obvious that he is no longer. He makes an overtly political, highly charged summary of the state case which contains nothing new except additional venom. His political reputation has long been discredited except by the lunatic right-wing fringe. He is no longer a great courtroom orator or, as he had once been, a rabble rouser.

We have decided to lead no evidence of our own and to make no detailed reply to the state case. The defence case will be reserved for a higher court if we are committed for trial.

Vernon Berrange replies to the state case briefly, following the lines of his opening statement a year before. He castigates the patently political purpose of the case, and adds some caustic comments about the calibre of the state witnesses and their evidence. The state, he tells the court, has failed to provide even prima-facie proof of treason. The accused are therefore entitled to be discharged.

There is another adjournment while the magistrate considers his findings, and at the end of January 1958 he does what we have always known he would do – he finds that a prima-facie case has been established, and commits all ninety-one of us to trial in the Supreme Court. Bail will be continued.

For the time being, we are liberated from the Drill Hall. I return to my office in the hope of reviving my practice once again, but my enthusiasm has worn thin. There is no indication how long it will be before the Supreme Court hearing starts. We assume that when it does, it will again be in Johannesburg and 'moon-lighting' will again be possible for anyone who has anything to work at. I am earning less than I could have done filling supermarket shelves, but hoping that something will turn up. The hope is false.

We have underestimated the petty-minded vindictiveness of the government. We are summoned to appear before the Supreme Court in Pretoria in August – forty miles away from any of our homes or treason-trial lodgings, and forty miles away from our lawyers' professional offices.

It can only be by malicious intent. In Pretoria, there is not even a court which can accommodate a trial of this size. An obsolete synagogue has to be specially converted for the purpose. It is out in the suburbs, well away from the existing courts in Church Square, and from the centre of town. Spectators will be few and far between, and demonstrations outside unlikely. Justice might be done, but it is not going to be publicly seen to be done.

The Defence Fund has hired an ageing coach to pick up all the accused in Johannesburg and ferry us to and from court each day. It is a tiring, bone-shaking journey of over an hour each way. It puts an end to the prospect of carrying on work before and after court. My practice is once again at the end of the road after being coaxed to life three times and killed off three times. I no longer have the heart to try again, so I arrange for a friend to take over my small remaining work and abandon the attempt finally and for ever. My drawing board and other apparatus is retired to my bedroom, just in case . . .

The daily ride from Johannesburg to Pretoria and back becomes as routine as the Drill Hall day, except that bumping and shaking makes it impossible to read, write or do the crossword puzzle. At least we are free to choose who to sit next to and talk to. In the mornings when we board, spirits are good; but by the time we get back to Johannesburg in the evening, it is dark and everyone is weary and short tempered.

Days in the Old Synagogue take on the familiar tedious pattern of the Drill Hall. The place, now abandoned by its congregation, is an even more bizarre courtroom than the Drill Hall, though less basic and utilitarian. Its interior, with high ceiling and Gothicky windows, is undistinguished, and what had once been the women's gallery at the back of the hall has become the public gallery. It is smaller and friendlier than the Drill Hall and the acoustics are better, but that is no compensation for the long daily journey.

A three-man bench is to hear the case. We are rather uneasy about its composition, and particularly about Judge Ludorf whose appointment to the bench is generally seen as a reward for past political services to the National Party. The movement had clashed with him during the COP over an application for a court order to exclude the Security Police from a campaign meeting. Ludorf had been counsel for the police and had shown his political bias.

We had lesser misgivings about Justice Rumpff, the most senior of the three, who we believe has no political affiliations but holds strong Afrikaner nationalist opinions and had judged and convicted the leaders of the Defiance Campaign after their 1954 trial – some of whom are again on trial here. We decide to ask both men to stand down though our lawyers warn that we might end up with a worse panel. We decide to make the challenge anyway to expose the political bias at the root of the case.

The application for the two judges to recuse themselves is made by Isie Maisels QC[1] who is said to be Johannesburg's leading barrister but quite unknown to most of us. He probably knows only some of the lawyers amongst us – Z K Matthews, Nokwe, Slovo and Mandela. He has had no association with any of our organisations, yet his argument to the court strikes precisely the right political tone. His address is brilliant and succinct.

For three days it is met with the matching cold and penetrating intellect of Justice Rumpff. In the end, Ludorf agrees to stand down, but Rumpff will not. Ludorf is replaced by Justice Bekker who has a reputation for fairness and integrity, and fully lives up to it.

Rumpff too proves himself to be scrupulously honest throughout and to have one of the country's most rigorous judicial minds. We come to have confidence in them both, but somewhat less in the third member, Justice Kennedy. He is said to be a legal lightweight as well as a 'hanging judge' who once sentenced twenty-two men to death in a single case. He is not likely to carry much weight in any disagreement with his two colleagues.

Maisels heads a formidable defence team which not only includes old faithfuls – Fischer, Berrange, Bizos and Coaker – but is also bolstered by Sydney Kentridge, Rex Welsh and Harold Nicholas when special occasions call for them. The state line-up, headed once again by Oswald Pirow, is heavily outweighed. Maisels opens Act 3 with a devastating critique of the indictment – perhaps better described as a demolition. In almost every respect it lacks the particularity and clarity required by law. Rumpff analyses each criticism acutely but fairly. He is extremely sharp and not easily persuaded.

While the argument between these two intellectual giants sputters back and forth, the prosecution is virtually sidelined. Pirow's attempts to defend his indictment seem to lack conviction. It is as if Rumpff's interventions show that we are winning the argument.

---

[1] Later to become Chief Justice of Southern Rhodesia, now Zimbabwe.

After two months of fitful argument broken up by repeated short adjournments, Pirow suddenly throws in his hand and announces that the indictment is withdrawn.

Two years into the case, still facing trial but with no indictment to answer. The court stands adjourned again for an indefinite time while the indictment goes back to the wordsmiths. More months of waiting in limbo.

Near the year's end, new indictments are served on all ninety-one of us. They change the whole character of the case by separating the accused into three groups in an attempt to repair a fatal defect in the previous indictment. Those charged with conspiracy are legally responsible for the acts of all the others – but only from such time as they can be shown to have joined the conspiracy. The first indictment had ignored that requirement.

The three groups are now separated by the date of their alleged entries into the conspiracy. Apart from that, there is little new in the revised indictments. The first group only is summoned for trial in the Old Synagogue in January 1959. I am in the second group. No date is set for us or the third group. We are left waiting in limbo for the outcome of the first group's trial.

The case gets off to an uneasy restart, with repeated adjournments and breaks. Once again the court is asked to quash the indictment, but this time the request is refused. The issue is taken on appeal to a higher court, which agrees to quash indictments for Groups 2 and 3, but not Group 1.

It is August '59 before the case against Group 1 finally gets under way. The defence is concerned to challenge two fundamental allegations in the indictment. First, that there had been any intention to use force or violence to achieve the aims of the Freedom Charter – without which the charge of treason cannot stand. Second, that the aim had been to establish a communist state. Without that, an alternative charge of breach of the Suppression of Communism Act cannot stand.

I have nothing else to do, and spend time in the defence office helping to research the validity of Professor Murray's ideas of 'communism'. I read my way through books I have long intended to read but have not got round to, including the writings of Gandhi, Nehru, Nkrumah, Churchill, Roosevelt and others. All contain ideas almost precisely the same as those described by Murray as 'straight from the shoulder communism'. All have political aspirations along the same lines as those from Congress writers and speakers and the Freedom Charter, often using precisely the same words. I compare and contrast them with the ideas of such recognised communist authorities as Lenin, Mao Tse-tung, and Professor Murray. It is an interesting extension of my own political education and helps fill some of the weeks of waiting.

While I am in the defence office, the defence lawyers are studying the evidence relating to the two main issues – violence and communism – and preparing their strategy. To me, regardless of the state allegations, the position is crystal clear. No part of the movement has ever encouraged the use of political violence; everyone irrespective of ideology has consistently opposed it, both in public and in private. Nor has any section of the liberation movement adopted or been urged to adopt the aim of creating a communist state – except the Communist Party itself in its long-term aims. This is acknowledged by everyone on our side, lawyers included.

Even so, it seems to me that in their striving for the best possible defence case, legal influences are tending to bend the facts minutely. Non-violence, which has never been a philosophical or religious dogma but only the best realistic strategy for our times and circumstances, is being subtly elevated to an article of faith. Congress non-violence is coming to be regarded as an absolute principle, and that, *in extremis*, defeat would be accepted in preference to a resort to violence. Perhaps so for the committed minority of pacifists amongst us. But that had never been Congress ideology.

A similar leaning away from the facts is creeping into the defence over the other issue – Congress attitudes to communism. To me, the fact is equally clear that they have always been pragmatic, not ideological. Communism has been accepted as legitimate a creed for members to hold as any other. It has been neither endorsed nor prohibited.

But here, too, attitudes are bending subtly, depicting the tolerant, non-communist stance of Congress into a more defensible rejectionism or even mild anti-communism. There *are* anti-communists in the ranks; they are a small minority as are the true pacifists. Without any deliberate intention to distort, their minority views are being pictured as the general view by the desire to strengthen the defence case. Congress ideology is beginning to blur.

Its real guiding principles of resistance to injustice and oppression are in danger of being turned into a variety of anti-communist pacifism.

The trend is subliminal, never articulated. If it had been, it would have been generally rejected, probably even by the pacifists and anti-communists amongst the Congress membership. It is starting to influence not only the lawyers' presentation of the case but also the evidence for the defence.[2] It bothers me, but strictly speaking it is not *my* immediate concern but that of the first group on trial who are entitled to defend themselves as they see fit – as I hope to do when my turn comes round.

I am working full time for an architect friend, and part time in clandestine secretarial work for the Party CC, editorial work on the *African Communist*, and writing for all and sundry but especially *Fighting Talk*. 1960 is passing quietly until March, when a storm bursts without warning at Sharpeville.

The ANC has been preparing an anti-Pass Law campaign which would lead to a mass burning of passes. It was not a new idea. It had been tried without much success several times before, and now felt old and second-hand though it might be a way out of the doldrums of the Treason Trial years. Burning of passes would be a declaration of resistance to a whole panoply of oppressive laws which depend on them. To have more than a momentary effect it would have to be done on a grand scale right across the country.

The ANC believe that the people are ready for it; I am not so sure. Pass-burning is a high-risk strategy. It can lead directly to eviction from municipal housing, loss of employment, and 'endorsement out' or banishment from the cities for all who take part. The state reaction will be fierce and unrestrained. Many leading Party members share my doubts about success, but the decision is not ours but that of the ANC. Once they decide to go ahead, we will do whatever we can to help.

Plans for the campaign are well advanced and the starting date fixed when the PAC steps in to steal the ANC's thunder. The PAC

---

[2] Some defence witnesses did suggest to the court that they saw non-violence as the ANC's overriding principle. Significantly, that was not Mandela's view. He saw non-violence as practical and pragmatic, not an article of faith, as shown by his subsequent career as Commander-in-Chief of Umkhonto we Sizwe.

announces an anti-pass campaign of its own which will pre-empt the ANC's by a week. In a piece of petty partisan spoiling, it has turned down overtures to join the ANC campaign. Although the aims of both are identical, the PAC's tactics are different. On due date, their leaders will stage a public demonstration by returning their passes to the authorities and announcing that they will carry them no longer. If arrested, they will offer no defence, accept no bail and pay no fines. The militant and self-assertive spirit seems to be in tune with the popular mood in the towns, but practical preparations for the campaign are grossly inadequate.

March 21st – the PAC day of action. The only significant activity is in its two urban strongholds in Cape Town's Langa township and Vereeniging's dormitory satellite, Sharpeville. Outside the Sharpeville police station people gather slowly throughout the morning in response to the rumour that something dramatic about passes is about to happen – nobody knows quite what.

All morning nothing happens. The crowd grows steadily, and presses in against the wire fence around the police station. Inside the fence, a contingent of armed police forms up, facing them. People at the back press forward to see what is going on, forcing those in front tighter against the fence. They are noisy, curious, but not threatening.

Suddenly, in the midday heat, someone's nerve cracks. A policeman inside the fence raises his rifle and opens fire. That becomes the signal for the whole police party to blaze away against the people, who flee for their lives. Whether the firing started in panic or on an officer's orders is never established, but when it finally dies away there are sixty-nine men, women and children lying dead, strewn across the dusty veld where they fled. Almost all have been shot from behind. Hundreds more are wounded and bleeding, struggling desperately to drag themselves away.

It is one of the worst massacres in South African history, but no one will ever be held accountable.

Shock and anger reverberate around the country – the thunder before the storm. The scale of the massacre which marks the start of their campaign stuns the PAC into silence. Robert Sobukwe and other PAC leaders are being rounded up and imprisoned; their organisation is paralysed and silent.

It is left to the ANC to react with a suitable sense of outrage. It calls for an immediate nationwide strike in protest, without taking time to prepare – the popular response must depend entirely on spontaneous anger. The scale of the stay-at-home is the sign that Sharpeville has loosed a hurricane which is felt even in the corridors of state. There is a sense that sands may be shifting beneath the government's feet. Dr Colin Steyn, Minister of Justice, talks of the pass laws being scrapped. The ANC decides the time has come to end delay and start burning the passes, with its most prominent members leading from the front. Chief Luthuli, Nelson Mandela, Duma Nokwe and others burn their own passes in a public demonstration witnessed by press and radio, and call for people everywhere to do likewise.

It is said that birds and animals sense the onset of an earthquake ahead of the seismographs. Perhaps revolutionaries do the same. In these hectic angry days, everyone in the centre of the radical movement knows that popular anger and frustration is boiling over, and the country is on the brink of an explosion. The Sharpeville storm, far from blowing itself out, is whipping up like a cyclone, drawing people and government into the vortex. Protest strikers are staying away from work without waiting for directives from the politicians. Bonfires of burning pass books are blazing in the black townships.

In the apparatus of state, after a moment of self-doubt, all the old repressive arrogance which precipitated the storm returns. There is only one way the South African state knows for dealing with its people. That is brute force. A State of Emergency is proclaimed, and police and security services are let loose to arrest and detain at will, without charge or trial.

The ANC and PAC are outlawed by decree; furthering their aims is made a crime; security forces are given blanket immunity from the law, and laws protecting civil rights are suspended. Past and present political activists are summarily arrested without charge; thousands of ordinary black citizens are snatched off the streets and spirited away without anyone knowing where or why. As the prisons fill up, the new euphemisms of 'detainees' and 'detention centres' enter the language to conceal the reality: concentration camps for the enemy are back for the first time since the South African War.

A night after the Sharpeville massacre, Kathy Kathrada phones with a coded message about rumours of impending police raids.[3] We have a working arrangement: those with telephones have lists of others to whom such messages must be relayed. The arrangement has its limitations – few of our people in the black townships have access to a phone. I relay the word by phone to those on my list that I can reach, and go out to track down the others. The message for them all is to sleep away from home. By the time I have worked through my list, it is too late to find a place away from home for myself. I decide to take a chance and go home. These alerts had often proved false in the past. There is no reason why this one should be any different.

It is and it isn't. There is no night-time knock at our door, but in the morning we discover there have been raids on homes all over the country and many arrests. The news is on press and radio but without any names. Hilda and I spend the day trying to find out which of our friends and political colleagues have been arrested. There is no way of finding out where those arrested have been taken, but police spokesmen have told the press that more 'detentions' can be expected.

We can make no pattern to account for the arrests. Some prominent activists have been passed over; some who were politically involved years before but have long since dropped out have been taken. We do not doubt that we figure somewhere on the state list of 'undesirables' and while arrests are continuing we are living on the brink. With four children to look after we can hardly bolt from home, even temporarily. We agree that one or other of us will sleep away from home each night – past experience has bred a fatalistic belief that police raids take place always at dead of night.

We have grown so used to living on the edge of crisis that we do not act now with urgency. Inertia has set in. We have learnt to contain our fears of disaster, and live in hope. For a few days, we keep up the semblance of normal life for the benefit of our children,

---

[3] Kathy and I have worked together in many political events since the 1948 Votes for All Assembly, and have been in the Treason Trial together. His flat in Kholvad House has become a gathering point for comrades in search of a chat, a meal or an overnight bed. He is well placed to pick up every rumour and leak of information.

even though we know that our time is running out.

The day after the arrests, I tell my employer that I will not be coming to work until further notice. He understands that this is to do with my politics, but not that I am telling him that my world is about to implode. It is five months before he sees me again. In downtown Johannesburg, there is nothing to suggest that the country is teetering on the brink. Business life is going on as normal.

I am trying to make contact with whatever remains of the movement, but there are not many places to go. The offices of the now outlawed ANC are sealed, its officers and most of my political colleagues are missing. There is no way of knowing whether they have been arrested or simply gone to ground. I try the barristers' chambers in the hope of finding Bram Fischer. All I can discover there is that a legal loophole has been found which appears to make the night's arrests illegal.

The police have apparently jumped the gun and used their powers under the Emergency Regulations before the Regulations have been legally validated by publication in the Government Gazette. An urgent application for the release of some people being held at Marshall Square is being made to a judge in chambers.

The state attorney has argued that the arrests comply with the spirit of the law since the Gazette is already in the hands of the government printers in Cape Town. It will be flown to Johannesburg for the judge's perusal within the hour. The judge is not satisfied. The arrests cannot be ruled lawful until he has seen the Regulations in the Gazette for himself. The applicants are therefore ordered to be released forthwith.

Marshall Square is in a state of confusion. The police have had the judge's order. They are not yet sure that they are above the law – as they will be once the Emergency Regulations are in force. They do not dare defy the court order but are not willing to comply with it easily, so bureaucratic obstacles to release are being conjured up.

Detainees mill about in the charge office while the police insist that they cannot be released before their identities are checked and itemised receipts are written out for all articles of clothing and possessions. The minutes of their reprieve tick away. A few of the sharpest and most determined of them abandon their belongings and force their way out of the charge office. While the police are unsure how to act they melt into the crowd in the streets outside.

Time runs out for those who stay to argue or collect their belongings; the Gazette is delivered to the judge who repeals his order for their release. Perhaps one in five of the white males at Marshall Square has got away. None of the black or female detainees held in other places is even aware that the case has been heard, won, and lost.

In the late afternoon I track down some survivors who have taken refuge in the Observatory home of Minnie and Ralph Sepel. The phoned alert had allowed Kotane, Harmel and Dadoo to disappear from their homes ahead of the police, as has the COD Secretary, Ben Turok. So far as anyone knows, the Sepels, who are recent recruits to the Party, have never come to the attention of the Security Police. They have agreed to let all four stay in their house for the duration. That leaves Bram and me as the only members of the Party Central Committee still at large and able to move about.

When the Committee has to meet, it does so at the Sepel house – including one memorable Saturday morning meeting during which two uniformed policemen appear suddenly at the front door. The portly figures of Marks, Kotane and the rest of the CC members vanish through the kitchen and into the bushy hillside beyond before it is clear that the police are there to sell tickets for a police charity ball.

I never feel quite so safe there again, but for want of any better place, the 'underground' survivors of the Party CC live and function safely from there throughout the State of Emergency.

In the next few days I make contact with others who had been alerted and had got away. Jack Hodgson and Piet Beyleveld are holed up in separate places where they cannot stay for more than a few days. So is Julius Baker who walked out of Marshall Square in the confusion over the Gazette, leaving his books and belongings behind him. There must be others too, but the remnants of the Party cannot possibly take responsibility for them all. It is as much as we can do to keep the CC rump in a position to function. The others must either fend for themselves or take temporary refuge in Swaziland until the situation clarifies.

Each evening, Hilda and I have the same discussion; we must take cover ourselves; that will upset our children and disrupt their lives. We never get beyond discussing. We agree to make some arrangements for ourselves but are so reluctant to break up the family that we convince ourselves that we have to give priority to other people's problems. Hilda is coping with wives who need to contact husbands who have vanished overnight leaving unresolved problems of missing cars and keys, and access to banking accounts. I am organising cars and drivers to ferry people from their hide-outs to Swaziland. The phone is unsafe. We have to make all our contacts personally, fix times and places for them to meet, and send out cars on dummy runs to Swaziland to find out what road blocks or border controls are in place. It is postponing the day when, willy-nilly, we have to get away ourselves.

We agree that Hilda will leave home early each evening, sleep somewhere else, and only come home when the morning is safe. That will retain a semblance of normality for our children. I intend to do the same, but am always too tired to actually do so. Hilda does sleep away for several nights; nothing happens; we are encouraged to think that perhaps nothing will, and relax.

Refugees from various parts of the country have crossed the borders into Basutoland (now Lesotho) and Swaziland, and have established a small Congress community around Mbabane. Others are temporising about joining them, amongst them Ruth First who has three small daughters; her husband Joe Slovo is already detained. As a well-known communist activist and a thorn in the side of authority through her investigative reporting for the radical paper *Guardian*, she is in imminent danger but unwilling to make a dash for safety in Swaziland. By staying on she knows she is courting disaster. The CC is urging her to go, at least until conditions settle down and her position can be reconsidered. She agrees very reluctantly, and I arrange for her and her children to get to Mbabane.

The movement's active ranks are becoming desperately thin. All the organisations are decimated. Chief Luthuli, Walter Sisulu and Mandela are in prison. Oliver Tambo has left the country on instructions from the ANC, and is en route for Dar es Salaam within the first hours of the Emergency.[4] For him, the task of establishing a permanent ANC mission abroad is the end of his legal career and

---

[4]See *Into Exile* for an account by his companion Ronald Segal; and Hilda Bernstein's *The Rift* for his later memories of it. Both published by Jonathan Cape.

the start of a thirty-year stint in exile as head of the ANC and representative of the South African cause in the world outside. Dr Yusuf Dadoo has also left for London on the instructions of the Indian Congress, which is still legal but reduced to impotence by Emergency Regulations. The whole movement is living on borrowed time. Representation abroad will ensure its survival whatever happens at home.

Kotane is now the most senior – perhaps the only senior ANC member still at large. It falls to him to try and reassemble the remnants of the ANC outside of prison, and to reconstruct the organisation. It is impossible to do so and simultaneously to lead the Communist Party from the safety of the Sepel house in the white suburbs. He needs to make contact with people and groups everywhere, but especially in the heavily policed black townships.

He grows a beard, and exchanges his customary blue suit for blue overalls and a chauffeur's cap. It is a paper-thin disguise for a man who has never learnt to drive a car, and has to call on one of the Party's grass-roots activists, Wolfie Kodesh, as driver, runner and courier for him and the CC remnants in the Sepel house. Their attempt to pass themselves off as a white boss at the wheel with a black chauffeur alongside is also painfully feeble, but they get away with it. Throughout the Emergency Kodesh continues to operate as go-between and messenger extraordinary for the underground Congresses and the Party.

A few days into the State of Emergency, a quick meeting of the Johannesburg COD members still at large is convened with Wolfie's help. The COD is still legal, the meeting probably not, and my attendance in defiance of my bans certainly not. Some fifty members dare to attend. I present a brief account of the state of the movement so far as we have been able to establish. The underground leadership of the ANC has set the tone in a declaration that the organisation will not dissolve, and will carry on the struggle from underground. That spirit should be emulated by the COD, but without any recklessness or heroics. We are still legal; we must not court arrest, but continue to deliver our message loud and clear to the white population. Although many of our members are still finding their feet in the movement, their readiness and confidence are encouraging. They will not be backing away from the movement despite the threatening climate around us.

I reach home dog-tired. I am half intending to find somewhere else to spend the night, but find Hilda is still at home. She too has decided to sleep out after the children have been put to bed. Before that time comes, Julius Baker's brother Louis arrives over our back fence. He has been tipped off and has slipped out of his Benoni home ahead of the police. He has nowhere to spend the night, so Hilda surrenders her intended hide-out to him. There are other places and people we can turn to to take us both in for the night, but it is far too late to arrive unannounced on their doorstep. In any case, we are fed up with the whole thing. It has caused us a great deal of trouble on other nights, only to be shown by morning to have been unnecessary. We decide we will stay where we are.

At 3 a.m. we are woken by knocking at the front door, and the door-bell ringing. Special Branch men are there to arrest us both.

We have talked about just such a possibility with our close friend and neighbour, Yvonne Lewitton. She has offered to take charge of our children one way or another if the worst happens. There is no better person to leave them with than a professional child psychologist. The police stand by while Hilda calls her by phone. The call is answered instantly despite the ungodly hour, as though she has been awake and standing by the phone. She sounds quite calm and controlled. She will come round to our house as soon as possible – but not right away. 'The police are here too – they're arresting Archie!'[5]

The police search our house once again, perfunctorily, poking about in cupboards and drawers. It is nearly dawn; Toni and Bessie Kubheka are already awake and up. We are anxious to get away before our younger children – Keith aged three, Frances eight and Patrick eleven – wake up and have to watch us being escorted away to no one knows where or for how long. Finally the police have had enough.

Once again we leave house and children in the care of Toni and Bessie, who are waiting for Yvonne to arrive. We are driven off to Marshall Square and delivered up into separate men's and women's

---

[5]Archie and Yvonne Lewitton had been members of the Communist Party, Archie a full-time 'functionary'. They both dropped out in the 1950s for reasons I never fathomed, and gave up all political activity – until this unexpected arrest. Both died in exile in Britain in the 1980s.

cells.

In the white male cell there are around fifteen others, many of them my political colleagues. Some are – like Archie – former communists who have long since dropped out of politics. Some have even changed their political orientation entirely. They are all understandably disoriented, and shocked to find themselves summarily jailed. That active political opponents of the regime are here is explicable. But what have they done to deserve all this? They have had no part in contemporary politics. They cannot seriously be regarded as any sort of a threat to the state. The only possible explanation must be that the security services are still using lists which are ten years out of date – perhaps those they seized in 1946 during the miners' strike. We sit around all day speculating, not knowing whether we are to be charged with something or simply held without trial. No one tells us anything. In the evening we are driven off to the Fort to be locked up together with all those arrested earlier in the week.

13

EXERCISE BEHIND BARS
1960

All the male detainees at the Fort have some sort of a political record, most as current political activists but some as activists in times long past or 'fellow travellers' or members of obscure sects.

There are people who are quite unexpected, like Hymie Basner who I have scarcely seen since he stormed out of one of my first Party 'aggregate' meetings back in 1938. Since then he has ploughed a lonely furrow, been elected as the lone Senator to represent all Africans in the Transvaal and Orange Free State; founded a new African Democratic Party to rival the ANC with small success; undertaken the legal burden of a number of important political cases; and been an expert witness for the defence in the 1946 Mine Strike trial. He seemed to have dropped out of politics altogether.

Less surprising to find Jock Isacowitz who, with me, had been introduced to Marxism by Kurt Jonas at Wits University. Around 1940 Jock had joined the Party, served in the army with the rank of Sergeant Major and helped found the Springbok Legion. After the war he had dropped out of the Party and later helped found the new Liberal Party.

There are two other members of the Liberal Party, Ernest Wentzel and John Laing, both lawyers who I do not know, and the Reverend Douglas Thompson from the East Rand who I know from occasional encounters at the Left Club and COD affairs. And Louis Joffe, brother of Max who had steered me towards the Party. He is an old and frail veteran of the 1917 campaign against the Germans in South-West Africa, one of Smuts's internees at the start of the Second World War, and a former Party member until expelled around 1940 for 'factional activity'. I had been on the Conference sub-committee which heard his appeal, upheld the verdict and advised him to apply *de novo* for readmission. He was a stubborn old man who refused to do so and remained ineffectual and on the political fringe instead.

There is one of my contemporaries from university who I cannot now recognise. Vincent Swart had been one of Wits University's golden boys, a highly regarded poet with the romantic looks of a young Chopin who moved in a radical circle of glamorous girl students. I had heard that, since then, he had been the moving spirit behind an obscure Trotskyist journal called *For a Democracy of Content* and was puttering about near Alexandra township with a sect which claimed to be 'The South African Section of the Fourth International'. I had heard that he was drinking heavily but am not prepared for this stumbling, dishevelled and unshaven hobo with shaking hands and slurred speech who looks as though he has been sleeping rough. And is now drying out, 'cold turkey' in the Fort.

There are about twenty-five of us in the 'white male' section of the Fort. Other men and women, black and white, are being held in other places, but we have no idea how many. Conditions are basic and uncomfortable. Once three felt sleeping mats are laid out on the floor, touching each other in cells designed for one, there is just room for our single chamber pot. During the day we have access to a tiny enclosed yard on a lower floor where the light filters in dimly through a dusty steel mesh roof. In one corner is a cesspit where chamber pots are emptied each morning and food bowls scrubbed.

Poor quality food arrives from a distant kitchen in battered steel bowls which are laid out in the stair hall and left to congeal before they reach us. Ronnie Press, the scientist amongst us, makes a trawl through the lunch-time stew and mounts his catch of weevils, grubs and other creepie-crawlies on white card like a museum exhibit. He presents it to the Prison Commandant on his next inspection. It is received without comment and taken away.

Before long, we have an outbreak of diarrhoea. The prison

doctor looks at our tongues from a safe distance and hands out sulfa tablets. As the outbreak becomes an epidemic, dispensing pills becomes too onerous for him and he hands a wholesale supply of sulfa tablets to our two pharmacists – Archie Lewitton and Jock Isacowitz – to dispense as they see fit.

Around 4 p.m. the steel grille gates between our cells and the corridor are locked for the night. Lights go off around ten. Some time after midnight Ronnie Press starts shouting from the cell he shares with Monty Berman: 'Help! Help!' He sounds slightly hysterical. Berman, it seems, is pale and cold and cannot be roused. He is still breathing. None of our shouted suggestions of first aid have any effect. We shout for a warder to come and open up. No response. Someone starts beating the bars of his cell with his tin mug. We all join in, shouting for warders, rattling the gates and beating our mugs against the bars. The din seems to shake the building, but no one responds.

We keep it up for what seems like hours before a lone warder appears on the outside of the locked gate between corridor and stairs, shouting: '*Stilte!* Shut up!' We shout back that there is an emergency; he must open the cell! Useless. He himself is locked into the stair hall for the night, without any keys. We start the din again and keep it up until someone finally arrives with keys. By that time Berman is showing signs of coming round. He is taken off on a stretcher. In the morning he has recovered. The doctor has diagnosed an allergic reaction to sulfa tablets.

We confront the Commandant at the morning inspection. Many of us are at an age where we are subject to heart and other life-threatening seizures. Unless the night-time regime is changed, we will hold him personally responsible for the consequences. He is unused to being confronted in anger by prisoners. He makes no reply, but new orders go out; our cell gates are left unlocked at night and a warder with keys is on call beyond the corridor.

The prison staff who have been treating us with suspicion as an alien red species are developing a new respect. Political prisoners, they are learning, are prickly and prepared to exercise to the letter every right allowed them under Prison Rules and Emergency Regulations. They are to be handled with care.

All our watches have been taken away. The time of day is to be ascertained only by the routine sounds of routine days. We have spent more than two weeks learning how to do so when the routine falls apart. It is about 2 p.m. It should be quiet with warders off having lunch. Suddenly there is the noise of men shouting and hurrying about, doors and gates slamming. It cannot be an escape – there are no alarms, though we can hear vehicle sirens in the streets beyond the walls, and the wail of emergency vehicles. The warders seem unusually hostile. Routine is the source not only of our sense of time but of all sense of normality.

Rumour spreads like wildfire. It is said that Verwoerd has been shot. It would be dismissed as false were it not for the turmoil around us. Is it possible that the old monster can really be dead? And, even more scaring, could the killer be one of *our* people? If so, it has terrifying implications for us all.

We can do nothing but worry and speculate. Hours later the rumour and gossip solidify into facts. Verwoerd *has* been shot while on a visit to the Easter Show at Milner Park. He has been rushed off to hospital – no one knows whether he is alive or dead – and not many of us care.

He has been the main formulator of apartheid. He has driven the nation towards its realisation with the certainty of a fanatic who believes himself to be divinely inspired. He has devised and led a ruthless attempt to create a white hierarchy which will rule the black majority for a thousand years, and shown a total disregard for the human suffering it has caused. He has expounded and defended it always with the most avuncular of smiles. I regard him as not just bad but mad; and his mad apartheid to be the most inhuman attempt at human engineering since Hitler's 'Final Solution'.

We learn only later that the shot was fired at point blank range by a white dairy farmer with a grievance. He is named Pratt. He is decidedly not 'one of us' nor of any radical movement, and is said to be mentally disturbed. The shot has passed through Verwoerd's cheek but has not deprived him of the power of speech, which is strengthening his supporters' belief that he is indeed divinely favoured.

Our fears that we might be made the scapegoats for the attempted assassination recede and the hysteria inside and outside the prison gradually dies away. We are back to the 'normality' of the Verwoerdian State of Emergency.

Days later we are told we are being moved to Pretoria, no reasons given. Some of our number with knee-jerk opposition to anything coming from the authorities, propose we resist physically. Few of us support the idea of a fight for the right to stay in the Fort's potentially lethal cells. Pretoria is unlikely to be any worse; it might possibly be better. We pack up and are locked into prison vans which are waiting in the yard.

Nothing happens while we wait on, interminably. The sun goes down and floodlights come on. We can hear men and women shouting excitably from across the wall of the women's prison. Some women detainees shout to us from a nearby van. They sound triumphant. The white women have flatly refused to move any further away from their children, and are staging a sit-down strike.

Force is the standard means of prison control. Assault and casual violence are a regular part of the process, especially when the prisoners are black but, even so, white supremacist standards apply. White male prisoners – even perverts or communists – are handled less harshly than blacks, women less physically than men and never by male staff.

The women's sit-down presents a new challenge to a regime which seldom has to cope with white women prisoners, and then generally only with alcoholics, shop-lifters and prostitutes. It has no experience of handling articulate, educated middle-class women who stand together for their rights. Senior male officers have been called in to plead and threaten, without result. The women have stood firm. The authorities will either have to back down, or revert to force.

Force it is. Female warders pick the detainees up one by one, carry them down a flight of stairs and across the yard to the vans standing in the yard. Few of the women are lightweights; and their personal belongings have to be packed for them and carried down. As they are pushed into the van, they are triumphant. They have given notice that they too are prisoners of a new type; politicals, who are prickly and not to be pushed about.[1] We sit

---

[1] One theory to explain the different responses of the men and the women is that the men had five lawyers to advise caution – Laing, Wentzel, Slovo, Wolpe and Basner – and the women only Shulamith Muller. Sharper reactions to separation from their families and children seems more likely.

waiting in the dark until the doors of the women's vans slam shut. At last the convoy takes off for Pretoria where the vehicles separate. The women are carried off towards Central Prison, and the men to Pretoria Local.

Things may be different for the women, but for us conditions in Pretoria are a vast improvement. We are held in two interleading ground floor dormitories with direct access to a fair-sized yard. We have our own ablutions block and small kitchen-scullery. The dormitories remind me of boarding school twenty years before, with the same rows of iron bedsteads facing each other and separated by wooden head-lockers, each with a hard mattress and grey prison blankets. After the Fort's felt floor mats, this is like four-star luxury.

A few detainees from Pretoria have arrived before us, two of them Liberal Party members I do not know – the Reverend Mark Nye who has been active in church affairs in Pretoria's black townships, and John Brink, a likeable and straightforward man of principle. Another is Mike Muller who I have known as a full-time, grossly overworked and underpaid official in Pretoria's black trade unions, and one-time member of the Communist Party. He is a man of dark moods with a chip on his shoulder. He believes the Party leaders and middle-class members have fought shy of making the financial sacrifices for the cause which he has made. Since he left the Party around 1947, ostensibly over differences on aspects of trade union policy, he has grown increasingly hostile. He claims that some Party members, particularly Joe Slovo, are trying to turn his wife Shulamith against him, and recently burst into a Congress meeting to drag her away. We make an attempt to maintain civil relations, but he clings to his hostility and keeps himself out of most of our communal activities. His is not the only difficult temperament amongst us, but it is the one that does not mellow with time.

'Detention' is like an amalgam of boarding school and army base-camp. It relies in the same way on purposeless rules and regulations, and the same routines of counting, cleaning and inspecting. It provides the same mediocre-to-bad food, and enforces the same intimacy with people one would not choose to spend one's life with.

The detainees coalesce into groups, some to walk the yard obsessively, some to read or study or play games with cards or balls.

Their only purpose is to pass time. Eli Weinberg marches round and round the yard singing liberation songs in his strong baritone, usually trailing a ragged chorus with him; Monty Berman takes charge of the food and transforms it into prison *haute cuisine* with expertise – and spices and additives bought by the communal purse; Cecil Williams rehearses, directs and plays the lead in evening rep theatre, struggling with an incompetent all male cast; John Laing trains and conducts a willing but inexpert choir to sing spirituals and barbershop harmony; and a painfully rehabilitated Vincent Swart gives poetry readings and expounds brilliantly on the mysteries of Gerard Manley Hopkins's poems.

These are the specialists. But there are also odd-balls, the oddest of whom is Raymond Thoms who was thrown in amongst us shortly before we left the Fort. It was difficult to credit his account of being arrested in the street while distributing COD handbills; COD was a small enough organisation for one of us to know him, but none did. His story was unlikely enough to suggest that he might have been planted amongst us to ferret out information.

I am deputed together with someone else whose identity I have forgotten, to try and find out more. We spend an entire afternoon with Thoms, probing. His story becomes less and less credible the more we learn. He had gone out with other COD members to distribute the leaflets; he knew none of their names and could not recall what the leaflets were about. Each one picked his or her own central city distribution point. He had picked the corner of Main and Von Wielligh Streets without knowing that the Special Branch headquarters was there. He did not know who had brought the leaflets to the group, except that he was short, red faced and looked 'kind-of-Jewish'. Wolfie Kodesh?

If he is on a spying mission, he is going about it in an odd way. He asks no questions and shows no interest in us, our views or what we do to pass the time. He is well educated, but is giving us a picture of someone unusually stupid or unusually sharp at appearing stupid. We give up. In Pretoria, Thoms takes to his bed with the blankets over his head. We have to bully him into getting up in time for the daily inspection. When the regulations change to allow books to be sent in for us, he receives tomes in classical Greek which are all he reads. He is reluctant to take his turn in washing the communal pots after meals, claiming it will make him sick. We insist; he takes part, turns green, throws up, and is never asked again.

Monty Berman is deputed to collect all our outgoing letters for the authorities to censor. One morning he shows me a letter addressed to Colonel Spengler at Special Branch headquarters. We decide that the Queensberry Rules are rendered inoperative by the State of Emergency, and open it up. Thoms is offering to answer any questions put to him in exchange for his release. We flush the letter down the drain.

A week later there is another. By this time there has been a statement by the minister that all detainees are to be interrogated, and those who answer to the satisfaction of the police will be released. We decide to pass this letter on. Whether anything came of it I doubt, but by the time Thoms is released and vanishes from sight we have given up trying to discover what makes him tick.

We elect a small committee to oversee communal chores and recreation. The Reverend Douglas Thompson asks our views about a non-denominational church service in the yard on Sunday morning. There are no church-goers on the committee but it sounds a reasonable idea and we agree. On Sunday morning we carry all available chairs and benches into the yard and virtually everyone attends. Douglas leads off with some familiar hymns; those who know the tunes sing while others hum along. He delivers a simple sermon which draws moral lessons from his own early life as a railwayman and his later incarnation as a socialist priest. It is a homily for tolerance, social justice and peace, richer in humanism than in religious doctrine, suitable for his unlikely congregation. As we leave the service, Jock Isacowitz says: 'If anyone had told me that I would find myself singing hymns alongside Rusty Bernstein, I'd have told him to get his head read!' I could have said the same about him.

The next morning the committee has a request from the Reverend Mark Nye to hold his services on alternate Sundays. I doubt if anyone on the committee could tell a high Anglican from a Methodist, but it sounds a fair proposal and is agreed. Apart from their Christianity, the two reverends have little in common. Thompson is down-to-earth and plain-speaking; Nye is intellectual and rather remote. The next Sunday he treats us to a theologian's sermon. He makes no reference to Thompson but takes his text from Corinthians: 'When I was a child I spake as a child . . . but when I became a man I put away childish things' – particularly those worldly and materialistic things Thompson had recommended the week before. It is intended to be a sharp put down not only for Thompson's broad humanism but also for the worldly concerns of the radicals and socialists amongst us. It is delivered precisely with a surgeon's cutting skill.

Douglas returns a week later, taking as his text the need for men to be their brothers' keepers. And so the war of the denominations goes on at arm's length, urbanely week after week, until Mark Nye is released. He is one of the first to go; Thompson is one of the last when there are only six of us left to rattle around between the empty beds in the echoing dormitories. The theological dispute enlivens several boring Sundays, but with little evidence that it may be saving any souls.

Each day we are barred from the yard for an hour to allow the white prisoners awaiting trial in the cell block opposite to use it. They have a statutory entitlement to 'exercise' time. The term is purely semantic. There are around twenty of them, almost all in their late teens or early twenties. They spend their 'exercise' time sitting on the concrete floor with their backs to the wall, gossiping. Through our windows we can hear their endlessly boring and improbable boasts of derring-do 'outside', their claims to have been unjustly framed, and the alibis they are concocting to prove their innocence.

A new face appears among them – a middle-aged man, somewhat portly and red-faced. At first, he holds himself slightly aloof. Some days pass before he joins their chatter, and within a few days he is cajoling them, urging them to get to their feet and to form ranks. They are not enthusiastic. He begins giving them orders: Quick march! Halt! About turn! March! The response is ragged and slightly shamefaced; they are just humouring him. He persists. Within a few days it appears that they are welcoming the diversion. More of them join the ranks and their movements smarten up. From the warders we discover that this is David Pratt, the man who shot Verwoerd.

Pratt's Army, as we call it, seems to lift the young prisoners out of dispiriting boredom and give them an interest in doing something, even something quite pointless. Pratt, single handed, is turning them back into social beings, breaking through their hopelessness and torpor. The prison authorities, supposedly responsible for their rehabilitation, look on without interest.

We had assumed that a man who chose to shoot the Prime Minister in full view of a packed arena would be wildly irrational. Pratt appears quite rational and calm. One afternoon, he is exercising his army in the yard while John Laing's choir is practising the Welsh hymn 'All Through The Night' in our quarters. Pratt detaches himself from his troops as though to review their march past, and stands close to our windows, listening. We end our song in quiet, almost hushed tones. Pratt stands there, crying. There is no way we can communicate with him, but thereafter we make a point of singing something nostalgic and sentimental for his benefit as his army exercises.

Our warders grow casual about locking the door that keeps us in and the others out during their exercise hour. Pratt must have noticed. He manoeuvres his army close to our windows. As they march by, he steps smartly aside, opens the door into our dormitory and seats himself on the nearest bed. He starts talking to us as if picking up on an interrupted chat. He is quite calm, quite lucid, and desperately anxious to talk. It is a matter of minutes before the warders realise what is happening and escort him out again. He offers no resistance. He is doing what little he can for the young men who are wasting away as they wait for trial. No one in authority is doing anything at all. In the tears and the Private Army we are seeing a far different Pratt from the crazed assassin depicted in the media.[2]

Our only source of outside news is a tiny transistor radio which Harold Wolpe smuggled into the Fort in his belongings. To conserve the battery which will be hard to replace, he agrees to use it only for monitoring the news. News of what is happening outside is as vital to us as food and drink. We organise a daily monitoring and give a verbal news summary to everyone each evening after lock-

---

[2]Pratt was charged with attempted murder, found guilty but insane, and sent to a penal mental institution for life. Conspiracy theory suggests that this was more convenient than permitting him to defend his action as justifiable reprisal for the Verwoerd regime's crimes. Verwoerd recovered and returned to the scene of those crimes. Pratt died in his prison.

up. We know that the women detainees will need to know what is happening in the outside world as much as we do, but our only contact with them can be via the Old Synagogue where the Treason Trial is still grinding on.

Leon Levy is being taken there under escort each morning. So is Helen Joseph, from the women's wing of Central Prison. We start a regular news agency. Each evening I transcribe the news summary in tiny letters on a strip of tissue which is rolled up tight and concealed in a cigarette. Leon – a non-smoker – carries it past the guard in a genuine pack, and through the daily body search. In court he hands the slip of paper on to Helen, who carries it back to the women concealed in the 'bun' of hair on the back of her head. It is never detected.

Six of us who have become known as 'double detainees' have wives in the women's prison.[3] We agitate from both sides for an opportunity to meet to sort out unresolved problems of children, houses and debts. It is several weeks before the agitating pays off and the six 'double detainee' men are taken to the women's prison half a mile away. We are allowed a half-hour meeting with our wives across a stout mesh screen, packed shoulder to shoulder in a small visitors' room.

Only personal matters may be discussed – no references to politics or prison affairs; warders listen in over our shoulders. Everyone starts talking at once in a noisy free-for-all. There is no privacy. We all eavesdrop on each other's conversations, and join in. In reality, there is nothing for us to settle that time has not already settled. The important thing is for us and our wives to know that we are alive, well and coping.

The 'double detainee' meetings are repeated each week. They become part of the routine; the warders lose interest in our chatter and stop paying attention. At one such meeting, Hilda positions herself deliberately as far as possible from the warders. While the other couples keep up a noisy exchange for the benefit of the warders, she tells me *sotto voce* that the women have had enough. They have been in prison for more than two months, and have demanded

---

[3]Bermans (Myrtle and Monty); Heymans (Anne and Issy); Weinbergs (Violet and Eli); Mullers (Shulamith and Mike); Kalks (Margaret and Willie); and Bernsteins.

that they be released forthwith. They have decided that if they are not, they will start a hunger strike. They have fixed the starting date and arranged for the press to be informed. We men and all other groups of detainees can decide for ourselves whether or not to join them. Whether we do or not, they are going to go ahead as planned.

I take that message back to our committee which decides to try and consult the other detainees, the overwhelming majority of whom are the black men. We must find a way to discuss our course of action with them. In the Old Synagogue, the Emergency Regulations have put at risk the confidentiality between lawyer and client; the defence lawyers, having failed to get guarantees of that right, have withdrawn from the case by agreement with the accused.

Nelson Mandela is now leading the accused in defending themselves. He tells the court he needs to consult with some of the named 'co-conspirators' who are in detention, and the court orders the prison authorities to make facilities available. On a Sunday morning Joe Slovo and I are escorted across to the prison wing where the black male detainees are being held. It is a historic breach of the rigid prison apartheid. Nelson, Walter Sisulu and Kathy Kathrada are sitting on floor mats in a cell, waiting for us.

We have a short and happy reunion, but our real business is the women's hunger strike. Everyone applauds the action they are taking, but there are formidable problems in the way of the black detainees joining them.

Our ANC comrades are only a minority of the hundreds of men who have been casually picked off the streets, often for no more reason than being seen reading an anti-government handbill. It might, even so, be possible to get them to join a hunger strike, but not without a long campaign of persuasion. Their rations are already grossly inadequate, far worse than ours; they have been demanding more and better food, and will not easily be persuaded to give up the demand and go on hunger strike. And the PAC members amongst them will almost certainly oppose any action which has been suggested by whites and is to be conducted in co-ordination with whites – even white detainees.

We can appreciate their position. They understand ours. We agree that our group will join the hunger strike if there is a majority amongst us for doing so. They will not, because to do so can only cause dissension and division in their group. We are of one mind – but even in the levelling circumstances of prison, we are separating our actions across a racial divide.

Joe and I report back to our group. There is some division of opinion. Those who can be called the pro-Congress faction are all for joining the hunger strike; the non-Congress faction is split by doubts and hesitations which cut across party affiliations. Liberal Party members Jock Isacowitz and John Brink vote for; John Laing and Ernest Wentzel defer to their employers who are providing financial support for their families, and abstain. The Reverend Mark Nye says he will not take part. He has wrestled with his conscience. God's will has brought him into prison; he will do nothing to frustrate His will even though the reasons for it are obscure. He will not act to secure his release from the place to which God has called him. It is a reasoning I find difficult to accept. If God's will passes all understanding, who is to say whether He would be for or against the hunger strike? If God has brought him here, who is to say whether it was in order to have him take part in the strike or to abstain? Faith? Or sophistry?

In a free vote, a substantial majority votes to join the hunger strike. Some who are not willing to join in have serious health problems. So do several who have voted to join in. There are men with heart conditions, high blood pressure, stomach ulcers and other complaints. Medical advice received through visitors is that long-term fasting can cause serious, possibly irreversible damage to their health. We recommend that they take that advice and opt out. Many of them do so reluctantly, but not all. In the end, around two-thirds of us are committed to the strike. We will be sharing space with the other third who will be eating as usual. And with their food.

More medical wisdom – later rubbished by experts – is that we all risk permanent damage to our health if we do not have a small daily intake of salt and glucose. We agree that our fast will have to permit us a lick of salt and two glucose sweets per day, plus as much water as we choose. Our hunger strike starts on the day fixed by the women. Unfortunately, the Treason Trial is in one of its periodic adjournments, which interrupts our message service via the court. We assume the plan is unchanged and that the press and prison authorities are in the picture. Our own action will be drawn to the authorities' attention by the return of two out of every three meal bowls to the kitchen, untouched.

The first three days are the hardest. By the time they are over and we have settled into fasting without much pain, the prison is putting out disinformation that our fast is being faked; that we are sharing rations so that the returns can be used as 'evidence'; we are eating food we had stockpiled in advance. They do not have much confidence in their own propaganda. They continue to supply the full complement of food bowls, but the quality suddenly improves. For the first and only time in our detention, there is a supply of oranges which we return – not without pangs.

Though we are living with food and people eating normally all around us, after three days we are acclimatised to fasting. The pangs of hunger are gone, but the sight and smell of food close at hand remains. The fasters fall into two groups: those who cannot bear to see or hear talk of food; and those, including myself, who talk of little else without having any real urge to eat.

Four or five days into the fast and energy is running low. In the shower room, the fasters can be seen to be wasting down to skin and bone, making the eaters by contrast appear obscenely fat. The smokers are puffing away as heavily as ever, but everything else is tapering off. The obsessive walkers and ball players are flagging, and physical exercise stops; so does the daily round of cleaning and polishing which is now being voluntarily taken over by the eaters alone.

Without meal breaks and physical activity, time drags by more slowly than ever. Small groups turn inwards on themselves, plotting privately. John Laing, who had formerly been involved in secret broadcasts from a 'Freedom Radio', is scheming with Monty Berman to create its successor. Joe Slovo, Harold Wolpe and others are scheming escapes, exploring the space above the ceiling, tapping walls and mapping buildings and guard-posts. Ronnie Fleet, who has been a deck-hand on a fishing trawler since being banned from his trade union job, is bending my ear with a scheme for a sea-going yacht which the movement could use to carry people and equipment in and out of the country. All the schemes have a slight air of unreality, of fantasy growing out of light-headed hunger.

No one is really suffering. Eating has become no more than a

Scenes from the 1946 Miners' Strike: confrontations between police and miners

Left: Bram Fischer with daughter Ilse, 1964

Below: Arthur Goldreich, Harold Wolpe and Abdulhai Jassat in Dar es Salaam after their escape from Marshall Square, Johannesburg, in July 1963, with the Tanzanian representative of the ANC, James Hadebe

Times Media Limited

Camerapix

Above: Cecil Williams – theatre producer, Springbok Legion officer, communist and principal of the 6th SA Division education college, Italy (July 1961)

Right: Joel Joffe – civil rights lawyer and solicitor for all the accused in the Rivonia Trial, 1964

Above: Advocates Vernon Berrange and John Coaker, who appeared for all 156 accused during the 1956–61 Treason Trial

Below left: Crowds gathered outside the Johannesburg Drill Hall, December 1956, in a demonstration to mark the opening day of the Treason Trial
Below right: Chief Albert Luthuli, President of the ANC, outside the Old Synagogue, 1959

Museum Africa (Times Media collection)

Sunday Times

Above: Ivan and Toni Strasburg, Rusty and Hilda Bernstein leaving the Magistrate's Court, Johannesburg, June 1964 and (*right*) being greeted by his daughter Toni on his release on bail

Sunday Times

Keith Bernstein

Left: Hilda Bernstein, 1986

Below: Frances Bernstein, age 12

Eli Weinberg

Above: George Bizos and Govan Mbeki sharing a joke, April 1991

Below: Arthur Chaskalson and President Nelson Mandela at the opening of the Constitutional Court, February 1995

Above: Rusty and Hilda Bernstein with their sons Patrick and Keith, being given a send-off from Dar es Salaam airport by Oliver Tambo (right), and local ANC representative James Hadebe

Below: Return to Lilliesleaf Farm, Rivonia, 1994 for the first time since the 1963 arrests. *(L to r):* Ahmed Kathrada, Rusty Bernstein, ANC security man, present proprietor of Lilliesleaf, Nelson Mandela, Andrew Mlangeni, Walter Sisulu

one-time habit of which we are now cured. How long we can carry on without it no one knows. We have never contemplated a fast to the death, and don't know whether the women have or not. We carry on until the eighth day, when the prison Commandant appears at a morning parade, triumphant. The women, he informs us, have ended their hunger strike; there is no longer any reason for us not to do so too. There are shouts of disbelief and 'Lies!' It is impossible to accept that they would have done so without some cast-iron guarantees about release. We tell him that we do not believe him, and will carry on the hunger strike until we hear the truth from the women themselves.

There is a weekend, and on Monday the Treason Trial resumes. In the evening, Leon Levy returns from court with the facts as told by Helen Joseph. The hunger strike *has* been called off. One of the women had developed heart problems, an outside doctor had been called in and had advised that her life and that of others could be endangered if they did not start eating again. Fortuitously, that had coincided with the authorities' decision to split the group; eight of them were to be moved to Nylstroom Prison where they would be unable to keep in touch with those left in Pretoria. They had all agreed, very reluctantly, that it was better to end their action in unity than to let it fall to pieces. They had been promised that a process of interrogation would start forthwith and releases would follow.

Our action has always been seen as complementary to theirs. Their action has ended; ours has been going on for ten days and whatever point we have been making is now made. We decide unanimously to call it off immediately. It is almost suppertime. As usual, a full complement of food bowls has been delivered to us. We have been advised that a fast should be broken slowly, so we start off gingerly with thin slices of bread and jam. The advice is impractical; once the dam wall is broken, there is no holding back. We eat our way rapidly through all the food we have – without any ill effects. The heady indulgence releases a mood of mild intoxication. We are celebrating something, perhaps just food or perhaps ourselves, as well as Joe Slovo's birthday – probably his thirty-second. We carry on revelry late into the night, singing songs and exchanging jokes and anecdotes, and – for once – the prison does the decent thing and leaves our lights on long after the usual ten o'clock black-out. Perhaps they too are celebrating that the strike has been ended without a riot.

Almost from Day 1 of our detention, we have been demanding the right to see our children, but have been repeatedly turned down on the grounds that any such visit would be damaging to the children. Unexpectedly, another volte-face by the authorities. We are told that 'double detainees' will be allowed a single visit from their children. They will be taken first to the men's prison, then to the women's.

After waiting and pushing for this for so long, when the day actually comes I am filled with as much dread as anticipation. I have to screw up my self-control to avoid breaking down and crying at the sight of them – I don't think they have ever seen me cry. If I do so now it will be bad for my own sense of self but probably even worse for them. Waiting is worse than any appointment with the dentist. I am scared to death but cannot wait to get there and end the pain.

The dreaded meeting takes place – I know that because I have been told, but my memory of it is blank. Did I break down? Did my children? I do not know. I have closed the lid on my memory and thrown away the key. I remember being taken along a corridor to the visit, and walking back in a cold sweat with my hands trembling. It should have been the best half hour of my months in prison; perhaps it was. But in my memory it seems to have been the very worst.

Outside the prison, the crisis is easing. Strikes and pass burning have come to an end, conditions are returning slowly to normal. If detention ever served any state purpose, it does so no longer. Humanitarian and economic pressure is mounting at home and abroad for the State of Emergency to be brought to an end. It had been introduced in an instant of panic. The panic is over, but there is no strategic plan to bring it to an end. Formerly, our detention had been said to be essential for the security of the state. A formula has to be devised to end it without government loss of face. It is announced that all detainees are to be interrogated by the Security Police, and will be released after they have answered 'satisfactorily'. The process is to start forthwith. It obviously has less to do with intelligence gathering than with getting the government off the hook. Like the Emperor's clothes, it might serve to cover the nakedness of policy.

In Pretoria Local Prison the process starts some weeks after the children's visits. We hold a general meeting to discuss what we will do. There is general agreement that we will not co-operate or answer any questions whatsoever. There is a suggestion that we might perhaps answer questions only about ourselves and not about others. That meets with no support. It had been tried by some people when the Liquidator was compiling his list of 'communists'. They had found themselves on a slippery slope without any foothold before the bottom and total surrender.

The first of our group are taken away for interrogation, and do not return. Later we see them gesticulating from the windows of the cell block opposite where they are being held, presumably to prevent them reporting to us what has gone on. Their interrogation could not have lasted long. Day by day, others are taken to be interrogated, and reappear in the other block, shouting through the bars to let us know that they have answered no questions. The numbers in the cells opposite is outgrowing the space available; interrogation is producing no intelligence and the plan is beginning to fall apart.

By the time I am summoned, the interrogators are hostile and angry but are already showing signs of defeat. Their first barked question shows that they realise they are flogging a dead horse.

Question: Are you prepared to answer all our questions?
Answer: No.
Q: Do you realise you can be held here indefinitely until you do?
A: Yes.
Q: Will you now answer?
A: No.
End of interview.

Three months into the State of Emergency. Politically, things in the country are quiet and the government is back in control. But investors have been pulling their money out of the country, the value of the Rand has plummeted, stock exchange prices are falling, and consumer boycotts of South African goods are taking hold internationally. The economy is in danger of going into free fall. There can be no return to stability while the State of Emergency continues, but the government will lose all credibility if it admits it has had no purpose and simply ends it. It will have to be phased out quietly.

The first of the white women detainees are released, Hilda amongst them. The others follow in twos and threes along with the first of the white males. There is no publicity, and no apparent pattern to the order in which they are released. Our dormitories empty out, beds are left unoccupied. The place takes on the feel of a sinking ship, as our comrades slip over the side one by one. We who are left clinging to the wreck are a dwindling crew whose numbers fall steadily until only half are left. Then ten, then six, rattling around in an echoing place. All that is needed to make the shipwreck complete is for the lights to be switched off.

Finally, only Joe Slovo and I are left. We have run out of things to talk about, and spend most of our days in long silences, waiting. It is mid-winter. Pretoria is unpleasantly chilly. I spend most of the day reading in the yard, moving my chair to stay in the moving patch of sun.

There is a locked steel door nearby giving access into the adjoining hospital yard. An elderly warder whose name I think is Van Vuuren stands by all day to open it whenever anyone bangs on it and shouts: *Hek!* That only happens once or twice in a morning. For the rest of the time he shuffles from foot to foot, examines his finger nails, and swings the great bunch of keys attached to his belt. He also is idle, just waiting. Occasionally we exchange a few words about the weather.

He asks me what I am reading, and nods sagely over my answer. I feel I must reciprocate and ask him how long he has been in the prison service. Something like fifteen years, 'But only four years on this gate!' And I am going out of my mind here after four months! He says he is due for retirement after two more years. I say I suppose he will look for a small farm – which is the Afrikaner equivalent of the Englishman's retirement dream of a small corner shop selling newspapers and tobacco.

'A farm?' he says. 'A farm? Never! Man, when I get out of here I'm going to get myself an easy job.'

Joe and I are released on the same day, shortly before the State of Emergency is formally ended. We have spent almost five months in detention. It is time for me too to look for an easy job.

14

TO PUT UP OR SHUT UP
1960 – 61

South Africa had changed in those four months. The tension and confrontations, which five months before had felt like a prelude to revolution, were gone. They had left behind a deep gloom in the white middle class about the economy and the future.

The mood in the movement was more difficult to assess. The whole Congress scene had changed. The previously legal and open ANC had vanished, its offices closed and deserted, although it had promised not to disband but to continue underground. Its former office bearers and activists were back in town after months in prison or in hiding, and were reconstituting their political inter-connections without the offices and facilities they had formerly known.

The modes of political activity were being re-invented to escape the law. Meetings which had once been public were starting up again but secretively, behind closed doors and only with carefully selected participants. Security, secrecy and caution had become the watchwords of survival. They cast a furtive shadow over every chance or deliberate encounter.

Even in the still legal sectors of the movement, such as the Indian Congress, COD and SACTU, secretiveness was spreading like an infection. All of them tended to shrink unconsciously away from the limelight of publicity, and were taking to semi-clandestine styles of work in order to remain within contact with the ANC now underground. The Party had been less strained in adapting itself to post-Emergency conditions. It had almost ten years' experience of underground work behind it, during which not a single member had ever been successfully prosecuted for membership. For Party members illegality had become the norm, and techniques of working within it had been practised and perfected.

But Party modes of work had also undergone their own change since the Emergency. From our start-up until the Emergency, we had kept totally silent about the reconstitution of the Party. There had been no public disclosures of any sort, no statements, no admissions by anyone of the Party's existence or acknowledgement of membership of it. Yet everyone close to the movement seemed to have sensed that it was there, somewhere, and to have accepted that somehow it was exercising an influence on things.

The secrecy had been suddenly ended in the midst of the Emergency when the rump Central Committee issued a statement from underground in its own name, declaring that the Communist Party existed and was back in business. It explained, for the first time, the Party's political aims, and its determination henceforth to be an underground player everywhere on the political stage.

Neither I nor any of the other members of the CC in detention had been party to that announcement, taken by Kotane and those members still at large. We were not in communication with them, and – at least to me – their reasons have never been clearly explained. I assume they thought that their declaration would encourage the post-Sharpeville mood of defiance and confrontation in the country; or perhaps that the changed objective conditions during the Emergency justified the reversal of our earlier agreement to keep our existence secret. Until that time there had always been a majority of the CC against the Party's 'emergence' as we termed it.

There were good reasons for that. The Party had been illegal while all its allies – including the ANC – were legal and operating in the open. Co-operation between us in those circumstances would have been fraught with difficulty; it would have embarrassed our allies, restricted their freedom of action, and might well have precipitated their own outlawing. Those considerations had less validity in the new conditions of an outlawed ANC. Perhaps for this reason, or perhaps simply because the balance of opinion on the CC had been changed by the detentions, it had been decided to end the secrecy. The Party emerged. And those of us in detention only heard about it when it was a *fait accompli*.

In opposing 'emergence' we had believed that one of its negative consequences would be a massive state crack-down on us while we were still too small and too easily identifiable to survive. In the event, we were proved wrong. 'Emergence' turned out to be a damp squib. There was no noticeable reaction from the state, and also no noticeable excitement amongst our allies or our supporters. It was as though they had all always assumed that the Party existed but chose, for their own reasons, not to say so. In fact, once everyone became accustomed to it, the Party's 'emergence' made relations between Party and ANC simpler and less hedged about with concealments. And it dispersed some of the mutual suspicions about hidden agendas and motives which had tended to come between Party 'insiders' and non-communist ANC 'outsiders'.

My own pre-Emergency architectural job had disappeared while I was in detention. After my release I had nothing to go back to. I lacked the will or the energy to try once again to build up my own private practice. All my previous efforts had ended in some disaster created by the state; there was nothing to suggest that this time prospects would be any better. I was still wondering what to do when the CC suggested that I return to full-time administrative and secretarial work in the Party, which would leave Kotane free to concentrate on the political functions of the General Secretary.

I was not enthusiastic. It would mean living without any ostensible employment or visible means of support, which would be a pretty clear signal to the authorities that whatever I was doing I must be up to no good. With some reluctance, I agreed to the proposal, subject to the condition that I keep up some semblance of an architectural practice and take time off Party duties to attend to it. In effect, I became a full-time Party officer without an office, and a very part-time architect operating from home.

The combined operation called for a strict separation of functions, and for great caution. We were quite sure our home was being constantly watched from a gardener's hut in the grounds of a Dutch Reformed Church institution immediately across the road. We knew we could be subjected to raids and searches at any time of day or night. There was no room for casual handling of documents, no space for careless contacts with colleagues, and no time for relaxing one's guard over comings and goings. I was living and working above ground and underground at the same time.

The Sharpeville crisis was over, but a new crisis was blowing up. Sharpeville and the State of Emergency had left South Africa isolated in the world and the target of international criticism. Harold Macmillan, visiting South Africa, warned the government that the 'wind of change' blowing across the continent required the ship of state to change its course. The Commonwealth at a meeting in London launched a fierce assault on the policy of apartheid and proposed excluding South Africa from the ranks.

Verwoerd's reaction was characteristically obdurate and intransigent. South Africa would neither change its ways nor remain within the Commonwealth as the butt of its condemnation. Its withdrawal from the Commonwealth would be immediate. South Africa would be asked to vote in a referendum for a constitutional change to a republic.

The referendum would be a classic exercise in apartheid. The white minority would be called on to vote. The black majority would be excluded. Constitutional matters were not for them; they would not be consulted or counted in the reckoning. Blacks, as Verwoerd had stated, had no place in South African society 'beyond certain levels of labour'. The decision of the white minority would be handed down to them, and they would have to live with it. The decision of the white minority on the republican issue would be final. The majority could either like it or lump it. This was more than simple macho posturing by Verwoerd. It was – and was intended to be – a shot in the eye for the Commonwealth, and a blunt warning to the black population that apartheid was not for changing.

For the majority of the population the matter at issue was not membership of the Commonwealth or a republic. That was a triviality beside the real issue: was the white minority to be allowed once again to determine the fate of the country without any regard to the opinions of the majority? Verwoerd had thrown down a challenge, and every section of black and radical opinion was prepared to take it up – including the underground ANC.

This was one pass that would not be conceded without a struggle. Behind the scenes negotiation gave rise to a broadly representative committee to mobilise resistance to the referendum.

It was fronted by the black churches through the African Non-Denominational Ministers' Association, though the unseen moving spirit was that of the ANC underground. For the moment it included the mainly white Liberal Party, represented on the committee by one of its foremost black members, the journalist Jordan Ngubane.

The referendum was held in October 1960; the white minority voted solidly for a republic, and the date of its formal proclamation was set for 31 May 1961 – Union Day. The committee decided to convene a mass protest conference at the end of March 1961 as the opening shot in a campaign against any constitutional change from which black opinion was excluded.

The main task of organising for the conference fell inevitably on the members of the ANC, who had maintained their organisational cohesion despite their illegal status. The campaign was developing well, up to the moment when the committee had to decide what plan of future action it would put before the conference. It was proposed to call on the government to recognise the unacceptable nature of a minority referendum, and to agree instead to convene an all-inclusive national convention to draw up a new non-racial constitution. If the government nevertheless chose to proclaim the Republic on the basis of the referendum, the committee would call a nationwide protest strike. Ngubane dissented, and resigned from the committee in a blaze of publicity, by implication taking the Liberal Party with him in what many people saw as a deliberate attempt to sabotage the campaign.

Still the campaign gathered pace. Its conference date of 25 March turned out to be propitious. In the Treason Trial which had been grinding on in the Old Synagogue, argument ended and the court went into recess for a week to consider its verdict. That meant that Mandela would be able to attend the conference in Pietermaritzburg. For several years he had been under a banning order which prohibited him attending any gatherings. Quite coincidentally, that banning order expired that same weekend. If it was not renewed, Mandela would be able to make his first public appearance in years – at the conference. The plan for him to do so was kept secret, and Mandela stayed out of sight to avoid the serving of a new banning order.

There were 1 400 delegates at the All-In-Conference in Pietermaritzburg. When Mandela appeared unannounced to deliver the keynote speech of the event he had not been seen or heard in public for years.

His appearance and speech electrified the conference. It set the scene for enthusiastic acceptance of a resolution for the anti-republic campaign to culminate in a national three-day strike on the eve of the proclamation of the Republic. He was appointed to lead that stage of the campaign and act as the committee's spokesman. Before the authorities could react to his unbanning, he was back in Pretoria to hear the verdict against himself and the other twenty-nine.

Another triumph – not just for the thirty in court but for all the rest of the ninety-one who had been under indictment for treason for over four years. At the end of March '61, the trial was over. The verdict was unanimous: Not Guilty. The bench of three of the country's most eminent judges was unanimous. The charge that 'the ANC had acquired or adopted a policy to overthrow the state by violence' had not been proven. Nor had it been proved that the ANC was, as alleged, a communist-oriented organisation, or that the Freedom Charter envisioned a communist state. The indictments which had been hanging over our heads for all those years were scrap paper. The marathon years were over – and we had won!

There were celebrations on the pavement outside the court that morning, and a noisy celebration party at the Slovos' home in the evening. Around midnight, police burst their way in through the windows in the way of TV cops, hot on the search for blacks in possession of alcoholic drink – a serious criminal offence at the time. Liquor of all sorts had naturally been in free supply – this was a celebration for blacks as well as whites.

But living under oppressive laws perfects the techniques of evasion. As the police burst in the evidence vanished. Not a single glass was to be found in any black hand. Some had been quietly deposited in amongst the empty glasses and bottles standing on every sill and table top; some had passed smoothly into 'legitimate' white hands. Partying went on while the police blundered about, and carried on after they had left, empty handed.[1]

Mandela disappeared after his brief appearance at the All-In Conference. His office was closed. Only a few of his auxiliaries

---

[1] In the aftermath, the Minister regaled Parliament with lurid tales of inter-racial orgies in the homes of named families, ours included. The Nationalist newspaper *Vaderland* repeated the story. We sued for defamation and received a printed apology plus £200 each (£3 405 in all) in settlement. All our windfalls were donated to the *Guardian* weekly.

knew where he was living as he moved about from place to place, leading the preparations for the strike. He surfaced from time to time to brief the press and radio, no longer looking like the sharp-dressing lawyer he had been. He had grown a heavy beard and often showed up in a workman's blue overalls. It was a disguise of sorts, but not one he was likely to get away with. His unusual height and athletic build made him easily identifiable, but he seemed to bear a charmed life as he shuffled his base between homes of white and Indian sympathisers.

The government mobilised a massive show of force to try and head off the strike. Part-time Citizen Force units were called up, and encamped in public places. Strong army and police patrols traversed the townships with armoured vehicles, and helicopters and fighter planes flew low-level sorties overhead. The intention was to intimidate. Employers joined in, threatening instant dismissal of any workers who stayed away during the strike, others offering temporary dormitory space for those who claimed to be 'intimidated' about coming to work on the day of the strike.

The strike went ahead. Mandela and some of his committee were sequestered together in a hide-out in Johannesburg where they could receive reports but could not see things for themselves. They were wholly dependent on what was being reported by press, radio and their own lay observers scattered around the country who often lacked reporting expertise and whose observations were restricted to their own small localities. Throughout the day, the state radio was reporting failure – Durban working! Cape Town working! No stay-away in Port Elizabeth! Jo'burg almost normal! The press echoed the message. The strike that had been called for three days was reported to have failed on its first day.

Mandela's committee faced an agonising decision: should they stand by the call for three days and watch the action simply peter out? Or should they accept that the call had failed, and call the action off forthwith and in good order? There could be many explanations for the poor response – intimidation by armed forces, coercion by employers and, above all, the recent memory of killings and mass arrests that had followed the Sharpeville action. Perhaps all these factors should have been foreseen. Perhaps the call for strike action had underestimated them.

But such post-facto analysis would have to wait till later. The immediate reality as presented in the media had to be responded to instantly. That media picture was decisive. Whatever different view might have come in from its own observers on the ground, they were too few and scattered to outweigh the view of the media. If the first day had been as bad as reported, the next two days could only be expected to be worse. The committee took a responsible decision, and formally called the strike off after one disappointing day.[2] It was a courageous decision, but left a sense of deep depression in the movement.

It fell to Mandela as organiser and spokesman of the strike committee to make the public announcement. That evening he emerged from hiding to record an interview for foreign television, his back against the wall in appropriate symbolism. He appeared glum, weary, and patently depressed. That picture of him would be shown again and again over the years in televised reviews of his life and times. The people, he said, had not conceded the day to a white republic. They had been intimidated not to strike but did not accept defeat. 'If the government reaction is to crush by naked force our non-violent demonstrations we will have to seriously reconsider our tactics. In my mind, we are closing a chapter on this question of non-violent policy.'

It was the first guarded but public warning from Congress that the days of non-violent political struggle were coming to an end.

Mandela was not wont to act without consulting his colleagues. For the rest of that year underground he was in touch with the ANC leadership, discussing the movement's future. A new consensus was developing, for which Sharpeville and the State of Emergency had been the turning-point. The whole policy of non-violence had been called into question when the government abandoned all pretence at democratic rule and turned to the use of naked force. Congress activists everywhere were questioning the policy of non-

---

[2] Months afterwards, it became clear that the decision had been taken on false and misleading information. Accurate passenger figures for buses and trains later revealed that the strike call had been more widely answered than the committee believed. Hundreds of thousands of working men and women in almost all centres had stayed home on Day 1. They might perhaps have done so again on Days 2 and 3 had the strike not been called off. The committee made a brave decision, but on a basis of distorted reporting.

violence which had been the core of their politics ever since the ANC's formation in 1912. Mandela was not alone in his conviction that ANC policy would have to change or the organisation would lose its support and credibility.

Around the middle of the year, the issue was before the ANC leadership for a formal decision. Though hope of a peaceful social transition had been severely dented, the NEC decided the organisation would not abandon its non-violent path. But it recognised that many of its members wished to go further and explore the possibilities of armed forms of struggle. Their right to do so could not be challenged, provided they did so not in the name of the ANC but under the mantle of a separate, independent organisation. It was accepted that Mandela, a member of the NEC, could go ahead to form such an independent body on his own initiative, but was to keep the NEC informed of developments.

The Party had been quicker to recognise that the era of non-violence was drawing to an end. Until 1960, we had always supported the Congress commitment to non-violence, but on a purely pragmatic reckoning. We were not bound to it, as the ANC was, by commitments of programme or philosophy, so shifting course was easier for us. The matter had been on the agenda of the Party National Conference held in Johannesburg at the end of 1960. It had been squeezed in at the tail-end of the conference and inadequately discussed because undue time had been taken up with a report of the deepening rift between China and the USSR as revealed at an international meeting of Communist Parties in Moscow.

Our Party had been represented there by Dr Dadoo who was then permanently stationed abroad; and Michael Harmel who had travelled and returned using an Irish passport issued because his father was an Irish citizen. Until he reported back, we had not appreciated the depth of bitterness and hostility between the Soviet Union and China. Both countries had provided vital assistance and encouragement to liberation movements worldwide.

In our ignorance, we had imagined that whatever differences there were would take second place to their common commitment to the liberation struggle, and could be smoothed over in comradely debate. There was little enthusiasm amongst us for the recent theoretical pronouncements of Chairman Mao – most of us favoured the Soviet position – but our delegation had no mandate to take sides. We had maintained friendly relations and solidarity with both sides, and our members distributed both country's publications illegally, and at some risk.

Harmel had returned from Moscow just in time for our own conference in Johannesburg. Discussion of his report back on the confrontation between Soviet and Chinese delegations overran the time set aside for it on our agenda. What we had thought to be a reconcilable difference of opinion had been revealed to be a deep divide. Each side had been encouraging the formation of factions of its own supporters in other countries, undermining the unity and integrity of the Communist Parties.

Parties in several countries had split into two opposing entities. Harmel had told the conference that our members were regularly risking imprisonment by distributing both Soviet and Chinese publications. We could not continue to do so if they published attacks on each other which would create dissension in our own ranks, and provide a basis for the formation of factions and splits within our Party as they had done elsewhere.

The Chinese delegation, he reported, had been extremely obdurate and had even refused invitations to informal discussions. They had not appeared to be free agents, and would decide nothing without prior reference back to their leaders in China. They had apparently been waiting for word from Chairman Mao. And when that word finally came, they had walked out of the Conference, and presumably out of the international movement. It was bad news for us. It could cause dissension and division amongst our members and supporters, so we spent far more of our conference time on it than had been scheduled.

It was our first conference since the banning of the ANC had changed the balance between the legal and the illegal sectors of the movement. It was our first opportunity to consider the situation created by the State of Emergency and its impact on the issue which was coming to dominate all others in the movement's thinking – the place of forms of armed struggle.

We managed only a short discussion before the conference had to end. We took what was no more than an interim decision. The CC would consider the matter further, but in the mean while it was to set up small specialist units in all districts to familiarise themselves with the practice and techniques of forms of armed struggle. The Party and the ANC were moving in the same direction, but not quite on parallel tracks.

That was also our first conference since our 'emergence', and it brought to light some of the difficulties created by it. From our inception, we had operated with no more than a short statement of aims and principles. For our own small membership, that had been enough. But now that we had emerged into the public arena, we felt a need to define ourselves for the public – and also more fully to ourselves and our new recruits. What precisely were our aims and objectives? Or the strategy and tactics by which they could be achieved? Why were we independent of and yet closely allied to the ANC? Conference felt the time had come for a properly considered statement of the Party's policy and programme, and appointed Harmel and Kotane to prepare a draft for discussion.

They made slow progress – security surveillance had become tighter since the Emergency. Both were banned from meeting each other or any banned people. It was unsafe for them to work from their homes, and the alternative places were few. Everything the Party was trying to do at that time was running into similar difficulties. Places for meeting, places to work or to hide out were becoming scarce; mass raids were sowing fear amongst sympathisers who had once provided them. The combination of life above ground with political work underground was becoming unsustainable. We were desperately in need of a safe house of our own which would free us from dependence on other people's generosity and courage.

Some members of the CC searched, and came up with what seemed to be a suitable place. It was an unoccupied small farm in Rivonia, with a substantial modern house, some separate out-buildings and servants' quarters, and about ten acres of farm land. Rivonia in those days was beyond the municipal limits, a so-called 'peri-urban area' of market-gardens and bungalows on five to ten-acre plots. The buildings were far enough from neighbours and the road not to be overlooked. The CC decided it would do. Somehow our treasurer, Bram Fischer, organised the funds – those of us who had no 'need-to-know' were not told where or how – and Lilliesleaf Farm was bought by the Party.

We needed a nominal owner to comply with the legal requirements. Vivian Ezra stood in as the nominal purchaser, and Arthur Goldreich moved into the house with his wife Hazel and their children. It would ostensibly be their own private home. We would retain sole use of the outbuildings other than the servants' quarters. Arthur had been a member of the Party for some time, but had never been publicly associated with it.

Hazel was not a Party member. Whether anyone told her the facts about the place and its real ownership I do not know, but she must soon have realised that the outbuildings were alien political territory where people came and went without discussing with her what they were doing. Mandela was an old friend of the Goldreichs. He had stayed for a time in their previous home when he was underground and organising the May strike. He became the first person to move into a room in the outbuildings and work from there under cover.

When we acquired the place, the outbuildings needed some reconstruction to be made suitable for meetings, and for people under cover to live in. I was the obvious person to draw the plans, negotiate a contract with a small builder, and to supervise the works. It meant I was visiting the farm generally twice a week before Mandela moved in and for several months afterwards. Whether Mandela knew that the place belonged to the Party rather than to Goldreich I am not sure.

He had some inkling. His autobiography, *Long Walk to Freedom* says simply that the property '. . . had been purchased by the movement for the purpose of having a safe house for those underground.' Near enough. While the builders completed their work, he lived in a small room in the outbuildings, known to the Goldreich domestic staff and farm workers as David Motsamayi, and to the Goldreichs' children only as David.

Our old Party comrade Thomas Mashifane recruited a number of lads from his rural home to work as labourers on the farm, growing vegetables for sale. And another old comrade, Frank Jelliman, was recruited to be their foreman and general custodian of the property. They formed no part of the Goldreich household, keeping themselves strictly apart as did the politicals who came and went from time to time. The main house was the Goldreichs' private domain, out of bounds to anyone not specially invited in.

For several months while building went on, I would meet

Mandela there regularly, and spend time chatting to him. His evenings were usually filled with his political activities, but during the day he was short of both company and reading matter. He wanted books about the legal and illegal experiences of political movements in other countries, and about their theories. He was not reading so much as studying, especially on the theory, strategy and tactics of armed struggle. I lent him, amongst other things, a Chinese booklet called *How to be a Good Communist* written by Liu Shao Chi, and a first-hand account of the Huk Balahap guerrilla uprising in the Philippines titled *Born of the People*.[3]

He was making notes of everything, studying seriously and discussing the books afterwards. In the evenings, he was regularly leaving in disguise under cover of dark to meet with ANC leaders and members in different places. He was probably the most wanted man in the country at the time, and was taking great risks. But that was his style. He was one who led from the front. He never asked anyone to take a risk which he was not prepared to take first himself.

As time went on, I became increasingly uneasy about his personal security. More and more people were getting to know his whereabouts. Apart from the members of the Party CC who might run across him when they came there on their own business, there was an expanding circle of his aides, go-betweens and drivers, and also his wife Winnie and her drivers and aides. The circle of knowledge slowly spread as control of security at Lilliesleaf divided dangerously between the CC and Mandela himself. It was a new experience for all of us, and we were slow to realise the dangers in what was happening.

There could be few political secrets at Rivonia between Mandela and ourselves. We both knew, in general if not in detail, what the other was doing. It could not have been otherwise. There were Party members who were part of the ANC's National Executive, and ANC members who were part of the Party CC. Mandela knew

---

[3]Both books were in evidence in the Rivonia Trial, together with Mandela's own study notes of them. The Philippine book, supposedly by the one-time leader of the Huk, had been ghost-written by an American communist, William Pomeroy, who served with the Huk during their uprising, was sentenced to death, and then deported to Britain.

that we were setting up special units, just as we knew that he was enrolling ANC volunteers for his special force. By the middle of the year, our own groups in Johannesburg had been up and running for some time.

I had been to Durban for a planning session with the District Committee and their first few specialists to get units started there – a session which would have repercussions for me during the Rivonia Trial two years later. Mandela's first units were recruited some time later. They soon outnumbered our 'specialist' units, but lacked people with practical experience of armed conflict. Our 'experts' shared their expertise with them, just as we shared skills with the ANC in political matters. We were travelling separate quasi-armed paths without competing.

It had not been planned that way – it had just happened. There was no logic in two separate forces with separate commands, advancing in tandem towards a common aim. We were both aware of it. In armed action, unity would be as much a part of success as it had been proved to be in every unarmed action. The separation of our forces into separate entities could undermine our mutual futures.

It was obvious that our armed forces should be unified and brought under a single command as soon as possible, but that was not as easy as it sounds. It meant combining bodies of quite different character. The Party's specialist units were an integral part of the Party structure; they functioned like any other non-specialist unit, under direct Party leadership and rules. Mandela's units functioned as an autonomous organisation, outside of the ANC structure, and with its own independent leadership and rules. Unification could not come about by simple merger. It called for changes in both bodies, and new organisational concepts. If not for the mutual trust and fraternity which existed between us at a leadership level, it would probably never have been accomplished.

But it was. Through a series of discussions between representatives of both groups, a consensus acceptable to both was reached. Both existing units would be merged into a single force to be known as Umkhonto we Sizwe ('the Spear of the Nation', shortened to MK). The specialist Party units would be dissolved, and their members would be free to join MK as volunteers. All MK members would be free to remain members also of the ANC or the Party or both.

Umkhonto's command structure would be reconstructed with equal numbers appointed by each of the existing leaderships, and with Mandela as Commander in Chief. The National High Command would devolve authority to Provincial Commands.

Once the formula was agreed, the transition was quite painless. The composition of the High Command was agreed and included Walter Sisulu as liaison officer with the ANC executive, and Joe Slovo as the Party liaison. At headquarters in Johannesburg there were only two men with any real military expertise – Jack Hodgson with war-time experience in a free-wheeling hit-and-run unit known as the Desert Rats behind the German lines in the Western Desert; and Arthur Goldreich, who had served with the Jewish Palmach in its struggle to free Palestine from British occupation.[4] Both were seconded to Umkhonto.

In his autobiography, Mandela writes that Umkhonto '. . . recruited Jack Hodgson, who had fought in the Second World War . . . and Rusty Bernstein.' And again, on the subject of the MK constitution, '. . . we were joined by Joe Slovo and Rusty Bernstein, who both had hands in drafting it.' I assume he wrote from memory since there are, so far as I know, no written records of the period (except perhaps in police archives).

His memory and mine are at odds. I stand by mine, at least about myself. I was not ever a member of MK – I was already fully stretched to fulfil my other Party functions. But I was meeting Mandela and other members of the High Command constantly at Rivonia and elsewhere, and we discussed things together freely. I probably knew as much as anyone outside the High Command of what it was doing and planning, and from time to time lent a hand in some small way. But for the record: I had no part in the drafting of the MK constitution, but did have a small input into the text of the manifesto it issued on the day sabotage began. Now I have no recollection of which parts of it were my work, but they were there somewhere.

Towards the end of that year – October 1961 – Chief Luthuli was finally awarded the Nobel Prize for Peace for which he had

---

[4] I am not sure that they were members of the National High Command, which included *inter alia* Raymond Mhlaba, Govan Mbeki, Wilton Mkwayi, and others at various times.

been nominated while still in detention in Pretoria. The award ceremony was to take place in Stockholm in December. The news lifted all our spirits. It was obviously a deliberate rejoinder to the state persecution of Luthuli, and by implication an endorsement of the policies of the ANC and the liberation movement.

A message reached me through the ANC. The Chief had been much taken by my 'Call' to the COP, and asked for my help in drafting his Nobel Prize acceptance speech. I took it as an honour. I admired the Chief tremendously though I shared neither his political nor his religious beliefs. He was a man of real integrity, honesty and moral courage. There was no possibility of discussing the speech with him as he was confined by ministerial decree to his home town of Groutville, Natal. I was on my own.

I knew what *I* would say. But the challenge was to suppress all that and try to imagine what *he* would say. I wished I knew him better. I had been given such a tight time limit that I could not draft and revise and revise again as I would normally have done. I made some notes, and dictated my draft directly from them to Tiny Nokwe – Duma's wife – who hammered it out on the typewriter as I spoke. I have no copy of that draft – I doubt whether one exists – and I remember very little of its contents. I can recall writing that though the prize was awarded to Luthuli personally, it would be accepted by all as a symbolic reward for the ANC, for the whole of our liberation movement, and for the movement's dedication to a non-violent course.

But I could not avoid the grim irony of the timing. The award came at precisely the moment when the movement was moving away from those fifty non-violent years which Luthuli had described as 'knocking peaceably at a door which would not open'. Non-violence had always been a hard course to steer in a violent country. Now the tide was turning against it. Yesterday's non-violent activists were becoming today's trainees in sabotage and armed struggle. Yesterday's non-violent ANC had spawned today's armed liberation force. I could not avoid referring to that irony. I recall that my draft ended by calling attention to the paradox of an award for Peace being made in Stockholm while decisions on armed struggle were being made in South Africa.

I never discovered how Luthuli felt about my draft. When I saw the speech he finally made in Stockholm it was quite clear that not much of my text remained. I was not surprised. I knew Luthuli had strong opinions of his own and had no need for a ghost writer except perhaps for reasons of time. I regretted only one thing: that in his acceptance speech my ending had gone. There was no reference to the contradiction between the war clouds gathering at home and a Peace Prize being awarded abroad. I felt he had missed a unique opportunity to alert the world and South Africans themselves to the crossroads at which our history was poised.

By that time, Umkhonto had established units in the main cities. It had started training them for sabotage and in the handling of explosives, without any explicit long-term vision beyond a campaign of sabotage. There was a pragmatic idea that the new form of struggle would, for the time being, be confined to sabotage of government installations, but avoiding all injury to persons. It hoped to awaken the public to the prospect of serious civil upheaval unless the government changed course, and to spur the government on.

But if the government did not change course, where was sabotage taking us? There was a half-formed idea that somehow sabotage would prepare the ground for something more confrontational – perhaps guerrilla war or even formal armed struggle. The process by which this evolution would come about was never very clear. What *was* clear was that preparations for that next stage should begin even while sabotage was the only action on the agenda. Selected MK personnel should be receiving proper training in the art of guerrilla warfare, just in case. The Party, with its contacts with the socialist countries, started investigating whether they could provide MK with training facilities.

MK was not alone in the field. Young white militants from the ranks of the Liberal Party had formed a secret quasi-military faction called the Armed Resistance Movement (ARM), which appeared to have no programme of its own other than sabotage. We knew of its existence through clues picked up in discussion with some of its members who had been detained with us in Pretoria. John Laing and Monty Berman were both seeking for new ways to confront the apartheid regime. Both of them were temperamentally inclined towards deeds of derring-do rather than staid Congress-style campaigning. It seemed likely that they would be connected with ARM. Berman and his wife had once been members of the Party but had drifted away. We had been friends for a long time.

I was asked by MK to talk to him about the possibility that ARM might be planning some action which would cut across their own plans. They were. We suggested that they co-ordinate their actions with MK to make its impact more effective, and they agreed. They would hold their planned action until an agreed date and time. Apart from that, the two forces would act quite independently. They would do what they had been planning to do – which was to attack and bring down certain power lines on the Witwatersrand. And MK would do whatever it was planning to do. It appeared that their numbers were smaller than MK's, but their expertise somewhat better. In their ranks were several people with war-time experience in the South African army or in the Jewish resistance to British occupation of Palestine.

On 10 December Luthuli received his Nobel Prize in Stockholm, and a few days later he returned to Groutville – by coincidence on the eve of the date set for the first acts of sabotage – 16 December. The choice of date was not arbitrary. December 16th had major political undertones. For the liberation movement it was Heroes Day, the anniversary of many memorable past struggles and the annual day of rededication to resistance. For the white establishment it was the Day of the Covenant, which commemorated the slaughter of the Zulu impis and the ultimate Boer triumph over black resistance at the battle of Blood River in 1838. It had an appropriate symbolism for MK's dramatic entry into the fight against white supremacy. A number of MK units were already trained in the main cities, and appropriate state installations had been reconnoitred and targeted.

Late on the night of 16 December, MK and ARM units struck simultaneously. Earlier in the evening, Congress volunteers had been out pasting up copies of the MK founding manifesto in public places. The manifesto was printed in large format on one side of an A3 sheet, to serve as a wall poster which would be seen by people on their way to work next morning. Both printing and pasting were dangerous, but illegal techniques developed in earlier years proved themselves. All the volunteers involved returned safely. We thought we had ensured that, in the morning, the public would learn what the night's sabotage was about, what it implied for the nation's future, and who was responsible for it.

We were over optimistic. Some time before dawn the posters must have been spotted by police. By first light, police patrols were going through town tearing down all the posters they could find. By the time the population was on its way to work, there was scarcely a poster to be seen. Sabotage had been intended to shake the country awake, but the political explanation for it had been silenced. There were many disparate and scattered acts of sabotage across the country. Power lines came down; pass offices and government offices were attacked. There was only one casualty – our own comrade Petrus Molife whose home-made bomb went off prematurely in his hands. Some of the acts, particularly ARM's sabotage of high-tension power lines, were spectacular;[5] others passed with little public notice. All in all, they greatly boosted the movement's morale and self-confidence, but no public explanation of the night's events or of MK's purposes was made. That was a bad blow to our plans.

Quite irregularly, I was drawn into one of the night's operations as a by-product of my part in the political preparations. It was on a mission with Jack Hodgson and Joe Slovo to cut the main telephone cables between Johannesburg, Pretoria and the Reef towns. The cables joined together in an underground chamber on a main road just beyond the edge of the town. The others were trained in the handling of explosives; I was not. They went down through the manhole cover into the chamber, taped their sticks of dynamite to the cables, and lit the fuse. I was with the car above, bonnet open as though it had broken down, shielding the open manhole and ready to pass a warning and close the cover if anyone showed any interest. No one did. There was no hitch.

We drove away keeping watch for a blast or a flash behind us. We saw and heard nothing, and assumed the fuse had fizzled for longer than expected. Slovo claimed to have heard something far

---

[5]Liaison with ARM ended there. ARM carried on sabotage independently until the arrest of a Cape Town member, Adrian Leftwich, who broke down and gave information leading to the arrest of most of the other members. Some were charged, others fled. John Harris, alone and despairing, placed a bomb in the Johannesburg station concourse as a protest. He tipped off the authorities who failed to act in time. The bomb killed a woman and child. Harris was traced. In a last tragic episode in ARM history, he was convicted of murder and executed.

off, but two years later, in the Rivonia Trial, the facts were revealed by a police witness who listed every known act of MK sabotage, successful or unsuccessful. Amongst them was our chamber, where a routine inspection had brought to light an unexploded pack of dynamite taped to the cables.[6]

December 16th must be counted an operational success but a tactical failure. Contrary to our intentions, the sabotage created only a ripple of concern in the government or the country at large. The MK manifesto warning of a dangerous drift into civil war had been effectively blacked out. The country seemed to have resigned itself to living with political confrontation and violent repression. It was a disappointing result, but the movement had set out on a new course and was not backing out. MK units carried on with a low-key rolling campaign of sabotage, and the High Command started considering a transition to 'the next phase' – guerrilla war. For that, it had neither the material resources nor the trained personnel, and would have to seek help from abroad.

The African heads of state were to meet in Addis Ababa in February 1962 to form a standing Organisation of African Unity (OAU). The ANC National Executive, meeting secretly with Luthuli presiding, decided to be represented. Mandela was appointed to head a delegation which would include ANC representatives already abroad. He would have to be smuggled out of the country without a passport, and smuggled back in. It was a risky undertaking, but his mission could serve two purposes. It could establish the ANC firmly in the company of independent Africa. And as Commander in Chief of MK he could canvass the prospects of receiving training and material aid from Africa for an armed struggle at home. In January '62, he left the country secretly on his way to Addis Ababa, leaving the MK High Command to carry on without him.

---

[6]Elias Motsoaledi had bought MK's dynamite from a mine worker. Several operations where it was used miscarried. Whether the supplier had known it was defective or whether he was a provocateur or state agent is not known.

15

THINGS FALL APART
1962 – 63

After 16 December, MK's focus began to shift away from sabotage towards guerrilla war. There was no formal decision. It was something that seemed to develop spontaneously from the idea that sabotage would somehow lead to a 'next phase'.

The High Command arranged for some of its senior people to go abroad for advanced training, and MK units started recruiting young volunteers for guerrilla training. Special teams were arranging for secretive transport to take them across the borders illegally, and bring them back again at some indeterminate time when training was complete. Detailed intelligence studies of the country's military, economic and communication installations were being made and mapped. While all this was going on, the High Command was itself developing a strategic plan for the next stage, which it eventually adopted under the title of 'Operation Mayibuye'.

It was almost inevitable that much of the High Command's activity centred around Lilliesleaf Farm, though without formal authorisation of the Party CC. Mandela's own stay there had been agreed to by the CC, and thus, by implication, his activities in the ANC and as the MK Commander in Chief would be expected to be conducted from there. But the CC had never intended to turn the place from a 'safe house' into MK's semi-permanent headquarters, yet that is what it came to be.

At first, responsibilities for Lilliesleaf security had been overseen by Mandela and the Party. The High Command, which took over Mandela's responsibility for MK, appeared to assume it had also taken over the custody of all the Lilliesleaf security. Boldness and daring were necessary qualities for the cloak and dagger nature of their activity, but they seemed to encourage a casual, almost reckless disregard for security at Lilliesleaf. Things which need not have been done there, were, because it was easy and available. Things that should never have been kept there, were; and people who should not have known of its existence were taken there – perhaps because it was easiest at a time when there were few other alternatives. Unconsciously, MK was turning our safe house into a place of peril.

Disturbing reports were coming back to the ANC from the Addis Ababa conference. Mandela was having a rough ride. PAC leaders who had gone abroad well before him had established some claim to represent all black South Africans, and were doing what they could to undermine the ANC. Their credentials in Africa were not a response to their paltry political record at home but to their radical rhetoric. They identified themselves with that popular African theme of 'negritude' and turned it into a weapon against the non-racial ANC programme. They pandered to Africanist chauvinism; they attacked the ANC for conceding any white South African role in the liberation struggle, and voiced a strident anti-white and anti-communist orientation. Rhetoric and demagogy had given them credibility in many parts of independent Africa, and the support of political leaders who had little understanding of South Africa or the gulf that separated our reality and experiences from their own. Governments were leaning on the ANC to strike some form of unprincipled 'unity' deal with the PAC on the basis of its Africanist ideology. Mandela and his colleagues were struggling against the tide.

At home, too, the movement was reeling from the backwash. The separating wall between the ANC and MK which had been so deliberately established at home was blown apart by a single statement from one of the ANC representatives in East Africa, Robert Resha, whose claim that MK was the armed wing of the ANC had been reported worldwide. No one knew whether the ANC delegation's leaders, Mandela and Tambo, had authorised the statement, but they did not repudiate it. It was certainly a distortion of the truth. Perhaps Resha, who had been abroad for some time, was misinformed; perhaps it was a concession to the Africanist pressure being imposed on the delegation. Whatever its origins, it made every member of the ANC complicit in an armed struggle for which most of them had never given either agreement or consent. It was a body blow to the political rationale for the formation of MK as a separate organisation.

It was also a breach of faith with the movement at home, and a cause of short-lived confusion. To the outside world, the ANC represented the whole liberation movement. It was impossible for an underground movement at home to correct an 'official' statement made by an officer abroad, or even to explain it to the many supporters at home who were appalled by it. But the statement changed nothing in the reality of MK's structure or command. It only distorted the public perception of it, and of its relations to the ANC. There was little purpose in trying to put the record straight – toothpaste cannot be squeezed back into the tube. So the statement stood, and the movement adjusted itself to accommodate it. It was a sign that things were beginning to fall apart.

Mandela returned to South Africa early in August, crossing secretly from Bechuanaland (later Botswana) and returning to Lilliesleaf Farm. He reported briefly to the MK command that the delegation had managed to overcome obstacles posed by the PAC, and had established the true position of the ANC in the South African struggle. He had made working arrangements for MK personnel to receive guerrilla training in various places in Africa, and had held useful political discussions with leading political figures in Britain and elsewhere. Almost immediately thereafter he set out for Natal to report on his mission to ANC President Luthuli, leaving his diary and notes made abroad at Lilliesleaf.

It was a dangerous journey. Luthuli was confined to the Groutville area under surveillance, and Mandela was certainly being sought. He was not a man to avoid an obligation, however dangerous. He never claimed any special exemption by virtue of his position. On the contrary, he accepted that his position as a leader laid extra obligations and duties on him. He left for Natal, met the Chief, and gave him a full report to be relayed to the ANC National Executive. That done, he decided to meet the provincial

MK command for a briefing.

It was a bold step – some afterwards criticised it as unnecessarily bold, even reckless. But it was his own decision. Word of his presence in Durban had leaked to the police – many believe via a tip-off from the CIA. The police were waiting for him on the road back from Durban. On 5 August his car was stopped at a road block, and he was arrested with Cecil Williams who was the car's owner and driver.

Williams was released without charge soon after, but Mandela was charged in Johannesburg with leaving the country without a passport. He turned his defence into an indictment of the white bias which had corrupted South African justice and made the courts an integral part of the machinery of black oppression. It was a characteristically courageous and defiant stand which helped raise the morale of the movement and its supporters, but did not save him from a guilty verdict and a sentence of three years' imprisonment. That was a tremendous blow to the movement. He had a unique prestige and reputation amongst the people. He had become the public symbol of the ANC and of resistance to apartheid. There was no obvious successor to fill his place.

Throughout the year, times had become more and more difficult. The police had been given new powers to detain people without charge for up to ninety days, which period could be repeated over and over again. Members of organisations disappeared into limbo with no one knowing where they were or what was happening to them. They were being held incommunicado, without access to lawyers or anyone else. The police had learnt from their failures of interrogation during the 1960 Emergency, and sent personnel abroad to be trained by the CIA in its torture-based techniques of 'counter insurgency'. Torture of detainees in order to extract information became routine; reports told of victims reduced to the state of zombies by prolonged sleep deprivation during which they had talked involuntarily and without consciousness, like sleep-walkers. Some of the best of our comrades had cracked under torture. No one could be certain what places or information remained secret, what had been involuntarily given away.

We had not been prepared for institutionalised torture. Our codes of conduct were based on our mutual determination to take the consequences of silence regardless of the penalties. They had served us well for years – but they could not survive the new combination of sleep deprivation and physical torture. Information was leaking out – but no one knew what. Rumour became rife, and fed fears and suspicions. Someone had been detained and then released without charge. Could a deal have been done? And on what terms? Should he be trusted or shunned? Communication links were being disrupted as key personnel were taken out, some by security doubts and mistrust, others by detention, torture or imprisonment. Gaps in the chain of communication between units and committees were opening up, which could be temporarily stopped by reshuffling members and rescheduling. But not indefinitely. Our human resources were limited – and shrinking.

We were also struggling against a new assault – house arrest. A spate of ministerial orders had turned many leading activists into permanent prisoners in their own homes – and into warders over themselves. Those who were full-time political workers were ordered, under threat of long-term imprisonment, never to leave their homes by day or night or receive any visitors. Like convicted criminals, they were prevented from working for a living, but unlike convicted prisoners, were expected to survive without any state support.

Others – generally those with 'acceptable' non-political jobs – had been confined to their homes except for daylight hours on weekdays, partly or wholly cut off from contact with the movement. More holes opened up in our networks; the fabric was being torn apart and temporarily patched with *ad hoc* decisions. Interim replacements brought in to fill the gaps were often not fully ready for their new responsibilities but were pressed into service simply because no one else was available. Our rules governing recruitment and promotion which had served their purpose well could no longer meet the pressures. Disciplines and procedures were also starting to fall apart.

In October 1962, my own house arrest order arrived. It had been signalled in advance by the Minister of Justice in a speech in Parliament in which he sought to justify such orders. They were necessary, he claimed, to control a small number of subversives who the police had been unable to stifle despite their already draconian powers. He had named some of them, including Brian Bunting and myself. I began to think of house arrest as my personal piece of legislation, and had been expecting to be arrested. I was fairly confident I would find a way to live with it, as I had with earlier bans. I am not very gregarious, and would still have my family about me. House arrest would cramp my political activities – but there would certainly be ways around it, though the whole family would suffer straitened finances and restricted social lives. My architectural practice would probably grind to a halt, and Hilda would be left as the only earner in the household.

The Minister's threat worried my family perhaps more than it worried me. My brother and his wife arrived at our house to urge me to leave the country before it was too late. We argued about it for some time, with Hilda joining in between flying visits to the kitchen to see that our supper wasn't burning. She, I think, sympathised with my brother's arguments but was prepared to leave the decision to me. I would be the main victim of house arrest though it would affect her own and our children's lives in ways we could not foretell.

I tried to explain why I could not agree to leave. It was neither simple obstinacy nor fear of losing face. The thing was that I had helped create the situation which confronted us. I had myself persuaded men and women to risk their necks for our cause. Leaving now would be like deserting them, though staying would do nothing to save them. It would be a gesture and nothing more.

I have always disliked gesture politics, but that was not the issue. I had given the whole of my adult life to the cause of a new and better South Africa. That had taken precedence over everything else. I had invested in it everything I had – peace, tranquillity, prosperity and reputation, as well as much that properly belonged to Hilda and my children. I was incapable of just drawing a line under it and writing it off as a bad investment from which I could walk away. It represented most of what I valued in my life. I would hang on to it to the bitter end.

I don't know if I managed to make them understand what I was trying to explain for their benefit. I appreciated that they were trying to save me from myself, but in the end we agreed to disagree.

House arrest permitted me to leave the house only between 9 a.m. and 6 p.m. on weekdays; not at all on weekends or public holidays. I had to report to police headquarters at Marshall Square every weekday between 12 and 2 p.m. I was not to enter any school or industrial premises, or leave the magisterial district of Johannesburg. I was not to receive any guests at home, or communicate with any other banned or listed person, except – by bizarre dispensation – my own wife.

We were almost in need of that dispensation. Underground activity had imposed its own disciplines on us. Silence about everything was the price of survival. It could only be broken where there was compelling 'need-to-know'. Hilda and I had learned, over the years, to live with that imperative, cohabiting without communicating about secret politics. It was our protection for each other and for our comrades in the movement. What one does not know cannot be revealed by accident or extracted under duress.

We had cultivated the security of silence between us. It was years since we had told each other what we were doing separately, where we were going, who we were meeting – though after years together we could often guess. We discussed nothing secret in our house – the phone was tapped, the walls, the ceilings, even the car might be bugged. If we had to talk of secret things we would walk away to an unlikely open place. We answered our children's questions with meaningless and probably irritating nothings: 'Where are you going?' 'To see a man about a dog.' 'When will you be back?' 'Before long.'

We concealed from them and from each other whatever we could. It was not too hard for me – I am naturally taciturn. It was far harder on Hilda who is outgoing and enjoys nothing more than talk. But real in-depth talk between us on anything touching on our politics had been sentenced to death. Occasionally we might mention the idea of leaving the country while it was still possible. I had always rejected it. Hilda would not press it. She would allow herself to be persuaded against her instinctive concern for the safety of the children and the stability of the family. But I don't think she ever really agreed.

House arrest cast a shadow on everyone in the house. They all became clock watchers. They would fidget and worry as six o'clock approached and I was not yet home. They would get tense and worried at every footstep outside our door after dark. Special Branch men would arrive at any hour of the evening, demanding to be allowed in to prowl around and check that I was home, and not 'receiving guests'. It made everyone jittery, until finally I lost my cool. I confronted two of them who came to the door bumbling about 'just checking'. I demanded to see a search warrant, which they did not have.

'You're on my property without a warrant,' I shouted at them. 'Get off or I'll charge you with trespass!' and slammed the door in their faces.

They were taken aback, and went off. But a few days later they were back again. My shock tactics didn't have any lasting effect.

They arrived again one evening when my daughter Toni was entertaining some friends in the living-room. I was by myself in the kitchen. They took the names and addresses of all the teenage visitors, and the next day their parents were visited by police heavies and warned to keep better control of their children.

It was blatant intimidation, and Toni hit back by giving the story to the press. 'My father may be house arrested. I am not!' she told a reporter.

But many of her friends no longer came near our house. Nor did a school friend of my younger daughter Frances, who was living in a forbidding, red brick orphanage not far from where we lived. She had occasionally enjoyed weekends with us away from the institution, but when we invited her once again permission to visit us was refused. House arrest spread like blight, first to my family, and then outward on to our friends and our children's friends.

Even so, I was far better off than those house-bound for twenty-four hours a day, often in tiny township homes or small flats. I had a garden to go out into, and I could leave home on weekdays provided I got to Marshall Square between 12 and 2 to 'sign the book'. It was not just that life was more restricted than under earlier banning orders; it was more secretive.

There was danger everywhere, even inside our own home. There was uncertainty in every chance encounter, and in every attempt to make contact with the movement. I was banned from 'gatherings' – but who knew what constituted a 'gathering'? Lawyers suggested it could be two or more people 'with a common purpose'. But what was a 'common purpose'? A queue waiting for a bus? An audience at a cinema? No one knew the answers. I was not to 'communicate' with any other banned or listed persons. But what is 'communicating'? A nod of recognition in the street? A wave of the hand? Answering a telephone call? Life had become like an expedition through a minefield without charts or white taped lines to delimit where one can tread and where one dare not.

Even prison has its marginal sense of safety; there are rules and regulations; one knows the borderline between what is permissible and what is not. Not so house arrest where you must try to define the legal limits for yourself, without any legal guidelines or precedents. It is a minefield with no cleared safety zones. One learns, willy-nilly, to shrink back from everyone and everything. Phones can be tapped; we stopped using them. Letters can be intercepted, homes watched and car numbers noted. Neighbours can be questioned and colleagues detained and interrogated without reason.

I sought out furtive contact with other people during daylight hours. For me it was a necessity, but it was threatening for them and an intrusion into their normal working day. One drew back slowly until social contact beyond the family circle withered away to nothing. Even inside the home, social paralysis settled in after dark and at weekends.

Visitors willing to outface the police surveillance grew fewer and fewer. When someone did arrive to visit anyone in the family, I might not 'receive' them; I retreated to the privacy of the kitchen. Our children's friends dropped in uninvited in the South African way, to share a barbecue or to swim in our backyard pool. I retreated to the kitchen. If their friends stayed to share a family meal, I ate alone by the kitchen sink, but not at ease. At any moment there could be police at the door again, 'checking up'.

The tally of those under house arrest was growing steadily. Of that group which reconstituted the Party only Bram Fischer was still moving about freely in the outside world. Kotane and Harmel were under house arrest, Dadoo was abroad representing the movement, Berrange had retired to live in Swaziland. Others who had been elected or co-opted to the Party CC since that time and leading members of the ANC and other Congresses were similarly immobilised or dispersed.

The tidy patterns of organisation were giving way, most evidently at Rivonia. Govan Mbeki who was a member of the CC and the ANC National Executive was served with a twenty-four hour house arrest order. He disappeared suddenly from his home in Port Elizabeth and arrived in Johannesburg. He was now acting Secretary

General of the ANC as successor to Sisulu who was under house arrest in Soweto, and a member of the MK High Command operating out of Lilliesleaf Farm. Kathy Kathrada had been house-arrested in his upper-floor flat in Kholvad House, Commissioner Street. He too had refused to be his own jailer and made his way to Lilliesleaf Farm where he was brought into the Party CC.

Inside Rivonia and outside, the movement seemed to be playing an endless game of musical chairs. It was hard to know from day to day who held what post in which organisation, or who – if anyone – now controlled the comings and goings at Lilliesleaf Farm. The changing cast of characters living there was changing the nature of the place and the operations centred there. It was no longer a safe house for the Party and a selected number of its allies on the run. It was becoming a refuge for everyone who knew about it. And increasingly it was being transformed into a workplace and *de facto* headquarters for MK.

From Mandela's experience at Lilliesleaf Farm we had learnt the difficulties of maintaining an activist in the underground. Providing Mandela's team of messengers, drivers, and security officers and a network of safe places for meetings had strained the resources of the movement. It was unthinkable that we could summon up the resources now, in more difficult times, to provide for several such people simultaneously, yet house arrest was forcing that problem on to the agenda. There was no longer time for deliberation and planning. On the CC, decisions had to be made urgently, piecemeal, before our whole machine came apart.

Harmel, who had been editing the *African Communist*, was under twenty-four hour house arrest. The work could not be carried on from his home and we had no one to replace him. We would have to smuggle him out to Britain to carry on the publication from there, where the printing and distribution arrangements were already in place. Kotane was incarcerated in his house in Alexandra township, also under a twenty-four hour order. The ANC was calling for his services in their mission in Dar es Salaam. He could do nothing where he was and would also have to go. Jack Hodgson was similarly confined to an upper-floor flat in Hillbrow with his wife Rica as his only link with the outside world. MK were thinking about a staging post in Bechuanaland to assist the passage of their trainees who were to go abroad for guerrilla training. Jack, who was MK's chief training officer, would be ideal for the job. He too would have to be smuggled out to Bechuanaland. And so it went, week by week – more of our key people going out, leaving yawning political and organisational gaps behind.

The CC was clinging to the illusion that it could keep pace with events, and close the gaps by orderly promotion of new people to replace those being taken out. But the gaps were being created faster than we could fill them. Our committees were beginning to run short of experienced personnel, chains of communication began to falter, and units began to find themselves out on their own with only the most tenuous contact with the centralised leadership they had grown to depend upon.

But still the organisations pressed ahead. Senior MK personnel were being sent abroad secretly for specialised officer-grade training; Raymond Mhlaba, Wilton Mkwayi, Themba Mqota and Andrew Mlangeni were on their way to China; the first groups of recruits for guerrilla training were on their way to Tanzania and elsewhere.

One way or another, almost every unit of the Party, the ANC and MK was getting drawn into some part of the preparations for a future phase of armed struggle. Some were actively recruiting young men and women for military training; others were organising their assembly in Johannesburg and their transportation across the borders. A few promising activists – amongst them our comrade Ruth Mompati – were being sent abroad for advanced political education; and a team of specialists was assembling and testing out a radio transmitter which would be the underground voice of the liberation movement. Sabotage was going on sporadically, though almost all reporting of it had been blacked out by state pressure on press and radio. Without publicity, sabotage had no more propaganda value. Minds were shifting inexorably towards 'the next stage' of guerrilla war.

Organisational and political realignments were eroding the walls which had been so carefully constructed to separate the ANC and MK. Borderlines between them were becoming blurred, as were the borderlines between the ANC and the Party. People who had once been clearly identified as members of one or other organisation – ANC, Party or MK – were being pressed into new positions where their affiliations were no longer clear. Govan Mbeki, for example, was at once acting Secretary General of the ANC and on the MK

High Command and on the Party CC. Others were being drawn involuntarily into similar doubling up and tripling of responsibilities. Relations between the organisations had long been close. Now they were becoming incestuous, and the border demarcations between them ever less distinct.

The CC of the Party was changing almost from month to month. Mhlaba had gone. Kotane and Harmel were going. J B Marks was under house arrest and incommunicado. For the rest, only Fischer and Slovo were still at large; I was hamstrung by house arrest, and Mbeki and Kathrada, who were both living at Lilliesleaf Farm, were underground. One of the gaps had been filled by the inclusion of Bob Hepple, who was young, an advocate, and the only one of us all not 'named' on the Suppression Act lists of former communists.

Despite our good intentions, Party and MK affairs had become dangerously intertwined at Lilliesleaf Farm, so we felt greatly relieved to hear that MK had acquired a place of its own at a farm called Trevallyn not too far from Rivonia. I expected that MK would move its operations away from Rivonia, but that didn't quite happen. MK was apparently thinking of Trevallyn as the place where it could stockpile and manufacture materiel for the next phase of its operations. Though it shifted some records and operations from Rivonia, it left most of them behind. Those of us on the CC who were not part of the MK apparatus knew little about Trevallyn, but even less about what they were doing there than about what they were doing at Lilliesleaf. I knew that Mbeki and Mhlaba sometimes stayed in one place, sometimes in another, and that Sisulu had been staying at Trevallyn after he had escaped from house arrest and disappeared underground.

The times called for the tightest possible security, but security standards were slipping inexorably. We were all over-stretched, but safe houses give a strange illusion of security. Those living in them underground have the illusion that danger lies only beyond the fence, and that inside it there is safety. Once the illusion takes hold, the guard is dropped and security measures slacken. We had no experience of the phenomenon and were slow to recognise it while security declined. Although MK had acquired its own place at Trevallyn, members of the MK High Command had grown accustomed to using Lilliesleaf Farm for all purposes. What had started as a temporary haven for Commander in Chief Mandela had changed imperceptibly into MK's operational headquarters.

The Party CC should have taken a grip on the situation, but those of us not living there were never fully informed. We were not aware that people who should never have known of Lilliesleaf's existence were coming and going – amongst them an MK saboteur from Natal called Bruno Mtolo. We were not aware that MK's top security documents, including intelligence maps and Mandela's diary of his mission abroad, which should not have been kept at all, were being stored there.

In retrospect, it is evident that the 'safe house syndrome' was at work.[1] Lilliesleaf Farm seemed to be the easy option for every hard choice. It was, after all, 'safe'. I began to sense that, in the top MK echelons, there was a growing gung-ho spirit of recklessness – though in their perilous cloak-and-dagger operations they would probably have called it a necessary boldness. It was not shared by those of us who still lived and moved about in fear in the real world outside the fence.

There was, I suppose, a measure of recklessness in us all, which kept us going even while things were patently falling apart. We were living dangerously in the constant shadow of disaster. Every meeting, every decision or document carried the danger of imprisonment and perhaps even torture. But we concentrated on the goals, not on the dangers. We had reached the point which comes in every long-term commitment when it is no longer possible to give up. Too much time, too much energy, too much emotion have been invested in it. It has become the whole point of one's life – as this one had for me and others after more than twenty years in it. We had come too far and given too much to pull back now even if we wanted to. There was only one way to go – onward.

While Mandela was still abroad, the MK High Command had produced a strategic plan for the next phase of struggle, called Operation Mayibuye. It was a plan for the transformation of MK from a corps of saboteurs into a properly armed and trained military

---

[1] Amongst the Rivonia Trial exhibits was a copy letter from the acting ANC Secretary, Govan Mbeki, to all Regional Secretaries. It was top secret – topic now unknown. Its first page instructed that it be read immediately by the recipient and his chairman only, and then burnt. Mbeki's own copy was preserved in his 'safe house' file.

force; and for moving on from sabotage to rurally based guerrilla warfare. It proposed developing 'armed propaganda' units to function in the countryside, and procuring, manufacturing and stockpiling such armaments as land-mines and hand grenades. It was a committee plan with no single author, but its main proponents seemed to be Mbeki, Slovo and Goldreich. Whether Mandela ever saw the document before his arrest I doubt. Because it went far beyond the scope of the understanding between the Party and the ANC on which MK had been founded, everyone accepted that such a major policy could not possibly go ahead without the full backing of the ANC and the Party. Operation Mayibuye had to be circulated to the organisations for their acceptance.

Outside the ranks of the High Command it met with some immediate opposition, and inside on the High Command itself it did not appear to have one hundred per cent support. Sisulu, for one, had strong reservations. Whether the document ever reached the ANC executive as a whole I do not know, but it was certainly seen by and discussed by all those leading ANC people who were at and around Rivonia at the time, and by the Party CC.

Consultations were bedevilled by security considerations. Conditions did not allow large representative meetings or the careful counting of votes for and against. Such consultations as could be held were difficult, constantly dogged by changes of personnel on the various leading committees, and were often broken off for security reasons before they were complete. Operation Mayibuye would commit us all to the most far-reaching decision the movement had ever taken. The consultations had to be pursued no matter how long it might take.

MK were impatient to press ahead. Mandela's mission abroad had produced offers from independent Africa of the training facilities and material aid which progress on Operation Mayibuye would require. Those opportunities might fade if they were not taken up in good time. I sensed a feeling amongst the High Command that the rest of the movement was taking too long talking about things instead of setting the Operation into motion. We were being over-cautious and dragging our feet. In their impatience they tended to be dismissive of the obstacles – including the fact that their own Commander in Chief whose views were surely of crucial importance, was out of contact; and the fact that many of the most experienced people whose judgement would surely be vital, were incommunicado in prison, under house arrest or on missions abroad.

The process of consultation dragged on. Some people had their say in several capacities and places – Mbeki in MK, ANC and Party, as also Mhlaba who had recently returned from training in China. Sisulu sat in on the debate in both the ANC and MK, Slovo in both the Party and MK, and so on.

The Party CC was deeply divided. All our people on the High Command – Slovo, Mbeki and Mhlaba – were wholeheartedly for Operation Mayibuye; Bram Fischer, Kathrada and I against. Kathrada had a principled objection to violence except in strictly defined circumstances, and had never favoured even the earlier sabotage campaign. I have forgotten the basis for Fischer's opposition, and the position taken by the recent addition to the committee, Bob Hepple. And I don't think we ever knew the views of J B Marks who was under house arrest.

My objections to Operation Mayibuye were wholly political – I had no expertise in military strategy and tactics. I thought it lacked political depth. It proceeded from a wholly inadequate analysis of the real balance of power in the country, and glossed over real consideration of our own or the government's weaknesses or strengths. It seemed to me to be founded in military-style thinking, slicked over with a political gloss. It was based on a fairly simplistic military assessment of the logistic problems of guerrilla warfare rather than on a social and political programme which also encompassed armed force.

Whether I would take the same view today I do not know – I have not seen Operation Mayibuye for the last thirty years. But I have long had a contempt for military thinking and its obsession with numbers and with things. It is primarily concerned with manpower and fire-power. It tends to reduce everything to cold calculation of logistics, terrain and materiel, and to ignore the human factors of consciousness, morale, and ideas. Operation Mayibuye seemed to me to be military thinking at its worst. It could have been produced by almost any military theorist for a guerrilla command in almost any country. It was not a political plan which politicians might be competent to appraise, but a military plan which they would probably not be. Its political content was simplistic, quite inadequate as a basis for such a serious and irrevocable action as it would commit us to. I disliked everything about it, and said so.

In MK there was some feeling that a lack of courage explained the opposition to Operation Mayibuye. Perhaps so. It is very daring to enlarge the theatre of a war when under a succeeding all-out enemy attack. Our MK comrades were forcing the pace. Mandela had secured promises from abroad for the essential training and logistic military aid needed for Operation Mayibuye. MK was pressing for an end to discussions and for the movement to commit itself before those offers lapsed. On the CC, Slovo in particular was growing impatient; the High Command jumped the starter's gun and delegated Slovo to take the Operation Mayibuye document to Dar es Salaam and to seek its endorsement by the ANC missions and Party leaders abroad.

We were being bounced into a *fait accompli*. It is my clear memory that the document had still not been endorsed by anyone other than the MK command. The Party was still talking about it; so was the ANC. That is my memory, and it is also Sisulu's, though some MK members disagree.[2] The Party CC which could have refused to sanction Slovo's mission, decided not to veto what was a decision of one of our allies. Slovo left the country for Dar on his mission for MK. He was accompanied by J B Marks who had escaped from house arrest to join the ANC foreign mission in Tanzania. The more the movement pressed ahead, the more gaps opened up.

A group of technicians had successfully tested a mobile radio transmitter they had constructed. It was small enough to be moved from place to place by car, and required a length of inconspicuous wire to serve as an aerial. This was to be the movement's underground Radio Liberation. For its initial broadcast, Sisulu had prepared a speech explaining the radio's political purposes, which would be followed by an appeal from Kathrada for the Indian population to support the liberation struggle. Both of them were underground; finding a place where they and the radio apparatus

---

[2] Thirty years on, this is still in dispute. Mbeki and Slovo insisted that it had approval from all three relevant bodies. Sisulu, Kathrada and I deny it. I do not have formal statements from the others who were party to the discussions but from informal talks I believe that the majority is on our side.

could come together safely presented obvious difficulties. Who took the decision that it should be done at Lilliesleaf Farm I do not know – it was just another of the decisions 'reached' by mysterious means at a time when organisation was breaking down.

Lilliesleaf was an obvious and simple solution. Our technicians were sure the trial broadcast could not be traced during the short time it would be on the air, and the apparatus would be removed immediately afterwards. On due date, the aerial was strung across the outbuilding roofs, and Radio Liberation went out over the air.

For the operators it was a technical triumph. From the political point of view it was something of a fiasco. There had been scarcely any prior publicity, so its timing and wavelength were almost as secret as its location. There was no one monitoring to discover how far the signal reached, or to estimate the number of listeners and their reactions. Monitoring and report back could have been attempted and should have been. This was planned to be only the first broadcast in a regular series. It turned out to be the last.

Even though MK had jumped the gun and Slovo had left for Dar to promote Operation Mayibuye, consultations went on. There was to be yet another, with some of the remaining MK, ANC and CC members present. Organisation was being improvised from day to day, so that I am no longer clear about the precise status of that meeting or how the participants were selected.[3] Some of them were already underground, others not, and almost all of us were banned from communicating with the others. It had to be a very secret meeting. The venue was proving difficult to find. We argued over which places might still be safe, and which might have been given away by people being tortured in detention.

It was late afternoon. I was getting fidgety. I had a long way to go to reach home. If I was not there by 6 o'clock at latest I would be liable to imprisonment for a breach of my house arrest order. I was itching to get away, but the others were taking their time over the decision.

Someone proposed Lilliesleaf Farm. I refused. The security lapses

---

[3]In the Rivonia Trial, the state described everyone at Lilliesleaf on the day of the raid – that is, Mbeki, Sisulu, Kathrada, Mhlaba, Hepple and I, and also Dennis Goldberg – as members of the High Command. No evidence was offered to support this presumption.

there had mounted up – I was no longer prepared to set foot in the place. Stalemate. One idea after another was proposed and rejected; time ticked away. I seemed to be the one putting a spoke in the wheel.

Bob Hepple made another plea for Lilliesleaf Farm.

I said: 'Never again!'

He said: 'Just this once! The very last time!'

I should have stuck to my guns, but it was already dark outside and near to 6 o'clock. I said: 'But definitely never again!' and ran for my car. I made it home in the nick of time. The whole family was standing anxiously watching out for me through the living-room windows.

The meeting would be my last chance to oppose Operation Mayibuye. I wrote a careful critique of its defects, including its political failure to consider how world opinion and friendly independent governments across the border could be brought into play. I remember little more about it, except that it made little or no reference to the logistical or purely military elements of the document, and based itself on what I saw as the political needs and possibilities. I was going to put it before the meeting at Rivonia which was scheduled for 2 o'clock on 11 July.

On that day I left home around midday to call on an engineer in the city who was doing some structural design work for me. Thereafter, I would go on to report at Marshall Square before 2 o'clock as I was compelled to do every day. It was something that I always dreaded. It was impossible for me to enter the place without fear that I could vanish into that lock-up and never come out. Each day I screwed up the last of my courage to go through with it.

With fear gnawing at my insides in anticipation, I backed my car out of our driveway, my critique of Operation Mayibuye tucked away out of sight under the floor mat. I was going to leave it there while I parked some distance from Marshall Square before reporting. I drove a few hundred yards, and got cold feet. I turned around and drove home again. I had made two secret hiding places in the house, but my time was getting short. Instead of using them I took my document into the garage-workshop and buried it temporarily in a heap of greasy nuts, bolts and bits of old iron. I would make my criticisms of Mayibuye from memory.

I called on my engineer, and went on to Marshall Square to

sign their 'House Arrest' book. When I was first house arrested there were dozens of people who each had their own pages. Now those pages were almost all ruled off, their signatories imprisoned or out of the country. There were only two pages still in use – one for Helen Joseph, the other mine. I signed, and came out without any undue alarms. I drove out to Rivonia, making sure that I was not being followed.

The road passed by the local police station which looked like some outpost of empire – a small white-washed building under tall eucalyptus trees, standing in a quadrangle of red earth. It was usually sleepy and almost deserted. That day I saw several policemen lounging about amongst a few parked vehicles, including a panel van with a dry-cleaner's logo. I thought nothing of it – my warning antennae must have switched off as I left Marshall Square – and drove on to Lilliesleaf Farm. I parked close to the cottage as usual. The others – Mhlaba, Mbeki, Kathrada, Sisulu and Hepple – were all there. We chatted for a few minutes about how we could raise funds for families and dependants of our people in prison, and then turned our attention to business.

Someone produced a copy of Operation Mayibuye. We had scarcely started to talk about it when a van swung into the driveway and drew up outside the main house. I recognised it instantly as the dry-cleaner's van from the police station. I told the others; everyone sat frozen, watching the van through the window. Its rear doors opened up and policemen tumbled out.

I was – as usual – slow to react. Someone – I think Mbeki – seized the copy of Operation Mayibuye from the table, stuffed it into an unlit heating stove and tried to set it alight – unsuccessfully. Mbeki and Sisulu scrambled out of a rear window and started to run towards a clump of trees behind the cottage.

The police divided; some went into the Goldreich house and the others came our way. I had no idea what might be in my pocket, but I had disciplined myself to carry political papers only in my right hand pocket.[4] I had just enough time to take everything from

---

[4] I once blundered into the COD office in the midst of a police raid. I was ordered to sit and wait to be taken home for my house to be searched. I sat at a desk which had already been searched, slipped the contents of my 'political' pocket into an open drawer and slid it closed with my foot, undetected.

there and place it amongst the miscellaneous papers on the table when the police burst in. Some of them chased after Sisulu and Mbeki and caught up with them. The rest of us were arrested.

Hepple and I were handcuffed, marched off to the van and locked in – I could not see what happened to the others. We remained in the van for several hours. We could hear policemen blundering about outside and clumping in and out of the Goldreich home. They were shouting to each other in excitement. 'Look at this!' and 'Jesus! Look what's here!' They obviously thought they were striking gold, but what it was we could not see.

Then the van door opened and a man in handcuffs was pushed in and the van relocked. He looked like a rabbi or a rabbinical student: thick wire-rimmed glasses, dark suit and hat, short beard trimmed to a point. He announced himself as 'Goldberg' and was considerably chirpier than either Hepple or I. I had met Dennis Goldberg several times before – but without the rabbinical trimmings. I had heard that he was in Johannesburg, on the run from Cape Town and expecting MK help to get across the border to Bechuanaland. He said he had been kicking his heels and reading in the Goldreichs' living-room when the police burst in.

Dennis was a victim of the casual MK security which had helped turn Lilliesleaf from a safe house into a trap. He had been active in MK in Cape Town before having to run for cover. I only discovered much later that the High Command had drawn him into a risky assignment connected with Operation Mayibuye while he waited in Johannesburg.

He was a qualified engineer. He had been asked to explore ways of buying or making castings and explosives suitable for hand grenades and land-mines. In his rabbinical disguise and under a number of false names, he had visisted several suppliers and obtained estimates of cost. It had been a dangerous exercise, carried through with considerable ingenuity and daring. He had left a trail a mile wide behind him – I believe his MK seniors owed him better supervision and guidance than he got. He had been let loose on his mission in what seemed to me a carefree, almost reckless disregard for security – more evidence of the 'safe house syndrome', which also accounted for his casual relaxation in the Goldreich house that afternoon.

We sat in the van, hot, uncomfortable, depressed and deeply

fearful for the future. But more than fear, my feeling was of emptiness as though I had used up my last reserves of energy and belief. I had no more reserves of optimism or hope to keep the motor fuelled. For so long I had lived with tension and danger that I was no more conscious of it than of an ill-fitting shoe – which only really begins to hurt when it is taken off. Arrest had relieved the tension and uncertainty; the danger remained, but I was as empty as a burst balloon. Anything could happen now, but everything had finally passed out of my control.

We sat there with nothing much to say. Characteristically, Dennis made jokes to cover up his desperation. They got little response from Hepple or me. We knew nothing of what Dennis had been doing, and nothing about what was in the Goldreich home to cause such excitement amongst the police. Whatever it was, it was unlikely to have anything to do with me. Whether it did or not, I knew fate had finally caught up with me. Just by being there at Lilliesleaf I had made myself guilty of any number of crimes – like communicating with other banned people; participating in the affairs of a banned organisation; attending a gathering, and perhaps half a dozen more like that. There was no feasible defence, and no possible outcome except a term of imprisonment. I had been prepared for that for a long time.

But now there was a new and terrifying element in the reckoning: the element of guerrilla war, and the rest of the implications of the Operation Mayibuye document.

It was already dark when we were driven off to the Fort. Again! We were put in separate cells, with a mat, some blankets and a chamber pot. No food; no opportunity to wash. My watch had been taken away but I knew it was past six o'clock. It would be a terrible time for Hilda and the children. I asked one of the Special Branch men to tell Hilda where I was. He promised to do so, but did not. I scarcely expected that he would. I knew they would be worried sick, waiting, knowing that something disastrous must have happened to me but no way of knowing what. They had no idea where I had gone, who I was with or what I was doing, and no one to ask. The night was going to be even worse for them than it was for me.

I lay in the cell thinking about nothing else. There was no point in thinking of things over which I no longer had any control. What

257

would happen would happen. Late in the night I remembered that my bunch of keys must still be in my pocket; the police had forgotten to search me in the excitement of their coup. I went through my pockets. Nothing of any significance except my key ring with the keys to our house, to our car still standing at Rivonia, and to a post office box.

The box had been hired in a bogus name for all the Party's incoming mail from our London group, and for illegal periodicals from abroad, which I was supposed to clear. No one else had a key. If the key was found on me it would be traced by the police, and give them access to the Party mail until our London group could be warned to stop using it. There was nowhere to hide it; it was too large to swallow. I could think of only one way out. I dropped it in the chamber pot, and in due course emptied my bowels over it. In the morning, still unwashed and unfed, I was taken from the cell leaving the pot for others to deal with. Neither the post office box nor the key were ever mentioned by anyone thereafter. It was my last act as an underground operator.

Detectives took me home and searched the house. Again! We had been turned over and searched more times than I could remember. Our cupboards had been ransacked, our bookshelves stripped, our typewriters confiscated. They knew as well as we did that there was nothing to find except perhaps a newspaper cutting or periodical which was now banned even if it had not been when they last searched. That was not something to worry about. A charge of 'possessing' banned material would add little to the weight of offences already around my neck. The thing which did worry me was my critique of Operation Mayibuye, buried amongst the nuts, bolts and old nails in my garage.

Hilda was not home. She had gone out early in search of information, and returned while the search was in progress. She was followed by our friend Tony Hall who was a reporter for the *Rand Daily Mail*, and a photographer. Hilda and Toni were veterans of many a police search, but this one must have been more grisly than others. I was dirty, unshaven and wearing the clothes I had slept in; and at the end I would not be left to tidy up but be carted off together with whatever books and typewriters they decided to take. The police were not searching seriously, only going through the motions. I had some bad moments when they went into the garage and scratched around in a desultory way, trying not to get their hands too dirty. They lifted up the tray of nuts, bolts and the critique of Operation Mayibuye to see if anything was underneath – and moved on. They found nothing of any consequence anywhere.

I had a few moments to talk to Hilda about things like household accounts and the whereabouts of our car. The police stood at our shoulders, listening to every word. I was told to pack a small case with clothes and toiletries – but no books! Keith, little Keith, our six-year-old Treason Trial boy was in my bed with a bad throat, watching with enormous round eyes, not saying anything. My half-packed case stood open in the bedroom while the police pottered about picking up and putting down books. When they were looking the other way, Keith slipped silently out of bed, picked up one of my books and slipped it into the case. A policeman spotted it there a moment later, and removed it. 'No books!' he told me. Keith waited till his back was turned, and slipped out of bed again and slid another book into the case. Neither of us said a word.

I had managed to stay cool up to that moment. But that almost broke me up. I had to fight with myself to avoid bursting into tears – which I suppose would have been terrible for Keith, and possibly worse for me. It would have been the end of my resistance, a signal of submission to those macho policemen and the state power they represented. I was hanging on to myself by my finger nails when I gave Keith a last farewell hug – without tears. A hug for Hilda – there was nothing to say – and I was driven away, not knowing when, if ever, I would see either of them or any of my other children again. That was quite definitely the worst day of my life.

I was taken to Langlaagte Police Station, my case was taken away, and I was locked into a fairly large cell. I was the only prisoner there. The cell gave on to a small yard, encased in wire like a bird-cage, but it had air, light, and a distant view of open veld beyond the wire. There were four iron beds without mattresses, and two filth-encrusted blankets which had been peed, spat and vomited upon – presumably by the drunks who are the usual occupants of police cells. I stayed there alone and unwashed for two days. There was a cold-water tap in the yard; I asked for soap or a towel to be taken from my case. Nothing happened. The Special Branch were unseen, but giving the orders. No soap. No towel.

Food was brought from the staff canteen by a uniformed

policeman, less hostile than the Special Branch. Twice a day it was a great slab of white bread topped with two greasy fried eggs. I ate with my filthy hands – no cutlery by order of the Special Branch – and tried to clean up with cold water. I could not make out whether they were trying to humiliate me, break my spirit or just hoping I would die of neglect. Whatever it was, I was in very poor spirits when, three days later, the Special Branch men returned and carted me and my unopened case off to Pretoria Local Prison.

16

TO SIT IN SOLEMN SILENCE

1963

I am locked into a tiny cell in the prison wing which once housed Pratt's army. It contains a small wooden table, a wooden stool, a chamber pot and a sleeping mat. By piling the stool on the table I can climb up and peer through the barred window opening – though that is strictly *verbode*. Several of the glass louvres are broken and the sharp highveld wind whistles through. Through bars and dusty mesh I can see the yard and the windows of the dormitory I had been in three years before.

The warder in charge of the detainees is a baby-faced thirty-year-old, very hostile, but controlled. It is rumoured around the prison that he has been denied any promotion because he once assaulted a prisoner. He is easily roused to a rage which drains the blood from his face and turns him deathly white. He understands English but only speaks Afrikaans to me – to give orders.

There are rules about everything. Blankets and felt sleeping mat must be folded in prescribed pattern after the early morning bell. They must stay that way till after supper. Shoes are to be left outside the cell door at all times. A small steel bowl for drinking water may be filled during exercise periods; it must last for twenty-four hours. All noise, whistling, singing or calling out is forbidden. Everyone has obviously been ordered not to speak to us except to issue instructions. Nothing happens without the noise of keys clanking, boots thundering down corridors, doors slamming. But without words.

Three times a day the cell door opens fractionally, a boot from outside propels a bowl of food through the opening, and the door slams shut. Twice a day, in mid-morning and mid-afternoon, the door clangs open, a warder says: '*Kom!*' and I am led down the corridor and into a yard. It is enclosed by three-storey high cell blocks on its long sides and by high barbed-wire topped walls at each end. In the centre of the yard is a waist-high brick wall enclosing a w.c., a cold water tap and a shower rose. I have half an hour in which to wash, shave, excrete, exercise and smoke cigarettes. He watches every move, wordless in the entrance doorway. Then again, '*Kom!*', and back to the cell, with the rest of the day and night to kill.

I have been given a small blue card recording my name and prison number. There is a space for 'Charge'. Someone has entered 'ninety days'. My watch has been taken away. I have no books, no paper or pen, nothing to do – and twenty-three hours a day to do it in. Time passes unbelievably slowly. There is deathly silence inside, but distant noise and clamour somewhere outside. I learn to tell the passage of time from the routine sounds outside – from the sound of prisoners polishing the corridor floor, from the clatter of steel food bowls being set down, from serial opening and closing of cell doors, and from the far-off thud of booted feet thundering up or down stairs.

Thundering feet on distant stairs start the working day. Shouted commands drive the black prisoners down from their upper floor cells to a day's hard labour, and drive them back up again amidst blows and curses at the end of the afternoon. The coming of night is marked by the black prisoners singing somewhere far above, singing movingly and in perfect harmony until all lights are switched off. And then a single powerful voice rings out from somewhere amongst them: '*Amaaaandla!*' – the voice of the ANC – perhaps Mandela? And then the answering bass chorus: '*Ngawethu!*' (Power! It shall be ours!) And then silence.

Nights are interminable, fifteen hours between supper at 3 p.m. and breakfast at 6 a.m. In the graveyard silence there is nothing but the occasional squeak of a warder's rubber-soled shoes as he patrols the corridor and peers in through the Judas-holes in the cell doors. Occasionally, when the wind is in the right direction, I can catch the sound of chimes from a distant clock, and for a moment

I can calibrate my internal clock to time in the real world outside.

But prison time has to be read without clocks or watches. Knowledge is power, and knowledge of time is strictly reserved for warders. Prisoners learn to tell the time from the routines. In my cell, I create my own time schedule, calibrated to the slow passage of a sliver of sunlight from the louvred window. It tracks slowly across the cell walls, moving perversely, from west to east until it disappears altogether close to suppertime. I start to divide the day into hours, and then hours into minutes by noting the light as it moves from one small scratch on the wall to the next. But it is better not to. Counting the minutes makes time pass even more slowly. The day goes by faster when there are only hours to live through.

Daily routines scarcely change. But the rules are changed just as one is becoming comfortable with them. At first, personal belongings must be packed away during the day in plastic bags and the table top left pristine. Then the rule changes. Everything – clothes, toiletries and food, must be neatly laid out on the table top – no bags allowed. For a time, cigarettes may be kept and smoked only in the cell; then they are to be held only by a warder and smoked only in the yard. Foodstuffs brought in by visitors are sent back unless they are in factory-sealed cans or bubble-pack plastic; then cans and sealed packs are sent back and eveything must be open for manual examination.

And so it goes, constantly changing and constantly upsetting. Whether it is deliberate or an indication of administrative confusion is never clear. The one rule that seemingly never changes is the rule prohibiting everyone from exchanging words with ninety-day detainees, except to give essential orders. Silence is obligatory.

I am settling in to the daily routine when it is broken without warning. Two Special Branch officers enter the cell in silence. They look me up and down slowly, deliberately, saying nothing. They have the hostile and supercilious stare of Hollywood FBI agents; only the mirrored sunglasses are missing. They leave again in silence. It has been menacing and frightening. Two days later they are back, with a photographer. He sets up his tripod and I am ordered to stand against a wall, facing the camera. I refuse. I say there is nothing in the ninety-day regulations which authorises anyone to photograph me. They don't argue. They just ignore my objections, push me up against the wall unshaven and uncombed, and hold me there while the photographs are taken.

The silence of the cell is less disturbing than the deliberate silence of the human beings who come and go. I know that it is part of the process, designed to break my morale; but that doesn't make it any easier. I calculate that I am speaking less than twenty words a day, and begin to wonder whether my vocal cords will dry up and wither if this goes on. I dare not try talking to myself; my cell may well be bugged and I may let slip something I do not want to. I have never been very talkative, but now I begin to hunger after talk, after conversation more strongly than for either food or drink. I know that Dennis Goldberg and Bob Hepple are close by – I can see their shoes outside their cells when I go out to the yard. They are on either side of me, in cells separated from mine by vacant cells.

I have learnt to know the intervals between the night warder's corridor rounds. Late at night I call out through the ventilator between my cell and the corridor. There is a long silence; then a guarded response, first from Goldberg and then from Hepple. We exchange only a few words. We cannot be sure whether anyone out there is listening in or whether our conversation is being bugged. Just breaking the silence, establishing a communication route is important. What we say can have no influence on anything that is happening to us, but at least we are back in contact. We do little more than exchange signals – words are muffled and distorted by the ventilator. Whistling is better. Dennis and I seem to know the same tunes. In the evenings we routinely whistle duets to reassure ourselves that we are still alive and in touch. 'In An English Country Garden' becomes a call sign by which we summon one another to the ventilator.

Each morning a group of men pass my door on their way to the yard. They talk together as they go, but the words are too muffled for me to understand. By prising up the cover of the Judas-hole I can identify Harold Strachan, Ben Turok and Jack Tarshish who have been sentenced to terms of around three years of imprisonment for offences connected with MK. The sentences had been made under the Explosives Act before the vastly heavier penalties of the Sabotage Act came into force.

I feel envious of them and their prison terms; they at least can talk. They are communicating. I feel as though I would trade my ninety days incommunicado for their three-year sentences with human contact. I catch odd words as they speculate about the ownership of the shoes outside our cell doors. It is impossible to call out to them – they have a warder in tow – so I trace their footfalls to the stairs, to the floor above and to immediately above my cell.

After the night warder has passed I try tapping on the wall – I cannot reach the ceiling even by standing on the table. There is a faint tapping from the floor above. Contact! If there is a code to the knocks from above I cannot decipher it. Perhaps it just means 'Signal received'. I try a slow sequence – one tap, pause; two taps, pause; three taps. Surely whoever is up there must realise this is A,B,C. He does. Someone up there taps back in code: 'Who's there?' It takes several nights before they know who we are down here, and why. But we are communicating! A small gap has been opened in the curtain of isolation.

I had imagined I would be able to cope with ninety-day detention. I can put up with the physical discomfort and the poor food, and even with the absence of light and sun, and the ubiquitous authoritarianism. I had experienced most of them before. But I had not realised the effect of total isolation from all human contact and communication. I had lived through periods of loneliness during my months of house arrest, but those were in relative solitude. That is still a kind of living. It accommodates such reliefs and distractions as reading, writing and music. It allows for occasional human communication and the sight and sound of the world outside. Absolute solitude is different. It is a blank, an emptiness in which the body functions while the mind decays. I had been mentally prepared for loneliness, not for absolute isolation.

There is nothing to do, day or night; nothing to exercise the mind except thinking. And only two things to think about: what might be happening to Hilda and the children; and what terrible end will I face when this solitary confinement is over. Both are upsetting. There is no possible answer to either question, and no way in which to influence them. Thinking of them only raises more and more nightmarish possibilities to undermine my morale and reduce me to a quaking bundle of fears. I have to force my mind to turn away on to other things. But in this tomb-like silence, what other things? I return constantly to the same terrifying grooves. Thinking is destroying me. I have to find mindless things – any things, however purposeless – to drive out thinking.

I take to pacing my cell obsessively – three paces, about turn, three paces, about turn – for hour on hour. I count as I go, mentally computing distances. If one pace is two and a half feet, three paces plus an about turn make nine feet; a mile is 1 760 yards which is 5 280 feet which amounts to 587 laps. I keep counting the laps, counting and counting until my concentration wanders and the figure slips from my mind. Still, I pace on as relentlessly as a hamster on a wheel. There is no point to the counting or to the mental struggle to convert the count to miles, yards and feet except that it prevents thinking and it kills time. I set myself a time which must pass before I can stop, and measure the passage of time by the sliver of sunlight which traverses the cell walls. I convert time and distance to miles per hour and feet per minute, solely to avoid thinking of anything else.

I discover pointless activities which will occupy my mind and kill the time. There is a stray pin amongst my toilet gear. I sit for hours on the hard stool, straining my eyes in poor light in order to unpick alternate threads from a handkerchief. I reduce it to an ever more intricate pattern until it is nothing but lace and then a mess of distressed threads which is good for nothing except to be thrown away. With the pin I scratch away at the painted surface of a food can, millimetre by millimetre, until all the background is gone and only the letters remain. And then I scratch away each letter until there is nothing left but naked aluminium.

I force myself to follow a daily routine of such useless time-killers as these. Without them, thinking returns to torture me.

I recall that some time ago I had designed a ten-foot long slide-rule made up out of a coiled steel tape measure. That leads to another time-killing routine – a daily session inventing devices to take over some of life's lesser chores, like threading a needle which is something I have never mastered. Afternoons pass as I pace up and down, designing improbable gadgets in my head. One day it is a device for adding gummed reinforcing rings to punched holes in filing paper; another an apparatus to keep car batteries permanently topped up with acid; and then, most ambitious of all, a tool for cutting multiple dovetail joints in wood which keeps me working for days on end. I believe it is solved. I check and recheck in my mind and it seems perfect. I itch to get my hands on pencil and paper to draw it out,[1] and move on to another time-killing, thought-killing device.

I depend on these routine sessions to see me through the day – even if they amount to no more than pacing the floor, playing with pins, or dreaming up gadgets. They not only shut out night-mare thought but also all consciousness of passing time. Every day becomes exactly like every other, without any variation to mark off how many days have passed, or how many there are to go before the magic span of ninety is complete. I *have* to keep a record; I *have* to know. I take to marking off each day with a blob of toothpaste inside my shaving case. But there is no indication of whether the last blob was made this morning or yesterday. The sameness of each day erodes the memory, so that one is left only with uncertainty, and something new to worry over. Marking the date must be given its own slot in the daily routine.

There is a conspiracy in the prison to break into my routine before it is thoroughly established. An unspeaking warder enters and dumps a Bible on my table. It is more than a week since I have had anything to read. I cannot resist breaking off my routine pacing and start reading at once. It must be around thirty years since I last opened a Bible. I have never read the New Testament. I start in on it and read on as long as the light lasts. At this rate I know I will have reached the end long before the ninety days are up. I rebuild my routine to include a strictly rationed period of daily Bible reading.[2]

The rebuilt routine is again interrupted by a warder. Any dirty clothes I have are to be handed over for washing; someone has come to collect it. He says nothing more, and ignores my questions. I know that prisoners awaiting trial can send their laundry home; perhaps ninety-day detainees may do the same. I hand my dirty clothes over; the morning passes. Some time in the afternoon my routine is broken into again. A different warder delivers a bundle

---

[1] When I do, I see it is fatally flawed, an impossible object like something in an Escher drawing. Evidence of solitary-cell dementia!

[2] Even so, I read it twice end to end in the ninety days. I could not face a third. It did little for my peace of mind, despite the belief that there are 'no atheists in foxholes'. I was in a deep, deep hole, and still an atheist.

of clean clothes and a packet of chocolate and fruit. It can only have come from Hilda, which means she is alive and still at liberty out there. Thanks be. But the thoughts that I have been suppressing are out of the box again. What is happening to the children? How are they all managing? What is going to happen to us all?

Even that remote contact with Hilda should cheer me up, but it does not. It breaks down my defences. I begin to brood on the unutterable mess I have made of my life, and theirs. I am shaken anew by fear and worry over what might be happening to them out there. I am close to breakdown but I dare not give way to tears. Not for fear of losing face with some macho warders and Security men, but because I know that if once I let go there will be no way by which I will be able to redeem whatever there is left of my life. My hope and confidence, my sense of self and of my own integrity will drain away. If I allow myself to give way to self-pity I do not think I will survive.

I am still in low state when once again I am taken from my cell without explanation. Detective Sergeant Dirker who arrested me at Rivonia is sitting beside a desk in a prison office. He is a heavy, paunchy man with little piggy eyes, a small Hitler-style black moustache, a lock of black hair hanging Hitler-style over one eye. He is rumoured to be Prime Minister Verwoerd's brother-in-law. He is, as always, lowering and hostile.

We remain staring wordlessly at each other until Captain Swanepoel arrives and takes over the power seat at the desk. He is short and as powerfully built as a Springbok rugby forward. He seems to have no neck; his bullet head grows straight out of his shoulders. He has sandy hair, a fiery red complexion, and a well-established reputation for brutal treatment of prisoners. He also stares at me for some time, saying nothing. This must be a means of intimidation they have learnt from the CIA. At length he stands up and strips off his uniform jacket. Across his chest he has a leather holster and a large calibre revolver which he removes very deliberately and places on the desk close to his right hand. I am not sure whether he intends to shoot me or beat me up with it, or whether he is daring me to make a grab for it. With Swanepoel, anything is possible. I am scared stiff, and probably show it. It is mid-winter, but the sweat is pouring off me.

They start firing questions at me. No good cop/bad cop act

here; both are fierce, hostile and come down heavily. They want to know everything there is to know about Lilliesleaf Farm and anyone who had been there. I know that there is only one way to respond to interrogation: say nothing! Don't try lying. Don't try answering some questions and not others. Say nothing, whatever happens. Anything else is a short path to disaster. I am determined to say nothing. That determination had wobbled momentarily soon after my arrest, when my morale was at its lowest and I had toyed briefly with the idea of trying to lay all responsibility for everything at Rivonia on people who were already out of the country. As soon as my reason returned, I rejected the whole idea. I had no idea what evidence might have been found at Rivonia, and no idea what anyone else under arrest might be saying. I would only have talked my way into even deeper trouble. Fortunately, no one had bothered to interrogate me at that time. And now that they have, I tell Dirker and Swanepoel that I have nothing to say.

Even as I say that, I start thinking of our comrades Leon Levy and Wolfie Kodesh who had been detained well before the arrests at Rivonia. They may have been the country's first ninety-day detainees. After some weeks in detention they had both been given one-way exit permits and had left the country. I knew nothing of the circumstances, but it seemed probable that the exit permits were the result of some sort of deal. The idea is creeping into my mind that I too might be offered an exit permit if I play my cards right. And if I am, I will turn it down and use my refusal to bolster a future application for bail.

At the time, the idea seems rather smart, and I decide to follow it. I refuse, time and again, to answer any of Swanepoel's questions, but I try to imply that I might change my mind if there was something in it for me. I must be slightly deranged. They are shouting and browbeating and threatening me with the prospect of a death sentence. I am not much of an actor, but I am trying to persuade them that my refusal is not absolutely final.

It is a stupid mistake. I have made a trap for myself, and encouraged Swanepoel and Dirker to return time after time to try and break down my resistance. Every new session leaves me shaken and trembling, with all my worst fears and nightmares revived anew. It takes weeks before they stop the torment – but never make any offer of an exit permit. Though the threat of violence is always heavy in the air, they never resort to assault or physical violence.[3] I learn only one thing from them. They are preparing for a great show trial which will justify them and their state to the world. The accused must show no signs of torture. The state is intending to press a demand for death sentences for us all.

Again I am taken from my cell to an office where there is a middle-aged man in a dark suit and rimless glasses. He gives me the familiar cold, unblinking stare. I stand while he delivers a bored recital which he has delivered so often that he is word perfect. He announces he is a magistrate, appointed under the Act to make good the Minister's assurances to Parliament that ninety-day detainees would have their welfare safeguarded by a visiting magistrate. He knows and I know that it is an absurd charade. The state imprisons and strips us of our civil rights; and then sends its own flunky to ensure that our civil rights are not being abused.

He plays his part in the farce with a straight face. 'Is there anything you wish to say?'

There is a lot I wish to say but the opportunity has been sprung on me without warning. I am not prepared. I manage to say that I am being held in unlawful conditions; I have been deprived of any reading material without any such provision in the law. He doesn't look at me while I speak. He scratches away with his pen in what seems to be a ledger, apparently recording it all verbatim. His pen pauses when I pause.

'Anything else?'

I say I cannot think of anything else. He scratches away, and the interview is over.

A week later the whole performance is repeated, including his prologue which ends again with: 'Anything you wish to say?'

'Yes. I would like to know what happened to my complaints of last week?'

His pen scratches away. I had learnt to read texts upside down from sitting on my children's beds and reading bedtime stories to

---

[3] Not to me or any of the other accused – except Motsoaledi and Mlangeni who were assaulted in police stations, and said so in court. So did several of the Rivonia staff who gave evidence for the state. Judge Quartus de Wet seemed disinterested and asked the prosecutor to investigate. Nothing more was heard of the matter.

them from one side of the book while they looked at the pictures from the other. I read what he is writing. 'Yes. I would like to know what happened to my complaints of last week.'

He looks up. 'Anything else?'

I say: 'Don't I get any reply?' and I watch him write down: 'Don't I get any reply?'

Then again: 'Anything else?'

I do not feel inclined to take a part in this farce. I consider saying 'The visiting magistrate is a slimy, time-serving shit' just to see whether he writes it all down so calmly. But I am in enough trouble already and avoid the temptation.

The interview ends, as do all his weekly visits, which confirm my opinion that the visiting magistrate *is* a slimy, time-serving shit who is lending himself to the state's deception of the public. His only real purpose here is to keep his job and his pension safe.

And so it goes on, one disruptive intervention after another. Again the curt summons: '*Kom!*' I follow the warder out of my cell into a small visitor's room split in two by a counter and a heavy mesh screen. I wait on one side; Hilda is led in on the other. I have never doubted that she will be moving heaven and earth to get in touch with me by fair means or foul.

I have no idea how she has contrived it, and no knowledge of the angst and humiliation she has had to go through on the way. But I have clung to the belief that, sooner or later, she will fight her way through. And when she does, I will have to be ready to warn her of my critique of Operation Mayibuye which lies like a ticking time bomb in our garage. In my hours of idleness I have worked out a form of words which will tell her something she doesn't know anything about without alerting those who will be listening in.

The warder tells us we are allowed only ten minutes; we are not to mention anything other than family and personal matters or the visit will be immediately terminated. We cannot touch. We talk across the mesh while a warder stands at Hilda's side listening to every word. There is so much that we want to know and tell about each other and about the children. But it is like an unexpected long-distance phone call; it is difficult to rise above the level of 'How are you?' 'Fine. And you?' But at least we can each now see the other is alive and reasonably well. We talk trivialities about household keys and accounts which we do not need to talk about except to keep the talk within the official limits. It allows us to listen to nuances and hints which only we will understand.

I slide my prepared coded message about the Mayibuye document into the talk. Hilda asks no questions, but I see she is hanging on to every word, frowning and memorising to decode it later. She nods to tell me she has got it. And then our time is up. We exchange words of love and hope, and that is it. I had been hoping for such a visit with the feverish anticipation of a dope addict for his next shot. And like that shot, the exhilarating high has a short life. Almost as soon as I reach my cell again, the euphoria evaporates. I am unsure whether the visit has restored or further undermined my nerves, unsure whether the visit has left me feeling better, or worse.

Communicating may be vital for survival, but breaking it off is to die a little. Resuming communication with Hilda becomes an obsession. With the prison's maze of secrets and conspiracies, there has to be a way. I have been drawn into some of them. At breakfast time when my cell door is unlocked, an unseen 'trusty' slides a bowl of porridge and a tin thimble of brown sugar through the gap. I start shaking the sugar over the porridge and a match-head less than a centimetre long falls out, together with a minute sliver of the 'strike' strip from a match-box. The match head has been finely split into four slivers. I tuck them carefully out of sight wondering how they can be put to use. Later that morning, a group of prisoners are polishing the floor of the corridor outside my door. They chatter amongst themselves. There must be a warder somewhere, watching them. The outer flap over the Judas-hole in the door slides silently aside and two cigarettes drop through. Smoking in cells is forbidden, but after nightfall it is possible, and better for being illicit.

With a little practice I master the trick of using a sliver of match to light a spill of paper and so enjoy an after-dark cigarette. I never discover who has smuggled in the contraband, but matches and cigarettes continue to arrive every few days. The prison runs by rules designed to prevent mutiny or escape. They miss the point. Mutiny and escape are rare, but conspiracy against the rules is endemic. Beating the system restores the prisoner's sense of independence and manhood which the system denies. It makes co-conspirators of all the prisoners, regardless of their politics. They use their endless time to devise ways for pitting their ingenuity against the system.

'Exercise' time. A duty warder is leaning against the wall,

watching me from the yard doorway. There is a waist-high wall around the ablutions area. He can only see me from the waist up as I sit on the w.c. A stub of pencil half an inch long is lying on the floor close to the w.c. bowl. I retrieve and pocket it without the warder noticing. I have no idea who has left it there, quite deliberately. Perhaps Dennis who had been in the yard before me. It is worth its weight in gold. I have no immediate use for it, but it is as dangerous as dynamite, and might explode on me in the event of a search. Back in the cell I wrap it up in some polythene from a sweet wrapping, prise open the sealed end of my toothpaste tube and bury it in the paste.

When I have anything worth saying I can now write messages for Bob or Dennis on a scrap of rolled up paper left in the w.c. Now that I can communicate with them there is little that I can find to say. But I have half a way of communicating with Hilda. I have to find a way to get a written message out. I have no way to bribe or cajole a warder or a prisoner going out – I have no more access to them than I have to Hilda. The only other way out is a message amongst my dirty shirts. I examine every item of clothing in minute detail. Anything written directly on any of it will surely be noticed. I have to find a way of hiding it. I hold every piece up to the light as a warder might do. One possibility emerges – the double thickness of my shirt collars. I unpick a short length of the collar seam. I write a short message on a strip cut from a handkerchief and feed it into the collar between the layers of material. Once the collar has been rubbed flat and the loose ends of thread cut away, it has a reasonable chance of passing a routine check.

I hand it over to be sent out with my next batch of laundry. The next few hours are gruelling. I am tense and on edge in case it is detected at the gate. Nothing much it likely to happen to me if it is. They can scream and shout about it, perhaps even cancel my laundry privileges or put me on a spare diet. But the worst thing will be if they search my cell and confiscate my pencil, shutting down my one channel of communication with Hilda.

I sweat out the day, worrying myself silly. Nothing happens. By the end of the day I start luxuriating in my success, only to start another bout of worry. What if Hilda does not spot the message, and brings the shirt back to be checked on its way in with the message still in place? If she *does* spot it, she will surely decide to smuggle in a reply of her own in the next batch of clean clothes.

Thinking about the possible consequences of that for her makes me sick. I relive the tension of stepping into the lion's den at Marshall Square to sign the register, knotted up by doubt about ever being allowed to come out again. For that I had had no option. Hilda would be doing it voluntarily. And I know that nothing will deter her. I wait out the rest of the week wracked in fear for her, dreading the advent of Sunday and unable to think of anything else.

Sunday. A warder opens my cell and delivers a bundle of clean clothes. My hands are trembling, making it hard for me to examine my message-shirt closely. There is no gap in the collar seam! I decide I am making a mistake; it must have been a different shirt. I examine them all, feverishly. No gaps. I think I must be going mad. Perhaps there never *was* any message, only my fevered imagination. I am growing frantic and examining my shirts again and again, unable to believe it. There has to be a gap! And then there is – a piece of collar seam where the stitching is minutely different from the rest. It has been restored so delicately that it is virtually invisible. I unpick it once again, and inside is a strip of cloth with a letter from Hilda. We have cracked it and are in touch again! We are communicating! I am exhilarated, but still trembling like an old leaf.

I have a new intoxicating routine of writing to Hilda weekly. She is more inventive than I. Somehow – I no longer remember how – a freshly laundered shirt brings in a needle and some thread so that I too can restitch the collars I send out – though I am a clumsy seamstress. Before many weeks, the pencil is near its end. I send Hilda an SOS, and the following Sunday's delivery includes a ripe banana. Either she has forgotten that I have an allergy to bananas or it is not meant for eating. I slice it open carefully, gagging over the smell. Threaded into its length is the thin ink tube from a ballpoint pen. I hide it away inside a seam of my leather shaving case.

I have a new routine – laundry out every Wednesday, clean laundry and some goodies in every Sunday. Sunday mornings are hard. I am on tenterhooks waiting for the sign that Hilda has come and gone safely, her contraband undetected. One Sunday I am left waiting and suffering. Something must have gone wrong. There is nothing delivered to my cell at the usual time before lunch; nothing during the afternoon or evening. I have a fearful day, followed by a terrible sleepless night. I know Hilda could not possibly have forgotten, or simply given me a miss. Something terrible must have happened. Perhaps she has been arrested or been forced to flee; the children might be alone and in a dreadful state. My imagination conjures up one fearful scenario after another until I bring myself close to breakdown. I try to convince myself that there could be a simple explanation – a car breakdown or the arrival of an unexpected visitor at home. I cannot carry on with my morning routine. And then, at midday Monday, the usual bundle of clothes and foodstuffs arrives, without explanation. I only discover long afterwards that it has been left lying in some prison office since Sunday morning.

Bob and Dennis have been moved into cells on either side of mine, and unidentified newcomers have taken over their former cells. We can now communicate by tapping on the dividing walls. In the mornings we are now all taken out into the yard together to leave yard-time for the newcomers, and threatened with fire and brimstone if we talk to each other – which encourages us to find a way to do so. We make a routine of walking singly, back and forth along the length of the yard as far from the warder as possible, so that in each lap we pass one another face to face. The warder can only see one face and one back. The back says something quietly without visible head movement; the face listens and perhaps lip-reads. We have manufactured a fractured semblance of conversation, but it is conversation which represents another small chink in the curtain of isolation.

We pass stubs of pencil or short pieces of ballpoint pen to each other via the w.c. postal route, together with messages written on tightly rolled strips of paper which can be flushed away after reading. There is conspiracy everywhere; but also counter-conspiracy. We are in the exercise yard when the authorities launch a pre-emptive strike by putting us all through a body search before we can return to our cells. I had left mine in good military order, blankets folded and stacked in prescribed format, clothes and toilet articles in full view on the table. I return to a disaster area. Blankets have been scattered and thrown down in heaps, clothes and toiletries strewn on the floor. Tubes of toothpaste and shaving soap have been opened and their tops left open where they fell; the roll of toilet paper has been unwound to the end and left wreathed over everything as though a typhoon has whipped through. The warders show no interest and make no explanation. It could have been a search for contraband or just a way to unsettle us. Prison jargon describes it as a '*skud*' – literally a shake. But whether shake-up or shake-down is not certain. It is part of their conspiracy against us.

Then Dennis vanishes! One night he is there, and the next morning he is not. There are no shoes outside his cell door, and he does not join us in the yard. There is no sound from his cell. After nightfall I try calling him up by whistling 'In An English Country Garden'. Silence. It is disturbing and frightening. I had come to take more comfort from my whistling and wall-tapping with him than I realised. A week or more passes without any clues. Then late one night I am awakened by shouts and the clanking of chains in the corridor. The door of Dennis's cell is unlocked, there is more clanking, and the door slams shut again. I wait till all is quiet and the last footfalls have died away before I try whistling our call-sign again. There is a long wait, and then a slow, somewhat off-key response, as though he can barely summon up the breath to whistle. Dennis is back.

The next morning he is brought into the yard, dishevelled, unshaven and in chains. His ankles are shackled and connected by a heavy chain to a chain belt around his waist. He must either drag the spare length of chain along the ground behind him, or lift it up between his legs and carry it in his hands as he shuffles along splay-legged. The sight shakes me to the core of my being. We have never been real friends; we are little more than acquaintances thrown together by chance. But in that awful place with its echoes of slamming doors and of shouting warders herding human beings like cattle with blows and boots, it seems to me to be the ultimate expression of apartheid: a human being treated like a mad dog. It is the saddest sight I have ever seen – the last straw. I know in that moment that I have had as much of the apartheid state as I can bear.

That evening I write a letter to Hilda to tell her how this day has changed me and my feelings about the country. I tell her that I have had enough and can take no more of this brutal country and its inhumanities. If I ever get out of prison now, my deepest urge will be to shake myself free of my love-hate relationship with it. Now, when it is no longer in the realm of the possible, I am ready to leave the country for good.

Much later, when we are able to talk freely together, Dennis tells me his story. He had been taken from his cell to a prison in Vereeniging where he was to be interrogated. The police had by then discovered Trevallyn farm and records of his investigations into the manufacture and supply of hand grenades and land-mines. Dennis is extremely ingenious. He devised a way to doctor his cell door so that the bolt did not slide home even when the handle was turned and locked. He decided to make a break for freedom. He opened his cell door during the afternoon, squeezed through a window on to a low level roof, and dropped to the ground. Unfortunately, he dropped past the window of a cell below, and someone raised the alarm. Warders had given chase across the veld and outran him before he could reach the plantation he was making for. He had been brought back and put in chains according to rules for escapees.[4] No one bothers to question whether they apply to a ninety-day detainee who is exempted from the usual prison rules – a legal subtlety of the apartheid state.

There comes a day when I am taken out to the exercise yard. I think I must be beginning to hallucinate; Jimmy Kantor is there. We are not allowed to talk but exchange nods of recognition. I do not know him well. I have met him socially on a few occasions through his sister Annmarie Wolpe and her husband Harold who have been close friends of ours. I know Jimmy as a chirpy, almost happy-go-lucky, and outgoing character. He is a well-known lawyer with a mainly criminal clientele, a socialite who mixes with the rich and beautiful people of fast society. His world is so far removed from ours that his presence in prison, amongst subversive politicals, is quite incomprehensible.

Next morning, I leave a note for him next to the w.c., which says little more than: 'Welcome! What the hell brings you here? You're supposed to get people out of here, not get yourself in.' I roll a tiny stub of pencil into the note, with the PS: 'This is like gold. Guard it with your life!' The next day his reply. Harold Wolpe and Arthur Goldreich have escaped from Marshall Square lock-up and are on the run. A nationwide manhunt for them is under way. Jimmy is being held either as an accomplice in their escape or as a

---

[4] Chains are left on day and night. Dennis found nights intolerable, and devised a way of picking the locks underneath his blankets and relocking them before dawn next morning.

hostage for their return. It is astounding news. Goldreich's arrest as the householder of Lilliesleaf Farm I can understand. But not Wolpe's, although I know he has been involved in some mapping and intelligence work for MK. I am desperate to know what it implies for all of us. But even if I could talk to Jimmy, I doubt if I would learn very much. Jimmy is strictly non-political. He has no interest in the ANC, MK or Lilliesleaf Farm and probably knows less about them than I do.

I have assumed that he would destroy my note without being told. But his experience of prison is all from the other side – from interviewing his clients from outside the bars. He has in fact taken my note back to his cell and hidden it between the pages of his Bible. A few days later there is a routine *skud* and the note and his pencil stub are both confiscated. Before I am aware that the prison know that I have a pencil somewhere, my cell is turned over and laid waste in the most thorough and destructive search ever. They do not uncover the ballpoint pen in my shaving case, so a few days later they repeat the exercise. Again the pen survives. I have no idea why they are giving me this going over. I assume that it has to do with Hilda, and that they are searching here for evidence against her. It means she must be in imminent danger, if not already under arrest. I am driving myself frantic with worry again, without understanding what is really going on.

Solitary confinement is getting to me. My hands are shaking all the time. I wake up in the morning feeling as though I have been punctured and all the air has seeped out of me. I have a terrible heaviness as though I am a hundred years old. I struggle for the energy to move or to do anything at all except sit and contemplate – and worry. I am aware that I am slipping, and that the boundaries between illusion and reality are dissolving so that I am no longer sure which is which. I wake in the middle of one night thinking I am hearing someone shouting in the corridor. He is effing and blinding in unmistakable London English in a place where all altercations are in Afrikaans. I hear barked commands and curses in Afrikaans, the sounds of struggle and of scuffles, and then a cell door slams shut and official boots retreat along the corridor. Silence. Have I really heard it, or been dreaming? I have to know. I try calling through my ventilator as quietly as I can: 'Who's there?' An English voice roars out: 'Sid Kitching.'

I am still not sure. I know Sid Kitching – I have not seen him for years. He is an immigrant from Britain who I think has been living in Swaziland. I had met him when he arrived in South Africa from Britain, bringing an uncensored and banned Chinese film as a gift to the resistance movement. He was always talkative, irrepressible, and what the army would call 'incurably Bolshie'. Can he possibly be here? And if so, why? Next morning he again shatters the funereal silence of the place by shouting to someone about his 'rights' as only a foreigner to South Africa would do, and demanding to see the British consul. And then, overnight, he is gone as suddenly as he arrived. Or have I dreamed it all? I never hear of him again.

I am becoming slightly paranoid and think I am losing my grip because of the diet. I write despairingly to Hilda for food which will keep me sane. I need it. There is a toilet roll beside the chamber pot in my cell. I had been warned by the warder who issued it: 'This has to last a full month!' Weeks later I am unrolling what remains of it and calculating whether there is enough paper to last. When I realise what I am doing, I come out of a trance. I tell myself I must be mad – there is no sense in this. I roll it all up again and forget about it. And a few days later catch myself counting the unrolled sheets again, and calculating.

I have a new fantasy. When my ninety days are over, I will only be charged with breaking my bans. I will be able to apply for bail and must prepare my argument for that. I worry away, day after day, on a case for bail, until it seems to me complete. It is based on my conduct over many years which shows unarguably that I am not likely to try and abscond. I had been charged with sedition and given bail during the Mine Strike of 1946; I had stayed and stood trial. In 1956, when most of my close colleagues had been arrested and charged with treason, I had made no attempt to escape, and had been arrested at home ten days later. I had again been given nominal bail, and had stayed and stood trial through all the years that the case went on. In 1960, when most of my colleagues were detained under Emergency Regulations, I had stayed at home until arrested, again some days later. Even after the Minister had named me in Parliament as one of the targets of the ninety-day law, I had stayed at home making no attempt to escape, and for more than a year thereafter I had reported to the police daily and observed a twelve-hour house arrest order.

It seems to me to be an unanswerable case. I half convince myself that I will be given bail, while in the back of my mind there is a black shadow of a *real* case I will have to face. I try not to think of that. I start building fantasy on fantasy. I will be granted bail and will set out to leave the country for ever. I have no passport, but I have an uncle who looks like me. I will beg, borrow or steal his passport to get me through immigration controls at a minor airport where I might not be recognised. The real give-away will not be my face but my walk. I must disguise my walk to prevent recognition. I start practising a splay-footed, slightly Chaplinesque walk in place of my normal pigeon-toed gait. I keep practising, back and forth for hours on end, as though my life really depends on it. I keep it up until I begin to feel – or to imagine? – that the joints between hip and thigh are working loose. I think I can hear them jangling in their sockets, and take fright. I may be crippling myself perman-ently. I have to stop.

The fantasy collapses. I know deep down that there is going to be no bail. I am taken out to see the magistrate again, and there in the corridor is Alfred Nzo. We can do no more than nod to each other from a distance. I know he is in a third consecutive term of ninety days.[5] I have a new nightmare: the same thing might happen to me. I do not think I can stand another ninety days of solitary confinement as Alfred has. I have to believe that whatever is going to happen will happen after ninety days. I check my toothpaste calendar and count the days remaining. I don't trust the result and count it again and again. And the result is always the same. But can I be sure? I might have missed making the mark on some days. Or even made it twice on others. Is the true figure greater or less than I have counted? There is no calendar with which to check. And in any case perhaps even ninety days is meaningless; I might have to go to 180 or 270. I have to know, but no one here will tell me. They tell me nothing and leave me to drive myself slowly crazy with uncertainty.

---

[5] Alfred Nzo, formerly Transvaal ANC Secretary, survived three consecutive terms of ninety days in solitary confinement before being released without charge. Later he became General Secretary at ANC HQ in Lusaka, and was Minister of Foreign Affairs in the Mandela government.

The regular warders go off on Sundays, and stand-ins take over. My calendar count is in the eighties when Bob, Dennis, Jimmy and I are taken out into the yard by a stand-in who either does not know the rules that apply to us, or does not care. We pass a few *sotto voce* words to test him out. He sits on a step and takes no interest in us. We start quietly conversing. Still no reaction. Suddenly we are in a huddle, talking together.

Talking! It is unbelievable, miraculous, like a return from the dead. I have not lost the knack of speech; my vocal cords have come through good as new. We talk together uncontrollably, interrupting each other and talking at once just for the sheer joy of it after so long. For our statutory half hour 'exercise' we are once again back in human society. We are wallowing in the knowledge that we are still human and can again do simple human things like talk and laugh and touch. This I know is real; one cannot dream this ecstasy and relief. I am drunk with it, for the few fleeting minutes before our time is up, and we are locked back into our solitary cells again. But the glow lingers on.

In those moments, I have learnt the bare bones of the Jimmy Kantor story. After the Rivonia raid, Harold Wolpe had decided to make a dash for Bechuanaland. He had been arrested at a farm on the South African side of the border before he could get across. He had been held without charge at Marshall Square together with Arthur Goldreich. Two young Indian comrades, Mosie Moolla and Abdulhai (Charlie) Jassat were in a nearby cell. Together they had bribed a young warder, staged a mock attack on him, and used his keys to let themselves out into the night.

The escape of two key figures in the much publicised Rivonia drama had been an immediate press and radio sensation. A national manhunt had been mounted without any result, except for a plethora of sensationalised accounts and theories about an apparently perfect escape. They had been reported from here and there, but they seemed to have vanished into thin air. The warder had been arrested and was being charged as an accessory to the escape.[6]

---

[6]The escape was a comedy of errors, with last-minute improvisations and missed secret rendezvous. Weeks later, Wolpe and Goldreich reached Bechuanaland by light plane from Swaziland, disguised as priests, followed later by Moolla and Jassat. See Hilda Bernstein, *The World That Was Ours* (Heinemann) and Annmarie Wolpe, *A Long Way Home* (Virago).

Jimmy has become the fall guy for the embarrassment of the Special Branch over the great escape. He was the principal of the legal firm where Harold had worked, and related to the owner of the border farm where Harold had been captured while trying to leave the country before the escape.

Many Special Branch men with whom Jimmy has been on first-name terms know that he has had no part in any political movements. But they need a scapegoat for their own incompetence, and Jimmy has been picked on – a proxy for Harold. It is a petty, vindictive act which has hit Jimmy very hard. He has been shaken by the unexpectedly vicious police hostility towards him, and by the fact that overnight he has been stripped of all the rights and privileges of an 'officer of the court'.

Jimmy Kantor is the real innocent amongst us in every sense of the word. His arrest has wrecked his social reputation and his family life, destroyed his legal practice and ruined him financially. I feel a sense of outrage at what is being done to him which I cannot feel for the rest of us who have at least done something of our own volition to finish up where we are.

Jimmy's victimisation carries on till our ninety days are done. Strangely, I recall so many trivial incidents and irritations of those interminable days. But of the ninetieth day itself I remember almost nothing. I can no longer picture the scene or recall the way in which those of us arrested at Rivonia were formally charged with sabotage, together with Jimmy Kantor, Nelson Mandela, Elias Motsoaledi and Andrew Mlangeni.

All I remember is that, before the day is out, I am back in the Pretoria Local Jail, in the same cell on the same corridor as before. But with a difference. I am no longer a 'ninety day detainee'. We are all now graduated into 'awaiting trial prisoners'. We are no longer incommunicado. We can speak and be spoken to. We can be visited by families and lawyers. And we can no longer be denied access to books or writing materials. I know how it feels to return to the world after hibernation.

17

IN A DEEP DARK DOCK

1963 – 64

We come together for the first time since our arrest at Rivonia. Even in the greyness of the prison interview room it is like a club reunion – handshakes, embraces and greetings.

I have not seen Nelson since his trial eighteen months before. Then he had been magnificent, a traditional Xhosa leopard-skin across his bared torso, his skin the colour of deep chocolate. Now his flesh has melted away. He is thin and rangy, but as erect as ever, his flashing smile of greeting unchanged. Robben Island has faded his complexion to dull yellow, and dressed him in the black convict's uniform of khaki shirt, short trousers and rubber-soled sandals. He had always been the best dressed and most clothes-conscious of ANC activists. Even in this mocking 'boy's' outfit he stands tall and distinguished.

We all show signs of wear, and are thinner, more subdued. With us now are two old comrades – Elias Motsoaledi and Andrew Mlangeni, ANC and MK activists who had been arrested some weeks after the Rivonia raid.

Eleven of us have been jointly charged, but there are only nine at this and subsequent consultations. Kantor is not with us. He has had no part in any of the matters which have given rise to the case. He has been dragged in to save the face of prosecutor and Security Police after the humiliation of the escapes from Marshall Square. He has taken on lawyers of his own – very sensibly – and will conduct a separate defence. Bob Hepple is nowhere to be seen. He has been taken from the Pretoria Prison by Security Police. The rumour in legal circles is that he is co-operating with the prosecutors. If they are breaking the rules to interrogate him now that he is already charged, they must surely intend to drop the charge and call him as a witness against us.

I am sad about that. I have known him since he was a child. I know that anyone is liable to crack under the stress of solitary confinement, but he has shown no sign that he has done so. Breakdown would be forgivable; testifying against his comrades would not. It would be seen as an act of cowardice and betrayal which will be remembered, and will haunt him. I hope that he will still pull back from the brink, but for the moment we are nine.

An impressive legal team has been gathered together somehow by Hilda and Bram Fischer. Our long-standing comrade Bram will lead the team. He has defended us and many of our comrades before. He understands the political issues as well as any of us. He is a leading member of the Communist Party and has been involved in the political events leading up to this trial. With him are other old friends and sometime defenders: Vernon Berrange who has returned from retirement in Swaziland for the case; George Bizos who has been with us in many of our political and legal battles; and Arthur Chaskalson[1] whom most of us are meeting for the first time. We know nothing of him, but Bram recommends him as a brilliant young barrister who is prepared to risk a lucrative career in commercial and insurance law to take a case against the tide of public opinion. It proves to be an inspired choice.

The rules require barristers to be briefed by solicitors, not directly by clients. Solicitors have been hard to find for such a political case at this time. Bram, in an inspired moment, has steered Hilda towards Joel Joffe. Most of us had never met him. Well before our arrest, he had given up his practice as a barrister and prepared to emigrate to Australia. His personal and household belongings had already been shipped out when Jimmy Kantor and his partner Wolpe were arrested, and their legal practice left in a leaderless shambles. Joel had been persuaded to step in temporarily to complete their

---

[1] Now Judge President of South Africa's Constitutional Court.

unfinished legal business. He had postponed his emigration when Hilda – a complete stranger – approached him to act as solicitor for an uncertain number of people in a case where no charge had yet been levelled and no date set. Joel, typically, agreed; he never seems to refuse help to anyone who needs it.[2]

This is an equally inspired choice. He is the mildest and least aggressive of men who combines a fierce sense of right and justice with great empathy. He becomes the lynch-pin of our whole defence, and something much more than a lawyer for us all. He is not only the organiser of our legal affairs but also makes himself the guardian of our families' personal and financial troubles. In the course of the trial he extends his responsibilities to the legal and personal troubles of many other victims of the police state and *their* families and dependants.

We have time only for a short discussion with them before being taken to the Supreme Court in an armoured convoy with motor cycle outriders and screaming sirens. There are armed men clearing our passage and holding back the traffic at every road intersection, as if in expectation of an armed uprising.

We are ushered into the court from the basement cells below. The prosecution team is already in its place, with Dr Yutar, Attorney General for the Transvaal, standing in the centre of a knot of prosecutors and Security Police. He is enjoying his moment, looking round at us and basking in the spotlight of publicity. There is a stack of bound volumes on the desk before him. As soon as the judge is seated he gives a Ciceronian sweep to his black gown, looks around to ensure the attention of the gallery, and calls 'The case of The State versus the National High Command and Others'.

He hands the judge a copy of the indictment. It is in four volumes, all beautifully bound, with hard covers and gold lettering. He makes a dramatic production out of handing similar sets to a few press reporters – although some had received advance copies the day before. And finally, a single copy without covers to be shared

---

[2]Before the trial was over, the Australian government revoked his immigration permit. His household and personal belongings were packed and standing at the docks for shipment. He made an eleventh-hour change of plan, and emigrated to Britain. See the detailed account in Hilda Bernstein's *The World That Was Ours*.

by all the members of the defence team. It is a calculated gesture of hostility or contempt – our introduction to the petty malice of Dr Percy Yutar.

Bram makes an immediate request for the case to be adjourned for six weeks to allow us to study the indictment. His manner in court is always quietly courteous, almost diffident, and apparently unemotional. He uses no oratory. His legal reputation rests on meticulously prepared and well-marshalled argument. Yutar objects to any adjournment. He has a naturally high-pitched voice which rises to a squeak when he becomes excited. Witnesses will be put at risk, he tells the judge. He 'fears for their lives!' Justice De Wet sits emotionless as a sphinx. He asks no questions about these fears or the basis for them but simply cuts Bram's request in half, rules that three weeks seem to him to be enough, and adjourns the court – our introduction to the personality and idiosyncrasies of Justice Quartus de Wet.

We have been incommunicado for months, without any news of what is happening outside. In these three weeks we begin to piece together the picture. It is not encouraging. The raid on Lilliesleaf Farm seems to have loosed a hurricane of destruction through the liberation movement. It is as though the police discovery of Rivonia has marked the turning of the political tide. Our movement is everywhere on the retreat and the state on the offensive, determined to smash down all that remains. The Security Police have been given free rein. Organisations have been trampled down; the jails are filled with the enemies of apartheid; hundreds are being held without trial, terrorised, tortured and killed. Restraints of law and concepts of human and civil rights are being obliterated in a wave of anti-communist hysteria, critics are being silenced by intimidation and courts corrupted into compliance. Already in the last weeks before our arrest we had sensed that our organisational network was beginning to unravel. Now the unravelling has turned into a retreat, and the retreat into something like a rout. We struggle to adjust our thinking to this new reality.

Except for Bram Fischer, our lawyers have little knowledge of the inner workings of the movement, and still less about the policies and activities that emanated from Rivonia. They are not encouraged by their reading of the indictment, and the more they learn from us the less optimistic they become.

The charge in the indictment is one of Sabotage as defined in the 1963 Act, which could encompass almost any extra-legal political action. We are alleged to have conspired together as a body called the National High Command to organise acts of sabotage, to train and equip guerrilla forces and to prepare armed action to overthrow the state.

The lawyers explain that the charge could well have been described as treason, but that would have involved a preliminary hearing in the magistrate's court. 'Sabotage' can be tried by summary trial in the Supreme Court.

Four of us – Mandela, Sisulu, Kathrada and I – have been through the 1956 Treason Trial. Until our lawyers persuade us otherwise, we imagine this trial might be a re-run since the political issues between the two sides are the same. But everything else is very different.

In 1956, our movement was at the peak of its public popularity in the after-glow of the COP and the Freedom Charter. It was filled with hope and confidence; our first reunion in the Drill Hall had a festival atmosphere. None of that remains. The mood around us is bleak with the movement in retreat and its support shrinking into the shadows. The issue now is no longer to vindicate the record of an exclusively peaceful Congress; it is to explain and vindicate a change to forms of armed struggle. We no longer appear as representatives of a legal political organisation, but of an outlawed ANC in regular co-operation with an outlawed Communist Party.

As in 1956, the allegation of violence is at the heart of the issue. But even that has changed its form. Then we were accused of having violent *intention*, though no acts of violence had occurred. Now we are accused of the actual use of or planning of some two hundred specific acts of violence and to have made active preparations for guerrilla war. Then, the allegations were false. Now they bear some semblance of truth.

This will be a very different kind of case. It is not just that the threat to life and liberty is more real, but that we feel that we are now carrying a responsibility for the fate of the whole movement and all those still active in it. The way we conduct ourselves must not encourage the retreat or contribute to it. We have an obligation to try and stop the rot, and to restore a spirit of confidence and of political purpose to the movement. Our members' future as much as our own may hang on how we conduct ourselves here.

While we have been in jail incommunicado, the authorities have been free to pour out propaganda to proclaim our cause dead and to traduce its purpose.

'The (Rivonia) arrests signal the end to all subversion' the press has been told by the Head of State Security. The Commissioner of Police has been more apocalyptic. 'The underground is smashed, its leaders apprehended, and nothing is left to be done except mop up the remnants.' 'Goldreich and his confederates had plotted a violent and hellish revolution . . . on a military basis', according to Dr Yutar. The state machine has had three months in which to demonise the movement and its leaders, to distort its policies, and to issue its death certificate. There has been no opportunity for any opposition voice to make itself heard.

In effect, the movement has been effectively silenced ever since police tore down the MK manifesto from the walls in 1960. Thereafter we had been unable to break through the blackout of censorship and intimidation in order to make a public explanation of the shift to violent forms of action. Public support was being undermined, hope and confidence in the movement was eroding in confusion and fear. We had not found any forum from which to make our reasons heard. Now the way is being presented to us – we can use the court as the platform from which to tell the whole story.

Our trial is already front page news and will be widely reported. There is a gap in the Suppression Act which, uniquely, allows the reporting of statements made in court by otherwise banned organisations or individuals. We will have the public platform we have been denied for several years. We discuss a strategy with our lawyers. We will seek to vindicate the movement and its policies rather than to exculpate ourselves.

They are not happy about it, and view the consequences more pessimistically than we do. The gossip in legal circles is that the prosecutors will be calling for the death sentence. That possibility is always somewhere in the recesses of our minds, but it is very much in the foreground of theirs. They are more than just lawyers. They have an empathy with us; they share our democratic beliefs and objectives, though not necessarily the ways we have acted to achieve them. They agree to follow our instructions on strategy though they are not convinced.

Amongst our problems is an indictment which charges us with responsibility for some two hundred separate acts of sabotage. None of us, not even the members of the MK command, know for sure whether these acts ever occurred, whether they were as described, or whether they were carried out by any of our people. Other groups, like the ARM, have been carrying on independent campaigns of sabotage. The only way for us to find out is to consult MK local leaders in different parts of the country, most of whom are themselves in prison. They will not feel free to talk, even to our lawyers, and we do not feel disposed to urge them to do so. MK's policy had always been to restrict sabotage to attacks only on installations of the apartheid regime, and where there would be no danger to people. It would seem to make little difference whether we accept an MK hand in fifty or a hundred and fifty acts of sabotage, provided they all fall within this policy ring-fence. We decide to accept tacit responsibility for any such acts which are verified by cross-examination.

The indictment has cast a wide net. It cites many of our members as 'co-conspirators' even though they are not before the court and cannot defend themselves. In the event of an adverse verdict against us, they could well face similar charges. We decide that we will not say anything about anyone still in the country. We will name no names. We will set out as clearly as we can the strategy and aims of the movement. We will make no denial of any true facts, and no apologies.

The lawyers' detailed study of the indictment leaves them shocked by its imprecision and lack of clarity – in their jargon its 'lack of particularity'. They demand 'further and better particulars' to inform us, in conformity with the legal requirements, precisely what part each one of us is alleged to have had in the 'conspiracy'.

The prosecution reply is contemptuous, a brush-off. The lawyers propose that the court be asked to quash the indictment for failure to comply with the requirements of the law. If such a travesty of an indictment is allowed to pass, they argue, it could prejudice our trial, and set a precedent for other cases in the future. We agree, though we feel less strongly about it than they do.

Legal consultations are difficult. They have to be held at the prison in an 'interview room' which appears to have been specially constructed for us. It is little more than a corridor, split in length by a counter and glass screen. The nine people on our side have to crowd up into a huddle to hear anything being said by any one of four lawyers on the other. We assume the room will be bugged, so discussion is restricted strictly to things we don't mind the police and prosecution hearing. Everything else has to be written down, passed back and forth under the screen, and finally incinerated in an ashtray.

At first the prison will not allow black and white prisoners to be interviewed together. They only back down when the lawyers threaten to apply for a court order to compel them. Then they insist that consultations break off for 'lunch' (at around 11 a.m.) and do not start again for several hours in order to fit the prison routine. All the lawyers come from Johannesburg. They have to kick their heels for hours in Pretoria before sessions can resume in the afternoon. In these and similar small obstructions, the prison authorities seem to have taken on the petty vindictiveness of the prosecution. 'Security' seems to have taken over the whole apparatus of state.

After three weeks, we return in armed convoy to the Supreme Court. A crowd of our supporters is waving and holding placards, but a far smaller crowd than that of the opening day at the Drill Hall in 1956. While we wait in the basement below the court, Hepple and Kantor join us. We are each assigned a number by the prosecution.

Mandela, who is Accused No. 1, leads the way up the steep stairs into the court. As he rises above the parapet between stair and public gallery, he looks round towards the public, raises his clenched fist and calls out: '*Amandla!*' From below, as we follow up behind him, we hear the public respond: '*Ngawethu!*' and orderlies shouting 'Silence!'

Walter Sisulu, Accused No. 2, is close behind. He too gives the clenched fist salute and receives the public response. I have no idea whether they have planned their actions or are reacting instinctively to the presence of their supporters. They have taken everyone by surprise. As warders and police rush about ineffectually, the rest of us make our way up into court, each one repeating the salute – all except Kantor and Hepple, who enter in silence.

A makeshift dock has been prepared for us between the public and the desks of the defence and prosecution teams. We are seated in numerical order in a single line, with a uniformed warder close behind each one, breathing down our necks like footmen at a royal banquet. De Wet takes his seat and nods to Bram Fischer for his opening remarks on the indictment.

Bram dissects the indictment patiently and meticulously, and makes his request for it to be quashed. He reports the defence requests for further particulars, and the prosecution's response: 'These facts are peculiarly within the knowledge of the accused.' This, he says, simply means: 'The accused are guilty; therefore *they* know what they have done and there is no need for the state to tell them.'

He speaks quietly without anger or invective, but his critique is withering. Yutar wriggles uncomfortably in his seat, head down and whispering to his assistants. For a while De Wet sits impassive, listening and taking notes. Then he appears to lose interest, lays down his pen, stops making notes and leafs idly through his copy of the indictment.

Bram recognises that De Wet has made up his mind, and brings his argument to a close. Kantor's counsel, Harold Hanson, takes over. He has also asked for further particulars about Kantor and been told either that the facts are '. . . peculiarly within the knowledge of your client', or simply: '. . . not known.' Kantor is charged in two capacities – on his own behalf, and vicariously on behalf of his partner Wolpe. Hanson has asked whether a particular act is alleged to have been committed by Wolpe or by Kantor, and has had the answer: 'Yes.' And to another question the answer: 'Dash, dash, dot, question mark.' De Wet intervenes, deadpan: 'In my copy there are four dashes, Mr Hanson.' He does not sound amused. Hanson sits down.

Hepple is not represented – he is a barrister in his own right. De Wet asks whether he wishes to be heard on the application to quash. Hepple is still getting to his feet when Yutar interrupts. He points dramatically towards Hepple in the dock, sweeps his gown around him like a toreador, and announces: 'All charges against Bob Alexander Hepple are being withdrawn! He will be the first witness against the accused!'

He looks at us in triumph. His announcement raises a flurry of excitement amongst the press and public, but not in the dock. We are prepared for it and sit in studied indifference. Hepple pushes his way out of the dock, mutters what might have been 'Good luck, chaps', and is gone.

De Wet calls Yutar back to the indictment. The attack on it appears to have caught him unprepared. He says the defence request for further particulars was never genuine; it was simply an attempt to embarrass the state. His normally high-pitched voice becomes shrill as he '. . . begs your honour, implores your honour' not to reject the indictment. He makes no defence of his draft. He improvises. 'If the court so desires' he will work late every night for a week to provide an answer to all questions. He offers to hand into court a copy of his opening address which will provide the answers to all the defence questions.

Our lawyers look at him as though he is losing his mind. An opening address is no more than his summation – some would say embroidery – of what he hopes to prove. It can roam beyond the boundaries of fact, to encompass speculation, guesswork and theoretical fancies. There is no legal requirement that it inform the accused with clarity and precision.

De Wet is not a patient man. It is said he is a government supporter. If so, he is not, like some South African judges, a simple apparatchik of the apartheid state. Bram is starting to voice a protest when De Wet cuts him short and tells Yutar brusquely that an opening address is not acceptable. The basis of his argument, he says, is that the accused are guilty. 'You cannot ask the court to decide the matter on that basis but on the basis that they are not guilty. Whether the defence genuinely wants the facts it has asked for is irrelevant. It is entitled to ask for them.' He rules that the indictment has failed to meet the requirements of the law and is therefore quashed. He leaves the court abruptly.

There is no longer any charge against us. Theoretically we should go free, but we are surrounded in the dock by police and warders. Captain Swanepoel pushes his way through, puts a hand on each one's shoulder and rearrests us formally. We are hustled down the stairs again, and taken back to Pretoria Prison. Our lawyers have scored a famous victory – but we are back where we started, awaiting trial. I am back in the same cell in the same segregated wing of the prison, with no one to talk to during exercise periods except Dennis. I have a lot of time to do nothing except read and write, and wonder about Bob Hepple who is missing from the yard.

I have known him since he was a small boy. His parents had been in a pre-war Communist Party group with Hilda and me. Occasional meetings in their house would be interrupted by a chubby, red-cheeked little boy in pyjamas and dressing gown, come to kiss his parents good-night. We were all 'dual members' of both the Labour and Communist Parties until the CP called an end to the practice and gave us each the option of opting for one party or the other. At that time Alex was a Provincial Councillor. He and Girlie stayed in the Labour Party. They remained honest, dedicated socialists, and we had stayed friendly after the parting of the ways though we seldom met. Bob was their only child.

Any testimony he can give can have little significance in the case against us, but for him to give evidence for the state will be a bitter blow to his parents. It will destroy his own reputation and self-respect and take his parents down with him. Giving evidence – any evidence at all – for the state will be seen as a betrayal and act of cowardice which will dog his life. Once he is freed of the pressure of imprisonment he might find the courage to draw back from the brink, as others have done before him. Hilda and Bram, who have helped his wife Shirley to stand strong during his detention, will surely now be advising her that Bob must leave before he destroys himself.

After the quashing of the indictment Kantor's application for bail is heard. His lawyers are confident of success. There had been nothing in the indictment to link him to any act of sabotage or to any part in the ANC or MK. Yutar asks that he be remanded in custody. De Wet is in testy mood and reminds him bluntly that, since the indictment has been quashed, there *is* no charge and therefore no basis for a remand in custody. Yutar improvises. He argues that if there is no basis for remand there can also be no basis for a grant of bail. De Wet slaps him down. He tells 'Mister Yutar' that the court is empowered to hear bail applications from anyone at any time – the change from 'Doctor' to 'Mister' seems to be quite deliberate.

De Wet is on the verge of granting bail, and is discussing with Kantor's counsel the sum which might be appropriate. But the police-prosecution do not give up their vendetta against Kantor with grace. There is an agitated whispered conversation between Yutar and senior Special Branch men; one of them hands over a scrap of paper, and Yutar re-enters the bail argument. He tells the judge that he had been prepared to agree to Kantor's bail, but the position has suddenly changed. Reliable information has just reached him of a plot to spirit Kantor away to Bechuanaland together with anyone else released on bail. He cannot – dare not – reveal any more, but must now oppose any grant of bail. Kantor's counsel observes that there is nothing before the court but Yutar's unsworn statement about an undisclosed scrap of paper from an unknown source. De Wet's prejudices show. No responsible police officer, he replies, would make such allegations without proper evidence. Bail is refused, and Kantor's fleeting chance of liberty is gone. Yutar hurries from the court amidst audible mutterings about 'perjured evidence' from Kantor's counsel.

It is a fearful blow to Jimmy, and an underhand one. He has set all his hopes on bail, and now he is to remain in prison for an indefinite time in a case in which he should never have been involved and in which he has little interest. His wife is pregnant with their first child; his legal practice is in ruins; his friends are turning their backs on him, and his finances are at rock bottom. He is on the edge of a breakdown, and yet he holds his integrity intact. His police contacts tell him that they can arrange bail for him if he tells them what passes between the rest of us in our talks in the prison yard. They suggest he can walk free if he tells them how the Goldreich-Wolpe escape from Marshall Square was organised. He knows something about it. He knows that Hilda has been involved, because she had gone to him for help in finding a place for them to hide after their escape. But Jimmy is not to be seduced, even though he is in total despair and on the edge of collapse. A good man fallen amongst revolutionaries.

Immediately after Kantor's bail application, the lawyers apply for bail for me, using the arguments I composed in my mind while in solitary confinement. But I have returned to reality. I no longer believe that I have a real chance of success, but the attempt is worth while. I have always stayed to face the consequences whenever I have been in imminent danger of arrest or trial. There is no reason to believe that I will change that pattern of behaviour now. But in the present highly charged political atmosphere, the hearing is something of a formality. The judge presiding – not, on this occasion, De Wet – is unmoved, and my application is turned down as I had really expected it would be. At least the press reported the argument quite fully, giving us a small amount of favourable publicity to counter the flood of hostile matter.

Weeks later, a new indictment is ready. It is not much different from its predecessor but has been padded out to make it look more informative. Several further acts of sabotage which have taken place while we have been in prison have been added. Our lawyers regard it as shoddy and inadequate as the one before, and propose to challenge it in court in the same way. We do not feel strongly about it. We know that, in the end, an indictment of some sort will be accepted by the court, and our trial will proceed. There is nothing to be gained by postponing the day except that the hysteria in the country might decline. We give the lawyers their head.

We have agreed with them the general character of our response to the charge. We will acknowledge that our organisations co-operated to form Umkhonto; that Umkhonto had organised a campaign of sabotage, and that it was considering the possibility of guerrilla action. That will not be disputed. We will defend our actions as justified, morally and politically, by the repressive and morally illegitimate nature of the state. We will enter only a political defence to what is essentially a political charge. This will not be a conventional defence, but it will not be a conventional trial. The manner of the prosecution makes it clear that legal conventions are to be subverted to uphold the power of state and to destroy those who challenge it militantly. This will be a show trial in which the odds will be weighted against us. The lawyers convince us that those odds will be improved if they attack the indictment once again.

We go back to court for the replay. The procedures have been changed. For the remainder of the case, De Wet takes his seat and calls the court to order before we are brought up from the basement. Any more salutes between us and our supporters in the gallery will now constitute contempt of court. The courtroom is less frenzied. Expectations of high drama have diminished. The men of the Special Branch no longer occupy most of the public gallery, though they still keep an admiring cordon around Yutar and his aides.

For a second time Bram patiently dismembers the indictment, repeating many of the criticisms which sank the previous version. De Wet hears him out in stony silence. This time he is bored and makes no effort to hide the fact. After a few minutes he stops taking notes and puts his pen down very deliberately.

Bram is still in full flow but senses De Wet's mood and cuts his argument short. So does Advocate Hanson on behalf of Kantor. Yutar is encouraged. With every one of his rejoinders to Bram's argument he turns towards the security men like an actor inviting applause. But De Wet is just as impatient with him as he has been with Bram. He dismisses the whole argument as if he has come to court with his mind made up. He dismisses the application to quash, no reasons given, and orders the case to proceed.

Bram asks for a further postponement to prepare the defence. Yutar opposes. We have been here before, but this time Yutar has prepared his ammunition. In collusion with prison officers, he has kept a record of each hour and minute spent by each of our lawyers at the prison. Not all the available hours have been used, which proves the request for a postponement to be frivolous. There is no precedent for such a spying watch on defence counsel but De Wet shows no flicker of interest. Yutar is again shrill and declaring his 'fear for the lives and safety of the witnesses'. He makes no mention that virtually all the witnesses are either detainees in police custody or policemen. He points dramatically to the dock and announces that: 'Already Bob Alexander Hepple has been threatened by the accused or their supporters and has fled the country!' He sounds triumphant about it. He is glorying in his propaganda coup which is nicely timed to catch the headlines in the evening papers. De Wet is quite incurious. He asks no questions but bluntly refuses the request for a postponement, and orders that we enter our pleas to the charge.[3]

We have decided our policy. Regardless of the admissions we intend to make, we will *not* plead guilty. To do so will appear to legitimise the prosecution, and might be interpreted by the outside world as an apology for our policies and actions.

Mandela is called first. He replies firmly: 'The government should be in the dock, not me. I plead not guilty.' If he had planned that in advance, he had not told us his intention. It causes some

---

[3]The allegation that he had been threatened was denied the same day by Hepple in a press interview in Dar es Salaam. There has never been any evidence for the allegation.

consternation in court, but De Wet lets it pass without comment. It is Sisulu's turn. In his own words he repeats Mandela's stance. This time De Wet speaks up. He wants only simple yes-or-no answers, not political speeches. Mbeki who follows shows no sign of having heard. He too blames the government and answers: 'Not guilty.' De Wet is realist enough to accept that there is little he can do except threaten us with prison. He says no more, and the demonstration goes on, each of us in turn pleading not guilty and finding our own form of words to turn the charge against the government. Only Kantor responds simply: 'Not guilty.'

We have spoiled what was to have been a big moment in Yutar's day. There is worse to come. Copies of his opening address lie tastefully bound and ribboned on his desk. He passes a copy to the judge, and an 'economy' copy to the defence team. Once again, the press has been given advance copies, but not the defence. He draws his gown around him with the familiar gesture, and prepares to read. We have noticed a microphone on the desk before him, and South African Broadcasting Corporation technicians fussing about. Bram interrupts to ask whether the court has given permission for the address to be broadcast. There is no precedent for this in the country's courts, and will the defence be accorded the same facilities? For once De Wet looks uncomfortable. His reply is muted. Permission *had* been given 'in order to inform the public', but in view of the defence objection 'that permission will be withdrawn'. Yutar disclaims all responsibility, and claims the initiative came from the SABC. We wait for the technicians to remove the apparatus. Yutar begins reading at last, but the suspense has been broken and the impact reduced.

The address is a tendentious rendering of the indictment in full shock-horror technicolour. It speaks of: 'a plot to commit sabotage, violence and destruction as a prelude to guerrilla warfare, armed invasion and the violent overthrow of the government in a war of liberation', all masterminded by the National High Command from headquarters at Lilliesleaf Farm. There is nothing new about it except a flight of fancy which has no basis in either of the indictments. 'Documents and witnesses will reveal . . . that the present year, 1963, was to be the year of liberation from the so-called yoke of the white man's domination.' The courtroom battle is joined and the first state witness takes the stand.

There are two things going on in court. There is the formality of witnesses and exhibits, and the shadow-play of the contrasting characters of judge, prosecutors and accused. The core aspects of the evidence will not be in dispute, but the personalities will take on the drama of confrontation. Now, thirty-five years after the trial, the detailed evidence is no longer of much interest to anyone except scholars of legal history. It has been recounted in greater or lesser detail in several books, most authoritatively by Joel Joffe in his book *The Rivonia Story* (Mayibuye Press), and with additional material and observations from Nelson Mandela (*Long Walk to Freedom*, Little, Brown & Co.); Hilda Bernstein (*The World That Was Ours*, Heinemann); and James Kantor (*An Unhealthy Grave*, Hamish Hamilton). The politics at the heart of the case are reminiscent of those of the 1956 Treason Trial, but the focus has shifted from the Freedom Charter to the narrower frame of force, sabotage and armed action.

Reminiscent of 1956 too is the parade of police witnesses with and without exhibits, and the back-up parade of lay witnesses – some honest but mostly charlatans, liars and frauds. But this time almost all the lay witnesses have been brought straight from the police cells where they have been held without charge and are testifying under duress. Several of them complain to the judge about threats and assaults suffered in police custody, but De Wet is dismissive. Nothing comes of their complaints.[4]

In a way we are entering unexplored territory. We are not aiming mainly to discredit the state evidence but rather to establish the validity of our own. For that, we will have to make a definitive statement of the facts, favourable or unfavourable, rather than have them emerge from distorted interpretations of witnesses and prosecutors. When state witnesses are telling the truth, the defence scarcely bothers to cross-examine. When the facts are unknown to us, as they are in regard to most of the specific acts of sabotage, the defence does no more than probe for a ring of truth. It is *our* evidence which matters for our purposes, not theirs.

Amongst the witnesses for the state is Detective Sergeant Card from Port Elizabeth who we come to call 'Card-index.' He runs

---

[4] I have tried not to repeat all that others have written about the course of the case. This is a personal memoir. I have confined it mainly to that small part of the case which is directly relevant to my own history.

rapidly through a list of dozens of people he describes as leading ANC and Umkhonto activists in the Eastern Cape, and ascribes to each of them a military rank or official post in the organisation. We know some of them but not all. Counsel asks how he has come by this information, and he replies: 'When they are in custody, I tell them what I know about them and wait for them to confirm it.' Bram objects to this evidence as hearsay and inadmissible. De Wet tells Bram, rather testily, that this is not a trial by jury. He can decide for himself what evidence is admissible and what is not; and that he will eliminate inadmissible matter when considering his verdict.

Card's evidence remains on the record. It is not clear whether it will be of any importance to us or not, but it shows us another side of De Wet's character – obstinate, self-willed, and intolerant of anything that might be a criticism of himself.

His ruling on hearsay gives a green light to the evidence of the state's key witness, Bruno Mtolo, who Yutar introduces theatrically.

'Are you a saboteur?'

'I am.'

We know little about Mtolo except that he has reputedly been one of Natal's most daring MK operatives. He claims to be a member of the ANC, Umkhonto and the Communist Party. Within hours of his arrest and with no apparent pressure upon him, he has changed sides and become a witness for the state. In the last few days we have seen him in the corridors around the court, at ease amongst the white police and sharing banter and cigarettes with them.

On the witness stand he is also at ease and cool. He gives apparently frank accounts of dozens of acts of sabotage he has personally committed, alone or with other members of MK. He has an exceptional memory. Dates, places, names of collaborators and technical details roll off his tongue without any prompting. He implicates almost everyone he has ever known in MK and in acts of sabotage, including his own brother who he says has gone abroad for military training with MK. He says he was once taken to Lilliesleaf Farm for discussions with the MK High Command, and claims to be the one who led the police to the place.

He is on the witness stand for days, talking not only of sabotage but explaining his notion of the ANC and the CP, and their mutual relationships. He portrays himself as someone victimised by the ANC and MK who failed to pay him the money he thought was his due.

Yutar feeds him his cue. 'How do the so-called leaders of the High Command live?' Mtolo says that the leaders were luxuriating while he was living a life of privation and poverty. He has been to Modise's[5] and Sisulu's homes and seen their fine furniture. He himself has nothing, but Sisulu has a car and has paid £3 000 for his own bail in another case, which is why he has defected and decided to give evidence for the state.

The High Command, he says, does not care about the ordinary members. '*They* ran away from Africa, and were not arrested!' He is a skilful liar. If he was ever in Sisulu's home – and his explanation for his visit to it is wholly unbelievable – he would know that it is an everyday Soweto home with everyday Soweto furniture and no car – Sisulu has never learnt to drive. Which he and Yutar must both know, just as they know that the 'runaway' MK leaders are in the dock under their eyes.

Yutar's questions and Mtolo's answers have the hallmarks of rehearsal before they are produced in court with small regard for truth. Between them, they are not producing evidence but gratuitous political smears.

Berrange is widely regarded as the country's most formidable cross-examiner. For several days he uses all his skills to test Mtolo's extraordinary memory, and fails to dent it. But he has an uncanny instinct for detecting the lies behind the evidence. He does not disclose his hand but asks in an almost casual tone about ANC-MK attitudes to risking human life in acts of sabotage. Mtolo explains that all MK operatives were instructed that every possible care must be taken to avoid any danger to people. Yutar and the police are well aware of this but have made no mention of it. Berrange acknowledges that that is so, and turns to one of Mtolo's own acts of sabotage – the bombing of an *induna*'s room at Durban's Addington Hospital when he was employed there. We know nothing about this event, but it is a puzzling breach of the policy on protecting people. Berrange probes away at the matter until finally

---

[5] Joe Modise, Minister of Defence in the Mandela government.

300

Mtolo shows signs of being rattled. He begins to contradict himself. He is a glib liar, but no match for Berrange with the bit between his teeth. Piece by piece the truth comes out. Mtolo had had a personal dispute with the *induna*. He had stolen some MK material, made a bomb and placed it in the *induna*'s room. He had acted alone. Not even his MK colleagues knew anything about it. And neither police nor prosecution have bothered to uncover the facts. It is easy enough to attribute anything to us.

Have they been just as casual with the truth over the hundreds of other acts of sabotage of which we know nothing? Are they just careless? Or utterly cynical? We try to understand Mtolo's reasons for his lightning conversion from a top MK saboteur to prime witness for the prosecution. Berrange's cross-examination provides the clue. Unknown to any of his MK colleagues, he has had a career in crime before turning to sabotage. His instant switch of sides when caught red-handed is an old lag's trick. For all his political posturing in the dock, he is a man without loyalties, ready to trade anything and anybody to gain his own immunity. There are no principles in his calculations – or for that matter in a prosecution which is prepared to use him.

I have a special interest in Mtolo. Amongst other things, he has told the court that he first heard of MK when he was told that someone had come from Johannnesburg to teach them how to make and use explosives. That is hearsay, but Yutar takes full advantage of De Wet's ruling to put it on the record. I guess Mtolo is referring to my meeting with the Party Committee in Durban, and 'improving' its purpose to suit the prosecution case. Yutar wants to know: who was this person from Johannesburg? Mtolo has been looking directly at me for days on end, and probably reading about himself and me in the papers as well. He must have been over this evidence with the prosecution beforehand, yet for the only time in his week on the witness stand, his hold-all memory fails. The name escapes him – or appears to escape him. He frowns, mutters to himself, gazes up at the ceiling and pauses before suggesting that it was something like Bunside or Berstone. Is this a real lapse of memory or some devious ploy? I am not sure. It should be of no account because hearsay should be struck from the record; De Wet may indeed strike it from his mind, but a more scrupulous prosecutor would not have called for it.

There are two other pieces of evidence to implicate me personally. One is provided by a young farm labourer from Lilliesleaf. On a Saturday afternoon about a week before our arrest he had seen a white man with fair hair on the roof of the farm outbuilding. The man was stretching a length of wire across the roof. Yutar asks him whether he can see that man in the dock. There are only three white men to choose from. I am the only one with fair hair. The witness ponders for a moment and then points to me. It is, I believe, an honest answer but completely wrong. The man in question is not in the dock. He is an expert radio technician called Lionel Gay. He *is* fair haired and built like me. But all this happened on a Saturday when I was confined to my home in house arrest. Even had I known of it I would not have taken any part in it. The method of the identification is patently unfair, prejudicial and unsafe, but Yutar uses it and De Wet lets it pass without comment.

The other piece of evidence is not just wrong but fabricated. It is provided by 'the investigating officer', Detective Sergeant Dirker of the Hitler moustache. It is designed to support the state scenario of events at Lilliesleaf on the day of the police raid. They have posited a long meeting; the document 'Operation Mayibuye' is said to have been on the table, and therefore the subject of the meeting; ergo, it must have been a meeting of the National High Command and taken a long time.

All untrue. The meeting had barely started when the police arrived. The Operation Mayibuye document was lying crumpled in the grate where efforts to burn it had failed. It was not a meeting of the National High Command. Police witnesses have tailored their evidence to fit their own scenario, and Dirker joins in. We have decided not to argue about where Operation Mayibuye was found – it is of no consequence. But Dirker underlines the concept of a long meeting by claiming that, when he arrived at Rivonia, he placed his hand on the engine of my car and it was cold.

He is lying. He makes no mention of an alarm in the car which blasts off when the bonnet is raised, or about its hidden cut-out switch. He does not know that my signature is in the police register miles away at Marshall Square, and the time recorded to show that I could not have reached Rivonia more than ten minutes before the police.

Berrange has met up with Dirker in court before. He does not

302

treat him gently. Dirker sticks stupidly to his story until Berrange reads out a judgment from another court where the judge had branded him a liar. Dirker's overweight body seems to shrink. He leaves the witness stand like a pricked balloon, and in tears. Berrange has enjoyed the encounter.

The whole case against me personally depends on these three factoids, plus my presence at Lilliesleaf Farm on the day of the raid. There has been a string of witnesses from Lilliesleaf Farm, some the Goldreichs' domestic servants and others farm labourers who have often seen me there. None of them has been asked about that, and none have volunteered evidence about it. The state case against me is complete, but it is riddled with holes.

All the state witnesses have been heard, but the facts about the movement have emerged, barely comprehensibly, in dribs and drabs. The police evidence has been largely formal, and generally reasonably factual. But most of the lay witnesses have larded their testimony with lies. Some are important lies; many are unimportant, almost irrelevant. But why this lying? It cannot be accidental – it is too systematic and too convenient to the prosecution for that. Yet the case is virtually cast-iron without any need for lies. It seems to me that the prosecution has never troubled to try and understand us. It has expected us to behave as usual criminals, to lie, provide false alibis and concoct excuses. And it has fashioned the state case to meet that expectation.

The evidence has been tailored to fit the indictment rather than the other way around. The evidence has been 'improved', and witnesses coached to deliver it. Evidence that is not admissible has been freely incorporated, and its delivery timed to ensure prime-time news coups for the state. The Rivonia Trial seems to mark the point of transition from the law as it was to the law as apartheid has deformed it. Even as it was, the law was never free of bias. Justice has always rested on a base of white supremacy and of inequality between blacks and whites. Yet it once conformed to established rules. The apartheid years have corroded the rules. They have changed the function of the courts from the dispensation of justice to the punishment of dissidents; and from the defence of the citizen to the protection of the state power.

In this case, the prosecution has bent itself to the dictates of the apartheid state. As I see it, the judge has not. For all his testiness and idiosyncrasies, De Wet appears to be trying to maintain a judicial balance and a judicial reputation. Unlike some of the more recent appointments to the bench, he is not a Nationalist apparatchik but a product of an earlier era. He is not one of the great law-givers. He is stubborn, self-willed, and guided as much by his notion of common sense as anything else. He is not a 'liberal' judge, but one with all the inbuilt white South African prejudices and certainties about blacks.

But within his limitations, he seems to me to be trying to hang on to the traditional South African legal style in a society where justice has already been sacrificed on the altar of 'security'. His impatience and his occasional hostile interventions enrage me. But I have some respect for the man, despite my certainty that, in the end, he will probably not be able to rise above himself and act with real political impartiality.

My feelings about Yutar are quite different. The longer the case goes on, the deeper my contempt for his vanity, the meanness of his spirit and his hostility towards us, our lawyers and our ideas. Like almost everyone on our side, by the time his last witness has been heard and he closes the state case, I have developed an obsessional dislike for the man.

Apart from some totally unbelievable lies from a few of the most stupid witnesses, there is no case whatsoever for Jimmy Kantor to answer. His lawyers apply for his immediate discharge. De Wet grants it without comment. Jimmy walks free from court at last, after many months in jail. The police have taken a bitter revenge on him for his association with the escapers Goldreich and Wolpe. The prosecution has colluded with them to ruin his life. There are no apologies. Only one or two of his police acquaintances mutter a shamefaced 'Good luck, Jimmy' as he passes them by. We have a short break in which to develop the case for the defence.

18

TELLING IT AS IT WAS
1964

We are all agreed that Mandela will have to be our chief witness. He had been first amongst equals in founding MK, and its first Commander in Chief. He could only give evidence on the facts surrounding its formation, but not on events after the beginning of 1962 when he had been on a mission abroad before being arrested and imprisoned. He has no first-hand knowledge of that period which includes most of the acts of sabotage, or of the circumstances surrounding the crucial Operation Mayibuye. There are others who can account adequately for the founding of MK as well as the later period. Would it not be sensible for Mandela to leave to them the responsibility for things he could not have influenced even had he wanted to?

Nelson will have none of it. I am not surprised. As long as I have known him he has acted on the principle that leaders have no special privileges, but have special obligations and duties greater than those of others. He rejects any special protection and insists on his responsibilities as titular head of MK. He will explain the ANC and its role in respect of MK, and defend them both in court. He will take on the full fury of the state attack – it is the obligation that falls on a leader. He puts his argument forcefully, and everyone – lawyers and accused – concede that he is right.

We are determined that the defence case is designed to give maximum publicity to our political aims and purposes. The origins of the armed struggle, which have been suppressed by censorship and repression, must be heard loud and clear around the country. It is difficult, almost impossible, to give a clear, coherent account from the witness stand where facts trickle out in fragments, separated by the formalism of question and answer. That cannot be good enough. We have to find another way. The only alternative is that a statement which cannot be interrupted for questioning be made from the dock. Such statements, untested through cross-examination, carry little weight with the courts. They are usually the last resort of a hopeless defence.

Nelson is a lawyer. He understands the implications very well, but decides he will make his statement from the dock anyway. We keep the news of this strictly to ourselves. He spends the rest of the recess working away at a draft, occasionally consulting us and our lawyers until he is satisfied. He shows us the final draft which ends with the sentence: 'I have cherished the ideal of a democratic and a free society . . . It is an ideal which I hope to live for and achieve.' And then, added in as an afterthought, the now famous coda: 'It is an ideal for which I am prepared to die.'

The prospect of a possible death sentence is never far from any of our minds. It requires a special courage to confront it starkly as Mandela does, and to throw down a challenge to the court to impose that penalty if it dares. We are uneasy about it. His blanket admission of responsibility for MK and sabotage is bold enough without it. Mandela listens to the arguments with his customary gravity. He is not posturing. He knows as well as any of us that he will be balancing on a knife-edge between life and death. But he is the leader, and in his mind the responsibility must be his. The coda stays as drafted.

By force of personality alone, Mandela is making himself a figure to be reckoned with in the court and in the prison. He is a convicted prisoner serving a sentence, yet several white warders turn to him for help with the essays they have to write to earn their promotion up the prison service ladder. There is a morning when we are all in the prison yard, waiting for transport to take us to court. A minor argument starts with some of the warders – I think about the handcuffs we are placed in before we enter the locked and armoured kwela-kwela. We object to the practice; it is unnecessary and demeaning. Mandela says as much in an unaggressive way. 'When your time comes,' one of the young warders tells him, 'you will do the same to us!' When! Not if. It is still 1964, and the name Mandela is only beginning to be known to most white South Africans.

When the recess is over and we return to court, the size of our convoy has been reduced, the overt hostility of prison, police and court officials seems to have cooled, and racial segregation in the cells beneath the court has been abandoned. Most of the cross-examination of witnesses will be undertaken by Berrange and Bizos, the legal arguments by Bram and Chaskalson.

Bram opens with a short summary of the defence. He is at pains to state very clearly and precisely those elements of the state case which the defence will deny, viz:

- that all those arrested at Rivonia were members of the MK High Command;
- that MK was a part of or the military 'wing' of the ANC;
- that the ANC was a 'tool' of the Communist Party and held identical aims and objects;
- that MK had adopted the military plan called Operation Mayibuye and decided to embark on guerrilla warfare at some specific time.

At the last item, De Wet looks up in surprise. 'That will be denied?'

Bram confirms: 'That will be denied. The evidence will show that, while preparations for guerrilla warfare were made from as early as 1962, no plan was ever adopted . . . It was hoped throughout that such a step could be avoided.'

He calls his first witness: 'Nelson Mandela who personally took part in the establishment of Umkhonto, and who will inform the court of its history up to 1962 when he was arrested. Mandela will make a statement from the dock.'

Everyone had anticipated Mandela would take the witness stand; no word of his real intention has leaked out. The judge is clearly surprised. Yutar is shocked. The clash between the leader of the ANC and the leader of the prosecution was set to be a great day in his legal career. He has clearly been preparing thoroughly for it. Volumes of the record of Mandela's evidence in the 1956 Treason Trial are stacked ready on his desk. It could have been a historic confrontation, but all prospect of it is gone.

There is a note of protest, even outrage in his voice as he jumps to his feet and addresses De Wet: 'My Lord, I think you should warn the accused that what he says from the dock has far less weight than if he submitted himself to cross-examination!'

Mandela is a lawyer. He does not appreciate being tutored in his profession. Nor does De Wet. He sounds acid. 'Mr Yutar, the defence have sufficient experience to be able to advise their client without your assistance.'

Mandela is already on his feet in the dock, adjusting his reading glasses. His calmness and apparent lack of fear had impressed me when we were waiting to enter the court. He still shows no sign of the weight upon his shoulders. His fate and that of all of us depends now on how he acquits himself. He takes his time. He shows no signs of nerves which even the most experienced public speakers are prey to at moments less testing than these. He seems totally at peace with himself, prepared to fulfil the special obligations of a leader without histrionics.

There is a hushed silence in the court, as though everyone present knows that this is not so much a plea as a moment of history. He starts reading at a measured pace, his voice clear and controlled. He is not seeking to arouse, as he is capable of doing, but to explain. When he makes an extempore speech he can enthuse and inspire, but when he is reading as now he loses the vital spark. His delivery is flat, unhurried and almost legalistic, but the whole audience is hanging on every word. He reads steadily for well over an hour.

Only when he is almost at the end is there a single touch of drama – deliberate or accidental. He reaches the tailpiece of 'an ideal which I hope to live for and to achieve'. There is a long pause. The silence goes on intolerably as though he has lost the thread. And then, with his voice lowered several tones, he adds his coda: 'But if needs be, it is an ideal for which I am prepared to die.'

There is a gasp of surprise, perhaps of shock amongst the public, and a drawing in of breath. He removes his spectacles slowly, and resumes his seat in silence.

Seconds pass. It is like waiting for the applause after the theatre curtain falls. De Wet waits inscrutable while the tension fades before he turns to Bram and says, 'You may call your next witness.' It sounds like advice rather than an instruction. Walter Sisulu takes the witness stand for what will surely be the crucial evidence in the whole case. He has been General Secretary of the ANC and a member of MK's High Command. He has been the liaison between the ANC and the Communist Party. He was party to the first discussions about the formation of MK and to the discussions on Operation Mayibuye. He probably knows more about the liberation movement's recent past than anyone.

Underneath his quiet, almost reticent manner, he is probably the most acute political strategist of us all – Mandela seldom takes a political decision without consulting Walter first. He is of small build, without either the physical presence or the charisma of Mandela, but he carries himself with calm and a retiring dignity. His formal education had ended in Standard VI, but he has the experience and ability to hold his own against Dr Yutar's Doctorate of Laws.

Bram takes him steadily through the evidence to confirm all of Mandela's account, and to fill in the account of the times when Mandela had been out of the action. His evidence amounts to an admission of guilt to the central charge but it disputes almost all the political characterisations made in the indictment. He denies specifically the four points Bram had said in advance would be denied, and amplifies the reasons for his denial. But he draws no veils over the truth; he makes no apologies for the movement or its policies; and he states very firmly that he will not answer any questions about other people.

We are making the prosecution's task easy, though Yutar seems not to realise what we are doing. He seems to me to be trapped in his own prejudices. He has paid little attention to the matters on which both Mandela and Sisulu have made complete admissions, and has failed to try and understand us or our motivations. He approaches his cross-examinations much as he would in any criminal trial, expecting to have to cope with the usual criminal denials, excuses and alibis. He accepts as axiomatic the moral rightness of the state and of white supremacy, and appears to see himself in the role of their avenging angel against us.

Before his cross-examination of Walter starts, George Bizos is taking bets that overweening self-confidence will lead him to focus on political issues – where Walter is the expert – rather than legal aspects where Yutar has all the advantages. Almost all his colleagues take his bet, and lose. Yutar almost disregards the fundamental issues which Bram has said will be denied and which Walter has indeed denied. He concentrates on political point-scoring and on political sneers against the accused and our organisations. He makes great play of the recklessness of MK and of the threat it posed to the public life and limb – though legally this is a red herring. The indictment makes no such charge; there is not a single instance of actual harm being caused to anyone; and his own witness Mtolo has testified to MK instructions to avoid all threat to people. But he hammers away at it relentlessly.

Another judge might perhaps remind him of his indictment, but De Wet does not. He lets it go on for some time, and appears to be taking some interest in the exchange between Yutar and Sisulu. He intervenes to recall that, during the war, a passer-by had been killed by a (right-wing) bomb placed outside the Benoni Post Office.

'If you are going to start bombing buildings,' he asks Sisulu, 'can you ever be sure that you have avoided killing or injuring people?'

Sisulu replies that an accident is an accident.

'Your argument is that as long as you have not got the intention to kill people, it does not matter?'

Sisulu: 'No, sir. I am not saying that it can't happen . . . but precautions are taken that it should not.'

This intervention, which supports the prosecution's attack, has a sinister undertone. Thus far, De Wet has been detached, even too detached over such strictly relevant matters as the admissibility of evidence. But he is changing, losing his detached air. Something has awakened his interest. Whether it is Mandela or Sisulu, their statements or their personalities, is hard to say. It seems to me that for the first time he realises that he is not dealing with crazed political fanatics but with men of ideas and of reason. Perhaps he is meeting up with a new experience – a black man conducting a political debate with the expertise and skill of any white politician. Politics appears to interest him. He is becoming involved.

If Yutar has a script he gives no sign of following it. He hops from one issue to another without any discernible logic – from murder and injury to Operation Mayibuye. Bram has told the court that we deny that Operation Mayibuye had been accepted or acted on, and Sisulu has explained the matter in detail. Yutar ignores this essential issue to ask: 'Who drafted it?' This has no bearing on the case. It can be of no interest to anyone except the Security

Police. Sisulu refuses to say.

> *Yutar*: Why not?
> *Sisulu*: Because I am not mentioning names.
> *Yutar*: I'm going to insist on a name.
> *Sisulu*: It doesn't help you to insist. I have explained that in so far as people who are in the country are concerned, I will certainly not answer.
> *De Wet*: You are not prepared to answer?
> *Sisulu*: I am not.
> *De Wet*: Very well.

Yutar still doesn't get it – or perhaps will not accept it. He hops to the question of the involvement in Operation Mayibuye of – with heavily accented sneer – 'President Luthuli, the Nobel Prize Winner for Peace'. Luthuli is neither mentioned in the indictment nor on the list of our 'co-conspirators'.

> *Sisulu*: I will not answer anything about Chief Luthuli.
> *Yutar*: What I am interested in is whether the new operation had been put before Chief Luthuli, and he agreed?
> *Sisulu*: You won't get anything about Chief Luthuli from me.

Yutar is intent on smearing someone, if not Luthuli then ·Canon John Collins of St Paul's Cathedral London and Christian Aid, who, he suggests, provided the funds for the campaign of sabotage. Sisulu brushes that aside with contempt.

Yutar hops again. Had an illegal ANC radio broadcast been made from Lilliesleaf Farm? Sisulu denies it. Why then was a radio aerial erected on the roof there?

'For experimental purposes. The actual broadcast had been done elsewhere to ensure signals were not traced back to Lilliesleaf.'

De Wet involves himself again – with his prejudices showing.

> *De Wet*: Some of your clever colleagues like Dennis Goldberg should have told you that they can only trace a broadcast if they know about it beforehand. If . . . they can trace the origin of a broadcast within a few minutes, then it doesn't matter where you hold the broadcast – they will catch you red-handed.
> *Sisulu*: It was not done at Rivonia. We were staying there, and we would have been exposing it to the police.

De Wet: So you don't mind the people who were working the broadcast . . . being caught, so long as you are not caught? Is that the position?

Sisulu: No. That's not what I'm trying to say. One does take the risk, but you would not put all your eggs in one basket.

De Wet: Isn't that rather typical of patriots – that they are always prepared to let the rank and file take the risk, and see that they don't put themselves in danger? Isn't that the position? . . . Exactly the same thing happens with people who are plotting a rebellion or revolution. They look forward to being the government in due course, and they see to it that they preserve their own skins, not so?

Sisulu: My Lord, we – to the best of our ability – want to preserve everybody.

Such political arguments are largely irrelevant to the case, but they have awakened De Wet's interest and his political opinions begin to show. They are typical of the views of the white ruling caste, revealed out of curiosity rather than overt hostility. Sisulu is being challenged by Yutar. Did the movement not simply aim to replace white government by black domination?

Sisulu: The only solution in South Africa is living together, black and white. There is no other solution.

De Wet: But doesn't that involve . . . control by the non-white element because they have more in numbers? Won't it mean black control?

Sisulu: Control can be exercised by both races together.

De Wet: You would never agree to that would you – you being represented by a white person?

Sisulu: Not to be represented. We don't want to be represented . . .

Yutar hops again. 'What is the membership of the ANC?'

Sisulu: When it was banned in 1960 it was 120 000.

Yutar: So despite your fifty years trying to persuade the Bantu . . . that they were being oppressed, you had a total enrolment of about 120 000 out of 12 million?

Sisulu: Political organisations don't get everybody, yet they represent the aspirations of the people.

De Wet: You think they should have the vote. But how do you know that the ordinary Bantu about town wants the vote? . . . You only know that you think he ought to have it.

Sisulu: I have not come across meetings where I have heard people saying: No, we don't want the vote. People always support the idea of the vote.

And so it goes on – Sisulu versus Yutar and De Wet, for five days. Against all custom, Yutar has ordered that Sisulu is kept in solitary confinement throughout the time he is on the witness stand. We have enough confidence in him to decide not to make an issue of it, and are vindicated. Walter comes through the ordeal magnificently. His testimony begins to shift the balance in the case. Guilt or innocence has become an issue in the background, and Yutar's attempts to denigrate the movement and us have begun to take over the foreground. But Walter has discomforted him. He has remained calm, forthright and imperturbable, undented by his contest with Yutar. Their encounter seems also to have roused a new awareness in De Wet. The judge is beginning to recognise that he is presiding over a case which could affect the whole country's future as well as our own.

We take the stand one by one. There are no differences on the facts or on our basic politics. The only differences between us are of personality, and sometimes of membership affiliations. Mbeki has the triple membership of the MK High Command, the ANC National Executive and the Communist Party Central Committee. He is soft spoken, courteous and scholarly. His manner is gentle but his political opinions are rigid and uncompromising. He covers the same ground as Sisulu, makes the same admissions and denials, and seems to awaken the same reactions from De Wet.

Kathrada, who is the youngest of us all, is by contrast the complete activist. There is no serious evidence against him except that he had been living under cover at Lilliesleaf Farm for some time. He admits to recording an appeal to the Indian community intended for broadcasting over the ANC radio. And denies absolutely the evidence of a taxi owner, a prize clown, that he ever hired a van to carry MK recruits to the Bechuanaland border. Kathy is a member of the Communist Party, but not of MK. He has been an opponent of the so-called 'armed struggle' on grounds of principle. In the witness box he is sharp witted, combative, alternatively humorous and aggressive. I don't think his manner endears him to De Wet.

Raymond Mhlaba is a leader of the ANC, of MK and the Communist Party. The only state evidence against him is that he was at Lilliesleaf Farm on the day of the raid and had been there occasionally before. And another taxi-driver's tale that he had taken an elaborate ride in Port Elizabeth to reconnoitre targets for MK sabotage in December 1961. The journey may possibly have happened. But even if it did, Mhlaba could not have been there. He was already out of the country and receiving military training abroad, and did not return until long after the event. On the witness stand, Mhlaba admits he had been on a 'mission', but will not say where; the answer could incriminate him of leaving the country without a passport. Yutar cross-examines: 'I put it to you that in December 1961 you were either in Port Elizabeth or in Leipzig?' So they know. But they have led the taxi-driver's evidence anyway. Yutar offers him an indemnity if he answers the question, but Mhlaba does not trust him and turns it down. It does his cause little good. He is a patently honest man telling a totally honest story, yet somehow he appears shifty on the witness stand, perhaps because he is slow spoken and is using English which is not his first language.

It is my turn. I do not have the same courage in this game of Russian roulette as the others. I do not feel at all calm – the press reports describe me as looking tense and nervous. I am. But whenever I have to speak in public, my nerves settle down once I am under way. Berrange leads me through my political c.v. – from the Anti-Fascist League to the Labour Party and then the Communist Party; and so to a close association with the ANC and ultimately Umkhonto. He gets me to define and disentangle the many committees, organisations and acronyms that have cropped up in evidence, and to explain the relations between them. For me, this is everyday stuff, easily explained. De Wet is listening intently. I imagine I am making some sort of order for him out of a political scene of which he knows almost nothing.

And so to allegations against me personally. I deny that I have ever been a member of Umkhonto or of the High Command, but admit to having had regular contact with both bodies. I deny ever being on the roof at Lilliesleaf Farm or taking any part in the rigging of a radio aerial. There is nothing else to answer. Mtolo's account of a visit to Durban by an unidentified 'Bunstead or Burstem' is hearsay and inadmissible. Dirker's tale of the temperature of my car engine has been shown to be lies. Counsel will argue later that both items should be ruled out of consideration altogether. My evidence is complete, and it is Yutar's turn to cross-examine.

I do not expect him to turn to these matters of evidence directly.

His method is to hop erratically from topic to topic. With the air of a magician producing rabbits from a hat, he springs on me one document after another, without any explanation of where they come from. They are not exhibits which have been formally identified by witnesses. Most of them appear to come from Communist Party sources. I am asked about each of them in turn, and whether I agree with the views expressed in them, or if not why not. There is no suggestion that I have either written them or seen them before, but I am comfortable about them. I am at home in my own game of politics, while Yutar is playing a game which does not appear to have any bearing on my case. He tires of that and hops to an equally irrelevant search for names and identities. Who attended that meeting? Who served on that committee? Who wrote that article? If he had been listening to what my co-accused had been telling him he would know he is not going to get any answers. But he has not learnt. I refuse to name any names; he grows increasingly indignant, and starts to lose his cool.

I have said in evidence that I have been a communist for twenty-five years, and a member of the legal Communist Party. Once again Yutar switches tack. Did I remain a member after the Party became illegal? I have been expecting the question and I refuse to answer on the grounds that I might incriminate myself. Yutar appeals to the judge who instructs me to answer the question. If I do not answer I will be guilty of contempt of court and can be sent to prison for eight days, then brought back and asked the question again and again until I do. Then he remembers that I have been in prison for the best part of a year already, and a thin smile crosses his face – it is the first semblance of a smile we have seen from him – and he adds: 'I don't suppose that will make much difference to you under present circumstances.' I say I suppose not, and there the matter ends. I sense that he is beginning to warm to me for several reasons. I am the first witness who comes from the same white, middle-class world as he does. I am also the only one who has been acclimatised by boarding school and army to an easy use of 'Sir' when addressing him or Yutar.

Yutar will not yield gracefully. If he cannot get me to incriminate myself, he can try and get me to incriminate someone else on my side. He produces another document. It is an article from the periodical *Fighting Talk*. It is years old – 1954! – and must have

315

come out of the police archives. It is not an exhibit in the case. It is titled: 'I think of Bram Fischer'. It gives a short biography of him as prelude to the writer's claim that when he is driven to despair by white South African intolerance and indifference to their black compatriots, thinking of Bram restores his hope. Here is an exemplary Afrikaner who has given his life to principled resistance to racism. The article carries the initials LB. Yutar asks if I wrote it. I say I did. He appears to go off again at a tangent. 'Who was the Secretary General of the Communist Party?' I refuse to answer. Bram is sitting at Berrange's side, directly in front of the judge's bench.

> Since you are unable to answer . . . perhaps we may conclude that it was the gentleman referred to in the exhibit before you. Please hand it to the judge.

Fischer is not charged or even accused. This is Yutar's most under-hand and despicable act – it cannot be called a smear because it is worse than that. It is a deliberate incitement to incriminate our leading barrister. De Wet cannot be unaware of what is happening, but he reverts to his earlier passivity and says nothing. That encourages Yutar to return to his earlier question: Was I a member of the illegal Party after 1950? Again I refuse to answer. He offers me a blanket indemnity for any offence disclosed. I ask the judge for a short adjournment to allow me to take legal advice. The lawyers go back to their law books and advise that Yutar, in his capacity as Deputy Attorney General for the Province, *can* offer such an indemnity, but his superiors in the Department of Justice will not be bound by it. Was he aware of this? I do not know, but I refuse the indemnity and refuse again to answer the question.

He switches track again. 'Have you ever accused the state of coaching its witnesses?'

I have no idea what this is about. I say that I probably have.

'Have you accused the police in this case of acting improperly?'

I say that I probably have.

I am beginning to realise what is happening. During the adjournment while Mandela was drafting his address to the court, I had written a letter to my sister in England. I tried to give her an idea of how the case was going. I had told her of two young witnesses who said they had been at a conference of the underground ANC in Bechuanaland. They agreed the proceedings were all in English. One understood English; the discussion had to be translated into Xhosa for the other. Both remembered two things only from their two-day meeting: that Tambo had opened the meeting and Govan Mbeki had made the main speech; and that they told those present to return to their districts and organise guerrilla groups. It was inherently unlikely. Bechuanaland security police had insisted on being present throughout the meeting. And Mbeki has told us that he opened the conference and Tambo made the main speech. They must have been coached.

I tell her of the witness who swears he drove Mhlaba around Port Elizabeth at a time when we all knew he was abroad. And of another taxi-driver with an elaborate tale of an all-day journey with Mbeki and others in which they stopped at various places to deliver and receive mysterious packages. Of the whole day in the car he remembers no conversation except about electric pylons, and no passengers' names except Mbeki's. Yutar asks for descriptions of the packages and the witness says he saw transparent plastic tubes filled with white powder. Yutar is not satisfied. He asks about it again and gets the same answer – transparent tubes and white powder. The witness returns to the stand the next day. He explains that overnight he has remembered that the tubes were actually opaque and the powder black – Yutar explains that the court translator was at fault. And Mbeki is adamant that if any such journey ever took place, it took place without him.

My letter tells of a man who says he drove Mandela to an illegal ANC meeting in Port Elizabeth – he is certain it was Mandela because he looked then just as he looks now in the dock. He too returns the following day, by which time he has remembered that the Mandela he drove that day had a heavy black beard. He was not clean shaven as he is now. So this was how the case was being put together. I had no doubt that witnesses were being coached, and that nuggets of falsehoods were being planted amongst the facts. I could see no reason for witnesses to lie unless they were receiving something for it – probably promises of release from custody. I had handed the letter in for censorship and posting by the prison in the normal way, and forgotten about it. Now it is returning to me, via the prison to the Security Police to Yutar.

Yutar puffs himself up in righteous indignation. How dare I make such scurrilous accusations against the police and prosecution? I remind him that Sergeant Card had said he tells his prisoners what he knows, and keeps them in custody until they confirm it.

> *Yutar*: Are you suggesting that the police force them to agree?
> *LB*: No. They just keep badgering them until they agree.
> *Yutar*: You say that the state coaches its witnesses. That is a reflection on the prosecutor?
> *LB*: I am afraid so.

He asks for my evidence of it. I tell the judge that I am being questioned about a letter written six months after my arrest, and cannot see any relevance to this questioning. De Wet says only that these are relevant questions and must be answered. I answer them by citing all the incidents I had given my sister.

> *Yutar*: You say directly that the witnesses were coached?
> *LB*: That is my deduction.
> *Yutar*: Did you ever say that: 'Apart from police witnesses and documents . . . all the substantial witnesses have been detainees who made statements under pressure . . . and subject to threats of either indefinite detention or prosecution'? Did you make that statement?
> *LB*: I did.
> *Yutar*: Is it true or false?
> *LB*: I think it is probably true.
> *Yutar*: That is a condemnation of course not only of the investigating officer (Dirker) but of the State prosecutor?
> *LB*: A condemnation of the state which has provided for witnesses' statements to be taken from them under duress.

Yutar's indignation carries him away. He is losing sight of the real case he is supposed to be conducting, and concentrating on the slight to his reputation. He fails to ask me a single question about any of the evidence his own witnesses have given against me, or about any denial of them in my own evidence. Without that, my denials must stand and the state witnesses' tales fall away. He sits down still fuming, his cross-examination of me ended.

There is Goldberg still to come. Unlike Mbeki and Sisulu he has not been in the leadership of MK but an activist operating under the guidance of the High Command. He has been deeply involved in technical investigations concerning Operation Mayibuye's logistical requirements, and has left a trail of evidence which is overwhelming. The lawyers do not advise him to take the witness stand, but it is up to him and he chooses to do so. They threaten him with fire and brimstone if he tries to joke his way through his testimony as he usually does everywhere else. Put to the test, he makes about as good a job of defending a hopeless cause as anyone could. For once, Yutar leaves the cross-examination to his assistant prosecutor, Mr Krog, who gets his only speaking part in the whole trial.

That leaves Mlangeni and Motsoaledi, neither of whom have been in the leadership ranks. Both are members of the ANC, and MK operatives involved in the recruitment and transportation of young men for training abroad. Neither of them has been involved in the activities or the decision-making at Lilliesleaf Farm. The lawyers explain to them the pros and cons of taking the witness stand, and both opt instead to make statements from the dock. Both their statements are short and moving. They reveal the motivations of the many men and women who are the backbone of the liberation movement. They explain how they came to dedicate themselves to the struggle for their people's liberation, and why – after years of non-violent political work – they turned in frustration towards MK and its use of political force. The last word is from Elias, who traces the gradual destruction of his life's prospects under apartheid:

> ... until there was nothing left for us to do except suffer. When Umkhonto was formed I was asked to join. I did so. There was nothing else I could do. Any African who thought the way I did about my own life and the lives of the people would have done the same. What I did brought me no personal gain. What I did I did for my people, and because I thought it was the only thing left for me. That is all I have to say.

Before they sit down, both Elias and Andrew turn to the judge to complain that they were beaten up by police after their arrest. De Wet has gone back into his shell of indifference. He asks the prosecutor to look into it, and adjourns the court. Nothing more is ever heard of it.

There is nothing left except the summing up by each side. Again, Yutar's desk is stacked with carefully bound volumes of his summing up, four volumes to a set. Again he presents a set to the judge, several sets to the press, and a single unbound set to the defence. It is expected that the prosecutor's summing up will review the strengths of the state's evidence and the weaknesses of the defence. In this case it should be simple enough. The three main defence witnesses have admitted and amplified the essential facts on which the prosecution rests, and have only contested the state's allegations of motive and intent. A four-volume summary seems unnecessarily ponderous, but the world's press is present and listening. This is the prosecution's big moment and it is not to be underplayed.

Yutar starts reading from Volume 1 of his address.

Although the State has charged the accused of sabotage, this is nevertheless a case of High Treason par excellence. It is a classic case of the intended overthrow of the government by force and violence with military and other assistance of foreign countries.

He is making a political speech without reference to the evidence. There has been no evidence at all of military or any other form of assistance from foreign countries. He is not examining the differences between state and defence testimony but repeating the politically slanted attack on the accused and their organisations with which the case had opened. He is once again justifying the allegations in the indictment not by reference to the evidence but by rhetoric and indignation. His summing up of the case is a repeat of his indictment, but heavily larded with infantile sarcasm and abuse.

The deceit of the accused is amazing. Although they represented scarcely more than 1% of the African population, they took it upon themselves to tell the world that the Africans in South Africa are suppressed, oppressed and depressed . . .

It is a great pity that the rank and file of the Bantu . . . who are peaceful, law-abiding, faithful and loyal, should have been duped by false promises of free bread, free transport, free medical services and free holidays. They forgot to mention free holidays.

True. We did not mention free holidays – or for that matter free bread, free transport or anything else from this flight of fancy. But that is of no account. He is not dealing with evidence but with fantasies of his own.

> It is tragic to think that the accused, who between themselves did not have the courage to commit a single act of sabotage, should nevertheless have incited their followers to acts of sabotage and guerrilla warfare, armed insurrection and open rebellion and ultimately civil war . . . They would then, from the comforts of their hide-outs . . . have surveyed the savage scenes of slaughter on both sides of the opposing forces . . .
>
> A man like Goldberg would have gone abroad to join the band of brothers which included that great and glorious guerrilla Goldreich, the heroic Harmel and Hodgson, Slovo the soldier, and the wise Wolpe. From a safe distance of six thousand miles or more they would behold the tragic works of their handicraft.

He is being carried away by his own rambling drivel, and manufacturing fictions out of his own head.

> The day of mass uprising in connection with the launching of guerrilla warfare was to have been 26th May, 1963.

De Wet, who has kept an impassive silence through this farrago, comes suddenly to life.

> Dr Yutar, you do concede that you failed to prove guerrilla warfare was ever decided upon, do you not?

Yutar does not concede. He has been too absorbed in his own performance to take serious note of Bram's opening statement or the evidence of Mbeki and Sisulu that guerrilla war *had* been discussed but *had not* been decided upon. He has not bothered to cross-examine either witness about it. He has plucked the date of May '63 out of the air. He improvises a response about 'preparations being made'.

> De Wet: The defence concedes . . . that preparations were being made in case one day they found it necessary to resort to guerrilla warfare. I take it that you have no evidence contradicting that, and that you accept it?

Yutar does not accept, but he has no evidence and backs off with an 'As your lordship pleases' and returns to the reading. He is now reading his own summary of Mandela's statement from the dock. De Wet stops him in his tracks. Mandela, he says, has admitted guilt on all charges, so a summary would merely confuse the matter.

Another 'As your lordship pleases' and he starts to summarise Sisulu's evidence. De Wet stops him again, for the same reason. He reads on, in disarray, his reading becoming more and more polemical and political, while De Wet goes back into his shell. Yutar seems to have lost all touch with reality. He is no longer a state prosecutor. He is St George slaying the communist dragon single handed, and a prophet – or perhaps a clown.

> For the edification of your worship, I have decided to nominate a shadow cabinet for the provisional revolutionary government.

De Wet is not the kind of man to take kindly to being 'edified', but he seems to have given up on Yutar and is letting him blow himself out.

> Goldberg, who was alleged to have run a camp for spiritual and health purposes, I name Minister of Health but he will have to learn the truth first ... Mbeki, Minister of European Affairs – to administer the white population as he claimed the Ministry of Native Affairs did the blacks; Bernstein, who wrote extensively, Minister of Information; Mhlaba, Minister of Foreign Affairs by virtue of his travels abroad.

And so on. This infantile stuff raises chuckles amongst his Special Branch sycophants and doubts about his mental stability with every-one else. He omits nobody: Kathrada Minister of Indian Affairs, Motsoaledi of Lands, Mlangeni of Transport, Hodgson of Munitions, and the country's first black barrister, Duma Nokwe, Minister of Justice.

> For the information that Bob Hepple has given to the police I would like to make him Minister of Informers. And Slovo ... I wish I had the pen of a Pope and a Dryden to describe the infamy of this man who – with Goldreich – was one of the worst traitors to infest South African soil.

And finally, Sisulu Minister of the Interior; Mandela Minister of Defence and Deputy Prime Minister; and Chief Albert Luthuli as President.

> I have not been able to find portfolios for all the men involved. But if they run true to form, if and when they come to power there will be a lot of internal strife resulting in many casualties, and they will be able to fill the vacancies which will inevitably arise.

A petty little man taking advantage of his position to dish out petty abuse. Even by the debased standards of prosecutors in the apartheid era he is plumbing the depths. De Wet's silent toleration of it reveals the levels to which the courts also have fallen.

Yutar is still not finished. He returns again to my letter to my sister, and my reflections on the prosecution.

> I deny, my Lord, that the State ever coached witnesses. I am a servant of the State. But I say now, and I am prepared to say it under oath: I have not been told what to say. I am an officer of this court, and I know your Lordship would not countenance . . . any conduct which fell short of that expected from an officer of this court. I am disgusted and revolted by the allegations which the defence have made about the conduct of the State.

I am reminded of Bernard Shaw's observation that: 'A nation's morals are like its teeth. The worse they are decayed the more it hurts to touch them.'

But Yutar is not finished yet.

> At the outset of my argument I said that this case was one of High Treason par excellence. Because of the people who have lost their lives and suffered injury as a result of the activities of the accused, it is apparent that this case is now one of murder and attempted murder as well . . . I make bold to say that every particular allegation in the indictment has been proved.

It is surreal. Two indictments and all the state and defence evidence is behind us. And now – now! – he adds in new allegations of murder and attempted murder. I am no longer able to feel anger. I can only laugh at this Walter Mitty who has cast himself as the avenging angel but is becoming an utter clown.

Arthur Chaskalson sums up for the defence. He is the complete lawyer – cool, reasoned, logical.

> The state has told your Lordship that this is a trial for murder and attempted murder, though the indictment alleges military training and sabotage . . . There has been a mass of inadmissible evidence which bears no relation to the indictment. The defence will not even deal with these allegations as they have nothing to do with the case.

There are however two matters of law which go right to the heart of the charge.

> The defence concedes that Umkhonto we Sizwe recruited men for military training and that members of Umkhonto committed acts of sabotage. The defence denies however that they committed *all* the acts of sabotage with which they are charged.
>
> The evidence is that Umkhonto's policy was only to commit acts of sabotage against government and public property which it labelled 'symbols of apartheid'. The evidence further shows, and stands corroborated by State witnesses Mtolo and Mthembu, that the clear policy of Umkhonto was sabotage without the loss of life. If one member of the conspiracy goes out and commits an act falling outside the ambit of the conspiracy, his fellow conspirators are not legally liable . . .

So much for Mtolo and the *induna*. Arthur analyses the evidence concerning every one of the more than two hundred acts of sabotage. It is a devastating criticism of the catch-all character of the prosecution. Of the 193 acts charged, there are only twelve in which the involvement of MK or the High Command has been shown. None of those twelve involved any threat to people or life.

Bram Fischer takes over. He tells the court that he has two crucial issues to argue. First, that though guerrilla warfare had been considered, there had been no decision to embark on it.

> *De Wet*: I thought I made my attitude clear. I accept no decision or date was fixed upon for guerrilla warfare.

Again, one down and one to go.

> *Bram*: That though certain sections of the ANC co-operated in the formation and work of MK, the two organisations were always separate and independently controlled.

De Wet intercedes again. This too is shown by the evidence and accepted by him. Bram has laboured mightily for days to prepare a meticulous argument. De Wet has accepted both his main points before he has even argued them. It may not make much difference to the verdict, but could be significant when he comes to sentence. And it could radically affect the thousands of men and women outside the court who have been or still are members of the ANC. For them, a clear distinction between membership of the ANC and MK could make the difference between a simple charge of membership of a banned organisation, and co-responsibility for sabotage and armed preparations. That could be the difference between life and death.

Berrange takes up the argument to the effect that the evidence against three of us – Kathrada, Mhlaba and me – does not sustain the charge. In his coldly controlled way, he is still fuming over Yutar's gratuitous sneers at us and his so-called cabinet list

> the relevance of which we have found it difficult to ascertain. The accused, with the dignity that has characterised them throughout this trial, have instructed us to ignore these remarks. It is however unusual, and not in the best traditions . . . for a prosecutor to deliver himself in this manner . . . Dr Yutar, in addressing the court, has in instances not accurately set out the facts, and in no instance has he tried to evaluate or analyse the evidence of the witnesses.
>
> The cross-examination of Bernstein covers 153 pages of transcript. This is not remarkable in itself, but what is remarkable is that, in those 153 pages, there is not one word of cross-examination as to the facts deposed to by Bernstein. The only direct evidence against him related to the erection of the radio masts . . . given by a servant at Rivonia who was in police custody under 90-day detention.

> *Yutar*: The witness was not in 90-day detention. He was in protective custody only.

There is no such thing in South African law as 'protective custody'. During my cross-examination Yutar had himself described this witness as a ninety-day detainee, and Berrange quotes that passage from the court record. The whole of the evidence about the radio masts had been denied by me, and Yutar had not questioned my denial.

The evidence is a matter of mistaken identity. This is the only piece of evidence against Bernstein. And on this basis he is entitled to his discharge.

He turns to the case against Kathrada. He had lived for a time at Rivonia, and recorded a speech intended for broadcast over the ANC radio. None of this proves participation in MK or any of its activities. Kathrada too is entitled to his discharge.

Mhlaba's case is more problematic. Berrange argues it as convincingly as he can, and asks that he too be discharged, but De Wet is clearly sceptical and not very sympathetic.

The prosecution has the last word, but now only on matters of law, not of fact. Yutar disregards the rules. He is in mid-stream of a recital of the evidence against me which he had failed to deal with during my cross-examination. De Wet cuts him short to remind him that: 'You are only entitled to reply on questions of law.' Yutar changes tack for the last time, to cite a government proclamation issued during the course of the trial, which declares the ANC and MK to be 'presumed' to be one and the same. The presumption had been made retrospective to cover the whole Rivonia period.

At the start of the case, Yutar had boldly told the court that he would not rely on that presumption: his case was so strong. Our lawyers had therefore not troubled to take it into account. Now Yutar seizes on the proclamation, and argues that Kathrada's broadcast for the ANC must be 'presumed' to be participation in MK. He had never mentioned it before.

De Wet finally loses patience, and asks icily whether Yutar expects the whole case to be reopened so that the defence can re-argue *its* case in the light of this sudden switch. Yutar may be a mean infighter, but he carries no counter punch. He makes a sharp U-turn. 'In the light of the court's view' he will abandon the 'presumption'; his case is still so strong that he does not need it.

Finis! Our ordeal in court is over. All that remains is verdict and sentence. The court is adjourned for three weeks.

Little happens in that interval. In my daily exercise period out of my cell there is only Dennis to talk to. There are regular visits from Hilda which both relieve and unsettle me. And for the rest, nothing but reading, writing, and thinking.

The day comes for us to return to court. I am showering and

shaving alfresco in a freezing courtyard, watched by the same warder Du Plessis who has been watching me in silence for the whole year. Gossip about my chances of being found not guilty must have reached him. For the only time that year he actually speaks to me as though I am human, and asks what I will do if I am released later that day. I remember putting the same question in that very yard to the warder Van Heerden who was near the end of his attendance on the hospital gate, and his reply: 'Man, when I get out of here I'm going to find an *easy* job.'

I tell Du Plessis the story. I get to the punch-line and add: 'I'm going to do the same. Get myself an *easy* job.' He has been watching me doing nothing for months on end. He looks at me solemnly and says: 'I think you're right.'

It is just talk. I know that, whatever the verdict, I am not going to be released. Even a verdict of 'not guilty' will change nothing. I will be rearrested, either in court or as soon as I set foot outside it, and charged anew.

The nine of us are together again on the journey to court for the first time in three weeks. There are handshakes and greetings but not much talk. We are all tense. We wait silently in the basement beneath the court, with only an occasional exchange of black jokes.

We wish each other luck as we mount the stairs for the last time, and take our places in court. We catch glimpses of families, wives and friends in the gallery but can make no greeting. The orderly calls, 'Silence!' De Wet is seated and waiting and the Clerk calls the case: 'The State versus Mandela and Others'. We rise and face the judge who waits a moment for silence before speaking. He is impassive as ever, inscrutable, his voice so sombre that it scarcely carries to the public gallery behind us.

I have recorded the reasons for the conclusions I have come to. I do not propose to read them out.

Accused number one – Mandela – is found guilty on all four counts.

Accused number two . . . on all four counts.

Accused number three . . . Accused number four . . . Accused number five – Kathrada – guilty on count two, and not guilty on counts one, three and four. Accused number six – me – not guilty and is discharged. Accused number seven . . . eight . . . nine guilty on all counts.

I will deal with the question of sentence tomorrow.

He gathers his papers and walks out. I feel relief from the tension but nothing more – only emptiness. For me, it is all so predictable, and devoid of any real meaning.

There is pandemonium in court, and people in the gallery are calling out: 'What did he say?' Police officers and warders are shouting against the crowd and trying to force us from the dock and down the stairs to the cells below.

19

IN A CLOSING NET
1964

For reasons which I no longer understand, it seems vital that I do not go down those stairs again. If I am going to be rearrested it must be in open court, in full sight of the press and public. I elbow my way through the ring of policemen around the dock – they are uncertain whether to restrain me – and push through to our lawyers in the well of the court. Detective Sergeant Dirker rushes over and starts to drag me away. He says I am under arrest.

Vernon Berrange intercepts him: 'After your disgraceful exhibition in the witness box, I take it you will not oppose bail when we apply for it.' Dirker is intimidated, and pulls me away, muttering a reply which I cannot catch. Captain Swanepoel comes across and joins him and together they hurry me past the empty dock and out of the court. My colleagues are already down in the cells below, and I have not even seen them go.

Suddenly I feel terribly alone. We have been together, on and off, for so many years, we have sat together, talked together and decided everything together during the whole year of the trial. We have learnt to depend on each other for advice, for strength and courage. Now, suddenly, it is all over. They have gone, without our being able to exchange a word or touch, and without any farewells.

It will be twenty-seven years before I see them again.

Things are happening too fast. I no longer feel in control of my own fate, but have become a puppet being pushed about by people like Swanepoel and Dirker. I am unable to celebrate my good fortune; I am still shocked and numb as they take me back to the prison to collect my few belongings. Apart from the warders, I see no one I know and talk to no one. I am put into the back of a car filled with Special Branch men and taken back to Johannesburg.

Swanepoel is bragging to the others as though I am not there. If he had his time over, he says, he would be a barrister – big money just for asking questions. The talk just washes over me. In Johannesburg, I am formally handed over to the uniformed police at Marshall Square, my watch is taken away again, and I am locked back into the cell I had been in in 1960. It is big and empty, with beds for six or eight. After the close confines of my Pretoria cell I feel very much alone, exposed and uneasy.

After Pretoria, the regime is relaxed, almost human. The uniformed police in charge show their resentment of the Special Branch men who treat them with the same above-the-law arrogance with which they treat the public. I am again 'awaiting trial'. Food can be brought in from outside and Hilda can visit. The desk sergeant suggests that she bring the children next time. Patrick is at boarding school in Swaziland, but I have an emotional reunion with the others in the comparative normality of an office. There are no visible minders. We are all rather stiff and uncertain with each other. I am still feeling too numb to do the occasion justice.

I know from the newspapers that all my colleagues in the Pretoria dock have been sentenced to life imprisonment. That means exactly what it says: life, without remission. It is too awful and depressing to contemplate, though there is comfort in the fact that no one has been sentenced to death. I feel as though something inside me has snapped and all my morale and confidence has leaked out. I am obsessed with thoughts of the comrades I know so well who are now out there somewhere, far away and out of reach. I should be rejoicing that I am not on Robben Island with them, but all I feel is desperate sorrow for them, and for their ideals which have all ended in pain. I keep wondering why it is that only I am here with something still to hope for. Why me? What did I do or say? What did I fail to do that I could have done or should have done? Guilty questions gnaw away at me, but there are no answers. Something has been lost – hope? morale? – I don't know what, and with it my inner spark.

I am at Marshall Square for about a week before my application for bail is to be heard at the Magistrate's Court. I have been too deflated to do anything about it, but Hilda has arranged it all. The charge against me is not yet clear. The charge sheet simply cites an offence under the Suppression of Communism Act.

It is Saturday morning. At the Magistrate's Court I am left to wait in a large bare cell in the basement. There are some twenty young men sitting on the floor, with others being brought in from time to time. They are all teenagers or in their early twenties – I am literally old enough to be their father. I sit on the floor with my back against the wall, listening to the talk around me. It is about how and why they have been arrested, and how they plan to talk their way out again.

They are all here for what they call 'bottles' or 'wheels'. These are the favourite petty crimes of white youths on Friday nights in Johannesburg. Selling a bottle of prohibited brandy to a black is the easiest way of raising a quick pound; and stealing a car for a joyride the easiest way to a night out. Some of them are already old hands with concocted and unlikely alibis ready; others are apprehensive first-timers. They all strike me as juvenile delinquents rather than criminals.

They are keeping their courage up before they are hauled off to court. All of them, guilty or innocent, claim they have been framed. They establish their places in the petty crime pecking order by talking of their past offences and boasting of time spent in jail. I take no part in the talk.

When they finish measuring each other up someone turns to me: 'What're you in for?'

At least he didn't call me 'Dad'.

I think 'Communism' might give the wrong impression, so I say: 'Treason'.

It is an instant conversation stopper. Everyone turns to stare. I recall the time one of my comrades gave 'treason' as an answer to a prisoner in the Fort in 1956, and the follow-up question: 'Did they catch you at it?' Here the follow-up is to establish ranking.

'How long've you been in?'

One-upmanship.

'One year.'

They have been talking in days, or at most weeks. They look at me in awe. This is out of their class. For the first time in my life I feel like 'The Man' in American crime novels – the big criminal in a gaggle of punks. They keep a respectful silence.

The numbers in the cell dwindle as they are called out one by one for their moment in court, until I am the only one and it is my turn. Hilda and Toni are in the court above, together with Vernon Berrange. It is a place for petty offences which attracts no reporters and no spectators.

Vernon makes a formal request for bail. The charge, he says, is not, on the face of it, particularly serious. The prosecutor does not agree. He says he has been instructed by the Special Branch to oppose bail, but does not know their reasons. Vernon will not let that pass. He has had the assurance, so he says, of the Investigating Officer, Detective Sergeant Dirker, that bail would *not* be opposed – he must be referring to Dirker's mumbled reply to him in the Pretoria court. He demands that Dirker be called to explain, and the court is adjourned while the prosecutor goes in search of him.

But Dirker cannot be found. Vernon insists that someone from the Special Branch be called instead. We adjourn again until the prosecutor returns to report that he can get no reply on the Special Branch telephone.

No one suggests why, but everyone in court knows that the Transvaal versus Western Province match for rugby's Currie Cup is about to kick off at Ellis Park. It is the sporting contest of the year – the South African equivalent of the FA Cup Final and the Oxford-Cambridge Boat Race rolled into one. It is well past the lunch hour. Everyone in court wants to get away, but the police state appears to have adjourned for the serious business of the afternoon. Vernon presses the magistrate for a decision; the prosecutor feels he has done enough and gives way; the magistrate thinks for a few moments and sets bail at £1 000. Somehow Hilda has arranged for the cash. Within the hour I am free and on my way home – by courtesy of Berrange and the South African Rugby Union.

In Pretoria, the state has perpetrated the last dirty fraud of the Rivonia Trial. Bram Fischer had been given an undertaking that his convicted clients would not be moved from Pretoria before he could consult with them and take their instructions on an appeal. The undertaking has been dishonoured. There have been no consultations, but all except Goldberg have been whipped off to Robben

Island a thousand miles away. Goldberg is still held in Pretoria's Central Prison reserved for whites. I know that towards the end of the trial the men had discussed the matter of a possible appeal and had decided not to make one whatever the verdict might be. It would send out the wrong message, and undermine the political purpose of their stance of apologising for nothing and retracting nothing.

But that was before. Now the lawyers want them to have proper legal advice and to consider their decision in the light of the verdict and sentence. If they have been denied consultation in Pretoria they will have to have it on Robben Island. Bram is already on his way to Cape Town where he will combine the consultation with a celebration of his daughter Ilse's birthday. He is in a state of exhaustion. The months he has spent in painstaking and meticulous attention to every detail of the case have taken their toll. He has made himself personally responsible for everything, with the single-handed assistance of his wife Molly. His days have been dedicated to the trial; his nights to working underground with Hilda and others to reconstruct the shattered Communist Party. He has been living in unrelieved tension, driving himself beyond the bounds of reason and good sense.

But that is Bram. He never thinks of self. His worst days must have been when the employees from Lilliesleaf Farm were on the witness stand. Any of them might point directly at him as one of the 'conspirators' they had seen there regularly. But he would not stay away though we all urged him to; the cross-examination could have been left to his colleagues. He had endured that week or more in agonising tension, waiting for an accusatory finger to turn his way; and for no reason except his own sense of duty. In the end no one pointed at him. On top of the other stresses of his life, that had stretched his courage and self-discipline to the limit. He has been holding himself together until the end of the trial by will-power alone. But he is now close to the end of his tether.

The afternoon passes between press photographers and reporters and learning to know my family again. As news of my release filters out there are phone calls from friends and relations, and a few close friends arrive surreptitiously across the back fence to welcome me home. I am in no mood for celebration, depressed by the thought of the men buried for life on Robben Island. The children are happy and climbing all over me, but I miss Patrick who is away at boarding school and cannot shake off my inertia. I go to bed depressed, only to be woken at first light by my next door neighbour, Ivan Schermbrucker, who is one of our closest friends. We and our children move freely across adjoining fences from his house to ours, but do not usually intrude into each other's bedrooms at dawn. I ask him what is going on. He sits down heavily on the end of my bed, buries his face in his hands and starts to cry.

I have never known him like this. He is usually strong and good humoured, given to explosive bouts of moral rage rather than to tears. He is a deeply human man who conceals a caring heart under a froth of curses and bloodthirsty promises to 'kill the bastards'. We both know from the pattern of the latest arrests that he is in imminent danger himself. People have been urging him to leave while he still can, but Ivan has been refusing to go. He cannot bring himself to leave friends and comrades who are in the same peril as he is but cannot leave. He is living on borrowed time, and so is his wife Lesley who has also been involved in much of his political activity. My immediate thought is that Lesley must have been arrested. I put out a hand to steady him until he can talk. And then he blurts out: 'It's Molly! Molly is dead!'

Molly Fischer is Bram's wife! Dead? So strong and alive yesterday, dead today? It is impossible to take in. She has been a close and much-loved friend of all of us for many years. She has helped us through all our troubles despite many of her own, and has been the strong prop on whom Bram has always leaned in his legal and political work. Selflessly and without any publicity, she has given the last year to Bram's single-minded mission of saving his Rivonia comrades from the gallows. Only those close to them know how crucial Molly's strength and support have been for Bram and all of us in these testing times.

And now, suddenly, she is dead on a road through the Free State on the way to Robben Island. Their car was nearing a bridge when a motor cycle came towards them on the wrong side of the road. Bram was driving. He swerved to avoid the rider, left the road and careered down the river bank into the water. Bram and his front seat passenger, Liz Lewin, had managed to struggle free. Molly had been trapped in the back. As they struggled to free her, the car had slipped into deep water. Molly had drowned before their eyes.

It is the last tragic episode of the Rivonia Trial.

If only . . . If only the state had honoured its pledges. If only they had kept Mandela and the others in Pretoria for a consultation, Bram and Molly might not have been on the road to Robben Island. Rivonia has laid a curse on all our lives.

This is truly nightmare time, and Hilda, Ivan and I are all in tears. If only . . . If only Bram and Molly had not felt such personal responsibility. If only our trial had not left Bram so strung out and exhausted. There is nothing we can do but weep. Much later we learn from Liz Lewin that Bram's first thought after the disaster is for those who wait on his mission to Robben Island. He *has* to call someone and explain. He starts dialling our number. Then he turns to Liz and says: 'Oh no! It's Rusty's first day home. I cannot do this to him!' So he calls Ivan instead. That is so typically Bram.

Relief at being home and free does not lift my depression. Molly is to be buried in Johannesburg, and Bram has asked that Hilda make the funeral oration. There will be many mourners – the Fischers are a widely loved and respected family – but Hilda and I are both banned from all gatherings. We apply to the Chief Magistrate for permission to attend the funeral.

Hilda is ready to ignore the ban and speak whatever the consequences. Her speech is already prepared, but everyone advises Bram against it. Her appearance could be an excuse for police intervention, and turn the funeral into a riot. We remain gloomily at home while the funeral takes place, and Hilda's oration is spoken by Vernon Berrange. The Magistrate's permission reaches us after the funeral is over. It is a bleak and depressing end to a bleak and depressing period in our lives, dominated by arrests, imprisonments and deaths and with no promise of improvement.

June 26th, Freedom Day – but not for me. I am back in court. There is still no detail on the charge and I am remanded for another three months. I spend the time at home, hibernating. I have no work, no expectation of work, and nothing to fill the day except signing the police register at Marshall Square between noon and two.

I have no desire to do anything. I sit on our front veranda in the bright mid-winter sunshine, back against the wall, basking motionless like a lizard. No one calls at the house any more. Most of our friends are in prison or in exile. The few who are not stay away from us to avoid the attention of our police 'minder' who is still watching us from the hut across the road. Special Branch men still arrive at the house unexpectedly at odd hours, claiming to be 'just checking' but keeping up the intimidation.

Bit by bit I learn something of the scale of the political debacle after the Rivonia arrests. It is as though a hurricane has swept through the movement we were part of, leaving a trail of destruction. There is no longer a cohesive movement. It has been ruthlessly broken up, and all our carefully constructed networks are no more. Only fragments of our organised groups have weathered the onslaught, a skeleton corps of former activists. Some are cautiously restoring secret links and others are keeping their heads down until the storm has passed.

The movement which we had believed we were representing in the Pretoria dock is now almost a thing of the past. One can get no sense of the overall picture. One can only guess which of the survivors have stayed and which have gone, which have kept faith and resisted and which have broken and collaborated. I sit and wonder about the self-sacrificial courage of Mandela, Sisulu and the others in the court at Pretoria and what purpose it had served. Had it encouraged the mass of the movement's followers, and strengthened their will to resist and resist again? Had it restored their confidence in struggle and given them an example of how it can be fought with pride even in the teeth of adversity? I don't know. I don't think we can ever know – but I look back on it with pride.

I learn a little about what Hilda, Bram, Ivan and a handful of others have been doing while I was in prison. They have taken enormous risks to try and reassemble the fragments of the Party and revive the organisation. It required courage and ingenuity to revive a few small groups, only to see them torn apart again by the Security Police. Though the results have been minimal they are a tribute to the spirit of the Party members, but not much more. There will be a time to resurrect the political dead, but perhaps it is still too soon. I tell myself that I ought to join in the attempt, but I cannot rouse the energy.

I justify myself. I am too notorious, too closely watched; I will give anything the kiss of death by joining in. I am no longer part of the activist fraternity but truly on my own. I should be thinking of things I can do, taking decisions, being dynamic. But I cannot rise to it. I can only bask and wait for my new trial which is only weeks away.

I ought to be preparing for it but I am growing fatalistic. Whatever the details of the case against me, I can see no chance that I will not be convicted. The evidence from Rivonia alone can convict me of communicating with other banned and listed people; of attending a gathering; of taking part in the activities of banned organisations; and possibly of leaving the Johannesburg Magisterial District – no one knows for sure where the boundary is or whether Lilliesleaf is inside or outside. Each offence can carry a ten-year sentence. I do not believe in fairies. I know my case is hopeless, and it will send me back to prison for years, perhaps for ever – if I do not get away. But I cannot rouse myself to decide anything or do anything.

Hilda and I discuss our future endlessly, and inconclusively. We are avoiding any decision, perhaps because we do not want to revive all the strains and stresses of the year we are still recovering from. Hilda, I know, has long been prepared to leave, but she has never pressed the matter while my instincts have all been against it. We know that time is running out and the chance of getting away is getting smaller by the day. The people Hilda has been working with in their attempts to re-create a Party apparatus are now being arrested one by one. The police net is moving close to her. A shocked Lesley Schermbrucker comes over the fence to tell us that Ivan has been arrested. Two others from her circle – Piet Beyleveld and Bartholomew Hlapane – have also been arrested and are rumoured to be talking and considering giving evidence against the others. We can no longer wait. Hilda *has* to get away from the house at once.

For reasons of their own, the Security Police favour night-time arrest. Hilda spends several nights sleeping away from home, but risks slipping back surreptitiously each morning to see the children off to school. She cannot bear not to see them though every minute she is in the house is an intolerable strain on both our nerves. A few days pass; nothing happens, so Hilda decides she has had enough and comes back to sleep the night at home. Saturday morning. The children have gone off to play with friends, and Hilda is in the kitchen doing household chores.

The phone rings and a stranger with a thick *platteland* accent asks for her. He tells her he has a message from a friend in Cape Town but cannot give it over the phone. Will she be in later if he calls? She says she will. It has to be bogus. At this time of fear and suspicion no one could be daft enough to announce – on *our* phone! – that he has a message too secret to be spoken of.

Hilda must get away from the house at once, before he arrives. I am under twenty-four hour house arrest at weekends and dare not leave the house. I am standing tense and nervous at our living-room window, watching the road outside, while Hilda potters about in the kitchen, preparing to go but not going, as if she cannot bring herself to it. A Volkswagen 'beetle' pulls up at our gate and two men climb out. I shout at Hilda: 'OUT NOW! Through the back!' as they walk up the garden path to our front door. I take my time, opening the door. They ask for Hilda and I tell them she is out, though I have no idea whether she is or not.

Out where?

She's gone shopping.

Shopping where?

How should I know?

When will she be back?

I have no idea – a couple of hours maybe.

They say they are coming in to check. I have been through this before and plant myself in their path and demand to see a search warrant – as I always do. They ignore me – as they always do – and shoulder me aside as though the law does not apply to them. They search the house and garden.

Hilda has vanished.

They leave without a word. They are probably already wondering how to report to their superiors without mentioning their tip-off telephone call, made simply to save themselves a little trouble. I know they will be back. And next time there will be no advance warning.

I have no idea where Hilda is, and dare not leave the house to try and find out. I have no choice but to wait for her to make contact – if they have not already stumbled across her in the street. I know we are now at the end of the road. When they come back, if Hilda is home they will take her away. And if she is not, they will probably take me for questioning or as hostage for her. We no longer have any choice. This is the final reality for us both; either we flee the country together or we go to prison separately for a long, long time.

I cannot leave the house, so the only person I can talk to is Lesley who can come over the back fence without being seen by our minder. She and Ivan have often expressed their objection to people leaving the country. For them it has been a matter of principle, an act of solidarity with all those others whose circumstances make it impossible for them to leave. They have lived up to their principles even when Ivan's own arrest was becoming certain. I respect their stand but do not join with it. I do not believe that any real political purpose is served by gestures or by self sacrifice. To me, staying or going has never been a moral principle which everyone should be persuaded to follow. I have stayed because it has been necessary to my personal sense of self-respect.

Lesley, I think, understands my position and accepts it as I do hers. She is not given to theoretical debate and does not argue with me now. She accepts that we must go and responds calmly and practically. She knows a reliable man who might take us to the Bechuanaland border and put us on course for Lobatse. Within two days the arrangements have been made.

I have managed to trace Hilda and can exchange letters with her through go-betweens. I tell her the arrangements. We tell no one except Toni, her husband Ivan, and my brother. Hilda feels unable to leave without seeing our old friends Borch and Vera Burchard for the last time. She visits them surreptitiously but says nothing about leaving. They know the life we have been living, and Borch senses the truth. He had been through something like this himself in Germany in 1931 when information about a Jewish grandparent came to the notice of the Nazis.

The next day he calls at my brother's office – they had never met. He produces a roll of banknotes and puts them on Harold's desk, saying only: 'This is for Rusty.' He is not a wealthy man. He lives by dabbling from home in antiques, in which he is an expert. One week they might dine on a Chippendale table and chairs, the next on plain deal and kitchen chairs if his business deal has been a success. For him, £300 was an enormous sum. It was a gesture of friendship which I would treasure for the rest of my life.

Lesley has solved one problem. The money solves another – I had not dared to draw the last remnants from my bank account in case it alerted the authorities. We are ready to go, but not before explaining it all to our children, face to face, and promising that we will send for them to join us as soon as we can. It is dangerous for Hilda to break hiding in order to meet them, but the risk has to be taken.

We arrange a rendezvous in an under-used picnic place not far from our home. Toni and I smuggle the children out through neighbouring gardens and into a borrowed car which is unlikely to be followed. We wait under trees until Hilda arrives on foot, wearing high-heeled shoes which I have never known her to wear, and a borrowed garden-party hat suitable for Royal Ascot. It is a minimal disguise, not very effective, but in their excitement at being with her again Keith and Frances do not appear to notice. Patrick is at school in Swaziland. He was on a camping holiday in Rhodesia when I was arrested. I have not seen him for over a year and he will not even know we are leaving until after we are gone. But the younger ones are visibly upset by our news, which they probably cannot understand.

It is an unhappy meeting but we dare not prolong it in that exposed place. We are all trying to hold back tears as Hilda kisses and hugs them for the last time, and then walks away alone on wobbly heels, not looking back. We wait till she is out of sight before I take the children home.

Toni and her husband Ivan (the other Ivan), who had married while I was in jail, are living with us. Toni has received the news of our leaving with a characteristic bluntness: 'I don't know why you didn't decide to do it long ago.' They have agreed to stay on in the house and take care of the children for the time being. It is suppertime. I say my own farewells to them all, and leave them at the table while I black my hair and eyebrows in private in my own inadequate attempt at a disguise.

It is already dark. I have packed a small canvas bag with a water bottle and some minimal essentials for Hilda and myself, and slip out of the house and across our back fence without seeing them again. There can be no going back. I have broken my house arrest order and left my home for ever.

As arranged, Lesley picks me up in her car not far away, drives me to the west gate of the University and leaves me there to skulk in the deep shadow of the trees. Hilda arrives soon after. We skulk together in fear, waiting for our get-away car and its unknown driver to arrive. I have visions of something sleek and fast, but a beat-up American rattle-trap comes up out of the night and pulls in. The driver gestures us to climb in the back – his young son is in the passenger seat beside him. We do not know him and do not exchange names as he takes off.

Hilda and I keep our heads well down, frozen in fear of being recognised as we drive through the town where we are both well known. We are on the main road out of the city and making for the West Rand and Bechuanaland. There is considerable traffic on the road. We shrink down in the back seat each time a car comes up to overtake, hiding our faces. We are very much aware that if we are stopped now for any reason, we are finished. We can find nothing to say to our driver, who we discover is named MacClipper. He seems very relaxed about the whole thing, but has nothing to say to us either.

We leave the West Rand towns behind us and we are nearing Mafeking (now Mafikeng) which is the last town before the border. Then he says sourly: 'The police are always stopping cars in this place,' and he pulls the car off the road on to the veld.

We can see the town lights in the distance, but the track he is following – if there is one – is invisible to us. He seems to be taking a circuit across the bare veld to by-pass the town. We bump and rattle across unmade ground not far from the black 'location'. Our headlights must be visible from miles away. We are tense, expecting to be followed or intercepted, but there is no sign of anyone taking any interest in us. MacClipper seems very sure of his route past and beyond the black shanty-town and back to the main road beyond.[1] The lights of Mafeking disappear into the distance behind us.

Around midnight, MacClipper finds the landmark he is watching out for and pulls the car off on to the verge. We get out as he tells us: 'We walk from here. I will go with you for the first mile.'

We leave his son asleep alone on the front seat, and he starts. We follow close on his heels. The night is pitch dark. There is no moon and nothing to be seen except the silhouettes of trees against

---

[1] We learn only later that MacClipper is an experienced cross-border smuggler when he is subsequently arrested and charged with assisting us and others to cross the border illegally.

the sky. We are apparently on a sandy track which muffles our footsteps. We must be passing close to some huts. We can hear dogs bark in the distance. He puts a finger to his lips to warn us to keep silent. The barking dies, the dogs are behind us and there is no sound except the crickets and the night insects.

We walk blindly on, until a cock crows somewhere ahead. MacClipper stops and points. 'You hear that?' We nod, and wait in silence. Another cock crows. 'You hear that?' He points again. 'Walk straight between those two and you will come to the border.' We shake hands and murmur our thanks, and then he turns round and is gone, back into the darkness. The cocks do not crow again.

We walk on blindly in the dark, trying to hold in our minds where the cocks had crowed, following the sandy path by its feel beneath our feet – if it was a path. We are in dry, grassless country where apparently nothing grows except the thorn bushes we blunder into in the dark. Long thorns tear at our legs and clothing. I try to keep a bearing on the stars, but I know too little about the night sky. Each time I look down to try and glimpse the path, my lode-star is lost amongst a million others blazing in the night sky.

We walk what we think is a straight course in the right direction, but there is no fence of any sort. We carry on, walking blindly without any certainty. The ground under our feet changes, and we are stumbling over mounds and furrows as if over roughly ploughed ground peppered with invisible holes. I go down into one up to my thighs. I know we have left whatever track there was and have no idea where we are.

We walk for over an hour. Far off on the horizon we can see the glow of reflected light in the sky. We decide it must be a town – perhaps Lobatse? We change course and head in that direction before we come to our senses and realise that a village of the size of Lobatse could not generate that much light. If it isn't Lobatse, it can only be Mafeking. We must be heading back when we are trying to head away.

We are well and truly lost in dangerous ground where we are in danger of twisting an ankle or breaking a leg through falling into holes. We no longer know which way is forward and which way back, but we walk away from the glow in the sky, tired and depressed. I have brought nothing that is of any help except a small pocket compass. Its dial is not illuminated. We risk striking a match to look at it knowing that the flare will be visible for miles.

We turn to walk west, telling ourselves that that way we must reach the border. But we are moving more slowly and falling into holes and blundering into thorn bushes which scratch and tear. But still no fence. Finally we give up and decide to rest until it grows light.

When dawn comes we are nowhere. As far as the eye can see, nothing but dry dust-land, withered scrub grass and thorn bush. We must still be inside South Africa. We start up again, walking west until we see some distant huts – black people's huts. They should not be hostile. We will have to take a chance. I leave Hilda sitting half hidden in the shade of some bushes, and go on alone. There are a few men moving about between the huts. I know no Sechuana, so I gather up my scraps of Zulu, pidgin and Afrikaans to make some sort of greeting and explain my problems. I have to improvise or use English for things like 'border fences' and 'guide'. I am not sure that they understand, but one of them says he will show me the way.

We collect Hilda and follow him along a sandy trail on which there are tyre tracks. Police patrols perhaps? I ask whether the police come past this way. They do, but they are 'OK police. No trouble'. I am uncertain about him. He has asked no questions about us, or where we have come from or why we are walking to the border. Could he be leading us to the OK police?

We are dead tired and very uneasy, but there is no choice but to go on. We come to a fence – or rather two. They are ordinary barbed wire farm fences running parallel, perhaps ten yards apart, nothing like the steel-mesh, razor-wired and electrified barrier I had in my imagination. I am still doubtful whether this really is the border, but he says it is. We thank him, crawl through between the barbed strands, and walk away as fast as we can. The fence is out of sight. We are out of South Africa and away. Or so we hope and trust.

20

OVER, AND OUT
1964 – 94

At that moment I am hit by the consciousness that I have lost my home. It is over seventy-five years since my grandfather made his way to the Witwatersrand and settled down to found a family. Whether he came to that rocky treeless place in search of gold, freedom or adventure, I do not know. It was a mining camp of tents and shacks. He was there when they laid down the first roads and pegged out the first building plots of what is now the city of Johannesburg.

My family has been there ever since. It has been my home for forty-four years. And now, in the night, I have pulled up my roots and shaken off the earth they grew in. We are transplanting ourselves, without any of the surrounding soil which sustained our life and growth. We carry nothing except a small canvas bag of our belongings, and a wad of Borch's banknotes.

Hilda's legs are giving way beneath her. My legs have been partially protected by trousers, but hers are badly scratched and torn by thorns. We have walked all night, and now the sun is growing hot and our water bottle is empty. Hilda cannot go on without rest. We are across the fence and probably out of sight of South Africa, but not yet far enough to be safe from kidnap – Bechuanaland's territorial rights are not likely to deter the South African police. We make it as far as a clump of acacias where there is some small shade. I leave Hilda there to rest while I go on to see what I can find.

A mile away I find a group of huts. I don't know what sort of reception I will get there, but I walk towards them anyway. Some blanketed men are squatting on stones around a small fire of thorn twigs. As though it happens every day, no one shows any interest in this tired, dishevelled white man who has arrived on foot from nowhere. Again I stumble through the ritual greetings; they remain hunched over the fire, giving only monosyllabic responses. There is no hostility and little spark of life. Nothing moves them. They seem to have given up on life; their eyes are dead; no one makes room for me at the fireside or invites me to join them. They are listless, wrapped up in misery. I do not need to ask why. There is no sign of any growing thing, only fields of withered and long-dead maize stalks from years before; no sign of any ploughing or planting. They are in the third year of an unbroken drought, defeated by it and just managing to cling on to the edge of life in the bone-dry dustland.

A woman emerges from one of the huts. She speaks some English – she has worked as a domestic servant in Johannesburg. I tell her that my wife is sitting under a tree in the distance and cannot walk much further. She takes me by the arm, and we set out to fetch her. She walks with a pronounced hobble, as though one hip is broken.

When we get back to where Hilda is waiting, she helps her up with a strong arm and supports her on the walk back to the huts. She brings out a small wooden stool from the hut so that Hilda can sit down while she boils a kettle on the fire and then bathes and massages Hilda's legs. She does not ask where we have come from or why, but she says that a few weeks before she had seen a man and a woman walking by, also carrying a bag. We know that Reg and Hetty September had crossed the border at about that time; perhaps she had seen them. If so, we may not be completely off track.

She fetches a small spoonful of tea leaves from the hut – they look as though they have been used before and been redried. She makes us tin mugs of hot water barely tinted with tea, and without milk or sugar. It is probably the only food there is in the place. While she is doing this, I try to draw the men into conversation. Do they know where there might be a telephone nearby – I need to phone our friends in Lobatse for help. No, no phones. A shop then? A shop might have a phone. No, too far. A school? No, too far.

Where is Lobatse? Too far.

They are not trying. It is not their problem. They are telling me in their own way to let them expire in peace. I try a different tack. I will pay money to anyone who can help us get to Lobatse – someone with a cart perhaps? No, no carts. How about a horse? No horses. A donkey? No donkeys.

For a while the woman listens while the men talk. Then she takes a hand. With my minimal Sechuana, I gather she is arguing about someone who *does* have a cart – she points 'over there' across the horizon. The men are sullen and unmoved. The horse has been taken out to the fields; they don't know where. The owner of the cart has gone with it. The woman stands behind them, arguing, contradicting, becoming more and more angry and insistent. She is the only one with the energy to carry on. She harangues them, lashing them with her tongue.

The men give up the argument and surrender. They are all clinging to life by the most emaciated of threads, but even in this dying place the woman is proving stronger. At last, one of the men gets up from his stone, reluctantly, protesting, and shuffles away to god knows where.

The day passes slowly. We doze in the sun, waiting for something to happen. In mid-afternoon a ball of dust approaches across the veld, and from it materialises a man driving a donkey cart. The woman has won.

She tells us: 'This is the man. He will take you.'

'Take us where?'

'To a motor car.'

'A motor car? Where?'

She points out into the distance in the nowhere land. The cart is little more than a board on two wheels, about a metre square. The owner speaks nothing but Sechuana; he says something but I do not understand. We clamber aboard for better or for worse, balancing ourselves on the edge with our legs dangling down almost to the ground. We thank the woman and press her hands in gratitude. I put some money into her hand, the driver whips up his donkey and we take off. There is no track. We bump across the open veld towards somewhere where it is said there will be a motor car.

Over an hour later there is – a modern American sedan parked by a cluster of huts in the middle of nowhere. Our driver points to one of the huts, which we enter rather tentatively. It is all quite surreal. Inside, facing one another across a kitchen table, sit a white man and a black counting out piles of banknotes and coins. We explain that we are trying to get to Lobatse. The white man says he is going that way when he has finished here, and will take us. The black man brushes a sleeping rooster off the pink nylon coverlet of a high iron bedstead, and suggests we sit down. They show no more surprise about the two dust-covered white travellers who have popped up with almost no luggage than we do at the rooster. They carry on counting the money and sorting it into heaps while we study a Blake etching of Nebuchadnezzar crawling on hands and knees which is hanging on the wall.

We have nothing to say to each other until it is time to leave. We say goodbye to the black man and set off in the car to Lobatse. We are on the road for more than an hour. Our driver asks us no questions but chats amiably enough about his work as a government agricultural officer. He explains that his work entails visiting rural districts and making payment of government subsidies to the local small farmers. We talk about the drought and about farming – he is avoiding asking anything about us or where we have come from or why. It seems he is anxious not to know anything about it. And when he drops us off in the centre of Lobatse at our request, he drives off without wanting to know where we are going.

It is a one-horse town with the charmless character of a sleepy South African *dorp*. There is a single street of shops with wooden porches raised up above the dirt street, stacked with iron pots, farm implements and sacks of grain. The shopkeepers all seem to be Indian. The road runs out through the shops to an edge-of-town filling station, and on to the north. There is a dusty crossroad that leads to the railway station and on to the South African border only a few miles east. We have the name of a Congress supporter we need to contact – an Indian merchant called Azad.

In a village this size everyone should know everyone, and certainly every Indian shopkeeper will know every other shopkeeper. We ask in the nearest shop for Azad's whereabouts. They look at us with sly suspicion and deny any knowledge of him. We try next door, with the same result. We can sense that we are being watched as we walk down the street. We are strangers, tatty and dishevelled strangers; who knows what we are up to? It is a border town where the South African police come and go with impunity, bringing the South African terror with them. Eyes and whispers seem to follow us around, and the feeling everyone is watching everyone else, and being watched. Paranoia.

An Indian lad in his teens follows us out of a shop and trails along behind us. When he feels it is safe, he comes up and tells us quietly where to find Azad. Azad is friendly, but does not know us. He sends someone to fetch the local ANC people, perhaps in order to check our bona fides. The ANC representatives are Maulvi Cachalia and Dan Tloome, both old friends and colleagues of ours from Johannesburg. They are maintaining a refugee house in the black slum area of town but think it will not be safe for us or for them if we go there. The place is kept under observation by both the South African and Bechuanaland police. We will also not be safe in the town hotel which is a regular drinking haunt of right-wing extremists and South African agents. They take us to a newish hotel on the outskirts of town which is safer, but more expensive. I still have Borch's bankroll in my pocket, so we settle for that.

Next morning we walk into town to declare ourselves to the Immigration authorities. Our route takes us past a filling-station. We are intrigued to discover the route of our all-night walk and long drive to Lobatse, so I ask the Indian proprietor whether he sells road maps. He does not, but he has one of his own at home, and offers to fetch it for us. We tell him it is not that important. He says 'Don't worry – I know everything!' and taps a conspiratorial forefinger against the side of his nose.

Perhaps he does. Perhaps that is part of survival so close to an unfriendly border. Certainly Tloome and Cachalia need to know everything, as does our other ANC comrade from Johannesburg, Fish Kietsing, now in charge of ANC transport in Bechuanaland. They are all very conscious of the South African police presence everywhere in this nominally independent country. They think we should be safe for a short while because there has been no publicity about our arrival. But they know this town, and are insistent that we must get away from it without delay.

There are few options. One is the road north. It is the only road which does not lead into South Africa or into Southern Rhodesia which has been known to hand refugees over to the South African police. It runs for hundreds of miles to a narrow neck of land – the Caprivi strip – which has a short frontier with Zambia. Most of the road runs through bush country, inhabited only by wildlife including lion, buffalo and elephant. In the event of a breakdown there a vehicle can be stranded for days or weeks before another vehicle comes along. It is a journey which can only be risked by two vehicles travelling together.

The ANC has been preparing such a voyage for some refugees who are waiting in Francistown, but has run into problems. One of their two vehicles has recently been wrecked by a bomb, and the other is stranded in the garage with a broken clutch. Kietsing believes that the garage's inordinate delay in getting a replacement part from South Africa is sabotage. He has no idea when the vehicle will be back in service.

The only other way is by rail. The line comes from South Africa and runs north through Bechuanaland before crossing into Southern Rhodesia on its way to Zambia. It is operated by South Africa's state railways. A few weeks ago, an Indian refugee from South Africa had been kidnapped en route and handed over to the South African police. We have made our way in, but have no idea how we will manage to make it out.

We must report our presence to the Immigration authorities before they discover us here without passports. Bechuanaland is still a British Protectorate, and its immigration and security man is called Sheppard. He is young, breezy and very British. We explain that we are only passing through, and will be leaving as soon as we can arrange it. He wants to know more than we are prepared to tell him about how we crossed the border and what we had been doing before. We tell him as little as we can to satisfy him. He uses what we come to know as his favourite phrase – 'Good oh!' – and urges us to be on our way as quickly as possible. His concern appears to be to get us off his patch before there is any friction with South Africa. He also warns us to stay away from the hotel in town, and to keep him informed about our movements.

For a few days we kick our heels, waiting for developments at the ANC's garage. Sheppard drops in almost daily, ostensibly to make sure we are safe but really to chivvy us up to leave. We would if we could. I phone every air charter company listed in the phone book in Bechuanaland and Southern Rhodesia. I ask about a charter flight to Zambia. They all prevaricate; they cannot say when they might have a plane available, but can they have my name and address to get back to me? Perhaps they are all one company operating under different names and have been warned off by South Africa. Or perhaps I too am becoming paranoid.

In a shop in town we have a chance encounter with a couple we had known quite well in Johannesburg before they left some years before. They are working in Lobatse, and want to know all about us and other former colleagues since they last saw us. They do not want to talk there, but arrange to meet us at the weekend. They are furtive, looking over their shoulders as they arrange to pick us up by car on a side road some distance away from our hotel. We drive some miles out of town before they feel it is safe to stop and picnic under some trees away from the road. Their talk is all of Lobatse's secret enmities and suspicions, and of being watched. Perhaps they too are paranoid.

Back at the hotel there are several phone messages from Johannesburg's newspapers. The story that we are in Lobatse is on the front page of the *Sunday Times*, and reporters from various places want to interview us about our 'escape'. In the hotel lounge we hear people talking about us – they do not yet recognise us. By the next day they will, and so will everyone else in Lobatse. We try to avoid meeting with people in the hotel and take refuge in the darkness of the recreation room where they are screening the film 'The Guns of Navarone'. It only adds to our unease. It is filled with suspense, violence and terror. Halfway through there is a tap on my shoulder. Sheppard. He beckons us out to tell us that there is talk in the downtown bar of a plot to kidnap us. He urges us to stay out of sight and keep our door locked – and to leave Lobatse without delay. He obviously relishes the role of secret agent, but can make no suggestions about how we might get away from town.

Next morning we walk into town to consult our ANC comrades. A yellow sedan car with South African Railway number-plates follows us around – we have seen it in the town several times before. Later in the day it is gone, but the following day there is a red Volkswagen 'beetle' apparently following us about. Regina Nzo and Tiny Nokwe, whose husbands are ANC leaders in exile in Lusaka, have arrived at the refugee house on their way to join them. They go off to Sheppard's office for immigration clearance, and come back to tell us of a red Volkswagen that had been outside the office while they were waiting there. Bechuanaland police had taken the white driver in, and had removed a shotgun from the car. Later the driver had been turned loose again and had driven off towards the South African border. I remember the old joke: Just because we're paranoid doesn't mean they're not trying to get us!

Our ANC colleagues have phoned Tom Nkobi, their representative in Lusaka, to see what he can do to help. Zambia is only weeks away from independence but Immigration there is still in British hands. We spend another day at the hotel waiting for his response. Sheppard drops in to see us. He is pleased with himself. He says he has been advised that Immigration in Lusaka has cleared us for entry – the impression he gives is that he has fixed it for us. Minutes after he leaves our ANC comrades arrive to tell us that Nkobi has phoned. He has arranged for a small plane to pick us up from Palapye Road on Monday morning – there should be no immigration problems. Sheppard has almost certainly been eavesdropping.

Palapye Road is a village a long way north. We have no way of getting there except by train. I know that Sheppard's police vehicles make frequent runs there and back, so I go to his office and tell him about the plane, which he purports to treat as news. I make the only request ever for his assistance. Can Hilda and I ride to Palapye Road on one of his trucks? He is smooth, sympathetic but full of regrets. 'Regulations, you understand . . .' I have not really expected anything else. I am sure he genuinely wants us gone from Lobatse but will not raise a finger to help. It might compromise the cosy British relations with South Africa.

It is Saturday afternoon. We cannot contact Nkobi by phone – we have only the number of his office which will be closed until Monday. We have no way to arrange for the plane's take-off to be postponed. There is nothing for it but to risk travelling to Palapye by train. The train leaves Lobatse around midnight every night, and reaches Palapye around dawn – except on Sundays. We will have to leave that night and hang around in Palapye for twenty-four hours.

No one knows of our plan except Tloome and Cachalia. I tell Sheppard in the hope that his security people will watch to see that we do not run foul of any South African trouble makers. We will not check out of the hotel or buy rail tickets in advance. Cachalia will go with us to the station, buy our tickets, and settle our hotel bill afterwards. Even if someone spots us at the station, it will be midnight. We should be off the train at Palapye and safely at the High Commissioner's before anyone is likely to intercept us.

We wait till near midnight before we make our way through Lobatse's unlit lanes and alleys to the station. It is little more than a rural whistle-stop – a long, single, unlit and unroofed platform with a small brick station-master's office near the South African end. We make our way to the farthest end before we cross the street on to the platform, and stand in the deep shadows of some tall wattle trees. The place is totally deserted, and pitch dark except for a single feeble light which hangs above the ticket-office window.

Hilda and I wait there while Maulvi goes off towards the office to buy our tickets. We lose sight of him. Then a car drives up at speed towards the station, its headlights raking the platform. It makes a sharp stop and some men climb out and stand in a group under the light. Then a second car close behind, and more men, big well-fed men in coats. South African security men in civilian clothes. We stay where we are, frozen. One of the men leaves the group and paces slowly, heavily, along the platform towards us. Colonel Britz. He paces past us not more than a few metres away, not looking at us but knowing we are there. We are holding hands tightly clasped. I have taken my Swiss army knife from my pocket, opened the large and small blades and hold it in my fist like a dagger. I have made up my mind. I have had enough. If he or any of his men try to lay hands on us I will use it, come what may. Britz paces slowly by, continues for a few metres and then turns around and paces slowly back, still not looking at us. He rejoins the group at the ticket office.

Maulvi comes back to us from out of the dark. He has not bought the tickets. A black railway worker has warned him that the white men are talking about us, and know we are going to board the train. We are standing there, uncertain what to do, as the train pulls in at the other end of the platform, its brakes squeaking. As it comes to a halt there is sudden noise, the sound of voices, carriage doors slamming and people getting off beyond the smoke and steam of the locomotive. I look everywhere for a sight of Sheppard or his men. Where in hell is he, with his smooth assurance and his security men when we need them?

Maulvi grabs our arms and says: 'Run!'

We turn and run from the platform, across the unlit street and into the darkness and the bush beyond. We stumble blindly past the backs of houses and through gates and yards. Maulvi must know where we are. He opens a house door without ceremony and pulls us inside. We stand breathless and petrified in a dark passage as he whispers explanations in Gujerati to a startled householder. We can hear the train whistle and begin to move out of the station on its journey north. The sound of people and of movement dies away outside. We sit in total darkness until the night is still again.

Maulvi decides it is safe for him to go out and see what there is to see before we make any move. He comes back to tell us that the cars and the South African men have gone and are nowhere to be seen. But he has encountered Sheppard who is cruising about in a car, and has been asked where we are. Sheppard already knows that we are not aboard the train, but he wants to make sure that we are safe – or so he says. Our man in Lobatse!

We make our way to Azad's house, and spend the rest of the night curled up on settees. In the morning Azad brings in a young white man, unshaven and in well-worn camping clothes. He has a fairly plausible story about fleeing from South Africa to escape arrest for 'immorality' with a coloured girl. He has heard – from Azad or who? – that we need a lift to Palapye. He has a truck and is going that way. We have no way of knowing whether he is genuine – but we are too hyped up and suspicious to trust anyone we do not know, and turn his offer down.

Palapye is as far away as ever and our time is running out fast. Hilda takes the decision to approach Azad. He has helped us in various ways and knows about our transport problem but has not offered to solve it for us. He will have to live in and with Lobatse after we have gone. But we have exhausted all our options so Hilda asks him directly for the loan of his truck. He agrees without argument. We decide to make no move till after dark, for his protection as well as ours. We will drive to Palapye through the night. Kietsing will come with us and drive the truck back – and bring along a few young ANC volunteers as protection, 'just in case'.

The whole operation goes smoothly. There is not another vehicle on the road. In the early hours of the morning when we are near

Palapye, we make a fire of twigs and sit around waiting for first light before driving into town. It is a village rather than a town – an African village. The cattle are being let out from their overnight kraals amongst the huts. They meander through the streets herded by small boys on their way to the grazing. The British High Commission's compound is like a last outpost of empire. A black policeman is raising the flag on a resplendent white mast which stands in the centre of a quadrangle of red earth and dust. A few square white-washed buildings are laid out with military precision with footpaths between them demarcated by lines of white-washed stones. Some barefoot men, probably convicts, are dragging thornbush fronds round and round the quadrangle to rearrange the dust in pristine whorls.

The officer in charge is expecting us – Sheppard must have been in touch. He is formal but quite unwelcoming. He is expecting a signal about our plane's arrival, and tells us to wait. We sit on the scrub grass beneath the wattle trees while the temperature rises steadily. We have not slept or eaten, but we buy tepid Coca-Cola from a roadside stall and listen for the sound of a plane.

Hours pass. Midday comes and goes, and our confidence that there will be a plane goes too. It is mid-afternoon before a signal is received and we drive out to the airstrip. It is a dusty earth track in the middle of the veld, with nothing to mark its purpose except a windsock. We catch the faint buzz of a distant plane, and watch a tiny plane turn and bump down to a dusty halt. It is a three-seater single-wing light craft; its pilot looks about nineteen years old. He says that air regulations compel him to land at Francistown for clearance before leaving Bechuanaland airspace. We say farewell to Kietsing and his bodyguard and take off.

I have a cold fear of flying. This is my first time in a light plane. We are bumping and rocketing about in the air, and my stomach is protesting. I am afraid I am about to be sick – or perhaps just die – but manage to hold on until we are circling Francistown airstrip. I am very uneasy about landing there. This is the airfield where a much larger plane had been destroyed by a bomb while waiting to pick up Arthur Goldreich and Harold Wolpe and fly them to safety.

Francistown is an outpost of the country's rabid white right-wing. We are parked a long way from the airport buildings, stretching our legs on the ground and watching two men coming towards us, in step. They are wearing identical kit – long khaki British army 'shorts', polished brown boots and Sam Browne belts. They come up, walk around us in silence, and exchange a few words with the pilot. Then one turns to me and says: 'Well, a thousand pounds bail. Do you think you're worth it?' They turn around and walk back, in step, like Tweedledum and Tweedledee. We are cleared to go.

After a time I realise we have changed direction and are no longer heading north. We are over a lake that stretches as far as the horizon. I can think of only one body of water as large as this in this dry country. It has to be Kariba – and it must be heading towards Southern Rhodesia! I am feeling sick with the plane's motion and sicker still with the panic notion of being kidnapped back to a South African prison. I can think of nothing I can do – and then we leave the water and are once again crossing land. A town comes into view on the horizon, the plane circles down towards a real airport with modern airport buildings, and our pilot speaks to us for the first time: 'This is Lusaka.' I want to believe, but I am still not sure.

From the side of the airport buildings people wave and call out to us. A man in British army uniform comes towards us. He looks like Tweedledum only podgier and redder, and announces that he is Napier-Bax – Lieutenant or is it Captain? – in charge of Immigration. He hands us each a notice that declares we are Prohibited Immigrants – PIs.

'I will not allow you to land here. You must get back on this plane and return to where you came from.'

I am unable to contain myself. 'We *have* landed!' I snarl at him. 'And we're not getting back on that plane to go anywhere.'

He says he can force us, if necessary. I snap back that he will have to – we are not going voluntarily and are not paying anyone to take us.

Our silent pilot joins in. He has flown all day and is not going to fly another mile. Napier-Bax is stymied. He orders us to follow and marches us off to his office. We explain to waiting friends what is happening to us, and the senior ANC people say they will go off and see what Kenneth Kaunda can do. He is Zambia's elected President Designate, but will not be in office until the country becomes independent in a week's time. Immigration is still in British hands. We wait while Napier-Bax phones in a situation report from the next office. The partitions stop short of the ceiling; we can hear every agitated word. I read the PI notice carefully, including the small type at the bottom which says that appeals against the order must be made within seventy-two hours on form P??. When Napier-Bax comes back to us I give him formal notice that we will be appealing against the order within seventy-two hours, and ask for the necessary form.

It seems that no one has ever done this to him before. He goes back next door and starts rummaging through drawers and cupboards, and then telephoning again in a search for the forms. 'I've tried to get them,' he reports, 'but they must have gone home. No one answers.'

He is getting ruffled when a message comes through. Kaunda has intervened, and the Chief Immigration Officer has agreed to postpone the order for seven days on condition that we give no interviews to press or radio. Our friends drive us off into town.

For the first time I have the feeling that we have really got away, beyond the reach of South Africa's Security Police. We have no idea where we are going – but we are out! We are in Africa, still close to our roots. If it were possible we might stay, stop running, but we have to be gone before the week is out. We are being forced into taking long-term decisions about our future literally on the run.

Sonia and Barney Gordon are old friends from Johannesburg. They have been living in Lusaka for several years, and take us into their home. The first thing to do is to telephone my brother in Johannesburg and arrange for Keith and Patrick to be put on a plane to join us – Keith because he is the youngest and Pat because I have not seen him since before my arrest at Rivonia.

The Gordons are amongst the few whites who have supported Kaunda and his UNIP Party during their struggle for independence. Kaunda and members of his cabinet-to-be drop in to the house casually to chat or have a drink. Amongst them is the Minister of Works who is facing an acute staff shortage in his Department when he takes over. White staff are packing up and leaving before a black government is installed. When he learns that I am an architect he offers me a post in the Department and promises to arrange for the PI order to be cancelled when the new government takes over. I jump at the offer and the prospect of settling down in Zambia.

In Lusaka Hilda takes the opportunity to renew her United Kingdom passport which she is entitled to by virtue of her birth in London. She now has a valid passport. Patrick and Keith, who have their own South African passports, arrive and join us – but our seven days are running out. Once again we find that it can be easier getting in than getting out. There is a strike on the railways, and in consequence all airplane seats have been booked and over-booked for some time ahead. Once again, our only way out is by road – but to where? The only long-distance road passenger services go south, but our luck is in. The ANC is preparing to transport some black South African nurses to Dar es Salaam, where they have volunteered to help the hospitals overcome their staff shortages. Some eight of them are already assembled in Lusaka and an ANC vehicle is being prepared. We can travel with the party on condition that I share the driving with Tennyson Makiwane who will be in charge.

If I had known more about long-distance driving in that part of the world I might not have jumped at the offer quite so readily. I had known Tennyson years before when he was junior to Ruth First as a Johannesburg reporter for the *Guardian* newspaper. He is now a full-time ANC official in the Dar es Salaam office, and confident that I will have no passport problems at the border – because of the ANC's good relations with the Nyerere government.

The ANC vehicle turns out to be an elderly Jeep pick-up which has been converted from military to civilian use by a canvas hood to enclose the back, and the addition of two hard, backless wooden benches bolted to the floor. There is just enough room for the passengers in the back to sit with their feet wedged in amongst a load of suitcases and four-gallon jerrycans of petrol. Three of us are wedged into the front seat.

Petrol points along the road are few and far enough apart to be marked on the road maps. Between them, there is nowhere to obtain fuel. We set out in typically noisy South African party spirit and encounter almost no traffic once we are out of town. The main road east is a dirt road in reasonable state. We leave a billowing cloud of red dust hanging in the air for hundreds of yards behind us. The dust gradually filters in through gaps and joins in the canvas.

There is red dust over everything – faces, clothes and hair, and between our teeth. The temperature in the closed interior is growing fierce, the sweat is pouring down, the festive spirit is subsiding and the passengers doze off. There are sporadic attempts to start community singing, and occasional black jokes to ease the discomfort. Our family is accustomed to long road journeys, but they have previously been in the comfort of sedan cars on tarmac South African roads. Our boys are not complaining, but they are miserable and finding the journey rougher and harder than we had expected.

Through the heat of day we travel through endless flat, uninteresting and seemingly uninhabited bush. We only stop for calls of nature, and from time to time in order to decant petrol from the jerrycans to the tank. There is nothing else to stop for. In mid-afternoon, those of us in front are watching the petrol gauge, and keeping anxious eyes on the mileage to the next petrol point. We are passing through what we later come to call 'Alice Lenshina country' after the local 'prophetess' who is leading a minor tribal rebellion against the government. We only know that she is said to have persuaded her followers that her magic powers will turn aside their enemies' bullets, and that the army has been sent in to 'restore order'.

We pass a few army trucks carrying dust-encrusted government soldiers, and finally arrive at the petrol point. It is closed. A man sitting on his haunches tells us there is no petrol; the army has commandeered it all for their own trucks. We know that there is no chance of our reaching the next petrol point with what we have, and no point in going back. There is nothing else to do but drive on. It is my turn to drive. At every minor incline I take the truck out of gear and let it coast in the hope of saving fuel, but I know it is useless.

We are watching the needle of the fuel gauge fall to zero, and then stop moving altogether. No one panics – it is too hot for that. We cruise along, calm and fatalistic, until the engine coughs and dies and we coast slowly to a halt. It is late afternoon in the middle of nowhere with not a sign of life – nothing but bush as far as the horizon. We all climb down and spread ourselves out on the prickly scrub grass at the roadside, waiting for a vehicle to come by. Nothing moves except the insects. I suppose our loud South African voices have carried a long way in the still air since eventually a tattered barefoot black farmer emerges cautiously from the bush to see what is going on. Then another, and another. Soon we have attracted a small crowd of chattering men and women who come out of the bush and stand a short way off, watching.

Our people try talking to them but without much success. Neither group understands the other's language. Tennyson has picked up some Swahili during his time in Tanzania. He manages better than any of us with the help of mime and gestures. There is a long exchange and then one of the men turns back into the bush and disappears. Both groups sit waiting to see what results. Half an hour later he is back, wheeling an ancient bicycle. By that time we have elicited the information that there is a mission station somewhere along the road ahead. It has a car and might have petrol, but no one knows quite how far. They use that all-purpose African measurement: 'Too far.' But it can be reached by bicycle which the owner will lend us if we promise to bring it back.

Cycle duty falls on Tennyson because he is the only one who will be able to make himself understood in Swahili. The daylight is fading. The bicycle has no light or luggage carrier, so we give Tennyson a small torch, a sharp knife to ward off wild animals, and a jerrycan. He takes off into the sunset, far from enthusiastic, steering a wobbly course with one hand and carrying the jerrycan in the other. The local people slink off one by one, back into the bush. We collect up branches and twigs and start a bonfire on the edge of the road. We sit and chat; we sing liberation songs from home, and we watch the sparks flying up into the night sky and the blaze of the milky way appear.

We are all townsfolk. We are enjoying the safari experience, but with some uneasy joking about lions and hyenas. It has been dark for a long time when we hear a truck approaching from the east. We can smell it coming – it must be carrying fish from Lake Victoria. We all stand and wave, and yell like banshees as it comes by. Perhaps they think we are hijackers. They drive past without slowing down, covering us in fish-flavoured dust. Back to the fireside until a long time later another truck approaches. We are beginning to get desperate and almost compel them to stop by crowding into the road. It is an army truck with a party of Zambian soldiers who keep their rifles close to hand. We explain our predicament to the sergeant in charge, using a polyglot mix of Zambian and South African tongues. At first he remains unmoved, but in the end he gives way to the pleas and blandishments of the nurses. The soldiers siphon a small amount of petrol from their truck to ours, and drive off.

Our petrol gauge is still around the zero mark as we go in search of Tennyson. He is sitting disconsolately on a rock several miles further on. He has a full jerrycan of petrol cadged from the mission station which is invisible in the dark. But the full can, torch and bicycle have proved to be more than he can handle. He has given up trying and is waiting for us to rescue him. We drive back to return the bicycle, and then turn round again to drive on into the night. We are near to the Zambian-Tanzanian border when we pass a sign advertising a roadside hotel. It is a small creeper-covered bungalow in complete darkness. We manage to rouse the manager, and negotiate the use of his only vacant room. The women push the beds together so that they lie packed together like sardines, across them. The boys, Tennyson and I curl up on the benches and the floor of the truck. It is dusty and hard but a welcome relief, though sleep is hard to come by.

By morning, it is obvious that our boys are much the worse for wear, and we still have at least another day on the road ahead. We go on and reach the border post. The Zambians pass us through; they are not much concerned about my lack of a passport since I am leaving anyway. They can leave the problem to the Tanzanians who have an identical post a few hundred yards ahead across a piece of no man's land.

They *are* concerned. I leave it to Tennyson to explain that we are on official ANC business, and the ANC in Dar will stand as guarantor for me. The immigration officer is friendly and trying to be helpful. He is obviously too inexperienced in his position to be sure of his authority – Tanzanian independence is still quite new. He knows about South Africa and the trouble with apartheid, but cannot comprehend how a white person can possibly be part of the liberation struggle. It is a situation beyond his experience and not covered by any rules. Tennyson suggests he radio Dar headquarters for clearance, but he has no authority to do so. The haggling goes on and on. I knew it might be easier getting out of Zambia than into Tanzania, but the prospect of being permanently marooned in no man's land between the two had never occurred to me.

That is a real possibility. We are approached by two Indian

360

teenagers, a boy and a girl, who ask for our help. They are also South Africans. They have run away from a boarding school in Zambia, for an adventure. Zambia had passed them out without passports. They had assumed that Tanzania would let them in, and that the ANC would look after them as it had many young refugees, especially because their father – an old comrade of ours, Salim Saley from Roodepoort – had always been an ANC man. But the Tanzanians would not let them in unless they could produce proper papers or financial guarantors. The adventure had turned sour. They have been living rough in temporary shelter in no man's land for several weeks waiting for their father to bail them out. They plead in tears for Tennyson to vouch for them. He might be able to do something but that would make them the ANC's responsibility which he is not willing to take on. We are in no better state. Without the ANC to vouch for us, we can go neither forward nor back. In our case, Tennyson gives the ANC guarantee. There is nothing we can do for these youngsters. We know their parents can afford to bail them out and that it can only be a matter of time before their ordeal will be over. The barrier is lifted to let us through and we drive on to Mbeya leaving them in tears in no man's land.

At Mbeya luck is with us. A light plane is on the runway being prepared for a flight to Dar. There are still seats available. We decide to end the boys' torture-by-road and put them on it together with Hilda. As co-driver I will have to stay with the truck. We wait at the airport until the plane has taken off, and then get back on the road to follow them to Dar. There is almost no traffic, it is as hot and dusty as ever, but there are no problems with petrol. By afternoon we are on a stretch of road which passes through the Morogoro Game Reserve. Notices warn motorists to keep a watch out for wild animals crossing the road. We do, but do not see any. They are more sensible than we are and are probably resting in the shade. It is again my turn to drive, with one eye on the empty road and the other looking out for animals. The accelerator pedal gives way without warning, goes right down to the floor and stays there. I try lifting it back up but it won't stay and flops back to the floor. We stop, and I crawl about in the dust inspecting the damage from below – I am so dust-encrusted already that a little more scarcely matters. A welded joint has come apart below the floor, and left the rod between accelerator pedal and engine trailing on the road.

From below, it is obvious that the Jeep was built for driving on the right, and has been adapted for driving on the left by moving the driver's pedals over and connecting them to the engine by transverse rods. There is no way we can repair a broken weld. The best we can do is to try and revert to the original left side for the accelerator control. We have no rods or wire. Rolling around in the dirt, I can connect the engine through a hole in the floor to the passenger seat position using Tennyson's necktie as the link.

The light is fading; everyone is getting twitchy at being stuck in the game park after dark, so we settle for that. Tennyson takes the passenger seat controlling the acceleration with his necktie. I drive with control of clutch and brake.

We are not totally in agreement about driving methods. I find myself pumping at the brake at moments when he is attempting to accelerate. When I brake before a bend he is as likely as not to be pulling on the tie so that we can take it at speed on two wheels. And vice versa. It is a nightmare drive through the dark, with a silent battle of wills at every bend and incline. It is fortunate that we have the road virtually to ourselves. There is nothing to be seen except endless dark sisal plantations beside the road. We roll into Dar es Salaam in the early hours, dead beat, and spend what is left of the night in recovery, dozing in armchairs in an ANC flat.

Hilda and the boys have been met at the airport by the ANC's Acting President, Oliver Tambo, and the local representative James Hadebe, and are installed in a small hotel on the edge of town. Patrick and I walk down through the hotel grounds to the beach so that I can wash off some of the dust. The beach is totally deserted. I do what I have always done in South Africa; I leave my shirt, shoes and towel in a heap near the shore line. And when we come out of the water they are gone. I have a spare shirt in my bag, but no shoes. I walk into town barefoot, go into the first shoe shop I can see and ask for a pair of socks. I put them on in the shop and ask for a pair of shoes. The shopkeeper shows no surprise. Perhaps this sort of thing is old hat in Dar.

I start doing the rounds of the travel agencies and airlines. There are plenty of flights available but not for someone without a passport. Several times I am reminded of a recent case of a man without a passport who boarded a plane somewhere in Europe, had been refused the right to land at his destination and had shuttled back and forth for weeks, unable to leave the airport until the UN rescued him. No one is prepared to repeat that experience. I try the shipping companies, with the same result. I am learning again that getting in is easy compared with getting out.

The ANC office does its best to help. For the whole week one of its officials guides me through every relevant office and department of the Tanzanian bureaucracy. Day after day we trudge from Police to Home Affairs to Immigration to Security and several more. Everywhere we are received politely; everyone wants to help the ANC; everyone knows about the evils of apartheid and supports the struggle for South African liberation. But a white member of the liberation movement passes all understanding. There is nothing in rules about such a thing, no known precedent, and no appropriate forms to fill in. There are a lot of questions, chiefly in Swahili, translated for me by my chaperon. Whether my answers lose something in translation I do not know, but each official makes extensive notes, presses my hand and wishes me well, and passes me on to another place as quickly as he can.

My ANC companion keeps telling me: 'Now we are getting somewhere.' Maybe, but I am not sure where – not even when we land in the office of the head of State Security himself. My comrade assures me that this is where the *real* decisions are made, though I have already decided that no such place exists. We go through the familiar routine of explanations, questions, incredulity and doubt. He runs out of things to say and reaches into his desk drawer and takes out a printed form. He picks up his pen and starts taking me through it systematically. The usual stuff – name, date of birth, place. Then: where did you go to school? School! I think back thirty years and select two out of a possible five or six. 'What places do you frequent?' Frequent? How about the Palm Beach Hotel and the Immigration Department. Passed. 'Do you ride a bicycle?' 'What are your hobbies?' 'What sports do you play?'

I can't really believe this, but he is going on. Occupation, distinguishing marks, colour of eyes, hair, skin, height, build, and anything else the official mind can conceive of. I am sitting across the desk from him, and reading the print at the top of the form, while he is writing down the answers in the appropriate boxes. It is a 'Wanted' form left over from the British administration. It advises all police stations of missing fugitives from justice. He signs it with a flourish and takes it off to another office along with two of my passport photographs. He comes back with a single sheet of paper headed CERTIFICATE OF IDENTITY. My photograph is pasted on with accompanying details of date and place of birth and so on. At the bottom in bold type it says: VALID FOR ONE JOURNEY ONLY. He stamps it, signs it and hands it over. The buck has finally stopped here, and we are free to move on.

We are still without a plan. Britain seems to be the sensible place to stop over while we clear the way for a return to Zambia. The direct flights to Britain are fully booked, so we settle for a broken journey with a few days stop-over in Nairobi. Zeke Mphahlele, who is the ANC representative in Kenya, meets us at the airport. He too is an old Johannesburg friend from the days before he went into exile and before he became a distinguished writer. He has spent those years in the United States and the capitals of Europe. He says he has booked us into a 'modest little hotel', drives us there and drops us off. Life in Geneva must have changed his values. The 'modest little hotel' is the Norfolk, a comfortable bungalow-style establishment and the city's most prestigious. He has booked us a suite which is far beyond our means. It is already evening. We decide to stay the night only, and make our get-away as early in the morning as possible. Our boys are seeing television for the first time, and cannot tear themselves away from even the most boring of political interviews with local politicians.

In the morning I try to settle our bill, but the hotel will not accept South African banknotes. There is an official embargo – which is good news politically but bad for us financially. We go into town to find a bank which will exchange what is left of Borch's bankroll. The first bank refuses to handle the notes, and so does the second which calls itself the Standard Bank of South Africa. I must have looked desperate, for the Indian teller follows us outside to tell us that our only hope is to find a money-changer, and directs us down a side lane to a bazaar stall. The Indian money-changer at first also refuses our money, but then relents and offers us around half the usual rate of exchange. We have no choice. We take the money, settle our bill and leave the hotel with only a few pounds left to see us through to Britain.

The only people we know in Nairobi are Eve and Tony Hall. Tony had been a reporter on the *Rand Daily Mail* when I was taken home after my arrest at Rivonia, and is now working for the *East African Herald*. We phone them to ask advice about cheap accommodation, and they invite us to stay with them and their three sons. For a few days we bed down in sleeping bags on their living-room floor, waiting for the last leg of our flight to Britain.

The plane is filled with British expatriates taking their children to boarding schools 'at home' after their annual holiday with their parents in Kenya. Since we left Zambia we have been enjoying our anonymity. The press seems to have lost all interest in us. But as we line up in the aisle of the plane at Heathrow and prepare to disembark, we can see television cameras being positioned outside to film people coming down the steps.

Our fellow passengers are looking around and trying to spot the celebrities on board. We pretend to be doing the same, but we fear the worst. As we come down the steps someone says: 'That's them!' The cameras start up, and I am grabbed by reporters. We are hustled off to a studio in the air terminal building, passing the crowd of friends who have come to meet us. They must have been alerted by the ANC or the Anti-Apartheid Movement, but we can only wave to them.

I am new to TV – it has never been permitted in South Africa. I cannot follow all the talk about BBC1 and ITV, but gather that I am to be interviewed for the evening news. I expect to be asked about the Rivonia Trial or our escape to Bechuanaland. When the interviews start they are scarcely interested in any of that. They are more interested in another story – the kidnap by South African agents from a caravan in Southern Rhodesia of a refugee named Barry Higgs. I have heard of it in Nairobi, but know less about it than the interviewers. They want to know what I think about it, and what Britain could or should do. Clearly we are already yesterday's news. We have had our fifteen minutes of fame.

The Anti-Apartheid Movement has cleared our passage through Immigration. I am given permission to stay for seven days on the strength of my 'One Journey Only' document. We can join our friends to celebrate, still uncertain of our future or how long we will be permitted to stay in London. Displaced persons, not quite residents and not quite tourists.

EPILOGUE

We live out of suitcases, first with relatives, then with friends, without a plan. Patrick's school vacation is ending. We try to persuade him that he is free to choose for himself whether to return to school in Swaziland till the end of the school year, or to stay with us wherever we are. He is an introverted and inarticulate adolescent, unable to communicate freely with adults. He opts to go back, I think believing that this will make things easier for us. We know he is unhappy, but he has made his choice, and we put him on a plane back to school in Swaziland.

Frances is still in Toni's care in Johannesburg. The plan had been for her to complete her school year and then join us. But she is miserable, and desperately wants to be with us. So Toni puts her on a plane to London, where she is miserable and homesick for South Africa, but with us. Not long after her arrival, we have a phone call from Johannesburg. Patrick has run away from school in Swaziland, crossed the South African border without a passport and hitch-hiked his way to Toni's flat. We take it to be a cry for help, and arrange for him too to be flown to London to join us. Our fractured family jigsaw is being put together again, piece by piece, while we are still drifting without a settled future.

My permit to stay is extended, first for weeks, later for some months. There is nothing left of Borch's endowment. My Johannesburg bank account has been closed and the small amount I left in it converted into traveller's cheques which Frances brings with her. We have spent all of it. Zambia has achieved its independence, control of immigration has passed from British to Zambian hands, but the PI order remains. All our attempts to get it cancelled disappear into some dark bureaucratic hole in Lusaka. I manage to talk to Simon Kapepwe, the Zambian Vice-Premier, who is in London on official business. He undertakes to see that the way for our return is cleared and the PI order rescinded as soon as he is back in Zambia. I am not surprised that nothing happens – our PI order must be low on the the list of priorities of a government which is still finding its feet.

The Colonial Development Corporation is advertising for architects to work in Lusaka for the Zambian government. I apply, and am called to an interview at the Foreign Office. I am seen by an obviously bored and detached British civil servant and his over-fed, overly self-satisfied Zambian equivalent. They show almost no interest in my professional experience or skills. They are interested in my 'background', which it is clear means my politics, and whether I am politically safe or red and dangerous.

The Zambian obviously disbelieves my story. His imagination cannot cope with the concept of a white man victimised for his part in a black struggle. He makes no effort to conceal his disbelief. They are just going through the motions. I know that my application will be turned down, and within the week I receive formal notice that '. . . the Minister regrets', although I know from friends in Zambia that they are having little success in finding architects.

Our funds run out, we are overstaying our welcome in other people's homes, and our children are missing out on their education. We can no longer hang on in the hope that something will turn up to clear our return to Zambia. The period of waiting and of drift is over. We arrange for our children to restart their education in London schools; I find a job in a London architectural practice, and we take a short lease on a furnished flat of our own.

Back in South Africa, Toni's husband Ivan Strasburg has been detained in a Durban prison in an attempt to induce him to testify for the state in a trial of some of his political colleagues. He has resisted successfully until that trial is over, and he is then released. He and Toni decide they have had enough, and leave to join us. We go to Heathrow to meet them but have to call up assistance from the Anti-Apartheid Movement and David Ennals MP before they are allowed to enter on a short-term permit. They move in to our flat for the time being. Our whole family is together in one place for the first time since my arrest at Rivonia.

We have settled. We are no longer refugees but have become exiles. Though Hilda was born here, she has been in South Africa for so long – over thirty years – that she too feels she is in exile. We have lost our home but are not trapped. We can travel abroad when we wish to, and do so for holidays, conferences and meetings about South Africa and apartheid. For several years I pass immigration controls with my Tanzanian document valid for 'One Journey Only' by persuading the officials that my journey has not yet ended. They are all prepared to accept the pretext as long as they have an official-looking document on which they can place their entry and exit stamps – and collect the visa fee.

I have to wait five years before I am eligible for 'permanent residence' status in Britain, and thus a British passport. Long before that, every inch of the now dog-eared Tanzanian document is filled with official stamps. Now I am trapped unless I can obtain a British travel document, which will only be granted in exchange for my Tanzanian museum piece. I surrender it unwillingly and receive a short-term UK Travel Document, which looks like a passport but isn't.

In involuntary small steps like this, we are putting down roots in an alien land while all our cultural, emotional and political being remains firmly embedded in South Africa. These new roots – Hilda's and mine – are feeble things, but our children's have taken and they are becoming British, willy-nilly. We speak the same language and share the same culture. We fit quite easily into British society, although slightly separated from it by our foreign accents and the exotic experiences which brought us here. Our children are more at home here than we are, and are coming to think of themselves more as British than South African.

We remain part of a tightly knit circle of South African *émigrés*, but our children go to school, mature, move into the native community, marry and raise families of their own. They are becoming British, while we of the older generation live lives apart, in a community of South African refugees and exiles, all of whom live with the dream of home.

Expectations differ about how soon it will be possible to return.

The most optimistic amongst us speak of five years, and keep their mental luggage packed and ready for the day. Most of us are less optimistic and think of ten years, perhaps more. But we are all certain that the day will come when we *can* return and will. We never lose that faith: if not in ten years then at least in our own lifetime.

The dream becomes more remote with time, but is never abandoned. We are for ever exiles. We do what we can from exile to sustain and develop the liberation struggle at home, and keep in touch with our comrades there, in and out of jail, and with the organisations of resistance and of struggle. We stop counting the years as the organisations and movements of *our* times pass into history. New struggles and new movements grow out of the compost of the old – Soweto students, Crossroads Squatters, the United Democratic Front. Our times are becoming times past – but yet we know our day *will* come!

Twenty years of waiting and of hoping, and at last the apartheid state starts to fall apart. Cracks and fissures open up in the great mountain of oppression, revealing to the whole world the blood-stained foundations on which it stands. Twenty-seven years. It is collapsing. Its prisons are emptying and the state machine is collapsing in disarray. Those of us who have lived so long in exile can return to rediscover our roots in the place we have come from, and start a new life amongst the generations who have grown up without us. But our children and their children have roots too deep in foreign soil to call this forgotten or even unknown country home.

Thirty years on. We go back for the first time to our own country. Apartheid is in its death throes, but still unburied. The first truly free non-racial elections are under way, and we are taking part in them and in the old regime's funeral. Our political careers have come full circle – from the outer regions of a radical minority sect to the heart and centre of popular politics. We are helping bring to power the first truly representative government the country has ever known after a lifetime of dreaming of it and working for it. We are at the beginning of a new era of restoration and recon-struction after a single long journey through the nightmare of apartheid.

Thirty years on: May 1994. We are standing on the terrace of the Union Buildings, Pretoria, together with hundreds of our comrades of those long years – those who have survived at home and abroad. They are all here, those men of Rivonia – all except Elias Motsoaledi who survived twenty-seven years on Robben Island and died of heart disease only days before this moment of achievement. But we are without Jimmy Kantor, who has died prematurely in exile from the stress induced by his trial. And without Bram Fischer, who has died in prison for his almost single-handed effort to reconstruct the Communist Party underground after its decimation at Rivonia.

This is their day, and ours. It is the day for which thousands of other men and women gave all their courage and strength, but fell before the final triumph. It is the day of vindication of all their faith and dedication in the struggle against power. We, the survivors, are the lucky ones – perhaps the luckiest generation on earth; for we have seen the peaceful triumph of the cause to which we have devoted our lives. We remember all those who set out on the great journey with us but did not live to see its end. This day is their triumph as much as ours, their memorial contribution to the living, and to the freedom and happiness of South Africa's generations still unborn.

It is a milestone at the end of a single journey. The flag of the hated old regime is being hauled down from the flag-mast, and the new flag incorporating the resplendent colours of the ANC is being ceremonially run up. It flies proudly over the nation's capital. The planes of a new South Africa are flying past overhead, and below them taking the salute stands the greatest survivor of all and the symbol of our hopes – our comrade Nelson Mandela, President of a new non-racial and democratic country, at the triumphant climax of one of the longest and most testing journeys in history.

SELECTED INDEX

Abse, Leo 65
Adams, Faried 168
'Advance' 22
Advisory Boards, Township 69,102
African Communist, The 133,134,
    189,246
African Democratic Party 199
Africanists 160,161
African Mineworkers' Union 69,89,
    90,91,92,95
African National Congress (ANC) 1,
    3,4,59,60,69,70,88,92,108,116,
    118,134,136,138,139,141,142,
    143,152,156,159,160,161,177,
    178,179,189,190,191,196,199,
    217,218,219,222,225,226,230,
    238,239,247,250,287,299,305,
    307,325,349,363
    National Executive Committee
    63,177,178,225,229,236,239,250
    Women's League 152
    Youth League 88,116,146,160
African Non-Denominational
    Ministers' Association 221
Alexandra (township) 101,105,116
Alexandra bus boycott 88,89
All-In Conference 221,222
Andrews, W H (Bill) 124
Anglo-Soviet Treaty 31,35
Anti-Apartheid Movement 365,367
Anti-Fascist League 19,20
Arenstein, Rowley 12,29

Armed Resistance Movement
    (ARM) 233,234,235
Army Education College 77
Atlantic Charter 88
Azania 161
Azanian People's Organisation
    (AZAPO) 161

Baker, Julius 119,120,194,197
Baker, Louis 197
Basner, Hymie 31,32,199,203
Bekker, Judge Simon 186
Benson, Mary 170
Berman, Monty 85,201,205,206,
    209,212,233
Berman, Myrtle 209
Bernstein, Frances 197,244,340,366
Bernstein, Harold 166,339
Bernstein, Hilda 12,29,45,50,60,69,
    85,95,96,102,156,164,165,166,
    171,177,192,194,195,197,209,
    216, 242,243,257,258,259,265,
    268,271, 272,273,274,276,279,
    284,285,293, 294,326,330,331,
    332,333,335,336, 337,338,339,
    340,341,343,344,345, 351,352,
    353,357,361,362,368
Bernstein, Keith 166,177,197,259,
    340,356
Bernstein, Patrick 197,330,334,340,
    356,362,366
Bernstein, Toni 85,86,164,165,197,

244,258,332,339,340,366,367
Berrange, Vernon 98,99,126,127,
    170,171,173,174,184,186,245,
    284,300,301,302,303,307,314,
    316,325,326,329,332,335
Berry, Abe 140
Beyleveld, Piet 139,144,179,194,337
Bhaduza, Schreiner 105,106,107
Bizos, George 170,186,284,307,309
Bopape, David 70
Bowles, Ellis 134
Boy, Det. Sgt 95,97
Briggs, Jimmy 33
Brink, John 204,211
British Empire Service League 78,79
Brown, Jimmy 51
Brutus, Dennis 140
Bucholz, Harry 94
Bunting, Brian 78,96,241
Burchard, Borch 339
Burchard, Vera 339
Burford, Ephraim (EJ) 19,20,22,41,
    42,43

Cachalia, Maulvi 171,348,351,352,
    353
Cachalia, Yusuf 136,144,171
Calata, Rev. James 178
Cape Coloured Corps 74
Card, Det. Sgt 298,299,318
Carnesson, Fred 78
Chamber of Mines 91,92,94,97,108
Chamberlain, Neville 16,18
Champion, George 9,110
Charter. See Freedom Charter.
Charter of African Rights 88
Chaskalson, Arthur 284,307,323,
    324
City Hall Steps 49-52
Clapham, Vic 140
Coaker, John 173,186
Cohen, Percy 135
Collins, Canon John 44,170,311
Coloured People's Congress (CPC)
    141
Communist Party of South Africa

9,24,25,28,30,31,35,40,43,53,56,
    88,89,91,109,113,114,115,123,
    124,131,135,137,160,188,196,
    218,219, 225,230,247,287,299,
    307
    aggregates 26,27
    Alexandra branch 55
    Central Committee 26,28,37,43,
    62,96,100,118,121,122,123,124,
    131,189,194,218,226,229,248,
    249,251
    night schools 40
    press 60-61
    Vrededorp branch 54-55
    Youth League 12,23
Communist Party of the German
    Democratic Republic 134
Communist Party of Great Britain
    36,37,134
Communist Party of Soviet Union
    32,35,36
Conco, Zami 143,178
Congress Alliance 139
Congress of Democrats. (COD)
    138,139,141,152,179,196,217
Congress of the People (COP) 142,
    143,144,146,148,149,150,151,
    152,155,156,157,158,159,160,
    169,171, 179,183,185,287
    The Call 149
    Working Committee 146,147,
    149,151,153,155,156,159,161
Cornelius, Johanna 18,41
Council of Non-European Trade
    Unions (CNETU) 58,63,95,115

Dadoo, Yusuf 3,4,29,48,49,62,63,69,
    89,96,99,121,123,127,131,151,
    160,171,194,196,225,245
Daniels, Adam 144
Davidson, Apollon 2,3,4
Davidson, Basil 65
Day, Det. Sgt 95
Decembrists 1,2
Defiance Campaign 134-137,141,
    142,185

De Wet, Judge Quartus 270,286,
291,292,293,294,295,296,297,
298,299,301,302,304,307,308,
310, 311,312,313,314,316,318,
319,321, 322,323,324,325,326,
327
Diphoko, Michael 29
Dirker, Det. Sgt Carl Johannes 268,
269,302,303,314,329,330,332
Dominion Party 33,151
Drill Hall, Johannesburg 167,168,
170,171,172,176,177,178,180,
181,184,287
Duncan, Patrick 135
Du Plessis, Danie 50,89,92,95,96,
127,128
Du Toit, Betty 50,135

Emergency Regulations 193,196,
201,210,279
Ennals, David 367
Ezra, Vivian 228

Fellner, Fritz 41
Fighting Talk 66,139,140,141,189,
315
Findlay, George 35
Findlay, Joan 35
First, Julius 119
First, Ruth. See Slovo.
First, Tilly 119
Fischer, Bram 2,4,29,89,95,96,99,
118,123,126,127,136,139,170,
171,186,193,194,227,245,248,
251,284,286,291,292, 293,295,
296,297,299,307,308,309, 310,
316,321,324,325,332,333,334,
335,336,370
Fischer, Molly 333,334,335
Fleet, Ronnie 212
Florian's Café 15
Fort, the (Johannesburg) 165,166,
170,198,199,257
'Forward' 22
Freedom Charter 142,143,144,145,
149,150,151,153,154,155,156,
158, 159,160,161,163,169,171,
187,188, 222,287,298

Gampel, Rica. See Hodgson.
Gathercole (Watts), Jack 25,26
Gay, Lionel 302
Glyn Thomas, Ivor 17
Goldberg, Dennis 253,256,257,264,
273,275,276,277,281,292,311,
318,321,322,326,332,333
Goldreich, Arthur 228,231,250,277,
278,281,288,294,304,321,322,
354
Goldreich, Hazel 228
Gordon, Sonia and Barney 356
Gordon, Max 41
Greek Seaman's Union 66
Grootewal, Cissy 114
Group Areas Act 151
Guardian 45,46,47,134,139,140,
195,357

Hadebe, James 362
Hall, Eve 364
Hall, Tony 258, 364
Hani, Chris 131
Hanson, Harold 291,296
Harmel, Michael 4,29,50,56,57,62,
71,96,123,124,127,134,171,194,
225,226,227,245,246,248,321
Harmel, Ray 29
Harris, John 235
Hepple, Alex 44,293
Hepple, Bob 248,251,253,254,255,
256,257,264,273,275,281,284,
290,291,292,293,296,322
Hepple, Girlie 44,293
Hertzog, J B M 32,33,34,162,183
Heyman, Anne and Issy 209
Higgs, Barry 365
Hlapane, Bartholomew 337
Hodgson, Jack 4,64,65,66,166,171,
179,194,231,235,246,321,322
Hodgson, Rica 66,139,144,246
Horvitch, Ike 127
House arrest 243-246

Huddleston, Trevor 151

Indian Congress (SAIC) 59,70,108,
    134,136,138,139,141,152,179,
    196,217
Inkululeko 45,46,56,57,58
International Defence and Aid Fund
    44,66
Isacowitz, Jock 15,16,66,199,201,
    206,211
Isitwalandwe 151

Jassat, Abdulhai 281
Jele, Josiah 131
Jelliman, Frank 228
Jenks, 'Caesar' 10
Joffe, Joel 284,285
Joffe, Louis 41,199
Joffe, Max 23,24,29,41,52,199
Jonas, Kurt 14,15,16,17,66,199
Joseph, Helen 4,139,179,209,213,
    255
Joseph, Paul 109,140

Kadalie, Clements 110
Kahn, Sam 113,121,125
Kalk, Margaret 209
Kalk, Willie 28,50,209
Kantor, Jimmy 277,278,281,282,
    283,284,290,291,293,294,296,
    297,304,370
Kapepwe, Simon 367
Kathrada, Ahmed 109,131,171,179,
    191,192,210,246,248,251,252,
    253,255,287,313,322,325,326,
    327
Kaunda, Kenneth 355,356
Kennedy, Judge Alexander 186
Kentridge, Sydney 186
Kepobetsoe, John 57
Kietsing, Fish 348,353,354
Kitching, Sid 278,279
Klenerman, Fanny 119
Kliptown. *See* Congress of the
    People.
Klugman, James 65
Kodesh, Wolfie 196,205,269

Kotane, Moses 3,4,28,62,63,70,89,
    96,118,121,122,124,125,127,
    131, 171,178,179,194,218,219,
    227, 245,246,248
Kubheka, Bessie 165,197

Labour League of Youth (LLY) 12,
    14,16,20,23,27,114
Labour Monthly 36
Labour Party of South Africa 7,12,20,
    21,22,28,30,31,33,34,41,42,43
Labour Party Club 25,42
LaGuma, Alex 179
Lai, Dougie 109
Lai, Alec 109
Laing, John 199,203,205,208,211,
    212,233
Landman, Gessie 29
Lansdowne Commission 90,91,92
Latti, Arnold 41
Lefela, Josiel 61
Lefela, Maphutseng 61
Left Book Club 12,13,25
Left Club 14,17
Leftwich, Adrian 235
Leibbrandt, Robey 39
Lekgotla la Bafo 61
Lenshina, Alice 358
Levson, Freda 170
Levy, Leon 179,209,213,269
Lewin, Liz 334,335
Lewitton, Archie 12,29,45,50,62,
    197,198,201
Lewitton, Yvonne 197
Liberal Party 135,137,138,139,151,
    199,221,233
Liberation 139
Lilliesleaf Farm 227,229,237,238,
    239,248,249,253,255,269,278,
    299,302,311,313
Louw, Eric 11,20,41,111
Ludorf, Judge Joe 185,186
Luthuli, Albert 4,141,145,146,149,
    151,178,183,191,195,231,232,
    233,234,236,239,311,323

Mabhida, Moses 131
MacPherson, Jessie 85
Madeley, Walter 33,34,41
Mai Mai beer hall 46,47,48
Maisels, Isie 186
Majoro, James 92
Makabeni, Gana 115
Makgothi, Henry 178
Makiwane, Tennyson 357,359,360,
    361,362
Malan, D F 32,33,111
Maliba, Alpheus 29
Mandela, Nelson 88,116,135,142,
    143,145,146,147,148,171,176,
    178,189,191,195,210,221,222,
    223,224,225,228,229,230,231,
    236,237,238,239,240,246,248,
    249,250,252,262,282,283,287,
    290,296,305,306,307,308,309,
    310,316,317,322,323,327,335,
    336,370
Marcus, Natie 120
Marks, J B 3,4,69,70,89,90,92,96,
    131,171,194,248,251,252
Marshall Square police station 95,
    193,194,197,242,244,254,274,
    277,281,283,294,330,331,335
Martienssen, Rex 14
Mashaba, Bertha 179
Mashifane, Thomas 228
Massina, Leslie 179
Matthews, Z K 4,142,143,145,146,
    178,186
Maybank, Frank 64,65
May Day 114-117
Mayekiso, Caleb 178
Mbeki, Govan 231,245,247,248,
    249,250,251,252,253,255,256,
    297,313,317,318,321,322
Meer, Ismail 109
Meyer, Chris 64,65
Mhlaba, Raymond 231,247,248,251,
    253,255,313,314,317,322,325,
    326
Miners' Strike (1922) 40
Miners' Strike (1946) 92-99,123,199

Mini, Vuyisile 178
Mkwayi, Wilton 231,247
Mlangeni, Andrew 134,247,270,
    282,283,319,322
Modise, Joe 300
Mofutsanyana, Edwin 28,45,56,57,
    70,89,91,96,102,103,104,127
Molife, Petrus 235
Mompati, Ruth 247
Moolla, Mosie 281
Motsoaledi, Elias 236,270,282,283,
    319,322,370
Mpama, Josie 28
Mpanza, James 102,103,104,105,
    106
Mphahlele, Es'kia (Zeke) 364
Mqota, Themba 247
Msitshana, Armstrong 29
Mthembu, Patrick 324
Mtolo, Bruno 249,299,300,301,310,
    314,324
Muller, Mike 204,209
Muller, Shulamith 203,204,209
Murray, Andrew 174,187,188

Naicker, Monty 171,179
Naicker, M P 179
Nair, Billy 179
National High Command 231,236,
    237,238,248,249,250,251,253,
    297,299,300,302,307,314,319
National Party 32,33,44,87,88,95,
    107,108,111,151,185
National Register 29,30
Natives' Representative Council 69
New Age 139
Ngoyi, Lilian 171,178
Ngubane, Jordan 221
Nicholas, Harold 186
Nikin, Sam 28
Nkadimeng, John 57
Nkobi, Thomas 4,351
Nkosi, Johannes 9
Nokwe, Duma 4,70,142,178,186,
    191,322
Nokwe, Tiny 232,350

Non-aggression Pact (Soviet-
  German) 31,32,35
Nye, Rev. Mark 204,206,207,211
Nzo, Alfred 280
Nzo, Regina 350

Odendaal, Venter 34
Old Synagogue 185,187,209,210,
  221
Operation Mayibuye 237,249,250,
  251,252,253,254,255,256,257,
  258,259,271,272,302,305,307,
  309,310,311,319
Organisation of African Unity
  (OAU) 236
Orlando (township) 104,105,117
Ossewa Brandwag 39,40,162

Palme Dutt, R 36
Pan Africanist Congress (PAC) 161,
  189,190,191,238,239
Pan-Hellenic Progressive Union 67,
  68
Pass Laws 9,22,189
People's Bookshop 25,119,120
Peters, Tommy 55
Pillay, Vella 109
Pirow, Oswald 11,20,29,41,111,183,
  184,186,187
Podbrey, Joe,140
Pollitt, Harry 36,37
Press, Ronnie 200,201
Pratt, David 202,207,208
Pritt, D N 113

Radford, Betty 45
Radio Liberation 252,253
Ramohanoe, C S 60
Reeves, Bishop Ambrose 169
Referendum (Republic) 220,221
Resha, Robert 178,238,239
Riotous Assemblies Act 11,29
Rivonia Trial 229,230,236,249,253,
  283-328
Robben Island 148,283,330,332,
  333,370

Roberts, William 96
Routh, Guy 16
Roux, Eddie 139
Rumpff, Judge Franz 185,186

Sachs, Albie 135
Saley, Salim 361
Salmon's Bookshop 13
Schermbrucker, Ivan 80,334,335,
  336,337,339
Schermbrucker, Lesley 334,337,339,
  340
Scott, Rev. Michael 105
Seedat, Dawood 48,49,63
Sepel, Ralph 194
Sepel, Minnie 194
September, Hetty 345
September, Reg 131,179,345
Sharpeville 190,191,220,224
Simons, Jack 100,127,128
Simons (Alexander), Ray 171
Singh, J N 4,96,109
Sisulu, Walter 66,88,144,145,146,
  147,148,165,171,178,195,210,
  231,246,248,250,251,252,253,
  255,256,287,290,297,300,308,
  309,310,311,312,313,318,321,
  322,323,336
Slovo, Joe 4,106,125,131,166,171,
  186,195,203,204,210,211,212,
  213,216,231,235,248,250,251,
  252,253,321,322
Slovo, Ruth 4,106,125,139,140,141,
  171,195
Smuts, Jan Christian 7,32,33,34,36,
  37,40,41,44,67,74,75,107,108,
  111
Snitcher, Harry 99,100,127
Sobukwe, Robert 190
Soldiers' Parliament 65
SOMAFCO 4
Sophiatown 48,101,117
South African Congress of Trade
  Unions (SACTU) 141,217
South African Indian Congress
  (SAIC). See Indian Congress.

South African Party (SAP) 7,8,32

Spengler, Col. At 137,206

Springbok Legion 65,66,70,75,78, 80,85,87,88,105,106,107,108, 111,136,137,199

Squatters' movement 104

State of Emergency 191,194,196, 202,214,215,216,220,224

Steyn, Colin 63,191

Strachan, Harold 264

Strasburg, Ivan 339,340,367

Strasburg, Toni. *See* Bernstein.

Suppression of Communism Act 26, 29,35,96,100,113,117,118,119, 120,125,132,153,176,187,248, 288,331

Swanepoel, Capt. Theunis 268,269, 292,329,330

Swart, Vincent 200,205

Tambo, Oliver 4,88,136,137,142, 144,145,146,147,148,171,176, 178,183,195,238,317,362

Tarshish, Jack 264

'Ten shillings a day' Campaign 58-59

Thibedi, T W 92

Thompson, Rev. Douglas 199,206, 207

Thoms, Raymond 205,206

Tloome, Dan 70,131,348,351

Tobruk squatters 105

Trades and Labour Council 25,42, 58,67

Treason Trial 167-181,182-188,192, 209,211,213,221,222
  Defence Fund 170,177,183,185

Trevallyn Farm 248,277

Tschauke, English 59

Tsehla, Hosea 92

Turok, Ben 194,264

Umkhonto we Sizwe (MK) 1,66,230, 233,234,237,239,246,247,250, 295,299,305,307,314,324,325

Umsebenzi 26,45

United Party (UP) 32,33,44,107, 108,111,113,151

Van den Bergh, M J 33,34

Verwoerd, Hendrik 48,202,207,220, 268

Votes for All Campaign 109,110, 111,192

Watts, Hilda. *See* Bernstein.

Watts (Gathercole), Jack 25,26

Weinberg, Eli 29,92,205,209

Weinberg, Violet 209

Weinbren, Ben 22,34

Weinstock, George 22

Welensky, Roy 65

Welsh, Rex 186

Wentzel, Ernest 199,203,211

Williams, Cecil 4,77,78,136,139, 140,205,240

Willis, Ted 23

Wolfson, Issy 28,41,50,127

Wolpe, Annmarie 277

Wolpe, Harold 4,125,203,208,212, 277,278,281,282,284,291,294, 304,321,354

Women's Federation 152

Xuma, Dr A B 69,160,178

Yutar, Percy 285,286,288,291,292, 293,294,295,296,297,299,300, 301,302,304,307,308,309,310, 311,312,313,314,315,316,317, 318,319,320,321,322,323,325, 326